REGIONAL FLASHBACKS

THE REGIONAL FLASHBACKS SERIES IS PUBLISHED BY THE
EUROPEAN ETHNOLOGICAL RESEARCH CENTRE
CELTIC & SCOTTISH STUDIES
UNIVERSITY OF EDINBURGH
21 BUCCLEUCH PLACE
EDINBURGH EH8 9LN

Ian MacDougall among the Border hills.
Courtesy of Mrs Sandra MacDougall

Border Mills:
Lives of Peeblesshire Textile Workers

BY
Ian MacDougall

EDITED BY
Caroline Milligan

in association with
THE SCOTTISH WORKING PEOPLE'S HISTORY TRUST
THE EUROPEAN ETHNOLOGICAL RESEARCH CENTRE
AND NMS ENTERPRISES LIMITED – PUBLISHING
NATIONAL MUSEUMS SCOTLAND

GENERAL EDITOR
Mark A. Mulhern

Published in Great Britain in 2023 by
European Ethnological Research Centre
Celtic & Scottish Studies
University of Edinburgh
21 Buccleuch Place
Edinburgh EH8 9LN

and

NMS Enterprises Limited – Publishing
NMS Enterprises Limited
National Museums Scotland
Chambers Street
Edinburgh EH1 1JF

Text © European Ethnological
Research Centre 2023.

Images © as credited and page IX.

No reproduction permitted without
written permission to the publishers
in the first instance.

ISBN 978-1-910682-51-7

*No part of this publication may be
reproduced, stored in a retrieval system
or transmitted, in any form or by any
means, electronic, mechanical, photocopy-
ing, recording or otherwise, without the
prior permission of the publishers.*

**British Library Cataloguing in
Publication Data**

A catalogue record of this book is
available from the British Library.

The rights of Ian MacDougall as author
of this book has been asserted by him in
accordance with the Copyright, Designs
and Patents Act 1988.

Cover design by Mark Blackadder.
Front cover: Winding on the warp
 threads, D. Ballantyne Brothers & Co.
 Ltd, Peebles © The Scotsman Publica-
 tions Ltd/From the collection at
 National Museums Scotland.
 Ref: 000-000-057-336
Back cover: Janette Harrower, a cutter
 at Caerlee Mill, Innerleithen © Fraser
 Simm.

Internal text design by
 NMS Enterprises Ltd – Publishing.
Printed and bound in Great Britain by
 Bell & Bain Ltd, Glasgow.

This product is made of material from
well-managed forests and controlled
sources.

For other titles in the Flashback and
Regional Flashbacks series see page 396.

For a full listing of related NMS titles
please visit:
www.nms.ac.uk/books

Contents

Acknowledgements VII
Editorial Note VIII
List of Illustrations and Image Credits IX
The Scottish Working People's History Trust X
Preface XI
Introduction 1

Chapters

1. Domestic and Community Life 13
2. The Impact of War 49
3. The End of Childhood: Into the World of Work 99
4. The Mills and Mill Owners 126
5. Life in the Mills 217
6. Reflections and Looking Forward 347

Appendix 1: The Mills and Mill Owners 369
Appendix 2: The Interviewees 371
Glossary 380
Bibliography 386
Index 389

Acknowledgements

The EERC are grateful to the Scottish Working People's History Trust for their partnership and support in bringing this book to publication. Particularly to Dorothy Kidd and Alan Reid for reading through earlier drafts and for their thoughtful comments which have informed the final shape of the text. Dorothy Kidd, Mark Watson and John Burnett were invaluable in providing explanation and description of a range of technical terms and processes. Sincere thanks are also extended to Elizabeth Bryan, Dorothy Kidd and Hannah Wood for their excellent help with resource gathering and to Fraser Simm, Nettie Simm, Ross McGinn and Louise Coulson for their enthusiasm, advice and hospitality in the pursuit of many of the photographs which appear in this volume.

Warm thanks and appreciation are offered to the twenty-nine mill workers who shared their knowledge, anecdotes, memories and thoughts with Ian and whose testimonies have provided such a rich resource from which to construct this text. And, of course, to Ian himself whose commitment to accuracy and to the people he interviewed meant that the core material for this book was not only enlightening, entertaining, detailed and empathetic but also comprehensive in its structure and content and furthermore reliable in both reporting what was said and in providing an accurate and true reflection of the voice of the contributors.

On a more personal note, for being interviewed and thereby helping me to know Ian a little and hopefully represent him more truthfully in this book, I extend sincere thanks to Sandra MacDougall, Alan Reid, Susan Reid and Hugh Hagan. Thanks too are extended to those friends and colleagues who shared their memories of Ian with me in informal conversations.

Finally, my sincere thanks to the brilliant team at NMSE Publishing for their support, good counsel and expertise.

Caroline Milligan

Editorial Note

The process of transcribing and then representing the human voice in written form is one which requires skill, commitment and attention to detail. The transcriptions used in this publication were prepared by Ian MacDougall and Susan Reid and supplied by the Scottish Working People's History Trust, under whose auspices the fieldwork was created. In conversation with the editor, Susan recalled that Ian paid meticulous attention to the transcribing process, striving for both accuracy and a true reflection of the interviewee's voice. Once completed, the transcriptions were sent to the individual interviewees and only considered complete when the interviewee had given their approval. Every attempt has been made to represent the interview material as it was collected and transcribed, while also striving to ensure the text is enjoyable to read. For this reason, hesitations and repetitions have been removed and words or phrases from another part of the interview may have been inserted to reflect the wider discussion and meaning therein. Square brackets indicate where the editor has inserted text to correct or clarify meaning or to assist the flow of the text.

List of Illustrations and Image Credits

Frontispiece: Ian MacDougall.
1. General view of Peebles showing mills.
2. Peebles, showing the Ballantyne March Street Mills, 1929.
3. Peebles, with Damdale Mill visible, 1947.
4. Innerleithen, Ballantyne's Waverley Mill, 1947.
5. Innerleithen, Waverley Mill, 1968.
6. Innerleithen, Leithen Mills, 1968.
7. Innerleithen, St Ronan's Mill, 1968.
8. Painting of Caerlee Mill, Innerleithen.
9. Innerleithen, Caerlee Mill, 1968.
10. The mill lade at Walkerburn, c.1954.
11. Walkerburn, Tweedholm Avenue East, 2009.
12. Walkerburn, Ballantyne's Tweedvale Mill.
13. A designer picking colours from sample yarns.
14. An in-giver.
15. A weaver checking the cloth.
16. The finishing department.
17. Inside one of the Walkerburn mills in the 1950s.
18. An Intarsia knitting machine in Caerlee Mill, 2013.
19. HM Queen Elizabeth II visiting Caerlee Mill, 1966.
20. Caerlee managing director, Arthur Oddy.
21. Advertisement.
22. Waverley Mill workers, c.1955.
23. The typing pool and friends, Caerlee Mill, c.1960.
24. The pressing department, Caerlee Mill.
25. Workers in the passing department, Caerlee Mill, c. 2005.
26. Dod McGinn working at a hand knitting machine, Caerlee Mill.
27. 'Ticklers'.
28. Peter Anderson in the Caerlee Mill yarn store.
29. Louise Coulson finalising an Intarsia design for production, Caerlee Mill.
30. Pat Laurie at a ribbing machine, Caerlee Mill.
31. Janice Dodds operating a buttonholing machine, Caerlee Mill.
32. End of a shift at Caerlee Mill, c.1980.

Frontispiece courtesy of Mrs Sandra MacDougall.
Image 1 courtesy of HES.
Images 2, 3 and 4 © HES (Aerofilms Collection).
Images 5, 6, 7, 9, 18, 19 and 22 © Innerleithen Community Trust.
Images 8, 20, 21, 23, 24, 26, 28, 29, 30 and 31 © Simm, 2021.
Images 10 and 17 © The Scotsman Publications Ltd/From the collection at National Museums Scotland.
Image 11 © Crown copyright. HES.
Image 12 © HES. Reproduced courtesy of J. R. Hume.
Images 13, 14, 15 and 16 © Scotland's Moving Image Archive.
Image 25 courtesy of Rose Johnstone.
Images 27 and 32 photograph: Fraser Simm.

The Scottish Working People's History Trust

Founded in 1991, the Scottish Working People's History Trust identifies and encourages the deposit in libraries and archives of documentary sources of working people's history in Scotland.

Its activities have included recording and making accessible the oral testimony of the lives of working men and women. The Trust has been responsible for a number of publications based on the collected oral testimony.

For more than twenty years the Trust's research worker, the late Dr Ian MacDougall, interviewed hundreds of workers in many occupational groups including miners, journalists, dockers, railway workers, farm workers, textile mill workers, librarians, co-operative society workers, shipyard workers.

In many cases, recording the experiences of working men and women allows them to be preserved for posterity in times of rapidly changing social and working environments. The experience of recounting their personal stories can also contribute to the recognition by those individuals interviewed that their lives have been meaningful.

The experiences of so-called 'ordinary working people' in Scotland deserve to be a better known part of our history. The Trust works to raise greater awareness of the important contribution oral recollections about work, housing, education, recreation and other life experiences can make to knowledge and understanding of our heritage. The Trust's collection and preservation of such records is accompanied by a commitment to underpin their presentation with scholarship of the highest standard.

The Trust will be pleased to receive proposals for future oral history projects. It also welcomes information about any documentary sources of working people's history in Scotland such as records of organisations and their members, photographs and other materials.

For further information about the Scottish Working People's History Trust please visit our website at www.swpht.org.uk

Preface

This book is the product of the work of many, though primarily it is the product of those who shared their life experiences and of the assiduous fieldwork of Ian MacDougall. In its approach and practice, oral history fieldwork is a seemingly simple discipline: hold a conversation; record a conversation; repeat with others focussing on a theme; transcribe the conversations; and, bring together those transcribed conversations in a book. That simplicity is, however, more apparent than real.

To hold a conversation in the first place requires contact to be made with a person with whom you most likely have no prior connection. When making this contact the fieldworker has to explain who they are, why they want to speak to and record the person and to say what will happen with the recording once made. All this takes time and care. This is the foundation stone upon which a work such as this book is built.

Once the conversation is to take place, the logistics have to be contended with. The key consideration here is for the fieldworker to enable the interviewee to be comfortable and at ease to allow them to say all that they want. It is therefore for the fieldworker to make the effort to go to the interviewee and to interview them in a setting in which they are most comfortable – often their own home.

The recruiting of interviewees and the logistics of interviewing then have to be repeated so as to build up a collection that tells us something of a theme and/or place. In this instance Ian secured the participation of twenty-nine folk.

Once the fieldwork had been created, it has to be securely stored and transcribed. To enable this, working with others is vital. In this instance, Ian conducted his interviews under the auspices of the Scottish Working People's History Trust. The Trust had established an agreement for their audio recordings to be held at the School of Scottish Studies Sound Archive at the University of Edinburgh. Within the Trust, the audio recordings were fully and carefully transcribed, with those transcriptions being held along with the audio recordings.

All of this is to say that the work that enables the production of a book such as this is relatively straightforward but that it requires care, knowledge and an ability to form links with bodies and individuals. All of this Ian did and did well. Not just for this book but for the many other books which resulted from his fieldwork over many years.

The EERC was delighted to continue our publishing partnership with the Trust – this volume is the seventh of those by Ian that we have published and is the first to be published as part of out *Regional Flashbacks series*. This series seeks to provide accounts of places and themes so as to enable us to understand something of life and society in Scotland on a regional basis.

For this book, we have sought to do two things: first, provide the reader with an insight into the theme of work in the Peeblesshire Mills; second, provide an insight into Ian's fieldwork practice. We have done this by being expansive, hence the length of the book. This is a reflection of the richness of the interviews, the range of topics discussed, and the salience of the information once marshalled into the six thematic chapters.

The *Regional Flashbacks* give a voice to folk little represented in the historical record. They seek to bring together direct, detailed experience about place, life and time within a framework that is readable both to the general reader and the scholar. We feel that this setting and approach mirror the approach and the work of Ian MacDougall.

As well as his deeply important work in the field of oral history, Ian was a teacher. When I took on the role of General Editor of this series, I met with Ian to seek advice and guidance on how to proceed. That conversation, held many years ago, has stayed with me and informs the continuing series of which this book is a part.

Mark A Mulhern

Introduction

by Caroline Milligan

When I was told that my next commission would be to work with Ian MacDougall on the present volume, I was doubly delighted. Although I had not met Ian I knew him through his publications and by reputation. One friend remembered his fearsome commitment to secure funding to publish a volume of oral histories of Penicuik papermaking employees[1] and another told me about how much she had benefitted from and enjoyed his tuition at Newbattle Abbey College. When I studied Ethnology as a mature student in Celtic & Scottish Studies at the University of Edinburgh his work was, of course, frequently referenced and quoted from. Later, as a member of staff at both the School of Scottish Studies Archives and then the European Ethnological Research Centre, his name was simply part of my day-to-day professional life. There was also the added bonus of the material we would be working on together: the Peeblesshire wool and textile mills. My own mum had been an out-knitter for a woollen firm and as youngsters my brothers and I all took turns on the knitting machine while she made dinner or sorted the washing – plain rows when we were younger then working patterns as we got older. This has left me with a life-long interest in textiles of all kinds. I was excited to have the opportunity to collaborate on this work with Ian and to have the opportunity to learn from him.

Unfortunately, within weeks of our planned first meeting, Covid-19 had arrived in the UK, shutting down all opportunities for Ian and myself to meet and, sadly, soon after that, on 11 April 2020 Ian died, only a short time after the death of my own dear eldest brother, Chris. After the shockwaves had eased the decision was made to continue with the book as planned, recognising that it would have a stronger ethnological focus than would have been the case had Ian and I been working on this project together.

The process then began. I started by reading and re-reading the interview transcripts learning as I did this not only about the mills and the mill workers, but

---

1 MacDougall, I. *Through the Mill: Personal Recollections by Veteran Men and Women Penicuik Paper Mill Workers*, The Scottish Working People's History Trust, Falkirk, 2009.

also about Ian. During this part of the process I often found myself second guessing what Ian might have concluded from this or that piece of information. Would he, for instance, have been disappointed that his enquiries about the reading habits of his interviewees were mostly met with an ambivalent disregard for reading and libraries? Or would he have been surprised by the general lack of interest in unions and industrial relations that this early read through of the interview transcripts seemed to indicate? Fortunately, over time, I realised the error of thinking this way. The more familiar I became with the interviews, the more I appreciated the nuance and complexity of what was being said and not said. Importantly, through working closely with the interview texts, I also started to understand Ian as a researcher. He had an enquiring mind and found his interviewees fascinating. If he was disappointed by replies to any of his lines of enquiry there was no evidence of this in the recordings. Importantly too, as Covid-19 restrictions were lifted and I was able to visit Sandra MacDougall, Ian's wife, and his close friends and collaborators, Alan and Susan Reid, I came to know Ian as a person. Sandra told me, 'Ian was motivated by the importance of gathering information and enabling ordinary working people to have their say and to be represented in the historical record'. What they said on a particular subject was valuable for its own sake, not because it confirmed or challenged any of Ian's own views or convictions. This is very much the attitude I have myself, and I felt a bit foolish for my earlier naivety. As well as Sandra, Alan and Susan, I learned more about Ian through a chat with Hugh Hagan, who had first met Ian as a mature student at the University of Edinburgh and recalled Ian as a caring, interested and committed man. I am grateful to each for their generosity in sharing their time and memories of Ian with me. The Scottish Working People's History Trust shared a link to an interview with Ian, conducted on behalf of the Trust by Elizabeth Bryan and I also watched a short interview with Ian on the National Library of Scotland website. Both resources were incredibly valuable. Hearing Ian speak about his work was key to understanding what was important to him and has hopefully helped to ensure that Ian has a strong and authentic voice in this book.

Whichever source I consulted, whether it was reading and re-reading the interview transcripts, listening to those who knew him best or listening to Ian himself, the picture of Ian that emerged was entirely consistent: a man of integrity and endless curiosity, and one who was driven by his commitment to record and share the memories of working people.

Ian left school at fifteen and had a varied career before settling into his passion for oral history based research. He was always interested in history and it is clear from his interview with Elizabeth Bryan that he enjoyed his work with the Trust, telling her that he wished he had started on his career as a collector earlier. The filmed interview is illuminating in a number of ways. Ian is modest about his individual role and is visibly more relaxed when recounting stories of people he has met along the way than when he is the centre of attention. When Elizabeth asked him specifically to select highlights from his collecting life he replied, perhaps unsurprisingly, that they all stood out, in a way. Throughout the interview, there is a special energy and enthusiasm whenever Ian is talking about his interviewees. One anecdote springs to mind: when Ian is talking about his time as PR Officer with Midlothian Council he spoke of visiting a lady who told him about Hoggie's Angels, which Ian had never heard of. This chance conversation led, in time, to the publication of an earlier edition of the Flashbacks series, *Hoggie's Angels: Tattie Howkers Remember*.[2] The ability to discover very specific local information from people directly was, said Ian, 'One of the great strengths of local history'. As Ian explained to Minnie Lavin, one of his Peeblesshire interviewees in this extract.

Well thanks very much indeed, Miss Lavin. That's very kind of you and you've got a good, clear memory of your working days and that, you know, provides another wee bit of the jigsaw that fits in with your sister's recollections and your brother's, and Duncan Adam's, and all these other folks that I'll be seeing. So thank you very much for your trouble. I hope I havenae destroyed your afternoon's arrangements.
No, no.

Ian's interviewees were always central to his work and he was diligent in keeping them informed and involved. This example, from Ian's interview with W. Lockie Robson, demonstrates this well.

I hope you dinnae think that I've subjected you to the third degree or anything!
No, it doesnae bother me in the least.
No, no, it's very interesting. What I find is that, you know, everybody has a different experience, even if you work in the same place at the same time. People see things in different ways.
Oh, Ah suppose.
Some folk remember things and others, you know recall different things. And it's only by interviewing a range of people, men and women, different age groups, people that worked in this mill, people that worked in that mill and so on and so forth, that you can get a kind of jigsaw that can be pieced together. And then there's a bigger, wider picture emerges. Some people remember things extremely clearly, others say, tell me that they don't remember much at all about this or that. So that's what I'm trying to do, is to see maybe a dozen folk in Innerleithen, get a different picture, a different story, a different recollection from each one of their working days and other aspects of living in the town as well. And then piece it together. So that's been extremely helpful. Last week, I went to see old Mrs Turnbull, who, as you know, is a 100 [years old].
Oh, aye.
And what struck me was the strength of her grip! You know, I shook hands with her

---

2   MacDougall, I. *Hoggie's Angels: Tattie Howkers Remember*, East Linton, 1995.

when I arrived at her door. I wouldnae say I was wringing my fingers but, my God, I'm surprised ...

Aye, she's been an active woman aa her life.

Aye. Oh, she's very active in many ways. And she could remember away back, of course, before the First World War, you know?

Oh, Ah've nae doobt, aye.

The last part of this extract shows so well how much Ian clearly loved people and loved learning about his chosen theme or subject through personal contact with people who had direct experience of a time or place. He was also, undoubtedly, a charming man and well suited to the role of interviewer. This is evident in the filmed interviews, the reflections of those who knew him best and in the interview transcripts. Alan Reid told me Ian could be tenacious and a little bewitching and, by way of illustration, shared a lovely story about a series of events Ian organised as Midlothian District Council's commemoration of the bi-centenary of the French Revolution. Focussed on the bigger picture, Ian seems to have been blissfully unconcerned about some of the finer details and, as a result, Alan found himself running about buying bread and wine and cheese, setting everything up and sorting out the technical details. 'Ian was a manipulator in the best possible way,' Alan told me, fondly.

Ian had a notorious ambivalence to computers, mobile phones, all technology – even email – as well as driving. The latter, Sandra told me, because he thought it would make him lazy. This lack of attention to those areas of life which others might consider vital could have hilarious consequences. At some point in many of the interviews there is a discussion about travel and comments along the lines of 'I'd better watch my time' are frequent. Often this is followed by a last question, a further discussion and the listener is left wondering how Ian could have made his bus at all. This short extract from his interview with Olive Davidson is a typical example.

'58. So just before you were married you were a shop steward for a time?

Uh huh. And then for that wee bit efter.

And a wee bit after, too?

Aye. Aye.

(Mr Davidson: Are you going on this bus?)

I better get that bus.

Four minutes.

Four minutes, OK, thank you.

(Tape is stopped)

Ian's charm and integrity are clear throughout the interviews and he is often met with great kindness, as evidenced by the number of offers of refreshments or interruptions for a cup of tea that are recorded. I doubt Ian ever got the bus home hungry.

Ian was always careful to be supportive and avoid making anyone feel uncomfortable. This can be illustrated with an example of when Ian is trying to ascertain a date, such as when someone was born, or started work, etc. He doesn't push too much but, recognising the value of attaching dates to events, however rough these might be, he will find a way of getting closer to an answer. Here is an example from his interview with Effie Anderson.

And that would be, that would be about 1938? Just before the War, was it that you started in the mill? You were sixteen
     Aye.
Aye, you were fifteen?
     Wait the now … Now, Ah've got masel kind o raivelled here.
Don't worry.
     When Ah left that private school Ah went to the County Hotel for a wee while. Not for long.
Ah! What did you do there?
     Waitress and cleanin. And that's when war broke oot, when Ah worked in the County.
In the County, right, right. That's the wee one along in the High Street?
     That's right, before ye come to the Tontine.

And Ian always acknowledged the difficulty of recalling the past, such as we can see in this example, when he is speaking to Archie Little.

Well, that's great. Thanks very much indeed for all your time and trouble. Your memory's far, far better than you thought it was! (laughs) You've remembered a great deal.
     Oh, the dates and things like that …
Ah, but don't worry about that. Everything becomes sort of merged into everything else as the years pass. It's difficult to remember precisely when things happened. That's great. Thanks very much indeed.
     (Laughs) Aye.

When I had asked Sandra if Ian would have been disappointed by the apparent lack of interest in politics and trade unions that he found among the Peeblesshire mill workers she told me that he would never judge a person for not being active in the union. Ian was however himself a very political person. He had been in the Labour League of Youth from an early age and he was often very critical of political decisions, such as Margaret Thatcher's stance on the unions. We see a glimpse of Ian's own political conviction only very occasionally in the Peeblesshire interviews.

One striking example is from his interview with Minnie Lavin.

That's what I'm coming to. Did the company wish you well at all, when you retired?
    No, no.
Tell me about that?
    No, they werenae, they didnae say 'You're leavin'', or anything like that, no.
Now what was that? Was that Dawson International by the time you retired?
    Yes.
It was Dawson International. The manager, nobody came? None of the directors?
    No.
Never said: 'Thanks for working for us for the last forty-six years?'
    Oh, no. (laughs)
Did they do that with anybody of the workers who left?
    Ah think most of them.
    (Miss Margaret Lavin: Well, Ah got a presentation.)
    Oh, you did.
From the management?
    (Margaret Lavin: I think it wis £2 for every year I had worked.)
Why did your sister not get a presentation?
    (Margaret Lavin: Well, Ah was with the Ballantyne's then.)
Aye, of course, aye. It was Ballantyne's. So Ballantyne were more likely, were they, or that was their practice, to thank the workers?
    (Margaret Lavin: That was their practice.)
But House of Fraser, Baird, Dawson International – Dawson International certainly didn't?
    Well, Dawson International didnae bother.
There was nothing at all. Nobody even came and wished you well, from the manangement side?
    No, no. Ye jist left and that wis it.
And that happened to all the girls and women who left, when Dawson International was in charge?
    Most of them. Well, Peter did.
Your brother. He got a presentation of some sort from the management?
    Aye, aye.
    (Margaret Lavin: He wis a chargehand.)
    Aye, he wis a chargehand. That wis why. I was jist a worker. (laughs)
Aye, but anybody below the level of foreman or chargehand got nothing at all?
    A: Nothing, no.
No thanks, no letter, no pat on the back, nothing?
    No, no.
Did you feel resentful of that?
    (Margaret Lavin: They'd just take it for granted.)

Ye jist accepted it.
There wasnae much you could do, I suppose?
No. Ye couldnae say, 'Well, Ah'm leavin. Cheerio!' or anythin. (laughs)
No, no, no.
Ye jist accepted it.
That was appalling that they could treat you like that, when you'd been working there forty-six years. So there we are. You know, if you had your time over again, would you go back into the mill?
No, Ah don't think so.

Ian was a caring, tenacious and conscientious interviewer and I have enjoyed working with the Peeblesshire interviews immensely. An example of how easily Ian established an immediate rapport with his interviewees is clear in his interview with Peggy Ferguson, held on 12 February 2004. Ian and Peggy seem to have recognised they were kindred spirits immediately. Just shy of her ninety-first birthday, Peggy was the last person to be interviewed for the Peeblesshire mill workers collection and the interview took place seven years after the rest had been completed. It is a lovely interview which demonstrates Ian's fine skills and it is for this reason, as well as the relevance of the content, that an extended extract from that interview has been chosen as the opening extract for this book. It is a fine example of the special atmosphere Ian was able to create in his role as interviewer and facilitator.

In the filmed interview with Elizabeth Bryan, Ian said that interviewing was the easy bit, it was the transcribing that was the difficult task. Susan Reid worked with Ian on these transcriptions over many years, including those for this book. When I met her in 2021, she reflected on her role. She said she was always impressed by Ian's respect for people: he was never condescending. When it came to transcriptions he was keen that these should be as accurate as possible in terms of dialect and set great importance in accurately representing the voice of the interviewee, which he felt had great dignity. Transcriptions of interviews were always sent to the interviewees before being declared complete. Great care was also taken to ensure the accuracy of any terminology used.

While Ian was undoubtedly a very accomplished interviewer, the interviews do reveal that he did, apparently, have one slight weakness: his mental arithmetic was not great. I have often found myself laughing out loud as Ian attempts to work out someone's age from their date of birth.

When I visited Sandra MacDougall to learn a bit more about Ian, I asked her about the motivations for his work. She told me that he was fearful that so many occupations were disappearing and with that, details of what those jobs were. He felt it was important for future generations to know about these jobs because for him history was not about kings or queens, it was about ordinary people. And while he was modest about his role he was also, as Sandra told me in a later letter, 'single-minded and determined, resourceful' and this is evident in his strong commitment to sharing the recordings and the outputs of his work. He kept up a fearsome record when it came to publishing and Sandra provided a listing (included in the bibliography) amounting to twenty-eight publications between 1965 and 2019.[3] He was greatly supported in these endeavours by the Scottish Working People's History Trust and by individual members who helped him in an editorial capacity. And, as he commented to Elizabeth Bryan, he was always delighted to hear that anyone had expressed an interest in listening to his recordings, which are now held as part of the School of Scottish Studies Archives, Centre for Research Collections, University of Edinburgh.

Before moving on to look at the structure of this book in more detail, one more extract from Ian's interview with Margaret Melrose reveals a little more about Ian. This made me smile when I read the transcription. In several of the interviews, Ian talks about borrowing items and is effusively reassuring that the items will be returned intact. This speaks of a man who was totally committed to his research and faithful to his commitment to his interviewees. It also hints at Ian's reticence with all things technological.

What I do is, I ask people's permission to borrow old photographs and I take them to the Queen Street Museum in Edinburgh, where they have a huge collection of photographs from all over Scotland. And they're always trying to build up their collection. They've really got some marvellous photographs. Fisher girls from Aberdeenshire or the Outer Isles, Shetland. Farm workers from the Borders, miners, forestry workers, railwaymen. All sorts of people. Men and women, you know. There are some quite old photographs and some more recent ones. And what I wondered is whether you don't have another print of this, a copy of this?

Ah had but Ah gave them away.

Aye, you've given them away, aye. What I wondered is whether ... I'm kind of hesitant because this is the only one you've got and you've got it in a nice frame. But whether it might be possible for you to let me borrow this some time?

Uh huh.

And I could get it copied. They copy it at their expense, Mrs Melrose. It doesn't cost you anything. It wouldn't cost me anything. They give me back the original, then I return the original to you, you know?

Uh huh ...

I mean, it's the first photograph I've seen of an Innerleithen family. I'm quite sure they wouldn't have anything like this before. And if it were possible for you just to jot down on a bit paper, you know, the names of your brothers and sisters—

Ah think it's aa on the back o it.

Oh, aye. Well, if you felt you could allow me – not necessarily today, you maybe want to think about this – but all I can say is that I've been doing this, on and off, for about

---

3   This does not include the many papers and articles Ian produced.

twenty-five years and I think, touch wood, so far only one item has been mislaid. And I must have passed in hundreds of photographs to them, you know. So if you like to think about that, I could maybe come back some other day. As I say, all I could do is to promise faithfully I would bring it back to you. And as I say, out of hundreds of photographs, only one has ever been mislaid, you know. But if you like to think about that maybe I could phone you.

Oh, Ah'll let ye have it.

Well, that's very kind of you. As I say, if that's the only one you've got, you know, I'm always slightly nervous.

Ma nephew has one. Ah can aye get anither yin.

For this study, Ian interviewed twenty-nine individuals – twelve women and seventeen men – some of whom were related to each other by birth or marriage. The eldest, Margaret Turnbull, was born in 1897 and the youngest, Wilma French, was born in 1938. Wilma was still working in the mill when she was interviewed. Most of the interviews were conducted between November 1996 and February 1997, with the exception of the interview with Peggy Ferguson, which took place in February 2004.

Each chapter begins with an extended interview extract which has been chosen because it has a particular focus in relation to the subject of that chapter. This is then followed by shorter extracts which explore more specific areas of interest that fall within the theme. The extended extracts allow us to appreciate Ian's skill as an interviewer and to enjoy the tilts and turns of the conversation as Ian strives to achieve a balance between encouraging his interviewee but not overwhelming them and also knowing which lines of enquiry to follow and which to leave aside.

As a template for the order of the main chapters of the book, the material is generally presented in the same order as Ian conducted the interviews, with questions moving from childhood and the domestic sphere through to working life and beyond.

Chapter one, on the domestic sphere, begins with an extended extract from Ian's interview with Peggy Ferguson which has already been touched upon. Peggy had obviously been preparing for their meeting, telling Ian that she had been reading his book on the gunpowder factory at Roslin.[4] Later in the interview, when Ian remarks on her fine memory she replies: 'Oh yes, it's referred to very often.' One can imagine Ian came away from this interview full of thoughts about the Peeblesshire work to be done. This chapter looks at life at home and within the social and community environment. The mill communities of Peebles, Innerleithen and Walkerburn were small, tight-knit ones where everyone knew each other and where most people were connected to the mills, with only limited options for employment outwith this.

---

4   *'Oh, Ye Had to be Careful': Personal Recollections by Roslin Gunpowder Mill and Bomb Factory Workers,* East Linton, 2000.

Many of the themes which will be explored in later chapters are introduced here: from the role played by the mill owners in daily life to how important gender was to the choices one could make.

In chapter two the impact of war on the Peeblesshire communities is explored. Many of the interviewees told Ian about their memories of the First and Second World Wars and the impact these conflicts had on their family life. In this respect, it was an extraordinary time to live in and Ian's interviews captured this period so well. This was a surprising theme to emerge from the interviews and one that could not be ignored. The chapter begins with a powerful testimony from Duncan Adam, whose father had died during the First World War and who then had to leave his own family to serve in the Second World War.

Chapter three considers the interviewees early working experiences and begins with an extended interview extract from Archie Little. Like so many of the interviewees, Archie left school at fourteen and was immediately immersed in the world of work. There were few exceptions to this. Many interviewees told Ian they had little choice about what to do when they left school and little ambition beyond getting a job in the mill. Most young workers would hand over their wages to their parents, often receiving a small amount of pocket money in return. But, of course, once you were earning a wage, you were also immediately able to claim a new level of independence and many of the interviewees were keen to embrace this. The recollections in this chapter are poignant, but also demonstrate so clearly the central importance of the mills in the Border communities.

Chapters four and five are the longest and most detailed chapters in this book, and rightly so as these cover the main focus of Ian's research. In chapter four we concentrate more closely on the mills and the mill owners, particularly the main mill families: the Ballantynes and the Thorburns, who dominated for much of the time covered by the interviewees' recollections. It is not a straightforward story: different branches of the families were often in charge of different mills; parts of the milling process – and therefore the associated workforce – might be moved from one place to another; mill buildings were burned down or were known by different names. Latterly, ownership changed, then changed again. It can all become a bit entangled and, in the words of Effie Anderson, I too often felt myself to have got 'kind o raivelled' as I tried to unpick the complexities of the interconnectedness between the mills, the mill families and the communities. I missed Ian's contribution most in this chapter, as his understanding of this complexity would have made this process far more straightforward and enjoyable.

In chapter five, what went on inside the mill is considered more closely. The routes that workers took through their time at the mill; the impact of change in terms of both ownership and technology and also the different processes across both cloth weaving and hosiery manufacture are explored here. Other important themes covered in this chapter include gender, industrial relations, changing working conditions and health & safety.

Before concluding an interview, Ian always asked his interviewees to reflect on their working life and so, in chapter six, we will consider some of the reflections and thoughts that were shared with Ian as he neared the end of an interview session. It is a fitting way to end this study and the reflections, when viewed from some decades later, can give us much to think about.

While the factors discussed in this book might seem to have sealed the fate of British textile manufacture to the pages of history books, the stories shared here speak of an industry that has always existed in a state of flux and maybe there is room for optimism. There are precedents. In a time when we all understand the need to be more sustainable in every aspect of our lives and also appreciate the heavy cost of textile manufacture on the environment, firms like Community Clothing are demonstrating that there is a way to manufacture cloth and clothing that uses innovation and new technology to develop sustainable, high quality and highly sought-after products, and to do this from a manufacturing base within the UK. But that's a book for another time.

The democratic nature of oral history recording must have been a powerful motivator for Ian. Oral history testimonies are a tremendous tool for learning, in detail, about our shared experience of life: often providing answers to questions which we, as investigators, would not even think to ask. And, while a book like this will select, interpret and re-present the material contained within the individual testimonies, there is always the original material there at the heart: ready to be listened to afresh, allowing anyone with an interest to hear directly from that person who was part of history at that time and in that place: in their own words and with the nuance and immediacy that makes spoken word testimonies so very meaningful.

Although I consider myself to be an ethnologist and Ian would have identified himself as an oral historian, our goals are very similar: to shine a light on the lives of ordinary people, to help rebalance the history books to provide fuller representation of all the people who make up our society in their own voices, to gather in what might otherwise be lost.

I trust that Ian would be happy that his work with the Peeblesshire mill workers has now been made available in this book. And we can conclude this introduction with a final quote from another of Ian's interviews, this time with James Howitt.

Well, that's great. I'm very grateful to you, Mr Howitt.
    Not at all. Not at all.
Thank you very much indeed for all your time and trouble.
    I hope you get something out of it anyway.
Indeed. But, as I say, it'll no be tomorrow!
        (Laughs) No! I can well imagine it. You've got a job on your hands!
Oh, aye.

I

Domestic and Community Life

The mill workers that Ian interviewed lived in communities where most of their neighbours and friends were also mill workers, or were related to mill workers. In many cases, their siblings, parents, even grandparents, were mill workers, or at the very least connected to the mills.

This chapter considers what it was like to live in a mill community by considering the domestic sphere and community. Included here are descriptions of housing and home life, schooldays and play, the role of gender in pre-work life and autobiographical recollections of the individual life within their social and community environments. The Peeblesshire mill workers' interviews often contain lively discussions around these themes and the extracts selected here can help us to understand and appreciate not only what life was like outside the working environment, but also the complex interconnections that existed between the domestic and working spheres in these communities.

Central to the domestic sphere was, of course, the home, and housing was a rich topic of conversation in many of the interviews. Some commonality of experience across the three communities can be noted here: most of the interviewees had childhood experiences which included cramped living and sleeping arrangements, shared outside toilets and only a cold water tap in the home. These extracts can help us to understand what it was like to live without luxuries which today would be considered bare essentials for living, such as a flushing toilet within the home, hot water straight from the tap or electric lighting.

There are distinctions across the communities too. In Innerleithen and Peebles, the housing tended to be provided by private landlords or the local council, whereas in Walkerburn, most of the houses were owned by the mill owners. The mill owners also had a role in the social life of the mill families and, as we will see in subsequent chapters, this interdependency is a recurrent and influential factor in the lives of many of those Ian interviewed.

The chapter begins with a long extract from the interview of Peggy Ferguson which touches on many of the themes covered in this chapter as well as giving an insight into Ian's fieldwork practice. Following on from Peggy Ferguson's interview, this chapter sets out extracts from other interviewees which provide a sense of what life was like in the world outside the mills and helps to set the scene for the chapters that follow.

Just ahead of her ninety-first birthday, Margaret (Peggy) Ferguson was the last millworker to be interviewed by Ian, completing the collection of recordings he made with Peeblesshire mill workers. Recorded in 2004, this interview took place seven years after the other interviews had been completed.

Peggy Ferguson, b. 1913, interviewed on 12 February 2004

Now you'll ask me questions?
Yes, I shall. We'll start with an easy one and not a very gentlemanly one, when were you born?
When was I born? 24th of the second 1913.
Right, so if I've got it right, you're coming up for your ninety-first birthday?
Ninety-first birthday.
Very good. You certainly don't look that, if I may say so.
Thank you.
Where were you born, Mrs Ferguson?
I was born just … do you know Howgate village, just before you come out at Leadburn? Well, just off Howgate the railway line went along beside the Howgate and there were cottages, railwaymen's cottages there. That's where I was born, the railway cottages: Milkhall Cottages. Well, I was born in '13, of course, so I don't remember much at all about the First War. The only thing that I can recall is the funny stuff they gave us for sugar! Funny how that stayed in my mind. It was a rough, brown, thick stuff.
Of course you'd only be a wee girl still when the War ended?
Yes, yes.
Now your mother was she born in Leadburn?
No, she was born around West Linton and her father was a grieve on farms. Before that she was in the laundry. There were a laundry, at Penicuik is it?
Yes, aye, at Auchendinny?
When I started to read your book about the gunpowder, do you know, for all the years that I've been around here, I never knew there were a gunpowder factory at Roslin. Never even heard of about it.
No, no. Not much, not a great deal known about it really. No records, aye. But your mother never worked in the gunpowder mill?
No, she … it would be Auchendinny, aye. Aye, it was Auchendinny. And the doctor told her to get out of it because it was six in the morning to six at night. And that was from twelve. She left school at twelve.
Oh, did she, aye? She'd go to school at West Linton, as far as you know?
I presume so.
I wonder how she got from West Linton to Auchendinny? That's quite a journey! There

wouldn't be many buses. Had the family maybe flitted to Auchendinny?

Perhaps, because being a grieve, they did move around a lot, you see.

Some of them moved every year, as you know?

Yes, they did, the farm people. Uh huh.

Sorry, I was going to say, were you the oldest of your family?

No, I wasn't. I have two sisters above me and I had two below me. No brothers.

Would you tell me the names of your sisters in the order of age, please?

The order, well, Janet, known as Nettie. And then there were Mary, known as Mamie. And then I was Margaret, known as Peggy. And then there were Helen, whose name never got abbreviated. (laughs) And then there were Sarah, known as Cissie.

That's grand. You came to Peebles as just a baby did you?

Just a baby. I can't remember. Do you know where we were first … down at Eshiels Cottages, Eshiels. That's down towards Cardrona and Innerleithen. And my mother had to walk up to there and my sister, Mamie, and I were both in the pram because we were so near. And she walked up that road to shop at Peebles.

At Peebles. How many miles is that?

Well, it must be about three.

And back again, of course?

And back again. They really had a hard life. I can't remember the house at all. But I remember her saying about her walking that road to shop and back, you know. And then we come into Peebles and we were up the old town. Now again, I can't remember that. My first remembrance of actual living in Peebles was when we went to Venlaw Court.

Right. Tell me about the house there then. How many rooms did you have?

Oh, it was just a but and ben. Now that's just opposite … do you know where the Post Office is when you come off the bus? Well, it was right opposite. It's a vennel. Very old, it's a very old …

Now was that a private landlord do you know? Not that it's important.

It was under a development company. And how I remember that was, I think I must have been the saftest o the family (laughs) because I got an awful lot of messages to do and I always had to go and pay the rent, and that name stuck in my mind. And they had an office in the High Street, along the High Street.

Can you remember how much the rent was?

Yes. I can remember. It was £12.4.0. a year and it was paid half-yearly. And it was paid off the Store dividend, the Co-op dividend.

Aye, aye, aye. That was the Peebles Co-operative Society?

Yes, it was a very well-going thing in Peebles. All the working people were in the Co-op. I can remember when the dividend was 3s.10d. in the pound, the old money, 3s.10d.

Aye, that was a good dividend.

Oh, it was a super. But it shows you what a good business they had in these days.

Right. How old would you be roughly do you think, when your parents went from the old town to Venlaw Court?

Well, my mother reckoned I was about four before I went to school, aye.

Right, that's great. Now tell me if you would, please, about the house at Venlaw Court?

Well, Venlaw Court, it was number 11, right down at the bottom. There were twelve houses there. And it had a room and a kitchen. The toilet outside was shared by two houses – a flush toilet. And there were seven of us, there were five, and next door, the Murrays, now let me think, there was Jessie, Peggie, Ruby, Ella, and then there were Tommy and Davie. What was the other one's name? There were four girls and three sons. And we all shared that toilet.

So that's sixteen of you?

Shared that one toilet. Oh, it was frozen every winter. (laughs)

Oh, what a job! How close to the house was it?

Oh, you just came out the door and crossed the cobbles. Because at one time, before even our time, it was houses on both sides. You know these closes in Glasgow and Edinburgh? They're tiled, they're cobbled streets and they're houses. Well, that was like that with houses on both sides. But all the houses on the one side were away when we went there.

When you were there … Was yours a block of houses?

Yes, they were all adjoining, they were all joined up.

So you were ground floor, all of you were ground floor?

And upstairs.

One up?

Yes, one up.

And were you on the ground floor?

Well, no. We were self-contained. We had the ground floor and the upstairs. But we were all joined.

Right. Each of you had an upstairs?

Yes, yes.

I'm with you now. And there were, I think you said, was it twelve houses?

Twelve houses. And there were actually two at the top on the right hand side but the other ten were on the left going down. You see, we were lucky because, well, lucky's no the right word because we were very poor – but we were all female. So, I mean, we weren't so bad because there were some houses had two beds in the kitchen.

Tell me then about the sleeping arrangements just as you remember them?

Well, we'd two double beds upstairs and ma sister [Cissie], she was very young, she was downstairs on this put-you-up bed.

Right, she was the baby?

Aye. I've still got her. The others are away and while she was young she was in

this put-you-up, but when she got a wee bit older she was put upstairs. So there were five of us up in that room. But mind you, it was quite a fair sized room and quite a high ceiling. There were two each in the double beds.
And then when Sarah came up she was …
And Sarah was on this put-you-up bed, you see.
Aye, I see. And your parents were always downstairs in the kitchen, down below?
They were in the kitchen downstairs.
But it was just the one room on the ground floor and one room above?
Yes, yes.
But that was normal in those days?
Oh, that was normal. It was normal.
What form of lighting did you have there, Mrs Ferguson?
Well, it was just gas light. Yes. In fact, well, after we were married, we got a wee house down there as well, you see. And it was at that time that, if they got so many names, they put in the electricity. And I can remember Tom [her husband] and I putting our name down to get the electricity.
When did you get married? What year?
'36. You'd an awfy job gettin a house. And by that time they'd built Dalatho. You know when you come in, you would pass Dalatho, big houses there. You know the Edinburgh Road, as you're coming in to Peebles? Well, that was built from '25, '27 to …
These are council houses?
Council houses. Yes. The majority are self-owned now. But they were built as council houses and in fact, well, Tom, he lost his father quite young and he stayed with a sister. And they moved from Biggiesknowe. Now, you would pass Biggiesknowe when you came up here. Did you come down the brae and over the Cuddy Bridge, yes?
I did, I did, yes.
Well, Biggiesknowe just carries on right through, you see. And they lived there. And the same situation as us. They had an attic room, I think. And they got a house at Dalatho, and I used to go up there for baths.
Well, that was the common practice.
When we were courting, I used to go up there and get baths because we still didn't have a bath, you see.
Tell me then, what did you do for baths? Was it a tin bath in front of the fire?
Oh, yes. Friday night was bath night. (laughs)
Was there a public baths in Peebles, you know, where you could go for a bath?
Well, there were some down at the swimming pool. It used to be down where … it's a biblical place now: the Evangelists. That's where the old baths were, the swimming pool. When we were a wee bit older we went there. We were often down at the swimming.
Aye. So you'd get a shower before you went in?

Because we were so near, we just went there for a shower. That was when you could afford it. Before we were working, we were in the cubicles and there were just a communal shower.

How much did that cost, do you remember?

It was only 2d. or 3d. I think, for the wee cubicle wi nothing. And I think it was a shilling or something wi the one wi the shower in it. When we started to work we went into the other one. In fact, the baths master used to get furious because, well, we were in the swimming club. If they thought you had possibilities, they used to ask you to join the swimming club, you see. So we were in till eight, half-past eight maybe, because we were taken after everybody else went out, to be taught all the different strokes. And when we came out, of course, we washed our hair and he would come in and, 'What are you doing in there? I want to get away home'. And we're still in. (laughs)

Taking full advantage of your 2d. or your shilling?

We used to take our stuff to wash our hair and everything while we were getting the chance. (laughs)

What else could you do? But as girls, you know, before you started working, your parents wouldn't be able to afford maybe to give you each 2d. to go and have a shower?

Oh, no, no, no.

So it was just a bath in front of the fire usually?

Oh, yes. That's right.

How did your mother do the cooking in Venlaw Court?

Well, I often look back and I wonder how on earth she managed! And, by Jove, we were well brought up. It was big pots of soup, mind, and stovie tatties and aa thae things. But how she turned out such food looking back, I often wonder.

Did she have a range, Mrs Ferguson?

Well, when I remember first, there were a swee, you know. Everybody had a big kettle always on the fire because there were no hot water. And there were always the big pot, the big soup pot. And then at the side there were a wee door and it was an oven … it was a wee range, yes.

Did you have a wee hot water tank at the other side with a wee spigot tap in front of it?

No, some of them had but we didn't, no. And then after a while we got just a plate wi gas rings, you know, a couple of gas rings. And that went on the top o this oven. And it was a long time after that before we got a cooker. But it just went into the kitchen in the corner. There were a corner area where the sink was and the shelves for aa your crockery and everything.

What a job for your mother though? Now how did she manage with the washing of clothes?

Well, often we were all in bed. Before we went upstairs we'd be just plonked on the kitchen bed, you know. And after we were all bathed, the tub would be refilled and she would wash all our things.

Was it Friday night she did her washing, after your bath?
>Well, we had a washhouse outside. But we hadn't a change every day like people have now. So that she had to keep washing things through for to have us clean for school each day, you see.

Did you get a change of clean clothes every day or just once a week maybe?
>No, maybe alternate days. Oh, ma mother was very fussy. Yes, maybe alternate days because we had, well, you'll have heard of liberty bodices have you?

Yes, my wife has told me she used to wear one.
>Well, ours were made with tweed, bits of tweed out the mill. And they were just like wee waistcoats and we had to be so tidy, every night we put our things in our – we all had our liberty bodice – and we would put our clean pants and what have you for the next day. We had to have things ready. You know, I'm the same yet. Old customs die hard.

Your mother was obviously a well-organised person?
>She was. She was very clean.

Do you think that might have been one result of her working in the hotel?
>Oh, absolutely, yes, absolutely.

She'd get a training there?
>She'd a very organised home life, too, because she was the knitter. She was the only girl and she'd four brothers and she knitted the socks for the whole caboodle, you know. She knitted socks all her life, aye.

Aye. Aye. Gosh. Now what about your food? You've referred to the soup pot there.
>Aye. Soup every day, nearly.

What would you normally have for your breakfast when you were a girl at the school?
>Well, it was usually porridge and, well, it was the oatmeal in these days and none o us liked it very much, you know. But other than that it was just toast maybe or something like that.

Did you have milk with your porridge?
>Oh, yes, we managed to get some milk. Actually, ma uncle, he got a farm down – you know – little farms for the veterans of the First World War. Smallholdings, down near Eshiels. And he was in the first one, which was near our old gasworks – this was ma father's brother, his youngest brother. Elliot. He was in farming as well. And he having the farm, we obviously got the milk from him, you see. So I expect we'd get it a wee bit cheaper as well.

Aye. So you had porridge and you'd have a drink of milk maybe or tea in the morning?
>Aye, we'd just have it like that or a bit of toast, aye.

Did your mother make jam?
>Oh, yes. My goodness, we were busy all summer holidays going for rasps and …

Gathering them from the hedges?
>Yes. And sticks.

For the fire?

We raided all the woods around Peeblesshire.
Was that a regular job for you?
A regular job. Bundles of sticks. We also took a bit of string or a bit o rope and trailed a big long branch home. (laughs)
Which your dad would saw up did he?
Oh, Ah've worked the crosscut as well. Because being on the rail … I'm digressing. (laughs) Being on the railway, you know, when they were re-laying a new bit, there were old sleepers. You know what the sleepers are? The old sleepers came out and they sold them cheaply to the workers. So he would bring home so many sleepers. Aye. He had a crosscut, you see, and he would say: 'Right, Margaret,' – he always called me Margaret – 'Right, Margaret – out!' And we sawed and they were all sawed in blocks, you see. But these were for kindling. You just needed a few bits because they were all oily, they got your fire going quickly.
Good burning wood?
Lovely, aye.
But it would burn away too quickly for logs maybe?
Yes, it was only used for kindling. And we did get coal but we also went for sticks, you know.
Because the coal would be costly?
Costly, and going for the sticks helped a bit. Ah've seen ma mother burning sticks all night if we came home …
A bit coal would give you a wee bit heat that the sticks wouldn't give, of course?
That's right.
Aye. That's good. So that was your breakfast and then when you were at school, you went?
Well, we came home at dinner time.
What did you get for your dinner?
Well, it was soup every day, except the weekend. A Saturday was my favourite day because we got a pie. (laughs)
Out the shop, or did your mother make it?
No, no, a shop pie. I was sent along to Goodburn's. Goodburn's had the best pies, 3d. they were, 3d.
That was quite expensive though?
It was quite expensive. That's how you didnae get them often. (laughs) That was a treat day.
Your mother gave you a treat. So you got a pie each? You didnae have to share it?
Oh, no. We got a pie each. (laughs) Sundays, my mother, for as long as I can remember, she always got a bit o meat boned and rolled. And there were no fridges, you see, so it was cooked on the Saturday and we had it cold wi chips or something on the Sunday. It was mainly mutton, well, they call it lamb now – everything's lamb now.

Aye, mutton was quite common though in those days?
>It was quite common, aye.

Now what about teatime, you know, when you came back from the school in the afternoon, what did you get to eat then?
>Oh, well, I've seen us getting a kipper or herring. They were cheap, ye see. We had a fishwife came round and, oh, I used to love to watch her. She was a wee wrinkled old lady. Her face was so brown with being out so much and she wore the fishwife's costume. She came from Musselburgh [Fisherrow], she'd the thick flannelette skirt, you know.

Quite an old lady?
>Quite full, aye.

Did she have a pannier with fish on it, and a band?
>Aye, she'd this leather band round her forehead which held the wee basket and she just swung it round and the knives had all wee slots, you know, and she could fillet, I think, just as quick as you like.

How did she get to Peebles?
>Train. She came by train. She was all day. It was a Wednesday, always. I remember it was a Wednesday. And she came in the morning and she was there till the five o'clock train at night. Every week, every week. The herrings were only 1d. each. And kippers – I don't think they were very much more. 2d. or something. It was a cheap tea and nourishing.

Aye, aye. So you liked fish?
>It was the old-fashioned kippers that you got. My daughter still loves an old-fashioned kipper.

Properly smoked, not just dyed?
>No these boned kinds.

Not dyed either – smoked?
>Smoked, there's quite a difference.

Aye, aye. You've got a good clear memory for that. So you always had something cooked at teatime?
>We always had something cooked – usually.

And then bread and jam, that sort of thing?
>Aye, aye.

Your mother had plenty jam always?
>But for supper, I've seen us makin stovies but no sausage or meat in, just onion and potatoes. And we got saps. Do you know what saps are?

Indeed, the bread soaked in milk?
>Bread soaked in some sugar and a wee drop milk. Well, often I'd just have a mug o saps.

So it sounds as if you got fed well, I mean, obviously you would feel hungry as a young girl, but that was between meals?
>Oh, well, young folk are always hungry. (laughs)

It wasn't because you missed a meal?

Oh, no. Oh, you didn't miss a meal. And you had to be there, too. I don't understand this new generation. They come out and in at all times, you know.

They all have different menus?

And they're very seldom all sitting round a table I think, you know. A lot of folk don't have tables now. Well, my mother … we were maybe poor but, by Jove, we had to sit at the table. There were none o this … The only time we maybe sat outside eating was in the summer. We would sit outside on the pavement.

Did you have a wee garden in Venlaw Court?

No, we'd no gardens, they were drying greens.

Aye, aye. Where your mother could hang the washing out?

And if there were no washing on them, there were kids playing. At one time there were thirty-two children down there.

And that was, did you say, twelve houses altogether?

Yes. I remember us counting one night and there were thirty-two at that time. It's changed days.

That's excellent. Thanks very much, Mrs Ferguson, that's a good clear memory. So you lived in Venlaw Court did you until you got married?

Aye, and after.

And after. Aye, because as you said, you and your husband got another wee house down there yourselves?

Yes. What a job we had getting a house. Sheer blackmail almost! (laughs) I remember, well, I was still in the mill. And I stayed in the mill till just before ma daughter was born. She was born the year the War started. And I worked, well, quite a while before she was born.

Sorry, you said you were married in 1935?

1936, it was the abdication year. And I came out the mill, I went up to that office. I was in the habit of going with the rent so they did know me, right enough. I said, 'Well, I think I'm entitled to that house because my parents have lived there,' you know and what have you. So I tormented them so much, I think they gave me it for peace! (laughs)

The same house?

No, it was next door to ma mother's. I think they gave me it for peace's sake. (laughs)

And then you lived in Venlaw Court with your husband?

Yes. Well, he was away in the Forces for four and a half years.

Aye. But you carried on living there till after the War?

Oh, yes. I was there for eighty-four years – I've just been up here three years – all in all, you know.

Aye. There cannae be many people lived in the one house for that length of time?

Well, I don't know, but that's how it was.

It wasn't the same house, as you say.

The only time I was away a wee while after we got married. We lived wi his sister, but it was in Peebles. And we came down. Ma mother said … well, you tried to keep on working as long as you could … and she said, 'Well, come to me for your dinner'. So I said, 'Well, on condition that we pay'. We paid ma mother so much for our dinner every day. So I was at Venlaw Court every day for ma dinner although I was living actually up at Dalatho, you know, up at Edinburgh Road. And it was just a few months and then we got …

The house next door? Literally next door?

Yes. I'll never forget it because after we got it, the woman who had been in it had did a midnight flit. And everything was still in her house. You know, we had to pack her stuff. But we were so anxious to get the house that we would've done anything!

Was that common in those days, a moonlight flit?

Well, I don't know if it was, I hadn't known anybody before that. But she did. She went away to Glasgow. She belonged Glasgow originally and she went away back to Glasgow. And, of course, we made contact with her because we had to send on her stuff. And I remember I said: 'Well, could I keep the stair carpet?' I would pay for it because it was up a stair, you see, and the cooker. Well, she said she'd been paying up the cooker to the town. You know, you could get a cooker through the town – rented. And you paid so much a month or something for it. So she'd paid two or three payments, she said. So I said, well, I would recompense her for that plus so much for the stair carpet. And I remember doing that transaction with her. I'm afraid my husband was a very easy-going person, very laid-back. (laughs) And I'm afraid I did all the business side of things.

But there's often a division of labour of that kind isn't there, with many couples?

(laughs) And I was always worried about debt so, of course I attended to the finance side of things. They were good houses. I was sorry to leave the house but this is sheltered housing up here. And when I came up to see this place and looked out at this view and everything – there are no views round Venlaw Court, I said right away, 'Oh, yes, I'll just come up here'.

…

And what was the aunt's name again, in Hawick?

She was Margaret Davidson. And that's my name: Margaret Davidson Armstrong.

You were called after her, aye, Aunt Margaret?

Uh huh, she had a little shop. She made the famous Hawick Balls.

Really, oh? She had the recipe?

Yes. And I'm afraid it died with her. It was never written down. And I used to sit at the table and she'd say, 'You can watch me but don't touch anything!

Don't touch anything!' (laughs)

You would quite enjoy being in Hawick then, if you got the chance to sook a Hawick Ball now and then?

Oh, aye. Oh, but she was very frugal, Aunt Peg. Tight, you would call it nowadays. And (laughs) I got a penny to buy this apple every day, you see. And when I got to the top of – it was Croft Road … Croft Road's right in the middle of the main street but you go down Croft Road, off the street. Well, I had to cross the road, you see, and the fruit shop was just opposite, then I went round a corner to go to Trinity School. Well, I didn't know that she always stood at the door to watch me crossing the road. So, after a while I got fed up always buying this apple and I thought, 'Och, I'm goin tae spend it on something else', and I didn't go in the fruit shop. Oh, what a row I got at dinner time. (laughs) So I didn't try that on again. And then after dinner she would give me maybe three or four sweets in a bag.

The Hawick Balls?

No, just … she'd other sweets as well.

She had a sweetie shop?

And you know, young as I was, I had to wash out that shop … the front room of a house made into a shop. So the actual front door of the house was on the street. There were two or three steps up and a lobby, then you went into this shop. And so I'd the shop and this lobby and the steps to wash. Young as I was, I had to wash that out.

So maybe that was one of the reasons that she asked for your transfer to Hawick?

Oh, yes! Looking back, aye.

It wasnae just the lack of company?

Aye, she wants a dogsbody as well! (laughs)

Aye, sounds like it.

But she was very, very strict. My slippers were as near the door as it was possible to have them, you know when you got in the door: 'Get the slippers on!'

…

[Back in Peebles] was there a hooter went or a whistle?

Oh, the hooters went. They started, ten past seven was it? There were three. You see, there were the two mills and Thorburn's mill, they would blow theirs and then Ballantyne's. Ballantyne's started at eight o'clock. March Street, that's the Ballantyne mill. But we were quarter to eight.

But the hooters went as early as ten past seven?

Yeah, about ten past seven. I think it was even before that. And then you got a warning one.

Why would they go as early as ten past seven if you didnae start till quarter to eight?

Well, ye had tae get up! Some o them werenae gettin out their bed! I remember the joke about that. Tom's friend was lying in his bed and when

DOMESTIC AND COMMUNITY LIFE

they met up in the mill he says, 'I was lyin in ma bed and I heard the second horn blowin'. And he says, 'Fancy, there's the second horn and ma mother's no wakened us yet!' (laughs)

Of course, living in a small town, you'd be able to hear the horn all over the town?
Oh, yes, ye heard them all over the town. Aye. By the time o the last one, if you werenae on the road you were late! (laughs)

Other Voices

In this extract, John Brown recalls the Walkerburn mill house his family lived in during his later childhood.

John Brown, b. 1920, Walkerburn housing

And it was the mill that owned the house in Galashiels Road?
Yes. They were mill houses and they were always going to sort them to put bathrooms in, running water and that, which they have done now, of course. It was a nice enough house, but you had to carry the water.

Where did you get the water from?
There wis a tap in the middle o the block, which done for the block. Well, there'd be eight at one side. Whether the eight at the other side used it as well Ah'm no sure, quite possibly.

At least eight, possibly sixteen households using the one tap?
It could have been, yes. Aye. I often carried the water. Two pails. Ah can remember once goin up the stair on a winter's night and Ah stumbled and Ah had to let go of the pails tae save maself. Ah jist let the pails go.

Were you soaked?
No too bad. But ye got a bit of a fright.

And did you go down several times a day to collect the water?
Well, Ah'd be about fifteen when Ah got the chance o a job. So Ah wis away all day. But Ah always tried tae get water at night, so as to save ma mother. Then, of course, you had tae have another pail for all the dirty water and everything, you know. Oh, when you think now, wi bathrooms and, oh, people wouldnae believe it! (laughter)

But these were the conditions in which you lived right up to the Second World War?
Oh, yes. Yes. Uh huh.

Hume Davidson's experience was, in many ways, similar.

Hume Davidson, b.1928, Walkerburn housing

Now when you were born where were your parents living in Walkerburn? Was it in this house?
No. It wis a house that's been demolished now. It wis just attached to the mill, just down there. If ee noticed when you got off the bus, there a car park.

25

Well, the house was in the car park.
So your earliest recollection is of growing up in that house?
Aye.
Aye. Now would you tell me then about the house. How many rooms did it have?
Jist the one room, Ah think.
A single-end?
Aye.
And it was a mill house?
Aye. They caed it the doocot. And through the wall wis the local coalman, who had his horse. Ee couldnae sleep at night for the horse kickin the wall – cause he had sair feet! The horse slept through the wall.
And all the family slept in that one room?
Uh huh. There were a bed recess, aye. There wis an upstair but somebody else lived in it. Tom Aitken lived in it.
And was that an internal stair then, to get upstairs?
Aye.
Aye. So they had to pass through your lobby was it, to get up to their house?
Aye, to get up to their ane hoose. (laughs)
(Mrs Olive Davidson: So in time they made that aa the yin?)
Aye. It wis eventually made the yin. But oo wisnae in it then.
How did your mother cook? Most people, but not everybody, had a range, with a wee oven?
Aye, well, Ah dinnae think oo had that. Oo had an open fire, just that. And then there wis the gas pipe there and ee had a ring.
A wee ring there, aye.
Aye, and ee could cook there. But Ah wasnae … Oo wisnae in that hoose awfy long efter Ah wis born. Ah think oo moved, when Ah wis aboot four, tae another hoose. Aye.
And where did your parents go then?
Oo jist went up near the hall. It wis called east end in thae days.
Now what kind of house was it there?
It wis a livin room and a bedroom. And an outside toilet.
And again what were the sleeping arrangements?
Ah think, if Ah can mind right, ma brother and I wis in the bedroom and ma mother and father were in the livin room. They had the recess.
Was it gas lighting there, too?
Gas.
Aye. And cooking arrangements?
Same thing. Gas ring.
Same. Gas ring and the open fire?
Uh huh.
Aye. And an outside toilet?

Shared. And then there were a well ootside. Ye went for your water ootside. There were a communal tap.

So there was no running water in the house?

No. We were never bothered wi burst pipes! (laughs) Everybody had a pitcher, ye know, there wis a pitcher wi a stoup on it, like's ye have for waterin the plants now. And ee went for water and ee had a pail with the slops. And ee emptied it doon and then ee filled the pitcher. (laughs)

Aye. So that was the early thirties? When you moved from there, there was no running water. Was that generally the case in the houses in Walkerburn?

Yes, aye. This block wis the same. There wis a communal tap jist oot there.

So when was water installed into the houses here and Gala Road?

Ah would imagine maybe the finish o the War. The owners started tae alter aa thir hooses, it would be '45. There were no electric light in Walkerburn either.

Did you get the running water in first?

Aye. Aye, that wis first, the water.

And then the electricity came in?

(Mrs Davidson: Well, Ah came here tae stey wi ma Auntie Mary, in 1951, and she still had gas lighting. This hoose.)

This very house? Jubilee Road.

Her auntie stayed in it.

(Mrs Davidson: Her bed wis in the recess there. And there wis a door there into a small back kitchen. And then there wis a toilet jist oot in the hall. And Ah slept up in the attic. And, ye see every house here wis jist a single-end. And then they were aa two made intae one, you'll see the differences in the windows and the way they're lined up. And then, this wis the last two to be made into one. Ma aunt got this house cause she worked wi the Ballantynes. She wis a maid up at the big house. And then when she died, Hume's mother actually got it through the mill, wi workin in the mill.)

Later in the interview, Ian asked about how the family managed to keep clean.

Well, there were different ways. When Ah wis a boy, oo wis taken in tae the Peebles Baths wi the Scouts or the Cubs. Ah wis a boy Cub then. An that wis a way o gettin a bath.

They were swimming baths? You'd get a shower?

So that wis yin way. An jist aboot everybody had a washhouse. So that wis another way ee had a bath. Each washhouse had a boiler. Some, the majority, wis worked wi coal, a coal boiler. An then they had a couple o tubs. So periodically ee had a bath in the washhoose.

Aye, in the boiler or in the tub?

Well, we ladled the water oot the boiler intae a tub, well, ee could maybe

have a zinc bath in front o the fire.
Aye. Friday night was bath night was it?
That's the one. That's another way we had oor bath.
You wouldn't go up all that often to Peebles, presumably, for baths?
No, no. Aye, oh, aye, a weekly bath.
When you were a boy, were all the houses owned by Ballantynes?
The majority o them. The better off folk maybe had their own house, but …
The mill workers by and large lived in mill houses?
Aye.

As the interview moves on a little, Ian, no doubt making connections in his own mind with other interviews and other times, then returns to this question of the Ballantyne's role in Walkerburn community life.

That's your clear recollection before the War, the village was very much Ballantyne's village?
Uh huh. Uh huh. Oh, aye.
Now roughly up to the War, what would the population be of Walkerburn?
It varied, the highest it ever was, Ah think, was above 1000. Maybe jist before the War. Everybody knew everybody in thae days, aye.
And many people presumably were related, too?
Oh, aye, aye. That's what they say when they come tae Walkerburn: 'You've got to watch what you're saying. You're probably speaking to somebody's relative!' (laughs) Aye, the Ballantynes were a great asset. There's the tennis courts, and then, come the festival, they produced aa the flags and the ropes and the tents and when the mills wis on the go they had lorries in the fancy-dress parade.
And was that a public holiday for you?
No, no. Nothing closed. It wis jist a follow-on you see. It starts wi Hawick. Hawick's in the first full week in June. And it comes Hawick, Selkirk, Peebles and then probably Walkerburn and Gala, you see. That's what it is. That's how it's timed. Oh, and they had a fancy-dress parade on the Friday night, and a bonfire. The dux boy lit the bonfire and there were a torch procession. And then on the Saturday there were running sports. In thae days immediately after the War, there were some good runners in Walkerburn. They were professional runners and they run [and they] got quite a guid turnoot. But it eventually faded away. Ah mean, they still have the sports yet, but it's mainly for the kids now.

Eric Pearce, who had lived in both Innerleithen and Walkerburn, contributed further details from his own experience.

Eric Pearce, b. 1927, Innerleithen and Walkerburn housing

I was born at Peebles Nursing Home. Everyone went there unless you were a home birth. We stayed in Innerleithen actually at the time. Ma father worked in the mill here. He was a wool buyer. And when I was about nine years old he got the chance of this particular house that we're in now, and we moved from Innerleithen down to Walkerburn – a mill house. But, about that particular time, I would imagine seventy per cent of the houses in Walkerburn were mill owned. In fact, one of my jobs in [Tweedvale] mill was I used to collect the monthly rents.

So your father was in his twenties when he left the Civil Service and got the job in the mill?

I would think so, yes. He always worked in the Walkerburn mill. The Innerleithen house was a council house. I don't think the mill owners in Innerleithen owned many houses as far as I know. Some of them did, perhaps, own a few blocks, you know, near the mill.

Meanwhile, talking about his childhood in Innerleithen, John Lunn recalled his home, first in a private let and then a council house.

John Lunn, b. 1936, Innerleithen housing

Where were you living when your earliest memories would be …?

In Bond Street, which is up the street that runs the other side o the main road, parallel to the gates to the Caerlee mill.

Was that a mill house?

No. It was jist the blocks o houses in Bond Street with a private landlord … it was quite a modern house in those days. It was a shared entrance with another family … both families had a toilet. And then we'd a small kitchen. Then ye went in and the corridor split and then that was your front door, if you like. And ye jist went straight intae the livin room. And then we'd a little kitchen and then a boxroom, bedroom if you like. Nowadays it would just be called a wee boxroom but that was the bedroom that ma brother and I wis brought up in.

So did your parents sleep in the living room?

In the living room. There was a bed in the livin room. And a wee bed in the boxroom. And we were quite lucky, we had a kitchen as well.

That's grand. Now what form of lighting did you have in that house in Bond Street?

Well, it wis gas, wi the wee gas mantles. We'd a gas cooker and— but we had the big range as well. She did a lot o the bakin in that. In fact, if Ah remember rightly, Ah remember her gettin the cooker when Ah wis aboot

maybe four or five year old. Before that, the cookin wis done on the grate.
Aye, aye. And did she have an oven?
The oven and everything wis in the range.
A wee hot water tank at the other side was it?
Aye. And the swee for puttin the kettle on and that. And then we got a gas cooker.
So what did you do about baths?
Ye had a wee bath a tin bath, and ye had a bath in front o the fire. Friday nights. Well, Ah had them more than that because Ah wis a bit (laughs) a bit messy at times, aye. There wisnae a hot water system or anything.
And did your mother have a washhouse for doing the washing in?
No. She went to one o the washhouses. There wis a washhouse in Chapel Street. There was one in Miller Street as well. Adams's in Miller Street. It wis the big one.
And these were privately owned?
Privately owned. Ah remember goin down there wi her, and aa the women and the smell o the soap and everything. We'd a barrow for takin it down in. Ma uncle made us a barrow. And we used tae take the washin down in it.
That was what everybody did, aye?
Aye, people did.
And you lived in that house in Bond Street until …?
Till Ah wis twelve year old. 1948. Then we moved to a council house in Horsburgh Street.
Now tell me about that house? How many rooms did that have?
Oh, it had two bedrooms, kitchen and a livin room and a bathroom. Still gas lighting. The houses were built in 1920. The house that ma mother was in was the one with the foundation stone on it.
Was that the first council house building in Innerleithen?
Ah think it must have been. Because Ah've seen old photographs and there were no houses this side.
Now you would be twelve years old then, so can you recollect your feelings on going into that house, from Bond Street?
Oh, aye. Ah mean, it wis a great thrill. Ah mean, the first thing Ah had was a bath! They didn't get electricity in there until, let's see, it would be about 1953.
What about the heating?
A coal fire. We'd the gas cooker and gas lightin.
And did you and your brother have a room each then?
No, no. But the room then wis big enough, we'd twin beds and that. When we were in Bond Street obviously we just slept in the one bed.
Now, what about garden? Did you have a garden in Bond Street?
Aye. The houses run up towards the church, the back o the houses. You go up the close, you know, there wis up the back and up the close and up the

stairs – an open stair. And then there wis gardens up the back. They were sort o communal gardens you know. They werenae fenced off or anything like that. But everybody had their own plot. Each hoose had their own plot.
Yes. It wasn't that you came from a house without a garden into one in Horsburgh Street that did have one?
No. Although when we went to Horsburgh Street, we'd our own garden. Your own front door and back door. So it was like goin to paradise really!

Andrew Brunton, whose family moved into their Innerleithen council house a few years earlier, in 1938, also recalls the thrill of moving there, aged ten.

Andrew Brunton, b. 1928, Innerleithen housing

So you moved to a council house?
Aye. It wis doon in Montgomery Street. We were first in. And ma mother steyed there up until 1984 wis it? And ma sister took the hoose ower. She had a hoose ower here in Caddon Court. But she got ma mother's hoose. So that hoose has been in the faimly since 1939 … 1938, actually.
Do you remember the flitting, moving into the council house?
Aye. Oh, it wis a great thing, uh huh. Bath, hot water, toilet in the hoose – ken, it wis aa great. And the scheme wis aa folk wi faimlies. And oo had oor gang, ye ken, as well, a crowd o us. In fact the scheme wasnae feenished when we moved intae it. It wis in thae days, when they build it there wis great big pits wi the lime. And of course, we wisnae vandals then, ken, but we created a bit o havoc, ye ken, wi that, and fightin an what not, ye ken. Flickin the lime aboot. So that wis jist kind o normal, par for the course.

In Peebles, there was a similar trend for moving into council housing once this became available.

Betty Muir, b. 1922, Peebles housing

Now tell me about the house in the old town where you lived, please.
Well, it's, actually it's up for sale at the moment. And it's been made into a three-storey apartment. Whereas when we were all small up there it was four different houses. And there wis a kitchen and a bedroom and a scullery.
Right. Now when you say four houses, was it four in a block?
Aye, in a block. You went in a close. The close is still there. You can still go in the same way. And there was one house to the left and one to the right. Ah think the one on the right was only a single-end, if I can remember rightly, and a wee back kitchen. Then you went right through the close and there were stairs up to two houses up the stair. Because we moved from the one down the stair in the close to one up the stair, which was still jist the two-apartment house but the livin quarter was bigger. It could take two double

beds forbye the rest o the room. It was bigger than the one down the stairs. Ah think Ah wis eight when we moved upstairs.

How many brothers and sisters did you have, Miss Muir?

Now, wait till Ah think on that snap. There wis ma older sister, maself an ma brother and Mary. There were five of us up there at that time. There were the two beds in the room and there was two of us slept in one bed and two in the other. And then there was a cot in the livin room, with the bed in the livin room as well. We slept head to feet, you know.

Betty also told Ian that the house was lit by gas and that cooking was done on a black range with an oven and hot water tank to the side. She then told him about the arrangements, helped out by grandfather Stewart, for keeping clean.

Now what about toilets and bath?

Outside. Outside toilet, round the back, yes, for the four, the whole four. It wis just underneath the stairs. Jist the one toilet, that's all.

For four households? You shared?

Yes.

Aye. And you wouldn't have any kind of bath or shower?

Well, we lived next door to ma grandfather Stewart, you see. He had the joiner's business next door. And after washin day on a Monday, we were all taken in there at night time. The boiler was filled up wi water again and boiled up and we all were put in the washin tubs and had baths in there.

Betty and her family moved to a new council house in 1934, affording the family more room, a bathroom and hot water. Electricity arrived a little later, in the immediate post-war period.

When we moved from the old town to North Street, well, we had wir bathroom and had wir own bath, yes.

You must have found that a huge change?

Oh, yes, yeah, it was, aye. There were three bedrooms there, forbye the livin room. And ma older sister and I, we had what was the middle room. And there was a wee fireplace and it wis lovely in the winter to get a wee coal fire in your bedroom. It wis a treat really. We had a gas cooker in the wee back kitchen, uh huh. And the hot water and then the bathroom, uh huh.

It would make life a lot easier for your mother?

Oh, yes, aye. A nice wee fireplace as well. Which was a change for her, jist a nice wee fireplace to clean out. No a big grate to clean.

It must have been a great transformation?

Oh, aye, aye, it really was. Ah can remember it great.

For Walter Scott, the move to the 'luxury' of a council house brought many benefits for his family. Life was still tough though, as his memories, especially of unemployment and clothing, illustrate.

Walter Scott, b. 1924, Peebles housing

> When ma mother and fither got mairried they stayed wi ma mother's folk. When they retired fae the ferm, they bought a wee hoose in Cross Street. And when ma mother got mairried, ma mother and father had a room there. And then, of course, Ah'm the auldest in the family, so Ah wis on the way and Ah think Ah wis born in the nursing home and … ma first year possibly could be in Cross Street. Then ma mother and faither got a wee hoose in Graham Street, which was a living room and one bedroom. That's ma first memory o home.

Was it just a wee cottage house was it? Or was it part of a terrace?

> Well, it wis a block. And they were aa the same. Ye went in the square, there were three doors and oor door wis on the right and ye went in a long lobby, [and] tae yer right wis the livin room. Along the lobby wis the bedroom and ye had yer toilet in the back kitchen.

Did you have running hot water?

> No, no, no, no. We had a range and the oven bit wis tae the side o it in Graham Street. Well, Ah wis there, ma sister wis there and ma brother Jack wis there. And ma uncle Wull, that wis ma mother's uncle, he stayed wi us … there wis a bed recess. Ma mother and faither slept there. Ma sister, she slept on a wooden chair that had three cushions, and it faulded doon as a bed. And the cushions went doon. She slept on that in the livin room. And ma brother and ma uncle and me, we slept in the bedroom through the back. Ah mean, ye didnae have jammies or anything like that! You slept in your shirt tail. The shirt you wore during the day, you slept in that at night.

Aye, because your parents wouldn't be at all well off?

> Oh, no.

Your father worked in the mill and, as you said, was often unemployed?

> Well, he wis often unemployed, aye. Sometimes, durin when he wis unemployed, he might get a job wi the electricity board – maybe diggin cables or somethin, ken, doon the Innerleithen road. Maybe he wis there for a fortnight, maybe a month, and then he wis off again. Maybe tattie howkin. But, I mean, that wis aa done on the hush-hush. Ah mean in thae days when they were on the dole they used to go and have to sign every day. This wis tae stop ye frae workin, see. So if say, the bureau office opened at half-past eight or, say, nine o'clock, he used tae be there early and sign on. And then he'd come hame and get his other claes on and away, maybe up tae Edderston or Edston or somewhere like that, and have a day shawin turnips.
>
> …

And then ma mother and fither got a hoose up Connor Street (about 1936–37). It wis a council house, aye, aye. That wis like luxury up there! We had three bedrooms, a big living room, a fair-sized kitchen, hot and cold water, everything. We didnae bathe! Well, durin the summer ye bathed in the Tweed swimming.

Did you go to the public baths in Peebles? You know, slipper baths?

Aye. Ma mother, she wis a great one for swimmin. And she taen me early on in life and learned me to swim.

Did you bath in front of the fire then, at home, in a big tub?

Well, Ah wouldnae say it wis a bath. Ye maybe got a wash doon. Ye jist had a wash doon. I'm sure ma mother used tae get a haud o us maybe aince a week, an off come the jersey and the shirt and you're standin there jist wi your belt and your troosers on. And ye would go ben tae the sink. And she would wash yer heid, yer neck, yer lugs, everything. Ken? Jist every part. Nae vest or pants!

You had no recollection of ever having underwear? No pants or vest, semmits, or whatever?

No.

Just the shirt and the jersey and the trousers? Aye. Socks?

And in these days ma grandfaither, he worked in the ware-room. Well, sometimes, ye know, say a piece came through and they only wanted so many metres and a bit wis cut off, he used tae pick that up and bring it hame. Ma mother used tae sew it up an make troosers for ye.

Aye. Your mother was quite good at sewing?

Oh, aye. She could sew and knit and aa that. Oh, she wis very handy that way. And, Ah mean, ye got a pair o troosers. Oh, ye were fair chuffed. But there were never any linin in them. And you get cauld weather like this, (whistles) your body wis raw! Short troosers. Oh, ye never got nae long troosers until ye startit workin.

…

Oh, Connor Street wis a palace … aye, ma sister had a room tae hersel, ma mother and faither had a room tae thersels. And when we went up there at first, ma mother's uncle he didnae come wi us at first. He went intae digs wi a Mrs Innes, in Graham Street. And ma brother and I, we had a bedroom. Ma sister had a bedroom. And then ma mother and faither went doon the stair. And then, of course, efter that, ma brother Dick he arrived, and then a couple of year efter that, here ma other sister arrived. So there were five o a family. And, Ah mean, the rooms up there were a fair size, ken. The big bedroom, where masel and ma twae brothers wis, well, we'd a double bed and a single bed. And ma sisters, they had twae single beds in their room. And ma mother and faither had the double.

Aye. So it was quite a transformation?

Oh, aye, aye. A different world aathegither.

For Anthony French, who was born into very difficult circumstances, home for most of his childhood was a single end in Northgate. As one of five children, overcrowding was an issue even with the close living arrangements described by other contributors as normal for the time. In Anthony's family, a temporary solution was for his eldest brother to go and stay with their granny, to share the load.

Anthony French, b. 1929, Peebles housing

You certainly didn't have any shower or bath in the house? Not in the single-end?
   No, nothing like that, nothing like that.
Did you ever go to the public baths for a bath?
   Yes. Yes. We went to the public baths for a shower and for a wash and for a swim. (laughs) Ah'm talkin aboot in the thirties.
And how often did you go? Do you remember, for a bath?
   It might've been unheard o tae have a bath. Of course, in thae days ye went swimmin in the Tweed as well in the summer. Well, it's maybe a sad thing to say but when Ah say Ah wis born in the Northgate, maybe that wis wrong. Ah wis actually born in the puirs house. The county buildins that wis the puirs house.

Ian also asked about other aspects of childhood and this next selection includes memories of schooldays and play, beginning with Betty Muir, who recalled her early schooldays in Peebles. Gender and discrimination are part of the story of the mills in Peeblesshire[5] and, even at school, we can see evidence of children being prepared for their future roles based upon gender, as either primary caregivers or wage earners.

Betty Muir, b. 1922, school life and gender

Now your memories of Halyrude may be a wee bit vague because you were only there a couple of years, three years?
   Aye. But Ah can remember goin to the school and ye got your wee tin o Gibb's Dentifrice toothpaste and your wee toothbrush. And it had your name on the tag and you hung it up in the cloakroom and ye'd tae clean your teeth every mornin when ye got there and wash your hands. I can always remember, jist a wee tiny Gibb's Dentifrice, a wee silver tin. Ah often wish Ah'd kept one.
Aye. You didn't have to pay for that?

---

5   From a modern perspective, noting gender stereotyping across all parts of society and different communities is a useful source of information and can help us to understand the role of tradition in perpetuating or reinforcing gender stereotypes. The Peeblesshire interviews, because of the time frame they encompass, show how this tradition changes and adapts over time and over the working life span of our interviewees.

No … ye got it, aye, and ye hung it up in the wee cloakroom and cleaned your teeth. And Ah remember we started off wi the wee trays wi the sand, for to do your alphabet. And we aa got your turn at feedin the big tank wi goldfish.

That sort of thing. So you enjoyed being at school?

Oh yes, aye.

And you got on well at the school?

Oh, aye, Ah liked it, yeah. And algebra and geometry, I mean, that wis jist beyond me. Ah jist managed to scrape through when Ah wis in that class. But other than that, Ah quite enjoyed school. Ah liked ma cookery lessons and the domestic science part as well. The only thing wis that one o the teachers we had there, she used tae bring aa her dirty washin for ye tae wash and do that, learnin her way. But it wis aa her dirty washin! Ah never liked that.

Aye, that was exploiting children?

It was, definitely. (laughs)

In the Peeblesshire interviews, staying on at school beyond working age was seen as a luxury that could not be contemplated. While some might have regretted this, Robert Gray certainly did not.

Robert Gray, b. 1926, school leaving age

Do you remember any feeling of disappointment that you hadn't got to Peebles High School?

Ah wis jist aboot swearin there! Ah'd huv been helluva disappointed if Ah'd had tae go tae Peebles High School! (laughs) Oh, quite frankly, Ah've got to be honest with you. Ah'd no interest in school at all. None whatsoever, no. The only interest in school Ah had was gettin out o it. Ah used to go there in the mornin and jist daydream until Ah got out at night. Well, ye see you know, the War started in 1939, and Ah left the school in 1940. Now, you know, Ah think in those days, that was it. The majority o boys actually thought, 'Oh, well, when am Ah gonnae get into the Army?' sort o thing. An that wis it. But then, of course, ye couldnae get in until ye wis seventeen so …

You didn't have any boyhood ambitions, to become a joiner for instance? You know, you told me you were interested in woodwork.

Not really.

Or work on the railways?

Not really. Ah went intae the mill, ye know.

You went straight to the mill?

Ah went up intae the Caerlee knitting mill, aye. Ah think Ah had ma summer holidays first. (laughs)

Other interviewees expressed similar sentiments.

Hume Davidson, b. 1928, school leaving age

And which school was that you went to?
   Walkerburn.
And then did you sit your Qualifying Exam when you were about eleven or twelve? Do you remember sitting that?
   No, Ah didnae sit it because Ah didnae want tae go tae Peebles. If you stayed at Walkerburn you got woodwork and technical drawin and that. Ah wis mair interested in that ... you could stay in Walkerburn School till ee wis fourteen.
Aye. Now when you were a laddie at Walkerburn School, and you remained on there till you were fourteen, roughly how many pupils would it have?
   Phew! Well, say aboot 150 or somethin. Because there wis a class o five-year-olds, and a class o six-year-olds and then a class o seven-year-olds and eights thegither. And then nines and tens. And then elevens wis in one and then Ah think there were, efter that, there wis twelve, thirteen, fourteen.

Anthony French, b. 1929, school leaving age

   Ah think, when ye look back, aa ye were interested in, wis, 'Oh, roll on fourteen, tae Ah get out the school!' An Ah think ye regret those words after ye go.
Aye. You sound as if you were not a keen scholar!
   (laughs) Ah think you could be right! Ah mean, Ah can show ye a photie fae 1937, an it wis a big, big class an there wis none o us really interested.

Margaret Gray, b. 1933, school leaving age

   Yes, uh huh, uh huh, to the wee school. And then went up to Leithenside School, yes.
Now the wee school again ... what was it called again?
   Maxwell Street School.
What about the qualy, did you sit that?
   Yes. I failed it! (laughs)
So sorry to touch on a painful subject!
   No, no. Ah wis like Bert [her husband], Ah couldnae have cared less. Wisnae interested ... aa ma chums, we aa flunked it, yeah, because we werena interested in it, yeah. We always all knew that we just couldnae ha cared less and that was it, you know. So we was aa quite happy that we didnae pass, because we would ha been aa separated, you know. (laughs)

Reflecting back on his own schooldays, Eric Pearce expressed a different view though.

Eric Pearce, b. 1927, school leaving age

You were quite determined to go, but looking back on it, have you had any regrets about leaving school at the end of your third year, rather than staying on?

Yes, I think I have really. I'm sure I could've done a lot better for myself. I mean, I don't say I would've been a brain surgeon or something like that. But I had the ability to do quite well. I mean, everything that I did academically I passed quite easily. In the later years I went to technical college and so forth, and that was no problem either.

You enjoyed that, too?

Uh huh. But, no, I think looking back now, I've possibly been in the wrong career all my life. But, as I say, I wouldn't advise any of my family to go into the mills nowadays because, obviously, it always has been one of the lowest paid industries with very little prospects at the top. I did as reasonably well as anybody in the mill, I would imagine. But when I look around, I can see people who were leaving school at the same time as me, that's done much better than me. (laughs) I did enjoy my days in the mill, especially the earlier days. Latterly it got a bit of a rat race.

This longer extract from John Lunn, who recalled his schooldays, gives us a broader insight into life as a teenager in Peeblesshire.

John Lunn, b. 1936, schooldays

Ye all had tae sit the qualy. Passed that and went to the High School.

Now in your primary days then, you know, up to the age of eleven or twelve, what do you remember about the school? Did you like the school? Were you a keen scholar?

Ah wasnae a keen scholar, no. Ah wis quite good at the school. But Ah wasnae keen.

Aye, you passed the qualy. Just a normal laddie?

Aye. As a matter of fact really, when Ah wis very small, Ah wisnae a good speaker. Ah'd a defect. Nowadays, you'd have went for remedial work. But it wis actually one o the teachers in the school, a Miss Murray, that taught me how to speak. But previous to that the only person that ever really knew what Ah ever said, until Ah wis about six year old, wis ma brother. Ma mother did, up tae a point.

Do you think that was a result maybe of a bad fright when you were a wee lad?

Well … Ah wis a blue baby to start with. An then when Ah wis six months old Ah had meningitis. There were an old lady that stayed next to us and that was every time she saw us up till she died, it was: 'Oh, remember, Ah took you to the infirmary in a taxi.' The Sick Children's, aye. That was when they discovered that Ah had meningitis. They would had tae have brought an ambulance either from Peebles or Gala. So the doctor decided jist tae get me there as quick as possible.

…

We had the river [the Leithen Water] at the end o Bond Street . And, in those days … where the car park is now there, was big billboards, you know. They don't have these things now. Well, they don't aroond aboot here. They might have them in the cities, you know. And they used to put up the adverts for the fags and aa these things. The men used to come every week and paste up the new posters and we used tae jist go along there and play. And then we played on the hillside – the kids still do it yet. They still play in the same trees and I suppose generations before us. We used tae put ropes up and have swings. Till somebody broke their arm, and then ye forgot about it for aboot six months and then before ye knew, you were back up, jist as bad as ever again! Ah've always been more interested in sort o outdoors life. Ah still do a lot o walkin and that. Still where ma interests lie.

Ye see, Ah wasnae keen on school. That was the irony, when Ah look back on it, that everybody was keen tae get to high school. It was a great honour tae get to high school. But Ah didnae want tae go tae high school. But Ah wis sent to high school. Because although Ah wisnae a great studier, Ah could do things naturally.

Aye. Obviously, or you wouldnae have passed the Qualifying Exam.

Ah never studied. Ah never studied at high school either. But Ah stayed in a double-A class.

Which languages did you take?

Latin and French.

And you enjoyed those?

Ah enjoyed those. But Ah couldnae do English, and in those days ye had tae have English. There wasnae aa this loody-do: 'Oh, Ah've got five highers.' Ye had tae do, Ah think it was five subjects tae get a higher or lower leavin certificate. And one o them was English. The other ones were Maths and that. Well, Ah couldnae do the English. So Ah jist decided, rather than do a lot o studyin, tae leave the school.

Aye. So you left as soon as you could at fifteen?

Aye, fifteen. Oh, Ah quite enjoyed it. Ah suppose Ah did. Again, Ah never studied. Ah mean, it wis jist one o these things. Ah went every day and Ah obviously did work. Because Ah wis able to stay in the double-language class right up to when Ah wis fifteen year old. But Ah enjoyed Latin and French and Ah enjoyed Maths. I mean, if somebody had said to me, 'You can go tae university', or 'You can go through life doin nothin else but Maths', Ah would've went there an done it for ever. Oh, aye.

But you sound as if you were reasonably happy at Peebles High School?

> Oh, aye, Ah enjoyed it. Ah made a lot o friends an that. We had a bus. We got a school bus.
>
> *And the school bus took you up in the morning? Because it's quite a long journey?*
>
> Aye. But it's changed even now, because what happened when we went tae the High School was, ye got the bus here. There were only one busload o folk went. Now there's four or five buses. And nowadays the buses takes them right up to the High School, whereas we were dropped in what's called the Eastgate, in Peebles: at the bus stop, where the Post Office is now. We left Innerleithen at twenty past eight and you were deposited in the high street at Peebles about twenty-five to nine. And ye'd tae walk fae there up to the High School.
>
> *That's quite a long walk?*
>
> Aye. And what used tae annoy us was that ye werenae allowed tae stay on the bus, ye had tae get off. There were conductors on the buses and ye were thrown off, and the bus went up tae Eliot's Park at the top o Peebles and brought the Peebles ones up to the school. We had tae walk! We were thrown off the bus. We were thrown off the bus at Innerleithen. (Ah suppose they were payin.) And it wis the same at night. Well, it wis easy enough to do unless ye started tae play football or something like that but ye'd tae be down in the Eastgate to get the bus at twenty past four.
>
> *So it would be quarter to five before you got home?*
>
> Oh, aye. An as Ah say, you were away from the house about ten past eight in the morning, tae get the bus.

Some of the interviewees spoke about how swimming in the Tweed was a popular pastime, not just for getting a wash. The next set of extracts say a little bit more about how the interviewees spent their free time, away from helping with the chores or – as we will hear more about in chapter three – earning money outside school to contribute to the family finances.

For many, like Margaret Melrose, a trip to the pictures to see a film was a priority, even if it meant a long walk to and from the cinema.

Margaret Melrose, b. 1907, leisure

> The pictures wis jist in the Memorial Hall.
>
> *Aye. It was just called 'the pictures', was it?*
>
> Aye. There were pictures at Walkerburn before they had pictures up here.
>
> *Oh, aye. Did you ever go to Walkerburn, did you?*
>
> Aye, we went to Walkerburn. It was a penny tae get in.
>
> *Did you go quite often to the pictures as a girl then?*
>
> No, no, no. If ee had the money.
>
> *And you'd have to go on the bus did you? Or did you walk to …*
>
> No, we walked doon and walked back. And run a pole and walk a pole, we

DOMESTIC AND COMMUNITY LIFE

used to say. Run a pole and walk a pole. The telephone poles comin up. Ye'd run yin and walk yin. Tae get home quick. Aye.

But, of course, it's not too far to Walkerburn is it?

Two and a half miles. But mind, it wis right at the end, the furthest end o Walkerburn.

Quite a long way for a young girl to walk?

Oh, we thought nothing aboot it!

For the Peeblesshire boys, it seems football rather than rugby was the favoured sport.

Robert Sanderson, b. 1929, sport

Ah wis in the Cubs, you know, when Ah wis a kid, for a bit. And then Ah wis in the ATC (Air Training Corps) for a bit, before Ah went to the Air Force durin the War.

Did the ATC have a football team?

Yeah, they did, yeah.

Did you play for them?

Yes, Ah did, aye, yes, aye. Ah played on the wing a lot then, aye. Ah played outside left usually, uh huh. Ah'm a natural left-footer.

So that was your first really organised team-playing, was it, with the ATC?

Aye, Ah suppose it was really, the ATC. That's right.

And then you went to do your national service and did you play a bit of football in the Air Force?

Yes, Ah did. Ah played for the station team and that, yes.

And even before you went to do that, you'd had one or two games in Peebles?

Aye, Ah played wi a couple o local teams, you know, as well, before that.

Aye. Was that juveniles, were they?

Aye. Well, the YM wis under-age juvenile, and then Ah played with another team that wis in the Peebles amateur league at that time, which doesn't exist now. Eh, Ah played outside left with juveniles but Ah played centre with the amateur side, uh huh. And Ah started wi the Rovers as an outside left, but Ah eventually became centre forward when Ah came out the Air Force. Cause Ah wis bigger and stronger then.

Aye. And what about Hibs? What position did you play?

Centre forward, aye.

About the ATC. Did you enjoy that?

Aye … Ah joined it to get in the fitba team. There were only three officers, but one o them wis the gym master at the High School. And it wis him that got me to join, to get on the fitba team, you know. But, previous to that, they'd had a very good team, the ATC. They got to the final of the Scottish Cup and that. But of course, they lost a lot of players wi bein called up an that, so. It wis after that.

He recruited you? He knew a good player when he saw one?

This is it. This is it, aye. So that wis the reason that I joined.

Duncan Murray, b. 1918, sport

What were your spare-time interests after you left school? You played football at the school: did you play football after you left?

Yes, Peebles YMCA.

So you were playing every Saturday afternoon were you?

Yes, oh, yes, oh, aye. We travelled down tae places like Duns and Coldstream, mostly through the Borders. Every Saturday afternoon. Ye wis either at home or away. The only difficulty wi workin tae a quarter past twelve on a Saturday wis ye sometimes had tae get away early, if ye wis travellin a distance. An this wis terrible, if ye were sayin, 'Could Ah get away at eleven o'clock the day?' Ye'd think ye wis askin for anything. Oh, terrible, it wis!

Were you ever refused permission?

Never refused. But ye'd an awfy job, an awfy fuss afore ye could get permission.

Was this the foreman you had to ask?

Well, the foreman, he wis all right. It wis the manager, Mr Euman he wis very sticky.

Were there quite a few of you asking to get away to play football?

Quite often there would be, yes. Oh, aye, ye wisnae always the only one.

There wasn't a mill football team?

No, no, no.

But you weren't a keen churchgoer or a regular attender although you played for the YMCA?

No, oh, no, no, no. But the YMCA in Peebles, Young Men's Christian Association, Ah mean, that wis a club. And we had a gym, we had a football team, we'd a first and a second team. And that wis a place tae go to at night.

…

Again, as an apprentice, did you go dancing?

Aye, Ah used tae go dancin tae the drill hall, on the Saturday night. That wis a regular Saturday night at the drill hall. And the pictures, aye, we'd three pictures, three cinemas in Peebles at that time, so ye'd a choice. The Playhouse, The Empire and the burgh hall.

So were you a regular cinema-goer as a lad, an apprentice?

Well, maybe in the wintertime. But in the summertime, we didn't go to the pictures. We wis always away up Tweedside or away walkin over to the Meldons or somewhere like that.

Aye, aye, you enjoyed outdoor activities and always had done?

Oh, outdoors, oh, yes, uh huh.

Playing, outside or inside, was not without its hazards, as these childhood recollections from Hume Davidson and Eric Pearce demonstrate.

Hume Davidson, b. 1928, childhood

Ah got knocked doon by a car an aa! It wis two old dears. Ma brother wis goin up the burn [Walker Burn] and ma father wis givin him a hand ower the dyke. So, Ah run across tae intervene and Ah ran in front o a car. And Ah got a broken ankle, Ah think. And the old dears they come in tae the hoose wi iz, and then they left two shillings when they went away. So Ah got two shillings. (laughs)

Aye. And a broken ankle. Were you carted off to hospital?

Ah don't think so. Ah cannae mind of bein in hospital. Another thing. Ah mind o tellin ee aboot the open fire. Ma mother's pal's brother wis a gamekeeper. And the wee boy used tae come down wi empty cartridges, shotgun cartridges. And Ah wis playin wi them, and Ah wis throwin them in the fire. And Ah threw maself intae the fire and ma hand went tae the bottom! Ah mind o that, cause Ah wis aa bandaged.

You've been in the wars as a laddie, then?

Aye. (laughs)

Eric Pearce, b. 1927, childhood

I remember once getting lost. A gang of us cycled up Leithen Road from Innerleithen, towards Dalkeith way. And for some reason I wasn't as good as the rest and I fell behind and they left me. So I got lost. And I remember there was a search party out looking for me as I was struggling home late at night.

Your parents would be worried to death!

Very worried. I think the local baker's van found me about five miles up the road from Innerleithen. I remember stopping at a little shepherd's cottage and asking if I was on the right road. And the lady kindly took me in and gave me a drink and a jeely piece with blackcurrant jam, and I hated it! But it was lovely that she did that, I was absolutely starving, I think.

You'd be quite worried being on your own?

Yeah! I think I was only about … I must only have been about eight at that particular time.

Just a wee lad. But you got home safely?

I got home safely.

No doubt your parents put certain limitations on you thereafter?

Yes, I think I was banned for quite a while after that.

I meant to ask you, did you have any sort of job yourself as a laddie before you left school? Milk or rolls or papers, anything like that?

No. But during the school holidays I always got a job with the forestry. There was about four of us here that had bicycles, and up at Cardrona, between

Innerleithen and Peebles up the back road there, there was a huge forestry plantation. And we used to go and cut bracken up between the rows of new forest trees. So that was always a nice, well paid job and a good job during the summer. We did that for several weeks each year, so I did it for about maybe three years.

And what were you paid for that? Can you remember?
It must've been away about thirty shillings a week. It was more than I got when I went into the mill! I was always surprised at that.

A lot more! More than twice as much?
A lot more, uh huh.

So that would be a good job for a boy then? And did you give that money from cutting the bracken to your parents and you got some pocket money? Or did they let you keep what you earned?
I think I was allowed to keep that, at that particular time.

Ian also asked the interviewees about their early holiday experiences. These tended to be day trips or outings organised by the mills, but there were exceptions – as these recollections demonstrate.

Walter Scott, b. 1924, holidays and travels beyond home

Did you ever get holidays as a family before the War? Or while you were at school?
Oh, no, no. There wis what they caed the store trip. Well, in thae days everybody in the toon wis a member o the Co-operative. And the Peebles Co-operative Society used tae lay on a train, and they used tae take ye tae Portobello for the day. That wis durin the school holidays – that wis your holiday.

Just the one day to Portobello. But as a family, you would never be able to afford to go anywhere else presumably?
No, no, no, no.

And was that the case for quite a number of other children in Peebles?
Oh, aye, aye. Naebody went holidays. Oh, hell, no. In fact, ye might no believe it, Ah would be aboot, oh, maybe seventeen or eighteen. Ah used tae have a pal here, Geordie Russell, and his folks belonged West Calder, and he came through here. His faither got a job as a butcher. And Geordie run tae school here and Ah run wi him gey near aa oor schuledays. And then they left, jist efter he left the school, and went back tae West Calder. And oo kept in touch and here, he invited me tae meet him in Edinburgh. Well, Ah wis shit-scared because Ah'd never been in Edinburgh! Except at Portobellae.

Ah'd never been in Edinbury. So, Ah mind Ah got the train and Ah arranged tae meet him at the top o the Waverley Steps. And that wis ma first recall of bein in Edinbury. But sayin that, that's a lie because when Ah wis maybe what, eleven, ten Ah wis in the Royal Infirmary for three weeks. Ah

DOMESTIC AND COMMUNITY LIFE

had a mastoid. And Ah wis in the Royal for three weeks and then Ah went fae there tae convalescent at Corstorphine.
Aye, Beechmount it was called.
Aye, and Ah wis there for three weeks. And then Ah came back hame.
Were you taken up by ambulance, road ambulance, to hospital?
Fae here? Aye. And then, fae the Royal Infirmary tae Corstorphine, we went in the cabbie, the pownie and the cairt. That's how we wis transferred.
There were quite a few of you in the cab?
Oh, aye. Maybe there'd be four, six o us, grown-ups as well. Anybody that wis goin fae the Royal tae the convalescin home.
But apart from that, you hadn't been in Edinburgh till you were seventeen or eighteen and met your friend Geordie Russell on the Waverley Steps? But that would not be uncommon for lads of your generation living in Peebles at that time?
That's right. Ah mean, in thae days in Peebles, well, it wis only half the size as what it is now, everybody kent everybody. Ye kent everybody's business. Or, if Ah met you in the street and you says tae me, 'Where does so-and-so bide?', Ah'd be able tae tell ye.
Aye, it was small enough to know everybody as closely as that?
Aye. Oh, aye. Ye kent where aa the shopkeepers stayed an everything like that, aye.

John Brown, b. 1920, holidays and excursions

But you never went to Dunbar or Portobello for a week with your parents as a boy?
Ah used tae go for a day wi ma parents jist tae the pool at Dunbar. It wis a lovely big pool. We used tae jist go and sit there. We used tae go on the train. And Ah can remember the ten shilling tickets. And, well ma mother had these sisters, and all ma aunts and cousins we used tae go – Ah think for a couple o years, there were these ten shilling tickets that lasted a week and ye could travel to Galashiels and round the Gala Water line to Edinburgh. And we used to go as far as Dunbar and North Berwick, things like that. That wis the holiday. But it wis very tirin. It wasnae tirin for us because we were young, but when you think o it now, for them. Cause you went out every day, you see, tae get the value o the ticket. Ah think it wis a couple o years we done that.

Later in the same interview, John recalls the excitement of a trip to London when he was a boy:

… there wasn't actually much rugby at the school, if Ah recall. Ah can remember goin a trip to Twickenham. Now, that wis a great occasion. [It wis] before the War. And, it wis ma mother and ma aunts. And, of course well, Ah'd never been in London, of course. Ah mean, we were jist lads. And we got the train at Walkerburn station, Friday, Friday night. Now what time? Maybe aboot six or seven o'clock at night. And right down tae Euston in London. Oh! It wis amazin. And, of course, ma mother and the aunts, they went sightseein. And it wis a lovely day that.

Was it a big train full o folk?

Oh, aye, it wis a big train. Oh, a big, special train, yeah. Right down to London. However, Jim Stirling, he wis a great rugby man, a First World War veteran, you know. So he took the lads, Walter Hardie, James Turner and maself, tae the rugby at Twickenham. And, of course ma mother and ma aunts went the trip round London. Then we met up at night wi them. And, well, Ah say night – after the game actually. And, Ah've told you about this Jim Craig that lived at Wallsend? Well, he's two daughters and they were sort o companions and they were in service in London and they had met us in the mornin and they saw us off at night again. (One o them was companion to Wills Moodie,[6] the tennis player.) And Ah think we left aboot twelve o'clock on the Saturday night[and] got back tae Walkerburn on the Sunday. Oh, That wis great.

Did Scotland win the match?

No. They got beat! Yes. But, obviously, of course Twickenham would be all changed now as well. But tae us, the thousands o people and that …

The following extracts further demonstrate the importance of locality and community to the sense of identity among the Peeblesshire interviewees. These extracts help to contextualise the subsequent rapid change which the Second World War and the post-war decades brought to the Border mill communities.

Myra Little, b. 1936, life in Walkerburn

And did you come to live in Walkerburn once you got married? And did you find a job in a mill here at that stage?

Yes.

So you weren't unemployed or without a job for a time?

No, no, no, no.

You just transferred from Selkirk to Walkerburn?

Ah got a job. Ah got a job.

Now tell me about what the mill was in Walkerburn and what you did there, you know, when you got married and flitted up?

Ah went on tae windin. Henry Ballantyne's.

Henry Ballantyne, aye, aye. And was it … a similar sort of job [and] a similar kind of mill to what you'd been working in?

Oh, it was a very similar mill. But there wis jist more freedom and Walker-

---

6 Helen Wills Moodie (1905–88), American tennis player.

burn had such a great atmosphere aboot it. The village itself in thae days had a great atmosphere.
You found it a friendly place?
Oh, very, very, very. Everybody knew each other. And it wis, it wis one o the greatest wee villages you could've got.
Aye. It was a much smaller, a much smaller place than Selkirk?
Oh, there'd only be what at that time, aboot 900 people in it? It wis a lot more than there is now: 900–1000.
It's fallen since you came forty or so years ago?
Yes. And everybody wis aa sort o related tae.
When you went to work in the mill, you said you found that quite a number of people were related, the workers?
Oh, everybody wis related.

Robert Sanderson, b. 1929, community rivalries

What I'm trying to get at is the attitude of people like yourself, who were born and brought up in Peebles, you know, towards Innerleithen and Walkerburn.
A lot of Peebles folk laugh about Innerleithen and that, havenae got a good word tae say about them, you know, in a sort o jocular way.
Aye. But it always seems to me, as an outsider and ignoramus, that Innerleithen is less obviously prosperous. Whether that is the case, I don't know. But it seems to be more a working people's town?
Innerleithen, you know, people that work in the hosieries and that, they've never, ever had short-time, you know, since the War. Until very recently, you know, it's always been boom, aye. So they've probably prospered a lot, you know. Likes o the mills in Peebles maybe struggled at times. But the hosieries have always done well, you know. Ballantyne cashmere and that have always done well, till jist this last year or so when things seemed tae have slowed down a lot. But they've always done well, you know, compared wi the other mill towns.
Aye. So Innerleithen has always been, at least since the War, relatively prosperous?
Yeah, they've never known bein laid off or anything like that.
It's Peebles and Walkerburn that have suffered?
That's right. Especially Walkerburn, especially Walkerburn. Aye, that's right. Peebles is very much a commuter town for Edinburgh now, you know. Because, if you sit here and that in a mornin between seven and eight, it's jist non-stop tae Edinburgh, you know. The opposite at five o'clock, you know, aye.
It must have changed a good deal in the last generation or so?
Oh, it has. And yet the population hasnae risen very much, you know. If you look back in records and that. There's so many new houses been built, you know, since the War and that. And they're goin to build, Ah don't know how

many hundreds more. There's a big estate goin on over the bridge there, next to Kingsland School, where all the prefabs were. They knocked them all down but they've started building. There's eighty houses goin in there.

Aye. Do you find you know, as a Peebles man, boy and man, that the town has changed a lot in your lifetime?

Oh, aye, very much, aye, very much. A lot o the shops are so vastly different, you know. Peebles, we'd thirteen grocers on the High Street. We havnae got any now, you know. You're all tourist, woollen shops or things like that, you know. Very much a tourist town. The main employer of local people is the Hydro. You know, there's more local people work there than work anywhere else. Well, March Street has about a hundred now. It might be 104, 105. But they're lookin tae keep it at a hundred, this firm that it belongs to now.

2

The Impact of War

Beginning with an account by Duncan Adam, this chapter continues with contributions from others on a theme which had such personal, communal and societal impact – war.

One of the more striking testaments revealed in the Peeblesshire recordings is the grim reality experienced by those interviewees who served in the Second World War or who undertook National Service, who also had first-hand knowledge within their own families of the devastation of the First World War. One interview that exemplifies this was Ian's conversation with Duncan Adam, held on 8 November 1996. Duncan's father died during the First World War and this event had shaped his childhood, influencing the choices he had and informing many of the decisions he made thereafter. 'I've no recollection of my dad at all', Duncan admitted. Yet, as this interview demonstrates, his father, or rather his father's absence, impacted on many areas of life, including the size of his mother's war pension and, therefore, what could and could not be afforded. This dictated how long Duncan could stay in education and what holidays the family could enjoy. When, in early 1941, with his daughter, Daphne, only three weeks old, Duncan was called up to the Second World War his reaction was perhaps unsurprising. 'Ah didn't want to go at all!' he said, 'Having had a father that was killed in the First World War, I was very apprehensive about the whole thing'.

Chronologically, this was the first interview recorded as part of the Peeblesshire mill workers study and it seems clear that this rich and detailed interview informed Ian's preparation for subsequent interviews in this series. Many of the themes explored more fully in subsequent chapters in this book are explored in this extended extract. These include Ian's interest in family connections within the mills, the subtle discrimination based on gender which was evident at every stage of life and the web of connections between the mill owners and the mill communities so evident, for example, in the recollections of the paternalistic attitude the owners had for their workforce.

Duncan Adam, b. 1916, interviewed on 8 November 1996

What about your father? What did he do for a living?
   He was a textile worker. He was a warper in March Street mills.
Now you mentioned earlier your father had been in the First World War?
   Yes, he was. He was conscripted.
Conscripted. 1916 or '17?
   I think so, yes, yes, aye. Aye, he was killed in 1917. He was in the Royal Scots. 7/8th Royal Scots, yes. He was killed at a place called Festubert,[7] which was on the front line. Just north of Arras, Festubert, uh huh.
Aye, it was a terrible battle that. Now your father had presumably been married maybe just before the War, was it?
   Yes. Yes. Ma sister, she was born in 1914. My mother was a widow with two children and her mother.
You personally have no recollection whatever of your father?
   No. I was only a year old when he was killed. I've no recollection of ma dad at all.
So presumably your mother must have had a terrible struggle?
   Yes. Aye, … she was a weaver in the mill. She had to go back to the weaving when ma dad didn't come back. She had to go back to the weaving – and ma grandmother, she kept the house.
That was your mother's mother?
   Ma mother's mother, yes, aye.
And did your mother remain a worker in the mill until she retired?
   She did, she did. She worked aa her days until she retired at sixty. There was a wee while she was off. But she went back. She went back and wove, uh huh.
So presumably – don't let me put ideas or thoughts in your mind, Duncan – but presumably your childhood and youth must have been fairly difficult financially?
   It must have been from ma mother's side. Of course she had a pension. She got a pension. She got a pension – mind you it was nothin to what they get nowadays – but she did have a pension. What between that and working, she managed. Because ma grandmother had no pension to start with. When I was wee, she had no pension at all. I can remember when granny got the pension. That was a great affair! Ten shillings a week! That was a fortune!
You don't ever remember her being distressed and upset? Maybe the anniversary of his death or something like that?
   No, no. I can always remember her sayin though, you know, the first Armistice, the first Remembrance Sunday, everybody was out, you know, and before that even, you know, when men were comin back and there were flag-waving and cheering, I can always remember her saying she had no flag

---

7   The Battle of Festubert took place 15–25 May 1915. This was an attack by the British Army in the Artois region of France on the western front during the First World War.

to wave and she'd nothing to cheer about. I can always remember Mum saying that.

Now were you aware of any other lads like yourself, whose father had been killed in the War?

Oh, yes, oh yes, because I'll tell you, the local Ex-Servicemen's Club used to run an annual treat for war widows. The war widows and their families were invited and there was a lot o boys and girls. Boys and girls were invited. We were invited to attend the matinee at the local cinema. And then after, there was a party, a spread and entertainment laid on. You got to know, you were a wee community actually.

Aye, there would be a lot of families whose father had been lost in the War.

That's right, oh yes, there were quite a lot.

Now was that held, was that provision once a year?

Once a year.

Was it on or about Armistice Day?

No. It was summertime. Aye, it was summertime. Well, it was light days anyway. I can always remember that because the party used to go on until evening and it was still light, still light.

And that was once a year?

Once a year, which was very generous of them. It was nice, a nice gesture.

Yes. And do you remember in your school class or classes, were there other youngsters who were in a similar position to yourself and your sister, who'd lost their father in the War?

Yes, oh, yes.

Quite a number?

Yes, quite a few.

And some would be sad cases, no doubt, you know, living in more straitened circumstances than your own family?

Yes, yes.

So when were you actually called up then?

January '41. I think. Ballantyne's never ever said, but Ah thought maybe they got me exempted for a wee while. Because all ma pals were away before me. But it was January '41 before I was called up. So I was quite lucky in that respect. I saw Daphne born. Daphne was born on 8th of January and I was away at the end. She was only about three weeks old when I was called up. In fact, Ah was called up before that actually, but Ah wrote to say that my wife was expecting and could they delay it, and they were very good. Ah got a wee deferment … they said Ah'd to register, you see. And Ah wrote and told them the circumstances. Not to worry, Ah wouldn't be called up before Daphne was born. So that actually happened, so it was quite good.

But what an experience, eh, just married and with your first child?

Three weeks and I was away, aye.

Did you want to go into the RAF?

Ah didn't want to go at all! Having had a father that was killed in the First World War, I was very apprehensive about the whole thing.

How did you feel about the War? Did you feel, you know, that it was your duty to go?

Oh, yes, oh, yes. Oh there was no doubt at all about that. I felt that I had to go. And I had to go because I didn't fancy what was happening in Europe. I was old enough to realise what was happening. Reading about it in the papers, you knew exactly what was happening there. It was terrible.

You took an interest in current affairs, but it didn't lead you to thinking of joining a political party yourself?

You read current affairs and kind o tied it up to how it was going to affect you.

Were you convinced maybe, or persuaded that a general European or world war was likely, Duncan, before it actually came?

Yes, oh, aye, even before 1938, I think, I realised that Hitler was up to something. But from 1938 onwards things was very apprehensive. I remember Munich and being terribly relieved at Chamberlain coming back and waving this famous piece of paper. But it bought us time. It gave us a year to build some Spitfires, etc. Mind you if he had gone and done his nut then as much as he did and into Poland then, I don't know if we'd have been ready for him.

And of course, you, as the son of a man who had been killed in the First World War, presumably always had this at the back of your mind? Your dad had been killed?

That's right. Is Nan goin to be left on her own? Always in your background.

Aye. A terrible business. So you were called up in early 1941, the end of January I think you said?

January, that's right.

Did you have any particular preference for the Air Force, the Army or the Navy?

I didn't want to go to the Army. No, the Air Force was a kind o natural choice. I fancied the Air Force. And if I could get into clerkin because I'd been a clerk, you know all ma time up to then. And I was accepted as a clerk. I went into Edinburgh, you know, when I was called up. And I got an interview. George Street, medical, etc., etc. And I can always remember, I was asked an equation: if $A = BC$, what does B equal in terms of AC? And if I could answer that I was fit for air crew!

That would be easy meat for you?

Oh yes, aye, oh, yes, because I had algebra. And they wanted air crew material? I didn't fancy air crew material.

You wanted, unlike your father, to survive the War?

Ah wanted to survive. I'd every reason to survive. That's right, aye.

Indeed. So did you become a clerk, then in the Air Force?

No. No. When Ah was called up I was told I was going to be a fitter, a rigger, that was the name. A rigger looked after the airframe. Everything else on the kite except engines and instruments. A rigger was responsible for that. Fitter airframe it became known as. I took tae it. The theory of flight was brilliant. You know, I suppose being interested in Science and Maths, it was easy. I discovered that Ah could use ma hands. The Air Force learnt me to use ma hands. Ah wis quite good wi ma hands, as well, I enjoyed the practical side.

Now where did you get posted to?

I was at Blackpool for square-bashing and training. That was all. Square-bashing and training. Came up to the flying boats on the Clyde. That was ma first assignment. I was there for about three years until they caught up wi me and sent me to India and Burma [now Myanmar]. (laughs) The flying boats were interesting though.

Was it Sunderlands? Catalinas?

Catalinas. The only thing we ever did in Sunderlands was, we did the main conversion. And in the cells, when they dropped the Merlin engines. They had Merlin engines and they dropped them and put in Pratt and Whitney twin loss, the Americans, and it was we that did the modification for that. Modified the cell that could take the Pratt and Whitney radium twin loss.

Right, right. But you really enjoyed that kind of work? And you learned a lot from it?

Oh great. Ah could have stayed in the Air Force, you know.

Did you think seriously about becoming a regular at the end of the War?

Yes, but Ah didn't like the rules and regulations. Ye had to do everything without question and you only asked about it after. You only could apply for redress after you'd done it. That's the bit Ah didn't like. Bull, bull.

You were demobbed in 1946?

That's right, aye, a long time.

But looking back on your life, Duncan, you don't have any regrets?

Oh no, no regrets, no. I enjoyed ma life. I objected to the five years, three months I'd to give the war service.

And yet, I suppose you found an interest there too, using your hands and learning the technology of aircraft?

That's right, using my hands and coming back to think, 'Well clerking's not really for you, Duncan. Try something', you know. And going to college, that was a challenge. And I did quite well at college. Ah got the prize for being the best part-time student at the college.

A very hard business, five years was a long time. And all these long hours you worked.

And Nan, she was very understanding. She probably felt it but she was very supportive.

Very supportive. You couldn't have done it if your wife hadn't been.

No way, no way.

No. Did you feel restless and unsettled when you came back from India and Burma?

Oh, I was pleased to be back. I was so pleased to be back and settled down. I realised how lucky Ah was because Ah saw so much deprivation in India and Burma.

Did that affect your views in any way?
>Oh it did. Ma first letter ever home was all censored. I described living conditions between Bombay [now Mumbai] and the railway station. I can always remember the railway station in Bombay. To go into Bombay, to visit for the first time, we had to walk to Malaxmi [probably Mahalaxmi] station. We saw people living in corrugated iron – Indians. People living in pieces o corrugated iron put together. Canvas. All the way in. I wrote ma first letter describing all this deprivation. Ma letter was all censored, it was all scored out. Nan never read it. To come back to a job, you know, and peace, a wife and family – oh, Ah was pleased to be home, pleased to be home.

Duncan, that was excellent. I'm very grateful to you and I hope I havenae disrupted the morning for your wife and yourself. I'm very grateful.
>Oh, no, no.

Other Voices

Beyond recollections about mill work in Peeblesshire, the impact of two world wars and fulfilling National Service requirements are a persistent and powerful theme in the interviews. The age of the contributors Ian interviewed often meant that they were sharing with him personal memories of both the First World War and the Second World War. As is shown in Duncan Adam's testimony, the death of his father at Festubert in 1917 was felt throughout his childhood, with this loss shaping his own attitude to his service in the Second World War – as he wondered if he too would leave his wife a widow and his young daughter an orphan. This, or similar scenarios, are evident in many of the interview transcripts.

This initial selection of extracts relating to the First World War can begin to set the scene for understanding the impact of war on the Border communities. Firstly, Margaret Turnbull recalls the outbreak of the First World War and the impact the War had on her life.

Margaret Turnbull, b. 1897, the First World War, Innerleithen

Do you remember the outbreak of the First World War?
>Yes. August, 1914.

Aye. And were there a lot of young fellows went off to the War from Innerleithen?
>Yes, aye. That's when ma boyfriend went off.

Did he go off to the Army? 51st Division of the Royal Scots. Was he in the Territorial Army?
>Oh, Ah don't know. But when he went away, he went to Haddington. And they wanted people, soldiers, to go abroad. And, of course, he stepped forward. And he went away to France in his own clothes. He hadn't a uniform. And a French girl tied his cap with a red, white and blue ribbon.

So your husband survived the War, fortunately?
>Aye.

Aye. But he was wounded?

THE IMPACT OF WAR

Well, jist that. Several times he wis in hospital, but not much. And then he came out, Ah think it would be 1919.
You would know some of the young fellows yourself, did you, who were killed?
Oh, yes. We knew them all.

Margaret Lavin b.1919, the impact of the First World War
What did [your father] do in the mill?
He worked in the throstle and he worked on the throstle all his workin days. That wis twisting the yarn. He never got the length of retiring. He died when he was forty-two in 1936. Because he had been gassed in the First World War.

Margaret Melrose, b.1907, casualties of war
Ah had three brothers in the Army.
And did they all come through the War?
Aye. Aye, the first, the auldest one, he got his leg hurt and he had a stiff leg. An he jist had tae trail it along. But he went back to the slatin after it. The Dawson one, he wis a slater, too. And the other one wis a plasterer. An there were two in the mill and one wis a butcher, served his time for a butcher.
And did Dawson die as a result of war service? He died quite young didn't he?
Well, he got gassed. He had the gas. It wis a bad dose o cold into pleurisy that finished him off.
So he probably was a casualty of the War?
Uh huh. Aye.

Robert Sanderson, b.1929, war and schooling
Now just going back to the primary school, did you enjoy the primary school?
Aye, Ah cannae say that Ah disliked it, you know. It wis likes o the last two or three years at Kingsland, you know, it wis durin the War, of course. Cause Ah left Kingsland in '41, so Ah had that two or three years there, you know, when teachers were brought out of retirement and we had old ones, you know. And it wasnae particularly inspirin, really. Same at the High School, really. Ah left the High School in '46, you know, just after the War.

In this next extract, Hume Davidson shares his own family's story of their involvement in the Second World War – providing an insight into the mind of a young person at the outbreak of the conflict.

Hume Davidson, b.1928, family connections to war
And were you the elder?
No, Ah wis the younger … ma brother got killed in the Army.
Oh, I'm sorry to hear that. Oh, dear.
Uh huh. He died o wounds anyway.

55

Oh, dear. Sorry to hear that. There were just the two of you?
>Uh huh. Ma brother went away tae the Army very quick. He went away tae the Army when he wis sixteen. And he told them he wis seventeen. And they told him tae come back in the afternoon and say he wis eighteen. So he joined the Army when he wis sixteen and they thought he wis eighteen.

So when would that be? Was he two years older than you?
>Now, he was born in '25. He wis three year aulder than me, aye.

Aye. So that would be the middle of the War, about 1942? Somewhere about then?
>Aye, he went away then.

He volunteered, obviously?
>Yes.

Aye. He didn't wait to be conscripted?
>No, no. That's what Ah'm sayin. He wis only sixteen.

Why do you think he volunteered?
>Oh, he would jist … A sense of adventure, aye. A sense o adventure, Ah think. And Ah think his mate maybe led him an aa. His mate wis aulder as him and says, 'I'm goin away tae join up'. And ma brother says, 'I'm comin wi you'. He liked the rifle, though. He liked the shootin. He joined the Black Watch but he finished up in the King's Own Scottish Borderers [KOSB].

And he was killed in the War?
>Aye. He got wounded at Blerick [Holland] in 1944, in December or November. And he died the 1st of January '45, died of wounds.

Blerick? I haven't heard of that place before.
>Well, it wis Blerick and Venlo. Aye, jist, jist near there. So he's buried, … you'll have heard of Eindhoven? Well, he's buried near Eindhoven.

That would be a terrible blow to you and your parents then?
>Oh, aye. Ma mother never moved for twae days.

Oh, dear! Of course, he'd still only be a lad of …
>Nineteen … aye.

Dear, oh, dear. Terrible. I'm sorry to touch on that sad memory, Mr Davidson.
>Uh huh. Oo wis ower, we seen his grave this year.

Oh? You've been over a few times?
>Aye. Uh huh. The local regiment was billeted in a place caed Helman [Helmond]. And ma father knew some o them that wis billeted there and ma father got an address. And he wrote tae this Dutchman and the Dutchman adopted his grave till the British Graves, War Graves Commission, took it over. And so oo still keep in touch. Ah mean, they're dead but the children are still livin. Oo wis ower at their silver weddin, jist twoor three weeks ago.

Very good. Well, that's good that you've got these friends there.
>Uh huh. Uh huh.

THE IMPACT OF WAR

Andrew French gives us this snapshot of life in Peebles during the Second World War.

Anthony French, b. 1929, life in Peebles during the Second World War

Ah well, even if Ah wis ten, in '39, and ma father went away tae the War at the beginnin o the War.

Right, he was away.

An, of course he wis at the munition dumps at Leadburn. That wis an ammunition dump up at Leadburn. They made the bombs. They had the bombs and everything, ye see. And he went away tae the RASC [Royal Army Service Corps] in 1939, 1940. Very early.

Very early. Was he in the Territorial Army?

No, no, no, no. The regulars. He wis conscripted ... he wis away for the six years, till '45.

So he was taken away quite early on?

That's right. So we were aa brought up wi jist ma mother.

Aye. Your father was away at a crucial time?

Uh huh. Uh huh.

It couldn't have been easy for your mother?

Oh, no. Oh, no. And in thae days, it wis tough in those days, mind. There wis no money in those days.

Aye. And you were only ten, when the War broke out?

That's right. That's right.

You weren't evacuated at all?

No, no, no, no.

People would be evacuated to Peebles?

That's right. Because we had friends that came fae Musselburgh. They were known as the Di Rollos. They had ice-creamers. And they stayed wi us durin the War for a wee while, as well. They were all interned, ye know what Ah mean? They were aa closed down.

Aye, aye, that's right. They were interned.

The Italians. Uh huh. They were all closed down.

Mill work during wartime

Every aspect of life and work was impacted by war and in this next selection of extracts we hear more about the impact of war on both production in the mills and the available workforce.

Walter Scott, b. 1924, changing production within the mills

Once the War started, thae boys were aa taen away.

And some of them would be killed, no doubt? And never came back from the War?

Oh, aye, oh, aye, aye. Ah can mind o two or three boys that didnae come

back, that wis actually in ma class at school.
Were there any changes in the mill, in production, what you were making, when the War came along? You know, did you switch the kind of cloth from one sort to another?
Aye, well, we did. We were on tae make a lot o khaki and khaki-serge. Aye. There wasn't much civvy stuff gettin done. Maistly it wis for the Forces.
That would be less interesting work was it?
Aye. Life wis a bit easier because ye got bigger beams. Ah mean, before that, ye were maybe workin wi sixty metres or somethin like that, which a single-loom weaver … that would maybe keep her goin a day and a half, two days. Whereas when ye got on tae the khaki and the Air Force blues, ye maybe got four cuts on a beam. So she wis bangin away. Wages went up.
Piece-rates, aye, piece-rates would pay?
Aye, that's right. There would be full employment then, aye.
Aye, the demand would increase for the company?
Aye, because insteed o a weaver havin tae wait on jobs comin, whenever she cut that job, oh, you stripped the loom, she wis in cleanin the loom. You got the beam in and it wis as hard as you could go tae get it goin again. And she wis away.
Maybe you wouldnae be allowed to work overtime, were you, as a laddie of fifteen, sixteen?
Aye, Ah think Ah wis allowed tae work aboot an hoor or an hoor and a half or somethin.
Aye, aye. And do you remember working overtime once the War came?
Aye. Oh, aye, because it made a big difference to yer wages when ye got a bit o overtime.

Minnie Lavin, b. 1925, production during the Second World War

After the War there were short-time.
Not during the War?
No. We jist wis on khaki.
Aye, Was that what you were doing mainly during the War? I mean, you'd just begun when the War broke out. As an in-giver, as a pirn-winder and as weaver, you were working mainly on khaki?
Khaki.
And these were government orders, were they?
Yes.
Was the mill making any other kind of cloth during the war years?
Sportex, aye, Sportex.
So there was some production for civilian purposes?
Uh huh. Not much, mostly the khaki.
Might have been three-quarters khaki and a quarter Sportex, something like that?
That's right, aye, ye got tartan for the Army [for kilts].

Was that a difficult job, weaving the kilts?
Yes, because the black and the navy blue were quite near.

Duncan Murray, b. 1918, pre-Second World War khaki production
So you worked your way through your apprenticeship and became a journeyman in 1938 and your wage, by then, was roughly about £3 a week?
Aye, it would be about that, aye.
And presumably you could add to that if there was overtime going?
Yes, aye, ye got paid for overtime at that time.
Can you recall, in that year or thereabouts, did you work much overtime?
Yes, we did, because by that time, [1938], we'd started on the khaki, makin it for the Forces. Oh, they were big orders. They were government orders. For uniforms for the battledress and overcoats.
What about Air Force uniforms? Did you get any orders for those?
We didnae do any o the Air Force stuff at all. Jist Army.
What kind of material was the khaki made up of? You know, was it a coarse material?
It wis fairly coarse, yes – no too coarse.
It wasn't as fine as some of your finest stuff?
Oh, no. It wouldnae, it couldnae, oh, no. It wis jist the kind o run o the mill wool.
The wool would come from the cheviots or the black-faces, rather than the Merino?
Cheviot. Oh, aye, there'd be no Merino in it, no. Oh, they wis big orders, oh, they were big.

Military service
Ian also recorded the testimonies of Peeblesshire men who had gone to war and those who had completed their National Service commitments. These extracts demonstrate how Ian's skills as an interviewer, together with his knowledge of war, were invaluable in helping to support the interviewees, allowing them to more easily share their memories.

Peter Lavin, b. 1922, Second World War experience
I jist joined the Territorials about six month afore the War broke oot, as I wis a drummer in the ex-servicemen's pipe band here, you see. One o the colonels came doon an they asked for all the band tae join the Royal Scots. The 8th Battalion. So they wanted us tae join, an there wis quite a number o us went away an joined up. I wis seventeen, and because I wis goin into the band I got in when Ah shouldnae have got in till Ah wis eighteen. An then when [the] War broke oot, we got called up. Right away, in 1939.
You were called up even before the War was declared?
Yeah, we were three days before the War. And he says, 'You people that's no eighteen', he says, 'you might get sent away home'. But Ah didnae. Ah got

kept in, because I wis in the band. An I wis right through the whole War.
And where did you go?
   Well, we were in the drill hall in Peebles an frae there, I think it wis aboot a week after, we moved down to Earlston, away down in the Borders there. An Ah wis there for more or less extra trainin, you know. An, I wis there for a while. We were livin in houses ... people took us in.
Oh you were living in digs, aye civilian billets, I'm with you. And was that the whole battalion who were there?
   Yeah, they were aa doon there an they were aa put in billets, yeah. I wis there a few month. An then what happened was, they came along and said that some o us that wis too young for tae go to France would be gettin transferred. An we got transferred from the Royal Scots to the Royal Artillery. An they went doon into Coventry.
How did you feel about being transferred? Were you upset about that?
   No, no, really because if Ah'd got a chance, if Ah'd been aulder, Ah'd been maybe sent abroad, you know.
Were you worried about that? Were you worried about being sent abroad?
   Well, Ah would've been if Ah had known I wis goin, but instead o that we went doon into this Royal Artillery doon in Coventry.
How did your mother feel about you joining the Territorial Army – because your father had died in the First World War, hadn't he? Was your mother worried about it? Did she try and discourage you?
   No. Well, when I joined, they weren't expecting a war to start up. But I think she was probably worried after that, you know, when the War broke out. Then I wis away an that wis it.
Aye. So you got down to Coventry and you were in the artillery. Was it field artillery you were in?
   Well, it wis a searchlight party for a while, an then they went onto the Bofors guns and I wis there when they blitzed the place. Gun-pits and searchlights were aa roond about Coventry.
Tell me about that then, what you remember about the blitz in Coventry?
   Well I think I wis on the searchlights that night and they came over and blitzed the place, of course, and we were tryin to pick up the planes. And then the order came through that wis tae put the lights out, cause they must have discovered that the lights were aa roond aboot Coventry. As soon as the lights went on they came into the middle o it. He knew what he was doin. It was quite a mistake. They knew where to go. An then frae there I went up tae the Orkney Islands. I went up there for fifteen month up in South Ronaldsay, for lookin after Scapa Flow an everything with the guns, you know.
Protecting the fleet up there?
   Up there, aye.
How did you find that experience? A kind of lonely place?

Well, there wis entertainers came up and aa the rest o it, but ye jist had to go oot for a bit walk if ye got time tae yersel. But they kept ye busy really. You know, ye didnae get much time for tae get fed up or that.

Did you feel homesick when you were in Coventry or in the Orkneys?

No, no really. There wis quite a lot o good chaps, you know, an that kept ye goin an everything wis aaright.

And you were all in it together, of course.

Yeah.

But you were still a very young lad. You were only eighteen, nineteen, twenty?

Oh, aye, I wis comin up for nineteen then.

So where did you go from there?

We came back down an we ended up at Polmont. That wis to defend the Forth Bridge and the Forth, and some o the places roond Edinburgh.

Again were you on the anti-aircraft guns there?

I wis on guns and they had searchlights there an aa. Then I got transferred away doon East Grinstead, … an fae there I went abroad – North Africa.

Oh, so when was that, when you went abroad then?

Oh, I cannae mind the date. The North African invasion had started when we got there.

Aye, November 1942. Did you take part in the landings?

No, they were landed. We took part in the Sicily and Italy landin.

So the North African campaign was almost ended?

Jist aboot finished … aye.

So it would be early '43 maybe?

Aye, somewhere about that.

And then you took part in the invasion of Sicily and Italy?

Sicily first, that's right, uh huh.

Aye, that was July '43. Were you in the actual landings?

Well, I wis in the landin, but no the first batch. We came in later on and then went right through Italy and aa the way up.

But again it was anti-aircraft defences?

Yeah, we were anti-aircraft and different things.

Where did you land in Italy?

Messina and then I went right up through Italy. I was at Veriano, and we could see Cassino about as far up as that hill up there, you know. Well maybe a wee bit further. Aye, I wis there when they blitzed it.

Cassino, aye. That was a terrible business, that.

We couldnae dae much mair wi it. Ye couldna cross the street. He had us aa covered aa the way roond.

A lot of lives lost there. So you went right up through Italy?

Aye. Ah wis in Rome for a while.

You came home from Italy?

The War got finished when we were in Italy. I think it wis '46, uh huh.
Of course you'd been away seven years by then?
Yeah, uh huh.
So that was a huge change in your life wasn't it, because you'd led a fairly quiet life, I suppose. You were saying you hadn't really had holidays in Peebles before the War, apart from the Co-op trip to Portobello. You'd never been away from Peebles, had you?
No, no really. No. Jist the Co-op's trip. Ma mother found a tanner and Ah went! (laughs)
So then suddenly there you were, you were whisked off to North Africa and Italy and Sicily and everywhere. Looking back on it, what effect do you think the War had upon you? On your thinking, on your views, your attitudes, your beliefs?
Well, a lot o us found out that ye can dae things for yersel. Everybody pulled thegither, you know. Aye, comradeship, that wis the word I wis lookin for. Aye. Everything wis aaright then, cause ye got thegither an then it broadened yer outlook too.
In what ways did it broaden your outlook?
Well, ye learnt quite a lot o things that ye never thought ye would learn, you know. And, well ye're mindin aboot it a lot, you know. I mean, they had the two minute silence the other day there and they were gettin a lot o us Legion folk to go but I didnae get there. An I wis jist thinkin, ye dinnae really need to go to that to mind o what happened. You know, you've got to go an put in an appearance but it preys on your mind aa your life.
So War made quite an impact on you?
Oh, yes, aye.
Were you ever interested in politics before the War?
Aye, no afore the War. After the War, well, Ah got in through the union. I wis on the union committee. And then Ah taen ower the chair o the union for the mill an Ah wis convener up there for a while an aa. Ah done a lot o work for the union. Well, politics wis jist a case o studyin it up, you know.
Did you ever join a political party?
Ah wis a member o the Labour Party for a wee while.
Was that after the War?
After the War.
You didn't join a political party before the War?
No.
No, no. So was the difference the War? Did that give you ideas about society and politics? Did you think about the world in a different way?
It gave ye an idea, it gave ye an idea that things should be better when ye come hame, you know. That's aboot what ye think aboot, you know. You try to improve things.

THE IMPACT OF WAR

John Brown also served for the duration of the Second World War, and shared this account of his training and active service.

John Brown, b. 1920, Second World War experience

Ah went intae the Army, well, joined the Territorials, the Royal Scots in 1939. Of course, we knew that war wis comin, you know. Cause we were called up on the Friday and Ah think the War started on the Sunday.

The Sunday, aye, aye. Two days before the War broke out, you were called up?

Yes, aye. We were called up.

And what led you into the Territorial Army then?

Well, it wis mostly tae be, well, all the chaps you knew, we knew we'd all be together. And, that wis really the idea.

Some of your friends had already joined, was that it?

Well, the 8th Battalion, well, oor fathers and uncles and that had been in the 8th Battalion in the Great War and they were restructuring the 8th Battalion again.

Before the Second World War, aye. And did you join because you felt very strongly about the political or international situation?

Well, at that time we knew we would be called up anyway and we would maybe have to go somewhere we didn't want to go. Whereas, if we joined up, well, we knew that we would have a choice.

Aye, I'm with you. You didn't join the Territorial Army because you were, say, very politically aware or active and worried about the international situation?

Well, not really, no. We felt we'd all be together, you know. Come what may, we'd all sort of be together.

So you remember the declaration of war?

Oh, yes, aye. Ah remember on the Friday night bein called up, aye. Cause some o the lads volunteered for guard duty. Volunteered for it. And marchin up and down wi the fixed bayonets, you know.

Was this at Innerleithen?

At Innerleithen. And some o them from the outlyin districts slept there. But we got a pass. You could get home to your bed and report back to the drill hall in the morning. And we would be here for a good two or three weeks. Forsyth's the baker wis the caterers. It wis lovely grub we used to get! So the instructors would be here for two or three weeks and they used to go up the hills and that, you know, and do rifle drills and things like that. And then oor first place wis Earlston. We moved to Earlston. And we were there jist before Christmas. And then we moved to Kinghorn.

And was it huts in Earlston that you were living in?

It wis civilian houses, but Ah remember we stayed with a retired schoolmaster, a Mr Carter, in Earlston. There wis four o us billeted there.

And then Kinghorn, was it barracks?

63

Kinghorn was civilian but they were empty houses, you know. Oh, it wis, by golly, it wis a cold winter there. It wis cold at Kinghorn. And then Ah wis in the advance party for Norway. We were goin tae sail from Newcastle but, of course, Norway fell, so we never landed. And then the next move, we walked from Kinghorn tae Galashiels – it took a couple o days, if Ah remember rightly.

Did you sleep out in the fields overnight?

Yes, bivvying, bivouac. And then we went down England, Marlborough. We went down to Marlborough.

And were you there for quite some time?

No. Jist about three month.

So you were moving about quite a bit really?

We were movin about, uh huh.

And then you went over to Normandy was it?

Yes. Uh huh. They used tae take drafts but they tried to keep each headquarter company together. Ah wis in headquarter company. There were so many of us went to [a place] near Leatherhead. And for the conscripts comin in, we were supposed tae be sort o instructors, you know. Showin them how to salute and things like that. Dish out uniforms, things like that. However, after two or three weeks, they discovered it wasnae suitable so we went back tae our units.

And were you doing sort of general guard duties?

It was, aye. They were [preparing] for the invasion, on sands. Ah remember goin out in the mornins wi the pioneers and we used tae build the steel scaffoldin to deter tanks comin in, you know. We were supposed to be one of the most equipped divisions in the country. (laughs) Ah don't know! But we were there for nine month. And Churchill got thousands and thousands o signatures, you know, petitions, for us tae stay there. (laughs)

Really? You must have been popular!

Aye, we must have been popular! (laughs) We used tae get a lot o odd bombs. There wis one Walkerburn fellow killed there by a bomb. And there wis another badly wounded. Ah can remember bein wi ma pal, Roy Kerr. He wis killed in Normandy. And we were in the Palace cinema, one o these old-fashioned cinemas wi big chandeliers. And they used tae put a notice up on the screen, you know: 'Air raid now in progress. You can leave if you like but the programme will continue.' So we jist sat the same as a lot o others and we heard the chandeliers shakin and we thought: 'Good grief! This is near!' So the next time, the chandeliers shook again we thought they were comin down. So we got out – and you had to carry a steel helmet with you and a gas mask, so we put the steel helmet on and here, when we got out, there's the bodies lyin. Ah thought: 'Oh, good grief! This is terrible.' And here it wis Burton's the Tailors and it wis dummies had been blown out on the street!

(laughs) They got the station that night. That was Lowestoft. Oh aye, there wis quite a few killed in Lowestoft.

So eventually you went over to Normandy, you were saying? And that was D-Day plus?

Yes. That was from Worthing. We were at Worthing. D-Day plus six, Ah think it was. We were supposed to break out o the, you know … the bridgehead.

And you were still with the 8th Battalion, Royal Scots?

8th Battalion, all the time, yes. All the time. Ah wis a lance-corporal by this time.

Now what about the fighting in Normandy? That would be quite fierce was it?

Oh, terrible!

Savage, costly, aye. Did you lose a lot of friends?

Yes. Well, as Ah tell you, ma friend wis killed there.

Roy Kerr?

Roy Kerr, uh huh.

Which village was he killed at?

Ah think it wis the very first day, when we went intae action, uh huh. Ah wis with C Company at the time. And he wis – Ah think – D Company. And we tried tae get thegither. And him and another Innerleithen [man], Johnny Parslow, they were carryin a stretcher with a wounded man and the three o them were killed.

Terrible. There was a heavy loss of life?

Oh!

But you weren't wounded yourself?

No. Many, many escapes, many escapes.

So you fought right through France did you? And into Belgium or Holland?

Yes. Well, actually, Ah never fired a shot.

Did you not?

No. Ah wis a stretcher bearer and we had sten-guns, small machine-guns, supposed to be for our own protection. Well, that first day we went intae battle, you had your sten-gun, you had all your equipment, you had your bandages, you know. And carrying a stretcher. Ah mean, it wis a stupid thing havin a sten-gun. There wis two o our stretcher-bearers shot by snipers and Ah think it wis because they had their weapons. After that, when we went intae battle, we never carried a sten-gun. Just a Red Cross band on our arm. We were unarmed. We had a thing that protected us under the Geneva Convention. Ah still have it, signed and that. Of course, we were still shot at and shelled and everything. But we never went intae battle again armed.

So you must have carried out many poor souls that were badly wounded?

Oh, terrible, terrible.

So you went right through France did you, and into Belgium, Holland?

Yes. Holland.

Where were you in Germany when the War finished?
> It was at a place, Bad Bramstetd, jist near Hamburg. We used tae go intae Hamburg. But we were at Lüneburg Heath.

Where Montgomery signed the surrender, aye?
> Yeah, we were at Lüneburg Heath. Ah can always remember the big canteen there and an oil painting o Göring. That wis the German barracks. They had everything there. They had fur coats and …

German Army uniforms … aye?
> Aye. And white shirts, because we got a few white shirts. (laughs) Oh, it was like a great big warehouse … a good canteen.

Aye, a quartermaster's store sort of place?
> Aye, everything.

And then when did you get demobbed?
> Well it wis the followin year. You see, well, Ah wis still pretty young then. The younger you were, well, the longer you were in. The older ones got out first, you see.

Aye. But you'd been away about seven years by then?
> No, six. Ah got married in '45, 8th o August '45.

You came home for that?
> Aye. But Ah still had tae go back.

Aye. So it was into 1946?
> It was '46.

And then did you come to live in Innerleithen at that stage?
> We couldn't get a house so we had tae stay with ma parents who were still in Walkerburn.

That was a very common experience wasn't it in those days, for many ex-servicemen? Housing was very, very difficult.

A few years younger than Peter Lavin and John Brown, Robert Gray enlisted at seventeen and became a paratrooper. In this detailed account we hear about Robert's training and subsequent deployment as a paratrooper, a soldier's understanding of the atomic bomb and about his time in Java and Palestine prior to him being demobbed in 1947.

Robert Gray, b.1926, Second World War experiences

You were in the forestry then from the age of about sixteen, seventeen until you went off to the Forces?
> Seventeen, Ah went off.

Did you volunteer?
> Yes.

You joined the Army. You preferred the Army rather than the Navy or the Air Force?
> Well, by that time, they were runnin down the Air Force, you know. Ah

mean it wasnae sae easy tae get in then, you know. And the Army was the one available, and that was it. The Air Force would have been ma first choice, if Ah'd been able to get intae it. But Ah couldn't.

And you didn't want to wait to be conscripted at the age of eighteen?
Well, no really. Because, Ah mean, they could bump ye into anything then, ye know.

You felt you had a choice when you could volunteer?
Uh huh. Once you got your basic trainin done, you know.

So where did you do that?
Dreghorn, up in Edinburgh for ten weeks.

And then were you given the option of joining particular regiments or were you just told?
Ah wis destined for the KOSBs, which is a Border regiment, of course, you see. And, of course, it's then [once you've done your basic training] that they come round wi the options – Do you want to do this? Do you want to do that? – you've got to volunteer.

So it was at that stage that you got off into the Parachute Regiment?
Uh huh.

Aye. And by that time, of course, the paratroops were becoming very much better known and very prestigious weren't they? Because that would be just before Arnhem?
Yeah before Arnhem came … British paratroops had been used before that an aa but not extensively. The first … Ah think Ah'm right in saying that the first organised sort of raid by British paratroops was at Bruneville [Bruneval Raid]. When they captured the radar installation there.

The radar installation, aye. Aye, that was quite a small operation?
Yeah. But it was a unit o the Parachute Regiment.

Yes, that's right, that's right. I think some landed from the sea and others were dropped in from the air, that's right. That's great. So you would then have quite a few weeks of specialist training as a paratrooper to undergo?
Yes. Aye, you do quite a bit, aye. You go tae what they call an army physical training school, you know. And that was in Derbyshire.

So that sort of toughened you up and prepared you?
That's right. And then you do your pre-jump training, which was aa done at [RAF] Ringway, [near] Manchester.

That's learning how to fall, how to land and so on?
That's right, that's right. And once you do that and once you do your eight jumps, they give you a red beret and 2s.6d. a day.

Aye. Wealth at last! (laughter) Was it the old business of being taken up in a balloon the first time?
Two, aye. The first two.

The first two jumps?
Yeah.

How did you find that, compared with jumping out of an aeroplane?

Oh, aye. The first one … ye don't know what's goin to happen to you. The second parachute jump oot a balloon is terrifying, cause ye know what's goin to happen to you. Because to jump out a balloon, you drop like a stone. To jump out an aircraft, the slipstream of the aircraft catches you and develops your parachute which is, you know an awfy lot easier than goin down out a balloon. It was terrifying, that.

I admire your courage.

I don't know why they ever made them do two out a balloon. (laughs) Ah suppose it was a case that: 'You've done it once, have you got the courage to do it twice?' Ah suppose. Somethin like that, ye know.

Aye. But that seems the more difficult of the two means, doesn't it, drop out of a balloon?

Oh, it's just terrifying!

Aye, terrifying! Whereas you would have thought they would only ask you to do that once you'd jumped out of an aeroplane?

Aye. Well, ye done the balloon first, ye know.

Maybe that was the psychology? If you couldn't jump out the balloon, then you'd be too nervous to jump out a plane? So it's better to give you the harder of the two tests first?

Aye.

I doubt if it had been me, I would have been saying, 'Sorry, I've changed my mind. It's the Navy I really want!' (laughs)

(Mrs Margaret Gray: Ye wouldnae get me doin it anyway. I can tell ye that! No way!)

Oh, I couldnae do that to save myself. It must be absolutely terrifying?

As Ah say, the second time, it was. It was terrifying, aye. Because ye knew what was goin tae happen to you. But then again, when ye get intae an aircraft the first time ye go out an aircraft, ye don't know what's goin tae happen tae ye. But as things progressed it got easier. It got easier again with the different type o aircraft, you know.

Oh? Was it Dakotas you were jumping out of?

Eventually, we got Dakotas. But ye done one out a Whitley, an old Whitley bomber, which was an aperture. You know, you went down …

Down through the floor, aye?

Aye. And then they went on to Dakotas, which was a door. Well, as Ah say, the frightening thing aboot it wis that ye were standin there – well, no standin there, but ye were goin out the door and the great big tailplane's there! You think it's goin tae hit ye!

Aye, that was always a danger, too, that the parachute might catch on it?

Aye, well, underneath. Then, of course, eventually they converted the big Stirling bombers, you know. And they jist take the sort of bomb bays away. Ye jist walk along and the floor disappears and that was that. It was quite good.

Anything that happened in the mill thereafter must have seemed absolute child's play! (laughs)

Aye, oh, aye.

Then you were in the paratroops right through the remaining part of the War?

Yes, aye.

When were you demobbed?

January, '47. The Far East. I was in India at the end o the War – Malaya [now Malaysia] and Java. As a matter of fact, when they dropped the atomic bomb, we were in an invasion armada off the coast of Malaya. We were goin to invade Malaya. And our target was Singapore, but we had to capture an airfield first.

Aye, aye. So what was the feeling among the lads on your ship in that armada, when the news came, you know, that the bomb had been dropped?

Nobody had a ruddy clue as to what they were talkin about. We'd never heard o anything. Somebody said 'They've dropped an atomic bomb' – and everybody's standin lookin at each other: 'What's an atomic bomb?' You know – nobody had ever heard anything about it.

Aye. It was a well-kept secret. But there must have been immense relief that the War almost immediately came to an end?

Well, once they dropped the second one. Once they dropped the second one, aye. We still invaded Malaya but, Ah mean, it was jist a case o roundin people up, you know. There wis the odd skirmish.

Yes. I suppose it would be difficult for the Japanese government to communicate to its troops in the field?

Well, yes. And then even although they did communicate, they were such fanatics that a lot o them didnae believe it. We didnae have a lot o problems in Malaya. The big problems that we had was down in Java. Because Java being the Dutch East Indies, the Dutch tried to go back there jist to take over and of course Sukarno and his outfit wouldnae let them in. Well, the Japanese were runnin about armed, Sukarno's outfit were runnin about armed. And ye didnae know what the hell was goin on.

So were you there for some time?

Yes. We wis down there in Java, oh, eight months. Something like six, eight months.

Were you involved in any fighting there?

Aye, skirmishes off and on, aye, mostly wi Sukarno.

Sukarno, aye, nationalists. Aye, it was a difficult time.

The Japanese mainly, it wis jist tryin to get them rounded up. But then ye couldnae get them rounded up because Sukarno was tryin to round them up to get the arms off them. And, oh, it was a bit of a shambles actually.

Aye, utter confusion, aye. So you were demobbed from Java was it?

No, no, no. Ah came back to Palestine. Ah did ma last eight month o army service in Palestine. Ah wis demobbed from Palestine, aye.

And that was 1947?
   Uh huh.
So you'd been away four years?
   Almost, aye.
Now what did you feel about your army service?
   Lookin back on it, Ah think that it was a very good part of ma life. And Ah saw an awfy lot o the world that Ah would never have seen.
You'd never have got to Java otherwise would you?
   No, no, no. Ah seen a lot o the world that Ah'd never ever have seen.
What sort of impact did the War have upon you? Did it develop your views in any way?
   Ah would think, yes. Ah think it moulded iz into a socialist really (laughs) the socialist that Ah am, you know. Because, Ah mean, that even in wartime and aa the rest o it, in the Army there was still an awfy sort o difference between the officer classes and the ordinary classes, you know.
Did you remain a private yourself?
   Yes, yes, aye.
You didn't reach the giddy height of lance-corporal?
   No, no, no, no. Ah'd no interest actually.

Duncan Murray joined up in January 1940 and by 7 June he was a prisoner of war. His account of his time as a POW is engaging and enlightening and throughout his account of moving from place to place, covering hundreds of miles, there is a strong sense of the anxiety this uncertainty engendered.

Duncan Murray, b. 1918, being a POW in the Second World War

   Well, September '39 until 15 January 1940 Ah wis workin in the mill over there. And then I joined up at Berwick in the KOSBs. Ah wis called up. But Ah did volunteer previous to that, because Ah had a cousin in the Navy, a regular. And Ah had another cousin in the Navy before that. So Ah went into Edinburgh to see if Ah could sign on in the Navy, ye see. Ah wis goin tae volunteer …
   Of course, what he said to me wis, oh, aye, he says, 'No, no, no'. He says, 'This is only goin tae last for six months'. He says, 'Wait till you're called up and put in for the Navy'. So Ah did that. But when Ah went in there, Ah had an interview with the naval man efter Ah'd ma medical, and he said, 'Well,' he says, 'there's only one thing …'
   Oh, aye.
   'What was your occupation?'
   And I told him.
   'Oh, if you'd been an engineer, blacksmith, electrician, sheet-metal worker, ye'd have got in right away. But,' he says, 'the only thing I can offer you is a cook'.
   Ah says, 'No, no me, Ah'm no wantin tae be a cook'.

So he says, 'Oh, well,' he says, 'I'm sorry, but that's all. You either go next door to the RAF or next door to the Army'.

So the first door wis the Army, so Ah went in.

So that's how you found yourself in the KOSB?

That's how Ah found in the KOSB, aye. Ah said if Ah had to be in an infantry regiment it had to be the Black Watch.

You were keen to get into the Black Watch. Why was that then?

Well, bein Perthshire, originally away back, and that wis the one that Ah always thought aboot, the Black Watch. Ye were supposed tae get a choice, but when they came through: 'Report to Berwick – KOSB.'

Aye, it was the luck o the draw, wasn't it? Were you a bit upset about that?

No. Ye see, aa ma pals that wis called up before me, they aa went down tae Berwick as well. Everybody in this area landed in the KOSBs.

How long did you spend at Berwick?

Aboot four months. Two months as a rookie and two months infantry trainin. Four months trainin. An Ah wis sent to the 1st Battalion in the May [1940] which was in France. And Ah never got to the 1st Battalion. Ah don't know actually where they were, but they were gettin evacuated at Dunkirk, ye see. So … when they were evacuated, we were landed in France. We boarded the boat at Southampton at four o'clock in the afternoon. An then we waited outside the harbour a bit to it darkenin and then oo moved in. And we wis supposed to land at Le Havre. But that mornin, when it wis six o'clock in the morning, it wis gettin bombed by the Germans, so we wis transferred to Cherbourg. So we wis landed there an then we got a train frae Cherbourg to Rouen, and frae there, that wis it.

That was as far as you got into France?

As far as we got into France. And then we couldnae get to oor 1st Battalion so we wis pushed intae the 51st Highland Division. So you ken what happened to it?

Aye. So were you yourself captured?

Yes, Ah was. (laughs)

So what regiment were you in then, when you were captured?

Well, we wis told the 51st (Highland) Division was to be left there. This was to try and boost up the French. So we wisnae actually in any regiment.

Aye, the sort of odds and ends from various forces, who never reached their own battalions, aye?

Jist odds and ends that's right. So we still had oor ane cap badge and aa that. But they were aa …

Aye. So you were actually captured at St Valery[-en-Caux].

Oh, yes, aye …seventh o June. Ah'll never forget that! (rueful laugh)

Tell me just a bit about the events preceding that. Were you heavily shelled for some time?

71

> Well, och, it wis jist a shambles, really. Ah mean, nobody seemed to know much. An then they decided that they thought the Germans wis comin. So we cut a hole in the hedge, go through and dig trenches on that side. So we'd trenches, slit-trenches on that side, slit-trenches on this side and they didnae even know where they were comin frae!

It must have been a pretty demoralising experience for you?

> Oh, aye, it wisnae half – no so much the shellin, it wis the mortars. They were the worst.

Did you lose any of your friends in those attacks?

> Uh huh.

So did the order come on 7 June to lay down your arms? Was that it?

> No. They were fightin a rearguard actually when we were captured. We come through and we wis makin doon this road and on either side wis cornfields. And then the next thing that we knew, there wis a plane come down and we wis telt tae scatter, and they jist machine-gunned up the road. And then we got up, organised again and got goin again, and then the next thing we kent we wis gettin machine-gunned again.

From the air?

> No. From a road. The Germans with their motorbikes and their sidecars and the sidecars wi their machine-guns were jist spraying the whole thing. And then your other side started firing fae that side. So it wis in crossfire.

Crossfire. In a hopeless position?

> Hopeless! Oh!

So did the officer decide that you just had to surrender then?

> Eventually, the officer stood up and told us like, he says, 'No chance!'

A terrible experience for you that?

> Oh, aye.

So the whole platoon surrendered?

> Yes, aye.

I mean, presumably some fellows had been killed by this machine-gun fire?

> Oh, yes, oh, aye, oh, aye.

Did you have quite heavy casualties?

> Wisnae too bad, no, because we wis well spread out, ye see. And, of course, ye dinnae group thegither too much when there's stuff flyin around.

No, no. What an experience for you. So you were told to lay down your arms on 7 June?

> Yes.

And what happened then? Were you marched back to Germany?

> We were marched back tae Germany. It wis actually Holland. Into Holland.

How long did that march take?

> That would last aboot two weeks.

And were you well-treated during the march?

> Oh, no.

Tell me about that? What about food and drink, for instance?
>That wis the thing, aye, food. Food was the main thing. They couldnae feed ye, ye see. Ye couldnae get any food.

So you'd be starving by the time you got to Holland?
>Oh, aye, we wis that.

You never got anything to eat in that fortnight?
>Hardly anything at all. An then ye wisnae allowed tae drink the water. But what can ye do efter that? Ye had tae drink the water, but ye never came tae any harm.

No, there was no stomach upsets or anything of that sort?
>No, no, no, no. Then oo got on to barges up the Rhine, then landed in Dortmund. And we went through there and the swastikas in the streets …

Did you find that a rather frightening experience?
>Well, Ah don't know, it's kind o … It's away in the background now. But at the time Ah suppose it would be.

Pretty depressing, to think the War was recently begun and here you were a prisoner?
>I know. That's right. See, there were only two things that could happen tae us when Ah went to France. Ah could either get killed or get wounded. Ah never, ever thought Ah would be captured. That never ever entered ma head.

And then were you put into a prisoner of war camp from Dortmund?
>Frae Dortmund, we wis put intae the cattle trucks and taken right across Germany into Poland and landed in Poland. Frae there, we wis put out to different workin parties.

Were you in Silesia?
>Ah wis in Silesia, yes.

Aye, but not to begin with, maybe?
>No, well into Poland.

What was the place you went to first?
>Toruń wis the name o the place. And then after that, we wis somewhere near Pozań or Poznań, I think.

You were moved around from time to time from one camp to another?
>Oh, yes, oh, aye, because ye … startin tae dig escape routes and tunnels and different things.

Tunnels? Were you personally engaged in that?
>We wis, yes, at one camp, yes.

So they moved you on, maybe every few weeks or …?
>Aye, every, maybe, nine months or up to a year, maybe, and then ye wis moved. So they kept keepin them, movin round.

And so you remained in Poland until the end of the War did you?
>Poland and then intae Ober Silesia. I wis in a camp in Ober Silesia for quite a wee while. And we lost quite a lot o prisoners there because it got bombed. It wis a big factory that wis takin benzene oot o coal.

You were made to work?
　Oh, yes, oh yes, aye, ye had tae work.
And who bombed the factory?
　Americans and the British. But it wis Americans that used tae come over wi their Flyin Fortresses. And, of course, they did what they termed 'blanket bombing'. And when they got near the place, they jist started droppin, and then another wave come in and droppin, droppin, droppin. And of course some o them landed on the camp. And of course ye'd always somebody that wis in the camp, like cobblers and different yins …
So a few of the lads were killed by this bombing?
　Aye. There wis a direct hit on yin o the air-raid shelters.
Oh, dear. What are you speaking about, ten, twenty, thirty men killed?
　Oh, anything up to about 200.
As many as that?!
　Aye.
In one raid?
　Oh, aye.
Aye, aye. It was just the once that they dropped bombs on the camp?
　Aye, on the camp. But there wis other ones that got it as well.
Oh, dear. That must have been terrible. So you were a prisoner there then from 1940 until early '45?
　'45.
Was it the Red Army that liberated you?
　No. It wis the Americans. By that time, ye see, we had tae move frae there and we moved out o the camp. And there wis the river Oder and we reached the Oder and couldnae get across. So they marched us back to the camp again, and the next day we wis marched out again. By this time, they had a bridge, temporarily across, and we got across. So we marched then again, and that wis the month o January 1945. And, by, it wis cold! And we didnae get much food at that time either. So ye walked on and on and on. Oh, we marched frae Ober Silesia and we touched intae a wee part, jist a part o Czechoslovakia and then frae there we finished up somewhere near, not far from Munich.
Oh, God! That must have been hundreds of miles?
　Oh, aye, it wis hundreds o miles, oh, aye.
In the winter, the middle of winter?
　Winter, aye.
Now did you see much destruction on the way?
　No. Not at that time, no. But we did, after oo wis on the road back. We come through Munich to come home. We were at the airport and, oh! Ah never saw anything like it! Flattened!
So you got to Munich and it was there that you were freed was it?

THE IMPACT OF WAR

    Yes, aye by Patten's Army, aye, aye.
That must have been a great day for you then was it?
    Oh, it wisnae half!
So that would be … was that January, February 1945?
    No, that wis aboot April, May.
So you'd been marching for two or three months really? On the move for two or three months?
    By that time oo'd already, oo'd got into a big camp here.
Near Munich?
    Aye, near Munich. We wis there for about a month or six weeks.
And it was from that that the Americans liberated you?
    The Americans, aye.
And you got home immediately did you?
    Oh, well, no right away. They had that many tae get away, that they had tae make it intae sections. So ye wis aa sectioned off and numbered. So we'd maybe be there aboot seven or eight days before we got out.
We're talking about hundreds of prisoners?
    Oh, yes, oh, aye – thousands. Thousands there, aye, it wis quite big. Oh, there wis quite a mixed lot. British, American, French, we worked with Polish civilians, yes.
But there was never any mention of concentration camps, Auschwitz, or anything like that?
    No, no, no, no, never mentioned that, never.
And you worked in these factories and places but you always were marched back to the camp at night?
    Oh, yes, aye, yes, oh, aye.
So it must have been quite an experience that? Because had you been away from Peebles much before the War?
    No. I'd never been abroad, it wis quite an experience, aye. Even the experience the first time when we went down to London, when we wis in the Forces. We went down to London to go to Southampton. Never been to London before. Ah'd never been out o Scotland.
Now conditions in the prisoner of war camp must have been pretty bad were they? The food would be very scanty?
    Oh, the food, aye. It wis only the Red Cross that kept us goin. If there hadnae been Red Cross parcels, Ah wouldna be here the day.
Terrible conditions?
    Oh, aye.
So you got back home then in … was it May 1945?
    May it would be, aye … it would be well intae May. Ah think it wis almost comin intae June. It wis after VE Day.
The bunting would be out in Peebles was it, to welcome you back?

No, there wis nothing. (laughs)
Your family would be delighted to see you?
Oh, yes, oh, aye, aye.
So did you find it difficult to settle down after that experience, at the end of the War?
It was a wee bit, yes, aye, because ye wis always on the move and ye didnae feel ye wanted tae settle down. Ye wanted tae keep movin. Och, aye, it jist took time.
Did you think of trying any other work after the War?
No, Ah didnae, no. Ah jist fell intae it right away when Ah come back.
You were quite glad to go back?
Yes, oh, aye.

In the next extract, Walter Scott, talks about his love of aircraft and remembers his time with the Arctic convoys. His lighthearted account cannot hide us from understanding the dangerous circumstances he found himself in on an almost daily basis on the aircraft carriers he served on. Also poignant are his remarks about returning to his civilian workplace: 'In thae days, ye see, once you got yourself intae a job, you stayed. Ye never thought aboot expandin o yourself.'

Walter Scott, b. 1924, Second World War experiences with the Fleet Air Arm
You were called up when you were eighteen?
Ah joined the Fleet Air Arm. Actually Ah wis wantin tae go intae the Air Force, because jist at the start o the War Ah joined the Air Training Corps here. And Ah quite enjoyed that. Of course, ye got your uniform, and Ah wis actually got made up tae a sergeant. Ah wis cock-a-hoop aboot this, ye see. And Ah quite liked it. And ma mission then wis tae go tae the Air Force. But when the time came for me tae get called up, they asked me, ken, if Ah'd been in ony organisations an that. Ah said, 'Aye, Ah wis trainin tae be a mechanic in the Fleet Air Arm'.
'Oh, you're just the very man we're lookin for.'
So they put me doon for the Fleet Air Arm. So that wis it. Ah wis away.
Did you feel disappointed about that? You would rather have gone into the Air Force?
Well, a wee bit in a way, but then Ah thought tae masel, well, Fleet Air Arm, you're on a boat, you're goin tae see different countries, and aa the rest o it, ken.
And you've got the connection with the flying.
That's right.
You were really interested in flying?
Ah wis, aye. No actually the flyin but the maintenance o the engines.
Had you flown before the War?
Oh, aye.
Where had you flown?

Ma auntie … that wis ma mother's auntie, we caed her auntie an aa, Nellie. She worked in service and she wis never married. And there wis a biplane, oh, quite a big thing then, came tae Upper Lyne. And, oh, it wis advertised, ye could get flights. Ah think it wis about a pound or somethin. Kids got, Ah think, for ten bob. And oo got a bus and oo went up tae Lyne and it jist mair or less took ye roond aboot Peebles and then landed, ken.

A great thrill for you though?

Oh, me flyin!

And was it that, that gave you interest in joining the ATC?

It might've been. Ah wis only a laddie then, aye. So that wis ma first time. And then once Ah wis in the ATC, Ah used tae go through tae Macmerry. They used tae take us through there. And Ah flew two or three times fae there, in Lysanders and things like that, ye ken.

So you were really interested in all that? Did that tempt you to think of trying to get a civilian job, before the War, as a mechanic?

No really, no.

You were quite happy in the mill as a young fellow?

Well, that's right, aye. In thae days, ye see, once you got yoursel intae a job, you stayed. You were in a job. Ye never thought aboot expandin o yourself. Once ye were intae the mill that wis it.

That was it, aye, aye. So you went off to the Fleet Air Arm?

Ah went fae here doon tae Staffordshire. An Ah did ma square-bashin and that doon there. And then Ah went fae there to Leigh-on-Solent and Ah did ma trainin doon there, as an air fitter, mechanic. And then fae there, Ah went tae Arbroath and did the practical experience then. Workin on planes. And then fae there, Ah went tae the Clyde and that wis where Ah joined ma first ship: HMS *Campania*. That wis an aircraft carrier. And Ah would be on there for, oh, hell … The first three runs we did doon tae the Med. Aa we were daen wis escortin convoys. And then we came back fae there and we thought we would aa get leave. But no. Nae leave. We wis sent fae there tae Scapa Flow. And then we did two runs, Ah think to Russia. And then when we came back the second time, then we got leave. And then we went back on again, and then we must've did aboot six or seven tae Russia [Murmansk].

Escorting convoys?

That's right. Oh, it was wild. In fact, well, the Jerries, they sunk a lot o boats. Oh, hell, aye.

Did you see ships sinking all around you? Aye. A distressing experience.

There wis nothing we could dae aboot it.

There was no way men could survive in those conditions?

Oh, no, no, no. They reckon if ye wis in the water for three minutes, that wis it. (sighs) Aye. And, see like, in the convoy, well, ye had cruisers and ye had destroyers. They were aa on the ootskirts. The convoy wis there. The aircraft carrier, she wis in the middle and that wis aaright as long as ye were sailin on. And then, when they were to put planes off for tae dae reconnaissance and that, you had tae drop back oot o convoy, and then ye would sail intae wind tae get your planes off. And then ye had tae get back in convoy again. And then, of course, when the planes wis due back, ye came back oot.

So was it a dangerous time when the aircraft carrier dropped back?

Oh, aye. Aye. It had nae protection.

That would be the time when Germans would strike presumably?

They were lookin for ye then.

Were you ever bombed in fact on the Campania*?*

Oh, aye. Aye. So, well, the Jerries wis bad enough but the worst doin wis the weather. Oh, aye. Sometimes ye couldnae get planes up, the ice wis that thick on the deck.

Terrible conditions! Bitterly cold! So you were doing that for maybe altogether about a year or more?

Aye, aye. '43–44, and then we came off the *Campania* that trip comin back. We got sic a doin. Ye see, she wis a utility ship. She had her flight deck built on top o the boat, like, ye ken. Well, we got sic a doin wi the weather, when she wis goin doon intae the water the flight deck got buckled up like that. There were nothin hale on the bloody boat! There were planes on the loose although ye had them lashed doon. They were smashed tae bits, ken.

Terribly high seas?

Oh! Ah mind o standin on the after end. Ah came oot and the boat must've been like that. Ah wis on the after end and all Ah could see wis bloody water comin. Of course, whenever that came ower of course the back end jist rose, ye ken. Ye were in bloody daylight again.

Aye. An extremely dangerous position, though? You might have been swept overboard?

Oh, ye could've been washed ower, aye. Oh, aye.

Did you suffer any loss of crew from being swept overboard?

No in that time, no. We had two or three casualties. When your planes wis comin in, ye had a catwalk at the side o yer flight deck. And you were on the flight deck and when they planes wis comin in, you had tae jump off into the catwalk. Well, where you were standin, you were this above, ken. Well, sometimes thae bloody planes, if the boat dropped when they were comin in, they would catch the wire but the bloody plane would go ower the side. And catwalk, men, and everything – intae the water!

Distressing. Did you lose any friends like that yourself?

Well, Ah knew chaps that had got caught and they never stopped. They just kept going.

Dead within three minutes of landing in the water, as you were saying.

Aye. Plus, well, ye ken how bad they were smashed wi the plane.

With the plane, aye. Terrible. You lost a few planes like that?

Oh, aye.

Did you ever land at Murmansk yourself, to go ashore? What was your impression of conditions there?

Yes. Bloody awful! Oh, aye. At Murmansk, the bit we saw, it wis mair or less like a rest camp for the Russian soldiers. There were great big dormitories. Well, we were never in them but ye could see faces at the windaes and that. An there were nae, like, tarmacadam roads, ken. They were jist rough. And as far as we were led tae believe, there wis one woman looked after each dormitory that would dae cleanin, cookin, whatever, for thae soldiers.

Soldiers, aye. A sort of rest camp?

Aye, oh, aye.

And of course, you wouldn't be able to speak with local Russian people, with the language problem?

No, no, no. We jist had a walk roond aboot it. It wis a day like this. A sunny day like this but snow aa roond aboot.

But bitterly cold?

Oh, cauld. Oh, hell, aye.

It was quite an experience for you then? Very different from Peebles?

Oh, hell, aye.

Aye. Did your war experience give you [a] wider view of things, do you think, looking back on it?

Aye. Ah often think o the chaps that Ah served wi. Ken, there were Welsh an a lot o English boys. Maist o them wis English, ye ken, that Ah wis wi. Ah often wonder where they are now. Whether they're still on the go or what.

But you'd never really been to Edinburgh till you were seventeen or eighteen. And then within a year or two of that, here you are, Scapa Flow, the Mediterranean, Murmansk, the Russian convoys. That must have made a huge impression on you?

Oh, aye, aye. Oh, aye. Ah wis quite pleased in a way that, when Ah look back, that Ah did go tae the Fleet Air Arm because Ah might hae went tae the Air Force. Ah might've been stuck in this country and never got naewhere, ken. Then again, Ah might've been sent abroad, Egypt or somewhere. Well, ye never know. But, oh, aye.

So you went into the Forces in 1942. And you came out '46–47?

Aye. '46, Ah think it would be.

But you'd no regrets about your war service?

Oh, no, no, no, no, no. Oh, no, Ah've nae regrets that way. Ah mean, Ah wouldnae like tae say that Ah lost three and a half, fower year, oh, no.

No, no. And it was something ... it was a vital thing, of course, you were doing?

Oh, aye.

Ian's interviews also captured valuable insights into women's experiences of war and remind us of the impact of the unprecedented changes wartime imposed on individual lives. Some found that their home environment or working life was directly impacted by war, while others completed military service which required them to spend time away from their home and family. From 1941, women over twenty-one were conscripted into either industrial war work or one of the auxiliary services.[8] This next extract, from Margaret Lavin, tells us more about this.

Margaret Lavin, b. 1919, Second World War experiences

You were in the mill, still in March Street mill at [the outbreak of the Second World War]? What difference did that make to the mill, if any?
    Well, it went back tae makin khaki and Air Force blue.
Uniforms for the Forces?
    Aye.
And what kind of work was that? Was it more interesting or less interesting?
    Oh no, no.
It was pretty dull work, was it?
    Uh huh.
Because you wouldn't have the same skills that you had with your normal work?
    No, no, that's right, uh huh. And we also did tartans for kilts for the soldiers.
And how long did that last? Did that go on right through the War?
    Well, there was thirteen of us all became twenty-one roond aboot 1940. And we were aa paid off because they were askin for people that age for the Forces or the munitions. And they knew that we would be gettin called up anyway.
Aye, because women were conscripted, I think, from about 1941. And you'd be twenty-two, twenty-one by then?
    I wis twenty-one when we were all paid off because they knew that we were gettin called up.
And how many of you were paid off?
    Thirteen.
So you were paid off. Was that a shock for you?
    It was in a way, but we knew that we would be gettin called up.
But did you know that you were going to be paid off?
    No, no.
And was there any attempt to get the management to change their mind about it?
    Oh, no, no.
You just all accepted it?
    Aye.
That's grand. So you were paid off when you were about twenty-one, in 1940? And

---

8   The choices were the Auxiliary Territorial Service (ATS), the Women's Auxiliary Air Force (WAAF) or the Women's Royal Naval Service (WRNS).

what happened then? Were you unemployed?

No, no. We knew that we were gettin called up so. There wis more than thirteen actually, but we were aa twenty-one. Jist roond aboot the same age. And we went to the Labour Exchange and we wanted to join the Forces. However, when we went to the Labour Exchange, they said that at the moment they weren't wantin anybody for the Forces. It would have to be munitions or the Land Army. So we said we preferred the munitions, you see. And they gave us three options: Woolwich Arsenal, Risley or Chorley. So we decided we would all go to Chorley. But you see some of the other girls that were paid off, they went into Edinburgh and they got into the Forces. We made the mistake of jist leavin it in Peebles, ye see.

Would you have preferred to have gone into the Forces?

Aye, uh huh. We were disappointed, but of course there was thirteen of us and we knew we would be all together.

You were all friends in the mill?

Uh huh.

So, the other girls who went to Edinburgh they were working in March Street mill, too?

Yes, uh huh. They had the sense to go into Edinburgh.

So they went into the ATS or the WAAFS or whatever, but you and your friends were sent to munitions.

Aye, uh huh.

Now where did you go then, to work?

Chorley. Lancashire.

Now how did you get to Chorley? Did you all go down on the train?

Train, uh huh. There was a train across there, the LMS, was across there, took us up to Carstairs or Symington, one of these places, an we got the train there. And we were met at Preston. And then we were taken to Exton. That was in the outskirts of Chorley.

What sort of munitions were they making?

Filling shells.

How did you feel about that?

We werenae very happy when we got there and realised what we were into, but we just had to put up with it.

Because all you'd been told up to then, was that it was munitions.

Aye, munitions. See they were desperate for workers for munitions then.

Near the beginning of '41, aye. So, it would be maybe about six months after Dunkirk?

Aye, somethin like that, uh huh.

So tell me about the factory.

It wis a new factory that they built. It wis six miles square. It wis huge really.

How many workers, roughly, were employed there?

Oh, there wis thousands there.

Men and women?

> Men and women, uh huh. There wis a lot of women but there wis quite a few men. We worked from seven o'clock in the mornin until two in the afternoon. And then the next week it wis two in the afternoon till ten at night. And then ten at night till seven in the morning.

So it was week about? You worked three consecutive shifts?
> Uh huh.

Aye, how long were you there?
> For the duration.

Right to the end of the War? Till after VE day?
> VE day, but we were home for VJ day.

Aye. You'd been sent back by then, the summer of 1945.
> Aye, uh huh.

So you were there for about four and a half years?
> Aye.

How did you find the work? Was it hard? Physically hard?
> Aye, it was quite hard.

You were quite tired at the end of the shift?
> Oh, yes, aye.

And you were filling shells with what?
> Gunpowder and yellow TNT. An of course, we didn't want to get into the yellow TNT because it stained all your hands and your face an ye were aa yellow. We were quite lucky, but one o our girls had to go into it and she did everything to get her books! In fact, she wis determined that she wis goin tae leave. An ye werenae allowed tae take cigarettes or anything like that in. Aye ye were searched, searched every time ye went in. And she took cigarettes in. An of course she wis found with the cigarettes and she wis instantly dismissed. But that's what she wanted. Ah never took cigarettes in. She got fined quite heavy. And then, of course, she was dismissed and they'd to go back there to the court.

Now which court was that? A law court? She was fined because it was an offence?
> Uh huh. Oh, it wis a dangerous thing.

I mean, she'd no intention of lighting her cigarettes, presumably?
> No, no. She jist deliberately took the cigarettes in and she knew that she would be found with them when she was searched, because you were searched at the gate every day.

That's grand. So you were there for four and a half years and I take it you didn't really like the work very much at all?
> Oh, no.

Was it dull and repetitive?
> Aye.

Certainly a big contrast with the skills you had been using in the textile industry?
> Aye, aye. But ye had tae be exact.

So you remained together, apart from that one girl, who brought on her own dismissal?
> Aye, more or less, uh huh.

Now where did you live when you were working there?
> Well, when we went there at first we were taken to a hostel. A government hostel. It wis newly built as well; two to a room. But eventually we got to know people that worked in the factory and they told us where we could get proper digs. An that wis in a wee village called Clayton-le-Woods, between Preston and Chorley. We got in wi these people. There wis one, two, three, four of us, and we went tae stay wi these people and we got on far better, and the people that we stayed wi had a baker's shop. So we were quite lucky during the War. We were well fed.

Now what about the other eight girls or so of the original group of twelve? Did they remain in the government hostel?
> They remained, uh huh.

So the baker looked after you quite well?
> Oh, aye. Aye. We really didnae want for anything.

Now how far was Clayton-le-Woods then from the factory?
> Oh, we had to get a bus. It wis aboot twenty minutes.

Now what about your wages in the munitions work?
> Oh, it wisnae very much really, because they were gettin more wherever they were makin planes. Ah think it wis aboot five pound or something.

Those who were building aeroplanes, they were better paid? Whereas munitions work was less well paid?
> Aye, uh huh.

You kept your wages?
> Cause Ah had to keep maself.

You'd have to pay for your digs and you'd have to pay for your hostel?
> Aye.

Were you left with much money in your own pocket once you'd paid that?
> No, not very much, no. Maybe a couple o pounds or so, which went quite a long way in these days. You only got a weekend off every three weeks.

You were working weekends as well?
> Aye. An it wis every three weeks, how the shifts coincided, that you got off.

It was hard work then, long hours?
> Aye, it wis long hours.

So you were working seven days a week, two out of every three weeks?
> Aye.

And got the weekend off every third week?
> Every third week. Aye. Well, it wisnae a whole weekend either, because ye would maybe finish Saturday at lunchtime, till your shift started on the Monday. It wis tiring but we managed.

Now what sort of entertainment, if any, did the workers in the munition factory have?

Oh, jist Music While You Work *and an occasional* Workers' Playtime *thing.*
Do you remember feeling unhappy when you first went?
No really. No, because there were thirteen of us.
Do you remember any of the girls feeling homesick quite badly?
Aye, there wis one. She did feel homesick.
What about relations with local people. Did you make friends with people living in Chorley?
Oh, aye, uh huh. There wis a crowd from the village went to the factory and we were friendly with them.
Did you get holidays there?
Aye, we got leave. Maybe a week or so. Ye got a pass for the train.
And did you get paid for that week's leave?
No, no.
So did you come home when you got leave?
Aye, aye.
And spent the leave with your mother and family at Peebles? And then went back again?
Aye, aye.
Do you remember feeling reluctant to go back at the end of your leave?
No. It didnae bother me really.
That's great. So you ended your work in the munitions factory in the summer of 1945, between VE Day and VJ Day.
That's right, aye.
Did you go back to March Street?
Uh huh. Ah had a letter askin me to come back. When the War ended, would Ah be still interested in comin back.
That was a rather different attitude from the one they'd shown when you were paid off?
Aye, aye.
So there was a letter awaiting you. They must have known that you were coming home. Was that it?
That's it, aye.

In contrast to Margaret Lavin, who seems to have taken her Second World War service in her stride, Betty Muir was initially very upset about leaving home. As she explained to Ian though, the experience proved an exciting and valued one.

Betty Muir, b. 1922, Second World War in the WAAF

After the War came. When Ah came back from the War, that wis when this Mr Wells asked me if Ah wanted to go back on to the job Ah had left, the birlin, or he says he wis needin darners and he said, 'Ah know that you can darn'. Ah said, 'Oh, well, Ah would prefer that if Ah could'. So that wis when Ah learnt the darnin.
So it was birling up to the War?

Up to the War, yeah and then Ah wis called up for the WAAFs.
Aye, so you remember the outbreak of the War?
Yeah.
And you carried on working in the mill for maybe another couple o years or so?
It was '42 when Ah went away.
When you were called up? Aye, you'd be twenty years old?
Yeah, yeah.
I think women were subject to call up once they became twenty-one?
That's right, I wis twenty because we were taken away in the December and Ah wis twenty-one in the January. That's right.
How did you feel about that?
Oh, Ah wis greetin ma eyes oot!
Were you? (Miss Muir laughs) *Was that because you didn't want to leave home?*
Home, aye, yeah. Ah wis a home bird.
And you were still a fairly quiet, shy girl?
Aye, yeah, yeah. That wis the first o me ever goin away maself anywhere, aye. And Ah always remember that, when Ah got into Edinburgh there wis a lot o ma workmates doon at the station – that wis when we had the railway here, doon at the LMS – the LNER. And they aa came doon tae see me away on the train. And ma mother wis there as well.
Was it to Edinburgh?
Goin tae Edinburgh. Aye, this wis when Ah had to go. And Ah wis tae be met in Edinburgh and it wis at the LMS station at the far end o Princes Street, when the station wis there. Caledonian Station. There wis this big bullet there then and we'd aa tae meet there. And Ah remember goin there and then there wis an NCO waitin for us. And she asked us aa for oor travellin warrants. And, of course, Ah went into ma handbag tae get it. Oh, Ah jist broke doon there and then. Ah hadnae got ma travelling warrant. (laughs) Ah'd left it at home. Cause Ah remembered where Ah had put it and Ah says, 'Oh yes, Ah know jist exactly where it is'.
She said, 'Well, if we phone the police, do you think they'll be able to get it?' I said, 'Oh, yes'.
So they phoned the police station for tae get tae ma mother tae get this travel warrant. In the meantime she got another travel warrant for me from the MPs that were on the station, and away on the train doon tae Gloucester. There were aboot twenty o us altogether, aa strangers.
Aye. That's where you were sent first, Gloucester? It's a long way to go?
Yeah. Aye, oh aye, Ah'll never forget that. Ah thought it wis endless that journey. And it wis at night tae, overnight, aye. There wis six of us from the mill that got called up at the same time. We went for our medical together and we aa were asked what we wanted to do. Well, we aa wanted to do mair or less the same thing. But they said we would have to wait till we got to

Gloucester to see if the jobs were available. We all wanted to be fabric workers, wi workin with fabric, you see. And we thought, well, we'd be fabric workers. That wis like workin with the balloons. But we all got sent to different places.

Oh, dear. You'd be heartbroken about that?

Oh, aye, yeah.

Do you remember feeling really apprehensive about going?

Oh, Ah was, yeah, Ah really was.

It really was a big step for a young lassie never been away from home?

Aye, aye, Ah know. And Ah remember sittin in this big hall wi aa the other girls when oo finally got to Gloucester and aa their names were gettin called and we'd passed my initial – M, and Ah thought, 'Oh, what's happened? Have they lost ma papers or anything?' But Ah wis aboot second last, Ah think, tae get called up. And Ah jist felt Ah wis bein forgotten. But then we were all taken to huts, different huts, and told ye were tae be up at such a time in the mornin. You would get called. Oh, Ah'll never forget wakin up that first mornin. Oh, it wis terrible. In December, in a Nissen hut. It wis cold. And wakenin up and aa these girls sittin pullin their pants on, you know, under the covers. Naebody wanted tae get up and get dressed oot o bed in front o each other. No, everybody wis shy as well. Oh, dear. And then, of course, ye were taken for a medical examination first thing the next mornin and ye had to lose all embarrassment there and then, because it wis a case o strippin and you jist saw everybody standin there. And that wis where ye lost all fear o bein embarrassed then.

Aye, just plunged in?

Yeah.

You didn't get any choice as between the WAAFs, the ATS or the WRNS did you?

Oh, aye. Aye, Ah wanted the WAAFs.

Do you remember why that was?

Ah've nae idea, no. Ah think it wis jist most of the girls from here went to the WAAFs. Ah think ye had tae be more clever than what Ah was anyway, tae get in the WRNS. Ah think ye had stiffer examinations tae get into them.

There was some belief, I think, that you had to have a relative in the Navy to get into them.

Ah know that there were stiffer examinations anyway. But Ah wanted tae go tae the WAAFs aye.

So there it was. And how long were you down in Gloucester?

Aboot five or six weeks. Ah jist cannae remember how long we were there. It wis jist for your basic training. Jist marchin and that, drill, aye. And then they were sorted oot and then findin out what ye really wanted to do.

Your trade or job?

Your trade, aye. Of course, Ah wanted to get the fabrics, so as maybe make up wi the other girls that Ah had went wi. But by that time aa the situations were filled. So Ah ended up bein a cook for the aircrew canteen. Oh, Ah enjoyed that, aye.

Were you interested in cooking before then?

No, no really, no. Ah got sent away for trainin. Ah got sent to Wolverhampton for basic training and then wis moved frae Wolverhampton to St Helens in Lancashire for to go to a cookery college. And Ah wis in private billets there. It wis one WAAF to one house. They had this one street and there were one WAAF allocated tae each house. And ye had your school durin the day and you ate everything that you cooked when you went there. The first thing wis your breakfast, then your lunch and then your dinner at night, before ye came back to your billet.

That would encourage you to be a good cook! (laughs)

Exactly, aye. Ye had to eat everything that you made. And then frae there, ye got a mark frae that school, and then we were sent to (RAF) North Coats.

And you did well at the school?

Oh, aye, Ah passed OK.

Because you were interested?

Yes, aye. And we went to North Coats at Grimsby and we sat another exam there and it wis quite a stiff yin. But Ah passed aaright anyway and Ah got into the aircrew canteen. Ah wis in the airmen's mess for a while first and Ah kept pesterin the sergeant that Ah wis under that Ah wanted intae the aircrew canteen because it wis smaller and it wis mair personal cookin, because the aircrews would come in, and there wis a huge blackboard on one end of the Nissen hut and they used to write up their names and what they wanted when they came back fae a flight, ken? Before they went they came in and they got their aircrew rations, which wis their barley sugar, chewin gum, sweets, more or less. That wis all.

The cooks provided these?

Aye, that wis aa in the canteen for them.

Which airfield was this where you were with the aircrew?

That wis at North Coats. Near Grimsby, aye.

So these were member crews?

Yeah. Coastal Command Beaufighters

And they sound as if they were given special treatment? Special provision of food anyway?

Oh, they were, oh, they were, aye, yeah.

And you were saying that the cookhouse or the canteen was about a third of a Nissen hut? That implies that there might have been maybe twenty men, aircrew, that you were working with? Would that be right? Something like that?

Oh yes, aye, yes. Ah think there wis only aboot twenty-four, Ah think. About six tables wi four. Ah think there wis only the six tables.

Was that a squadron of Beaufighters?

Oh, aye, I worked with a squadron. I wis wi 236. Now, we had to go on flights wi them. The first time Ah went up in a plane wi them was to Tain, up in the north o Scotland. They took their own cooks with them, ye see.

When they moved?

Aye, when they moved. And they took their own WAAFs that were fabric workers and any that worked aboot the planes as well. They all went with them. Every time the squadron went somewhere for a few days or a couple o weeks, you went with them.

On exercises presumably? So how did you find that?

Oh, Ah liked that, aye. Aye. The first time wis frightening. When we saw these big troop-carriers comin in, you know. But Ah enjoyed it.

Aye, that would be a new experience for you?

Oh, aye, exactly. Ah really enjoyed it.

So you were there for maybe about three years, were you, at North Coats?

Now how long wis Ah there? Ah wis there till Ah wis demobbed in '46, and Ah went to … Oh gosh … Ah moved frae North Coats. Maybe three years, aye. Because Ah went to another place in Lincolnshire anyway, before Ah wis demobbed.

Looking back on it, or if you can remember how you felt at the time, how did you feel about that experience?

Oh, Ah wouldnae like to have missed it, no way. Even when Grimsby wis bombed. Ah'll never forget the nights when they were bombin at Hull, ye know, tryin tae get the docks there. And Ah'd made friends wi a girl who came from Cleethorpes, jist along frae Grimsby. And Ah remember standin at the hut window and, oh, jist a mass o scarlet across in that direction. And, oh, she wis standin there sayin, 'Oh, ma mum! Oh, ma dad!' She wis cryin her eyes out. And tryin tae comfort her. And, of course next mornin she got permission to go home to see that they were aaright. And Ah got the day off to go with her as well. They were like a second family to me.

And they were alright?

Oh, they were aaright, aye, yeah. It jist looked worse than what it really was, aye. So that wis an awfy experience that. And then we were away frae there when oor site wis bombed, where the WAAF huts were. We were up at Tain at that time wi the squadron. They dropped bombs on the camp that night.

Was there anyone injured?

No.

You were all away?

No, them that were left were aa in the shelters. But they got one o the huts right enough. The top hut wis bombed. But Ah missed that experience of close-hand bombin.

You were fortunate then?

Aye, yeah, exactly, aye. Once ye made a friend ye were aaright, aye. But each time Ah got posted somewhere else Ah always seemed to be on ma own. If Ah made a friend, if we were both gettin posted, we were both goin different directions.

But that would help your confidence?

Oh, it did. Yes. Aye. Because it wis frightening even goin with your kit bag and gettin on a station and sayin, 'Where am Ah goin?' Ah'd no idea where Ah wis goin … Ah remember after aa ma first cookery trainin wis over and they asked you where you would like to be posted. Straight away Ah said East Fortune, because that wis a mobile station then. And Ah thought, 'Nearest home – get there'. And Ah knew another girl that had went away at the same time as me wis at Turnhouse. But Ah didnae want to be wi her, so Ah thought, 'Ah'll try East Fortune'. So Ah got posted tae East Fortune. But Ah wis only there three weeks when Ah got posted again! (laughs) That wis when Ah got posted down tae North Coats at Grimsby, and Ah wis there nearly aa the time.

So you sound as if you got a lot out of your service experience?

Oh, Ah did, aye. Especially, Ah had nine months at Torquay for the repatriation o the Canadians and the Australians. They were gettin repatriated frae there. And Ah wis billeted in the Toorak Hotel jist along fae the railway station. And we worked in the Grand Hotel. Ah would love to go back.

You've never been back to Torquay?

No. It's one o ma biggest wishes. If Ah come up in the lottery it's the first place Ah'd be off tae, tae see the Grand Hotel as it is now. That's another thing Ah should've looked oot for ye comin. Ah never thought to look oot thae things. Ah have snaps o us taken in the grounds. There were three different shifts o cooks there and we were aa taken in the grounds. But that wis like a holiday. Nine months. The Canadians were so good tae ye. And ye were allowed to use their canteens. This is strayin away frae your question.

No, no, no. But it's all part of your experience because it obviously made a big impression on you?

Oh, it did, aye. Ah really loved … for aa it wis wartime, it never bothered me.

You never thought of becoming a regular in the WAAFs at the end of the War?

No. Funnily enough, ye wanted tae get home, aye.

One other point that occurs to me that maybe it was fortunate in a way you were attached at Beaufighters, Coastal Command, rather than to bombers. Because given the terrible casualty rate, that would be a very emotional experience for you?

Well, that wis emotional enough, workin wi the aircrew because, Ah mean, they would come in there and put up what they wanted, an then if they didnae come back.

Did that happen quite often?

Oh aye, yeah. Quite a few, aye … never came back. And it would be ages before you could bring yoursel to rub their drawin off. Some would maybe draw a plate o ham and eggs: this is what they want when they come back. It wis ages before ye could rub it oot off the board.

It must have been heartbreaking?

It wis, aye. Oh, aye, ye got tae know them all.

After the extreme pressures of wartime, VE day was celebrated with a similar degree of exuberance, as Betty went on to describe for Ian.

Well, VE Day, Ah remember we had to barricade oursel in the canteen that night because the aircrew were goin mad! And they had aa these wee explosives and they were lettin them off outside the canteen and we were inside, terrified!

All the girls barricaded in?

Aye, aye. Well, there wis three o us. There wis two waitresses and maself, a cook, and we were jist scared, but it wis only little fireworks things, little bomb things, but we were terrified.

Of course, they wouldn't have done any harm.

But next mornin there wis a couple o them came in that had moustaches, and half the moustaches had got singed off with these bomb things that they were throwin aboot. And, oh, a few casualties wi them, but it wis jist the excitement o the thing bein finished.

So you never did meet up at North Coats with anybody who'd worked in the mill at Peebles?

No, nobody, no. Ah still keep in touch wi two girls. In fact, Ah wis doon at Stevenage two year ago. Ma next door neighbour had a sister doon there and Ah went for a holiday wi her. And this one o the girls that Ah wis friendly with, she lived in Stevenage as well. So ma next door neighbour's sister, she found oot jist where aboot in Stevenage her address was and she took ma across to see her when Ah wis doon. And, oh, it wis a lovely reunion after aa these years, forty-odd years. So we've kept in touch aa that time. And it's the same wi another one, but she moved to Australia. But we still keep in touch. And she wis home jist aboot three year ago and she came to Edinburgh and it wis nice.

Now did your wartime experiences leave you restless, unsettled, when you came back home?

No. No, Ah remember that, that Ah wis glad to get home, aye.

You didn't have any difficulty settling down?

No. When Ah went back to work, the woman that Ah worked wi on the birlin, before Ah went on tae the darnin again, she wanted me to emigrate to New Zealand. It wis at a time when they were aa beginnin to go oot to New Zealand tae work for the mills oot there. And she wanted me tae gin oot tae

her sister, who lived oot there and worked for the mills. She says, 'Ye'll make far better money oot there,' she says, 'and you're jist a young woman'. And she tried her damndest tae talk me intae goin.
Why did you not go?
Ah wis home and Ah wanted to stay at home.

Land work during wartime

In this extract, Effie Anderson, talks about her time at Cademuir forest during a period when, despite the War orders, the mill had laid off workers to cope with a slack period.

Effie Anderson, b. 1925, forestry work during the Second World War

So you must have got into the mill, maybe, about 1940, '41?
It would be … wis it 1940?
Do you remember Dunkirk?
Aye. Ma brother wis wounded in Dunkirk.
Aye, that was June 1940, aye.
Uh huh.
So you think you were maybe not long in the mill by then?
But the mill went slack and Ah'm tryin tae think how it went slack, because we done that much khaki. They went slack, and then Ah wis still on the bobbin machine. Ah hadnae been long in, when it went slack, so they sent us to the dole. And the dole sent us to the forestry. And Ah worked up at Cademuir. In the forestry for, oh, Ah would say maybe about nine month, ten month. And Ah loved it.
What did you like about the forestry then?
Ah think bein out in the open. Aye, Ah liked it.
So you weren't in the mill very long before you were sent to the forestry?
Before Ah got paid off.
It sounds as if you must have gone to the forestry somewhere about maybe 1940–41. So you'd be up at Cademuir for about a year? You were living at home still?
Oh, aye.
Travelling back and forth?
Walkin.
How many [girls], roughly, were there?
There wis aulder yins than me. There must've been six or seven o us sent up there fae the Labour Exchange. And there were a lot o conscientious objectors up there.
Were there? Men?
Men, uh huh.
Now what about the conditions in the forestry?
We used tae all meet up tae walk up together. Sometimes the lorry drivers

would gie ye a lift doon tae the High Street.
But normally, you had to expect to walk?
   Uh huh.
Of course, walking in the company of the other girls would make it more enjoyable.
   It wis aaright.

Life at home during wartime

Back in the Borders, there were other changes to life during the Second World War. In this next extract, Bob Anderson recalls the Polish officer who came to say with his family.

Bob Anderson, b. 1931, Second World War in Innerleithen

You mentioned that your mother had a Polish officer as a lodger during the War?
   Aye, that's right. She did, aye.
Now can you remember the Poles coming to Innerleithen?
   They came no long efter the War started. An when oo moved tae Miller Street, there were folk came and they asked how many rooms oo had. Well, oo had two bedrooms. There wis a bigger bedroom and a smaller bedroom. An, eh, they asked if we'd many rooms. Of course, ma mother had a bed in the livin room and the boys lived in the other room, so we taen this captain.
Aye, aye. So do you remember him coming?
   Aye, oh, aye. Captain Julius Sternok. He wis stationed here.
And was he quite a congenial character?
   Oh, he wis, he wis aye, he wis quite pleasant, aye. Oh, aye.
Ah never had much tae dae wi them, he jist slept there. An he got his meals oot, tae. Did you know anything about him?
   Well, Ah think he'd his wife some place, but Ah cannae mind where it wis. Cause Ah aye remember he had a fur cape.
Oh, yes. A fur collar was it?
   Aye. But it wis a lady's. It was a big, long fur, aye. He hung it behind the door and it wis in a white sheet, aye. Oh, he was quite friendly, aye. Aye there were an awfy lot o folk in the toon that had soldiers stayin.
Officers but also other ranks?
   Aye, aye, aye, uh huh.
Now there were some Poles in, was it Caerlee?
   Oh, aye. That wis the big buildin in Caerlee. It wis a hostel at one time, a part o the mill.
Aye. So some of them were billeted there?
   That's right, aye.
Were some in Leithen mills?
   Ah cannae mind o onybody in Leithen mills. There were that many soldiers billeted in Innerleithen.

The Poles maybe went off to fight in France after D-Day?
    That's right, aye, aye.
A lot of them were in France weren't they?
    (Mrs Joan Anderson: There's a lot o Poles still in Innerleithen now.)
Aye. That's what your husband was saying, I think, that after the War some of the Poles …
    Stayed. Aye, they married.
And do you remember any of them working in the mill?
    Oh, aye, we'd them working in the mill aside us, aye, oh, aye.
Quite good workers?
    Aye, oh, aye, they were quite good, aye.
They joined the union, too?
    Oh, aye, they were in, aye, aye. They were awfy for makin money. (laughs)
Were they?
    Oh, aye, aye, ony job. (laughs) Some o them had fower and five jobs! Aye. (laughs) Oh, aye.
So they were very hard-working?
    Oh, aye. Oh, they worked aaright, aye. Oh, they seemed tae aa get on, tae, didn't they?
So there's a wee sort of Polish community is there in Innerleithen?
    There's no so many now cause they've died off.
If there were any still alive of the original Poles who were here during the War, they'd be men into their eighties now?
    Oh, aye.
    (Mrs Anderson: Well, there's two that Ah ken. There's Joe up here. And there's yin in Miller Street. Ah cannae mind his name though.)
Aye. They both worked in the mill?
    Aye, they baith worked in the mill, aye, that's right, aye.
It would be interesting to hear what they thought of it, you know, coming from an entirely different background?
    Aye, uh huh.
    (Mrs Anderson: The yin in Miller Street, Ah think he worked in Waverley, did he no?)
    Waverley, aye, Ah think sae, aye.
    (Mrs Anderson: It was either Waverley or … But he was a tailor wasn't he?)
    He wis a tailor tae trade, aye, aye, uh huh. This wis the latter years, like. And he said that their family never ate for two days, tae gie him a meal when he went over there. They used tae say some o them had tae fight for the Germans at one time.
Yes, aye, they were forced into the German army. That's right.
    Forced intae the German army.
And of course that raised difficulties?

That's right, aye.
They could then be seen as traitors to their own country?
Aye. Oh, aye.
It couldn't have been an enviable position?
Oh, no. Oh, no. No.

National Service

The last set of extracts in this chapter concerns the experience of doing National Service, which was in force in Britain from 1949–60. There is a palpable change of tone in these extracts. While the interviewees might still be sent to dangerous places, for them the horror of the Second World War is over and for some, including Andrew Brunton, National Service provided an opportunity to learn new skills.

Andrew Brunton, b. 1928, National Service

Ye see, Ah did twae and a half year in the Airmy. That wis 1946.
Aye. You'd been in the mill for about a year before you went off to do your army service? Cause you left the forestry when you were seventeen?
Aye. Actually, Ah got the chance tae take deferment, ken. So Ah wis caed intae the office an Ah wis asked if Ah wanted a deferment. But Ah decided, no, Ah'll go in now an get it done wi. An Ah wis kind o a wee bit unfortunate. Ken, maist conscription service times were aboot a year and a half or roond aboot that. Well, Ah wis unlucky. Ah had medicals for demob, and there wis some crisis sterted. Ah cannae mind if it wis the Berlin airlift or something. There wis something happened. So Ah feenished up daein anither six or seven month.
So you actually did two and a half years. Aye. I think immediately after the War, '46, my brother was in the Army at that time and he did about two and-a-quarter years. I think that was the usual, you know, just over two years. From, I think, 1948 onwards, it was a fixed term. When you first went, it was not fixed.
Uh huh.
But in practice, it tended to be about two and-a-quarter years. But it sounds as if you did a bit more than that, as you say?
Well, Ah came oot in January '49.
'49, aye. So you must have done, as you say, about two and a half years?
Aye.
And what did you go into? Was it the Army?
Aye. Uh huh. Well, Ah wis in the Signals.
Aye, the Royal Signals?
Uh huh. Ah started off at Glencorse. Everybody did their basic training, ye ken. Ye went tae a camp for basic training. Ye did your six weeks and then ye got a lot o tests and what-not and then ye were sent oot tae different regiments.
Did you ask to go to the Signals?

No, Ah didnae, no. That wis ma last choice. (laughs) See, ken, like, aa ma uncles had aa been in the Royal Scots. An at that time, the only chance of ye learnin tae drive. Ah cannae mind if Ah asked tae get intae them, ken, Ah wanted tae learn tae drive.

Aye. But I thought you had been driving in the forestry?

Drivin a tractor. Aye.

Aye, right, so you weren't licensed?

No, no. Ah wisnae licensed, no. In fact, Ah drove that tractor on the roads an aa. Ah dinnae ken how it worked, ken. Jist fae the sawmill, ye ken, ye went fae the sawmill aboot fower, 500 yairds an ye were intae the forest.

Do you mean, you could drive? You knew how to drive but you wanted to get a proper driving licence?

Well, that's right, aye. There's a difference drivin a tractor away up in the forest an drivin on the road.

Aye, aye. Did you drive a lorry ever, in the forestry?

Ah got wee shots, ken. Like, that wis jist off the road, aye.

Aye, illicit, aye, aye. So the best way to learn to drive formally and get your licence, was to try and get into the Royal Scots was it?

Well, ken, Ah wanted tae go intae the Royal Scots.

So you were in the Signals. And, let me guess, you went to Catterick?

Catterick, uh huh.

And how long did you spend there?

Now – twae or three month.

Sort of basic Signals training?

Well, the Signals course. And then Ah trained as a wireless operator but Ah never, ever did any wireless operatin. No, Ah did later on. What happened was, Ah came back fae Germany. Ah went fae Catterick tae a – whit dae ye caa they camps where ye're waitin? Anyway ye went there an then Ah wis sent tae Germany. Ah wis in the Signal Corps a the time. So Ah went tae Germany an Ah wis detached tae the RAF. An Ah did a wee bit o teleprintin operatin. Jist a kind o basic thing. So, Ah did that.

Where were you in Germany?

Near Celle, we were right in the middle o a forest. It wis, eh, Wiesendorf.

That would be near Belsen concentration camp then?

Fourteen mile fae Belsen, uh huh. Div ee ken Germany, div ye?

I don't. I've never been to Germany.

Ye came up wi that very quickly, ye ken!

Aye, there was a concentration camp at Celle itself was there not? Russian prisoners of war, I think died there in huge numbers.

Ah tell ye what, there wis an awfu lot o displaced persons. They were employed in the camp daein jobs aboot the camp an that. But it wis only fourteen mile fae Belsen.

So you were there for what, roughly a year, I think it was?
> Aboot a year, aye. An then Ah come back an Ah wis in Pocklington in transit. It wis an auld RAF station. An Ah wis there for twae or three month. An then Ah wis posted again to the RAF doon in West Raynham. It was a kind o experimental place.

Did you enjoy your army service? Or did you feel it was a waste of time?
> Well, ye see … Well, a waste o time actually.

Uh huh. There were certain things you hadn't done before. You learned a bit about radio.
> Aye.

And maybe other things. And you got abroad? You wouldn't have been abroad before?
> No, no, no.

Hume Davidson, b. 1928, National Service in India

That's great. So you got this job in the mill and then you went off to do your army service? Just after the War? Is that right?
> '46. Uh huh. Ah did two years, a year in India with the Royal Scots. And Ah wis there when they got their independence in India and there were riots brekin out. Ah wis in Karachi, and we were flown tae New Delhi tae join the Royal Scots Fusiliers. And Ah wis there tae Ah come home. And when Ah got home we got promised we would get put back in the Royal Scots again, so we was put back in the Royal Scots and Ah got demobbed two years later in '48.

Now that must have been quite an eventful period for you? Because here you were, a laddie who'd been born and grown up in Walkerburn, you go into the Army and you find yourself sent off to India at the time of the troubles, the independence?
> (Laughs) Aye, uh huh. Ah but Ah never seen any troubles.

What were your impressions of India?
> Poverty. But Ah often thought that some o them would be worse off after we come home because a lot o them had jobs off o us, you know. Even sweepin our hut oot, our charwallahs, or dustywallahs, NAAFI wallahs. And they had jobs in the camp and we treated them no bad. The company charwallah wis a known man: if ee had no money ee went over and asked him for some money and he put it on the tab and ee'd pay it back on pay-day.

Put it on the slate for you?
> So Ah dinnae ken what would happen to aa thae folk.

Did you get much chance to go out and about in the streets where you were, in Karachi or in Delhi?
> Well, a lot o places wis out o bounds. You had tae watch what you wis daein. There were big notices up, 'Out of Bounds to British Troops'. Even some restaurants.

I've spoken to one or two other former servicemen, who've said that really they became aware of the terrible poverty in India and that this changed their whole attitude to all sorts of things here at home as well. You know, they became, if you like, politicised. They became aware of society in a way that they hadn't before. Was that your experience?

That's right, aye. Of course, when you wis young you just took it for granted. But Ah wis in New Delhi, as Ah say and Ah wis oot at Delhi Fort because the Muslims wis goin one way and the Hindus wis goin the other way and we were keepin them apart. And one o the places Ah wis at – the gate intae the Red Fort. Actually Mrs Mountbatten used to come up aboot every day – that's Lady Mountbatten. The food used tae come in and one o ma jobs wis tae direct the traffic at narrow bridges, because there were streams o Indians, and Ah seen seven deaths one day – kids, and they were gettin buried underneath o where Ah was, wrapped in linen. It wis starvation. And we used tae get oor packed lunch and oo didnae eat it in the camp. And cholera had broken oot so oo went away out intae the country. And anything we didnae eat we brought it back and gave it to the kids on the road. And some o them wis that weak.

Did that shake you?

Uh huh.

Anthony French, b. 1929, National Service training and deployment to Belfast

Now, when you were eighteen, you registered and then you were called up to do your National Service. What did you go into?

The Royal Scots. Ah never got any option. Ah went tae George Street for ma medical, an it wis jist a case you were goin intae the infantry. Either the KOSBs or the Royal Scots. So it wis the Royal Scots.

Where did you do your National Service?

Berwick-on-Tweed. But then we went fae there down tae Magdalene Fields, eh, doon tae Saighton Camp, Chester. Aye. That wis in 1947 an there wis three or four o us, even half a dozen o us, if ye wis underweight, ye were sent there tae get built up. It wis a physical development centre.

So you were underweight?

Aye, Ah wis jist, maybe if ye wis supposed tae be eight/eleven, ye wis maybe eight/five or somethin like that.

Aye. You were quite tall, of course?

Oh, aye. Ah'm somewhere aboot six.

Aye, aye, so you were quite a thin lad?

Aye. (laughs) When we went doon there, ye wis doon there for two or three weeks an they used tae assess ye. Ye'd run a mile. Then ye used tae learn aa the tricks o the trade. The first time ye'd run, ye'd maybe be nice and slow. An the next time ye'd run, then ye would maybe get that wee bit faster, which ye always had in reserve. And then they assess that and says, 'Well, at least he's goin the right wey. He's gettin faster'. But we were puttin on to the picture wi aa this carry-on, ye see.

Aye, the old soldiers told you what to do?

Aye. (laughs) An then we shifted intae the KOSBs. No choice, and put over to [Northern] Ireland.

You were just told you were transferring?

Uh huh. And we wis shifted over to Ireland in November '47.

Where did you go in Ireland?

Belfast.

Aye. What was it, mainly guard duties?

Jist everything like that, guards, anything. Ah wis up at Holywood Barracks outside Bangor. Ah wis up there for aboot, what, a year? Two chaps fae Edinburgh and masel.

Did you enjoy your National Service?

Efter Ah came oot Ah thought it wis the greatest thing in the world, but Ah wis glad tae get oot, ye understand?

Aye, aye. You never thought of becoming a regular?

No really, no, no. Ye were jist longin for the demob day.

3

The End of Childhood: Into the World of Work

The chapters so far have served to give us an impression of what life was like in the Border communities at the time our interviewees were embarking on their working lives. Wages were poor, housing was basic, the War was influencing all aspects of life and horizons were changing. At the same time expectations were often low as a result of poverty and the apparent lack of opportunities outwith the mills.

Significant too, is the role the mill owners played and this will be the focus of the next chapter where we consider what the interviews can tell us about the complex and inter-dependent connections between the mill owners and mill workers.

We have considered the domestic sphere in which many of our interviewees lived. The family budget had to be carefully monitored as any change in the family fortunes would have had an immediate impact and threats to the economic stability of the household were many and ever present. The interviews clearly show that the mills were in a near constant state of flux due to changing ownership, technological innovations and wider economic pressures. Additionally, the impact of the War was a present danger which could impact on the family in many different ways: the loss of the main wage earner or the economic consequences of the War on the textile industry being two most likely to have an immediate impact on the family unit. The consequence of one or more of these factors, evident in many of the testimonies collected by Ian, was that childhood was short and the choice of one's future was often no choice at all. As Betty Muir remarked to Ian: 'Ye had tae get oot tae work.'

This chapter will consider extracts from interviewee testimonies which illustrate the experience of living with this level of economic uncertainty, revealing some of the ways in which people coped with these pressures and constraints. Here, interviewees tell Ian about their childhood ambitions and the often hasty transition from childhood to worker. 'I left school on the Friday and started in the mill on the Monday' was a sentiment expressed in many of the interviews. The exception to this being if there was sufficient income in the family home, when a child might have been able to remain at school a bit longer. This may have happened if the father was in a suitably senior role to command a better wage, or if older siblings were already out and earning, thereby contributing to the overall economic comfort of the family. However, such cases were the exception in the experience of Ian's interviewees.

Many of the Peeblesshire interviewees told Ian that they had left school as soon as it was possible to do so. Sometimes, this was merely the way things were, with everyone simply conforming to expectations. In other instances, the parent or child might have expressed the necessit for the youngster to set out on their working life. With the parents, the motivation would often have been a desire to improve the fortunes of the family unit. With the children, it was more likely to have been a desire to escape the tedium of school or to move on and join friends or siblings who were already working.

This chapter begins with an extended interview extract from Archie Little, who was a few days from his seventieth birthday when he was interviewed by Ian in January 1997. Archie's recollections of work include driving a horse and cart from the age of ten and then lorries from around age fourteen. Ian must have marvelled at some of the anecdotes that he heard from his interviewees about their early working lives, not least those shared by Archie. No doubt, he would have been thinking of his own children when he listened to Archie describe how, at the age of fourteen, he would be out of the house from seven in the morning until seven in the evening, doing heavy log work up in the hills all day long, with only rounds of sandwiches to sustain him. Archie made light of his situation though, joking with Ian that, 'One o the hardest jobs durin the War, ye ken, was kennin what tae put on the bread!'

Archie was born in 1927, joined the army aged seventeen, was demobbed aged twenty-one, in 1948, and was working in the mill by 1951. Whether he's telling Ian about the time he climbed into the wagon of the bread van to escape the rain, or the challenges of delivering coal on the Sabbath, Archie's testimony is a powerful and entertaining account of early working life around the time of the Second World War.

This narrative tells a story of the threads that ran through Archie's life. His interest in driving, which was present throughout his working life, as well as the impact of war and economic circumstances on the choices available to him, and the choices he felt he was able to make.

Archie Little, b. 1927, Walkerburn, interviewed 10 January 1997

Ah got demobbed on ma twenty-first birthday.
So that would be January '48. You didn't think of remaining on in the Army?
Aye, we thought aboot it, Ah quite enjoyed the Army. Ah mind Ah got demobbed at York, and he says, 'Name, rank and number and date of birth?' So Ah telt him. He says, 'Many happy returns!' It dawned on iz it wis ma twenty-first birthday. So that wis the day Ah come oot. Ah returned hame and the British Road Services had taen over aa the lorries bar one! An ma uncle bought a farm, you see, and kept one lorry, which done the coal and sticks. So Ah wis put on that an aa the other drivers were taen away, of course. And Ah wis workin wi ma uncle quite hard, done a wee bit on the farm that he bought – Kirklands at Innerleithen. It wis quite a good farm. And he stayed in Montaza, a big hoose at Walkerburn. Ah'll tell you what it was. He caed it

efter the hospital [Montazah] that he wis in, in Egypt in the First War. So we stayed on the farm for a wee while efter he bought this farm at Innerleithen. And Ah worked a bit on the farm and then, when he wis ready, he moved. He moved up tae the farm and we moved intae his hoose doon here, you see.

Montaza. Was that quite a sizeable house?

So, aye, it's quite a big hoose. It's two-storey one side, three up on the other side because it's on the main Galashiels road, opposite the church along there. So he went to the farm and we went tae Montaza. And Ah worked, oh, 1950, Ah think it wis 1951, when there wasnae an awfy lot doin in the coals. And there were two coal businesses, so he sold his coal business tae a Mr Watson and Ah went intae the mill. Ah got a job in the millin, in the mill-hoose in the mill.

How did you get the job in the mill? Was there a vacancy that was advertised?

Ah mean, they were needin workers then anyway, so Ah went tae see them and Ah got this job. So, Ah wis in at the millin o the cloth, you ken. It wis quite an interestin job.

Now which mill was that?

That one there, Walkerburn – Tweedholm mills.

That was quite a change for you though, from your previous occupations which had been outside jobs.

Aye. But this place wis practically outside. The doors were open and aa thing, you ken. It's scourin the cloth and millin it, you ken, intae the right widths and aa thing. So Ah wis in there for maybe a year and a bit and then they decided tae get this big van. So Ah got the job on the van. Then they got a lorry. So, Ah wis drivin the lorries right up until Ah finished, till the mill actually finished – 1988, Ah think wis when oo wis a redundant then.

You'd be, you'd be just over sixty at that time?

Yeah. Aye. But then efter Ah wis off, they asked us tae come back again workin month by month shiftin machinery that wis in this mill, shiftin it tae Galashiels and Langholm and Edinburgh. And so Ah wis on that for about a year. And by that time, Ah think Ah wis aboot sixty-three.

Yes. So you finally retired?

So Ah jist retired then, aye, uh huh.

We also learn that Archie's working life actually started at an early age, as he tells Ian in this next extract. He also gave more detail about his life: in the forestry; with Walkerburn Co-operative Society; and with Ballantyne's mill at Walkerburn.

At the school, did you have any particular ambitions?

Ah don't know. Ah think it wis mainly on the drivin side that Ah wanted, because Ah used tae drive when Ah wis ten year old, you ken, Ah could drive lorries when Ah wis ten. (laughs)

This is your uncle's lorry?
　　No, auld Alan Watson. This bloke swept the road wi a brush and they put the leaves in wee heaps, ye see. Then auld Alan Watson came roond wi the lorry and shovelled them on. So Ah used tae drive the lorry fae heap tae heap and he shovelled them on, ken. (laughs)

Aye, aye. Was he a council driver?
　　No, no. No, no.

A private contractor?
　　Private contractor, aye. Aye, he let iz drive. And, oh, Ah used tae drive everything.

He was taking a bit of a risk was he not? A laddie of ten driving?
　　Oh, Dunc [his son] drove when he wis no able tae reach the pedals – standin up he drove. He wis aboot six when he wis drivin! (laughs) Mind you, there wasn't the cars on the roads then.

No. Now when you started work, though, you were saying you got your first job with the Co-op?
　　Aye.

And can you remember how you got that job? Was it advertised or you just went along or …
　　Ah think the bloke that wis on it wis called up tae the Army, Ah think, if Ah mind right. And they were needin somebody, ye ken. But it wis the horse an cairt from what Ah mind.

Were you disappointed at not being able to drive a motor to start with?
　　Well, Ah wisnae long there. Ah wis only there for a month. Ah wis drivin the motor right away when we went out tae The Glen,[9] ye see. It wis away in the wilds. Ah wis drivin there, drivin all sorts o things there, ee ken.

And roughly how many folk were employed in and by the Co-op when you were there?
　　Oh! twenty, Ah would think.

Aye, aye. And most of them would be working in the shop?
　　Aye, there were bakers there, you see. They had bakers and apprentice bakers. And then they'd butchers and apprentice butchers. Then the grocers and there were apprentices wi the grocers. And they'd the drapery and they had the shoemakers, ye ken.

Were there any other shops in Walkerburn at that time?
　　Oh, aye. Quite a few. There wis two chip shops. There's none now, like, ye ken. There was one, two, three, four – there would be aboot anither eight shops or something in Walkerburn then, ye ken.

Aye. So, you know, as an old resident of Walkerburn – when I say old, I mean somebody who has lived here most of your life – practically all of your life – you must find that the village is in a state of sad decline?

9　A country house and estate in Traquair, owned at the time by Lord Glencomer.

Oh, aye.

(Mrs Myra Little: Terrible.)

Well, you used tae ken everybody in the place, you ken. And they gaun away, they used tae gaun away off on holidays and they jist left their windaes and their doors open in thae days. You jist gied the key tae somebody else and they'd go in. But, oh, Ah dinnae ken half o them, no near half the folk in Walkerburn now.

But the closing of the mill must have made a huge difference to Walkerburn?

Aye. Aye.

(Mrs Little: It actually took away our sort o social life as well. It took away everything.)

So when you were with your horse and cart how far did you go round about Walkerburn?

Oh, Ah din the whole o Walkerburn and West Bold – Ah mind it wis like a stagecoach. (laughs) You sat up in the front thonder and it wis square, this bread van, and there were a wee slide, you could reach in and get a loaf oot, ye ken, save ye gettin off the van. Ah mind goin out tae West Bold and it wis pourin o rain, so Ah crawled in through the wee hole and Ah'm drivin the horse oot through the wee hole, ken! (laughs) And somebody reported a runaway horse! (laughs)

Did you enjoy that work?

Aye, Ah quite enjoyed it, aye. A lot o ma pals worked at The Glen, you see, this big estate – tae get away oot there. So as soon as Ah got a job there, Ah went away tae The Glen. Ah enjoyed it. You're away oot in the wilds, ye ken.

Yes, aye. And you were there about three years, roughly?

Aye, uh huh.

And how did you get to work?

Well, oo got the bus or bikes tae Innerleithen and then got picked up wi a lorry, an open lorry. By God, it wis cauld some mornings in, ken, an open lorry, you ken, jist an open lorry, sittin in the back, somebody else sittin between your legs. Everything wis open.

And you were sawing, you were felling timber, were you?

Aye. But ma main job wis, Ah got on tae the caterpillar tractors and stuff like that, ye ken, and Ah drove them. Ah quite enjoyed that.

Aye. And was that what you did from a fairly early stage? Within a matter of months maybe of starting?

Aye. Oh, aye, aye. Ah wis also in everything else in the forestry, cuttin and the horse and stuff, because every so long the tractor had tae go in tae the engineerin place and get aa done up, ee ken, and Ah used tae get another job, ken, when aa that wis gettin done. So Ah've done everything in the forestry.

That was quite dangerous work was it not, the forestry?

Oh, aye.

You were never yourself injured?
  No, no.
Did you work in the saw mill occasionally, too?
  Aye, aye.
So you turned your hand to everything?
  Everything up there, but mainly Ah wis on the caterpillar tractors. There wis a lot o winchin – it wis so steep. We used tae have a big winch on the back, ye ken – the second man had tae put it over his shoulder and pull the wire rope away doon. And somebody else wis fixin the trees on and Ah pulled them up, ye ken.
Pretty hard, heavy work?
  Aye, aye.
Now what sort of hours did you work in the woods then?
  Well, Ah went away at seven and came back aboot seven.
You left home at seven? So you started maybe about eight, was it?
  Aye, wait the now tae Ah think this out. Aye, we must've started aboot quarter to eight or somethin like that. And we worked tae … Oh, Ah think the Timber Girls[10] didnae work overtime, they worked tae aboot quarter tae five or half-past four, and we worked on after that. We were often workin seven tae seven, ken, travellin. We used tae try and catch the seven bus and we used tae flee on this lorry fae The Glen, try and catch the ten past seven bus.
Aye. That was a long day though? And you were just a young lad?
  Aye, a long day. Oh, aye.
And was that five days a week or six?
  Ah've seen us workin the Saturdays an aa.
And what were the wages there?
  Well, Ah wis quite lucky because I'd quite a big wage for ma age, ye see. An Ah think, Ah think Ah can mind o gettin, when Ah started, about £3, £3-odds, £3 a week.
Aye. And that included payment for overtime?
  Aye. But Ah must've got more later on because Ah can mind on makin £11, you know. That wis on piece-workin, on piece-work.
That was good money in those days for a laddie of sixteen, seventeen?
  Oh! Aye, that wis piece-work, cutting props wi a prop-saw, ye ken.
Aye. That was exceptional?

---

10 The Women's Timber Corps (Lumber Jills) was a separate branch of the Women's Land Army and was started in 1942 due to the German occupation of Norway causing a shortage of imported timber. Working slightly shorter hours (7am to 4:30pm) than the Land Girls, it was considered by some as a soft option, however Lumber Jills had to pass a stricter medical examination than Land Girls.

Oh, aye. Aye.
(To Mrs Little) You didn't realise your husband was so well off in his youth! (laughs)
(Mrs Little: Well, he wis only gettin aboot £8 a week, £9 a week, when oo got married.) (laughs)
Were you in a union when you were in either the Co-op or the woods?
Aye. Aye, we were in the Transport and General Workers [in the woods].
In the woods. You weren't in a union when you were in the Co-op?
No. Well, Ah wis only fourteen or fifteen when Ah wis there.
Were the other workers in a union, that you can remember?
Certainly in the woods they were in the union.
Was there a head forester who managed the timber side of things?
Oh, there wis, aye, aye. Ah think, there wis one or two worked on the estate. There wis one or two o them. A gamekeeper and foresters, aye.
But your employer was who then?
The Ministry of Home Grown Timber Production. There wis probably aboot a hundred o us workin there, ye ken. Oh, Ah dinnae know how many worked there, maybe no as many as that. No, no, there wisnae as many as that.
Maybe seventy or eighty?
Aye, including the forty-five Timber Corps girls.
And maybe about thirty to forty men?
Aye, aye, aye, aye. Ah would think so, yes.
Now what sort of work did the women do? Was it light, lighter tasks?
The same. No, no they cut trees and everything. No the big trees, but the fellin, peelin. There wis two o them on the saw and, aye, they din aa the work.
Did they do any driving at all?
No. No really, no.
It must have been quite a hard life for women was it?
Oh, Ah think they enjoyed theirsels up there, you ken, cause they were aa thegither.
So you were working on and about the farm and the coal and the sticks for your uncle for about three years?
Aye, aye.
Did you enjoy that work?
Aye, Ah quite enjoyed it. The only thing wis, the coal wis away ower the farms, you ken, away ower the Yarrow and Ettrick and thae places. It wis rationed at the time. Ah wis jist maself and the thing, jist yoursel, tryin tae fill bags o coal and lift them on to the lorry and stuff like that. If there's two o youse, you can dae three times the work o one. It wis heavy work for one. If there's two o youse you're aaright because you can pick them up, you ken. But it wis jist ower much, it wisnae ower much but, oh, Ah wis gettin behind. Ah used tae go oot on the Sundays an aa.
Did you?

Aye. Coal wis rationed, and folk were desperate for their coal. One time, Ah went on a Sunday and this auld wife wouldnae take it on a Sunday. She wouldnae take coal in on Sunday. So she had nae coal.

She was a Sabbatarian?

Oh, aye.

Aye. Oh, dear. So it was all round about Walkerburn but also as far over as Ettrick?

Oh, aye, Ettrick and Yarrow an aa, aye, aye. There's auld brigs that … Some gey scary roads up to some o thae farms, ye ken, wi a big coal lorry. And you're up on the edges there and it's rumblin away as you're goin along. Ah mind Ah went ower yin day and this place Ah wis goin tae wis across a bridge. And Ah'd a laddie wi iz. Ah said, 'Away and see what that bridge is like'. So he went ower and put his fit through it! (laughs) So Ah went ower and examined it and it wis kind o strengthened underneath, ye ken. He says, 'Aw, Ah'll stay at this side!' Ah drove up. (laughs) Aye, Aye, Ah reckon it wis 1951 Ah went intae the mill. In the millhoose, you milled the cloth, made the cloth fae the raw material intae, ken. The tartans and stuff like that, you had tae be very careful tae get the checks right, ye ken. You aye had the pattern, you had tae get the pattern, ye ken, right. An then, oh, it wis quite interestin.

But you didn't do that for very long before you moved on to the lorries?

(Mrs Little: You were on the lorries when we got married in '54.)

Were we? Ah must've worked aboot three year in the mill. (laughs)

But from what you're saying you were glad maybe to get away from that job and on to the lorries? Is that right?

Oh, aye. Yes.

Tell me what you were doing with the lorries?

Most o the time Ah wis takin yarn tae wee hosieries here, there and everywhere, ken, away up at Stirlingshire or somewhere like that and droppin somethin off at this wee hosiery and some o this at another wee hosiery. But then – was it twice a week? – Ah had big loads for Lesmahagow. Ah wis in East Kilbride a bit. Ballantyne's had a place in East Kilbride, ye see.

So, just after you married you went on to the lorries?

Aye, must've been, right enough, aye.

Did that continue until the mill closed more or less?

Aye. There wis a lot o different owners in that time.

But your work remained the same under successive owners?

Jist aboot the same. Jist aboot the same, aye. Ah emptied a lot o the mills when they closed. The Dawson group taen ower a lot and closed an awfy lot o mills. An awfy lot.

You emptied the machinery?

Emptyin the machinery away and everything that wis there, ken. Emptyin the mills in Hawick and Selkirk.

What did you think of that work then?

Oh, Ah wis gettin enough work, but it wis a shame the places were aa closin doon.

So that was your work though, always with the lorry, delivering yarn and sometimes cloth and, later, shifting machinery.

Aye. Shiftin machinery.

Was it into the sixties and the seventies when the mills began to close?

The first one that Ah can mind would be into the sixties. Aye.

So the industry was really beginning to run down from the sixties was it?

Aye, aye.

So how did the closure of the mill affect Walkerburn? What impact did it have on the village?

Aye, it had quite an impact because the places werenae sae busy. Because you got aa these workers in the mills in the shops and it affected them, ye ken. And the club.

This was the mill club was it? The workers club?

It's actually a memorial club, it used tae be, that used tae be the library, but it wis handed over tae a committee. And it had nothing tae dae wi the mills or onything, although it wis the Henry Ballantyne Memorial Club. Jist an open club, ye ken. And it seemed tae decline a bit efter the mills closed.

People would start to leave the village in search of work?

Aye, yes, aye. There wis quite a few left the village. And there's one or two. They built units there but they didnae employ very many folk in them.

Industrial units, aye?

Aye.

So, quite a number of people still unemployed in Walkerburn?

There were, but most o them got jobs in Wilson & Glenny's in [Hawick].

Aye. Were you glad to go? Or would you have preferred to have stayed on?

In the mill here? Oh, Ah'd have preferred to have stayed for a bit, aye.

So looking back on your years in the mill and you worked there from 1951 until 1988, so that was nearly forty years!

Aye, gey near it, aye.

Did you find it a satisfying job, an enjoyable job?

Well, as Ah say, it wis quite an interestin job when Ah wis in the millhouse, ken. Ah'd never been in before and it wis quite a good job. It wis yin o the best jobs in the mill, ye ken. But Ah preferred bein oot, ken.

So you found the driving satisfying?

Yes, aye.

You didn't ever really seriously want to do anything else?

No, and Ah didnae want tae get on the other lorries and go away for days at a time, ye ken.

Well, that's great. Thanks very much indeed for all your time and trouble. Your memory's far, far better than you thought it was! (laughs) You've remembered a great deal.

Other Voices

The following extracts tell of the impact of, and strategies for coping with, periods of unemployment, shortened working hours, or when there simply was not enough money coming into the family purse week by week.

Andrew Brunton, b. 1928, Innerleithen, coping with hard times and unemployment

Can you remember your father being unemployed?

Aye, aye, uh huh. He wis oot o work, aye, aye. Oh, he used tae take us walks. In thae days, if ye went up the tap o the street, the tap o Waverley Road, they were aye men standin at the tap o the street, unemployed.

Aye. Mill workers mainly?

Well, mainly, aye, uh huh.

Do you have any memories of the consequences of your father not having a job? You know, having to go short?

Well, Ah can mind yince, ken, Ah'd this auld overcoat and the linin wis torn. And ma mother sent iz a message and a ten bob note. Ah put it in ma pocket an it must've went through the linin. So, needless to say, there wis a helluva cairry-on, ken, with the ten bob! But the thing aboot this is, ma mother went to the polis station. And another unemployed man had handed that ten bob in to the polis station.

That was a lot of money in those days?

Aye. Ah can mind it. Ah can even mind the man's name. It fell at a man, Wilson and he handed the ten bob intae the polis station. Well, Ah'll tell ye another time. Ah turned no weel. An ma mother had a croon, ken, a five shillin piece. An she had tae get medicine. So we went up tae Sandy Russell's, the chemist. They were nae croons goin about then, ye ken. So she gave him the croon an he says, 'Mrs Brunton,' he says, 'Ah'll haud on tae that an if ye can redeem it ye'll get peyed'. But it never was redeemed, ye ken.

No. She'd never have as much as that again?

No, no.

So times must have been very hard in your boyhood?

Oh, aye, aye. Och, aye, it wis a case o goin oot an gettin turnip, ye ken, away oot an get a turnip oot the field, ye ken, at the ferms an things like that, ye ken. Ma uncle wis a great yin for goin tae the waterside, bring wid hame, saw it up, chop it up for kindlin or logs for the fire.

So this was your uncle who lodged with you?

That's right, David. Efter the War, aye, and even efter, Ah wis on short-time, ken. The mills were aye on short-time. There were aye something happenin. An Ah've seen iz poppin out an gettin fish, ye ken.

How common was poaching on the river in Innerleithen?

Very common, very common. It wis mair prevalent wi some faimlies as tae others, ye ken. There were kind o faimlies o poachers, ken. But Ah wisnae off a poachin faimly.

John Brown, b. 1920, Walkerburn, poaching

Ma father wis a great fisher. Oh! Ah remember as a lad going down the Tweed and, of course, there wis a lot o unemployment then. And it wouldnae be much for a ticket then for fishin. But ma father used tae take me and if he sees any[thing] sort o suspicious, you know maybe the bailie or that comin, he would hand me the rod, of course. (laughs) He'd be teachin me, you see. An Ah can remember it as well as anything and oh, what lovely trouts. He was a good fisher.

Now what about, speaking of fishing, was there … was there much poaching went on in and about Walkerburn?

Oh, there was quite a lot. Oh, there was a big lot o poachin, uh huh. There wis a lot o the men, you see, they had no work. And, they used to get sticks and that in Plora Wood, you know, for tae keep the fires and that goin.

Which wood was that, sorry?

Plora, jist passed Walkerburn station. An, oh, they used to have wee carts and that and, you know, collect the wood. And, oh, there used tae be a lot o poachin. But, no, Ah can truthfully say Ah never did any poachin. (laughs)

A favourite walk on a Sunday, [wis] tae walk up tae the cauld – that wis between Walkerburn and Innerleithen – and see the salmon. Oh, amazin sometimes.

It must have been very tempting?

Oh, it was! But there was a caravan wi the two bailies, you know, that came up. Oh, there wis, Ah would say hundreds sometimes, the salmon leapin. It was marvellous.

To watch it, aye.

Uh huh.

But a lot of the men and the young fellows went out at night did they, poaching?

Oh, yes. There wis a lot o poachin.

John's father had a less risky method of supplementing the family fortunes, as he told Ian.

Ah'll tell you: ma father used tae cut hair. Ah remember ma mother tellin me this. You see, there was no hairdresser at Walkerburn then. And this gentleman that cut hair, he said he was giving up. And ma father bought his clippers and that. You know, different things. And Ah can always remember ma mother tellin me that. Well, Ah remember he cut the hair. He had a shed. In fact, there used tae be a shop at Walkerburn station. Oh, it wis jist a tin hut, you know, but it wis a shop. And he bought that. Now what year would that be? Ah wis still at school, so early thirties, And then he got permission and he shifted it up tae the hut at Tweedholm Avenue. Oh, it wis a nice hut. And he cut hair. And for a haircut it wis thruppence.

Was that for a man or a laddie? A boy?

For both. (laughs) Even girls used tae get their hair cut. Thruppence!

Thruppence was it?

That wis old money, of course. And when you think now. Ah go up for a bit trim at John Dryden's and it's £3, an takes a couple o minutes! But you know, what a difference! So he done that in his spare time.

It was a spare-time job? It was never a full-time job?

No, no jist evenings, uh huh. And he used to shave the old men, you know. Ah think it wis thruppence for that, too.

The impact of economics was felt in many aspects of life. Here John speaks about how the cost of feed, maple peas, meant that his father was forced to give up John's pigeons while he was at war.

There wis a lot o pigeon fanciers in Walkerburn. There wis a big club. If Ah recall, Ah'm sure there wis aboot fourteen, sixteen members. Cause that wis a great thing, the pigeon racin, you know.

You were interested in that?

Ah have a certificate hangin on the wall. First in Scotland (laughs) in 1938.

So you'd only be eighteen?

Eighteen year old.

And had you always been interested in the pigeons?

Yes, aye. And two o ma pals used to keep pigeons as well. And, oh, there wis a lot o pigeon racins. But when Ah went away, ma father kept them on for a while, but it wis gettin the maple peas, it wis gettin the feed for them. And Ah remember he wrote tae me and said, 'Oh,' he says, 'Ah'm goin tae give the pigeons away'. And there were some good pigeons. This wis durin the War, when Ah wis away in the Services. When he wrote and said that Ah felt quite sad. However, when Ah came back Ah never started again.

Hume Davidson recalls how illicit means were sometimes called upon to supplement the family larder.

Hume Davidson, b.1928, Walkerburn, poaching and wild food

You always enjoyed working in the mill?

Aye, aye. But, mind ee, when oo worked doon there the dam used tae run. If ee opened the window you could see the salmon. And oo had a cleek stick in the mill and the windaes opened and ee could go doon and nip a salmon durin even the workin hours. There were a lot o stories but, Ah mean, the salmon, it wis an industry. And we caed that the back dam, and ee had a piece o stick wi a cord and a piece o wire, piano wire wi a swivel on it and hooks and a bit lead. And some o the fish that got taken out that dam wis unbelievable!

You couldnae do it from the factory building though?

No, no, no. This wis at night. But through the day, Ah told ee aboot the coolin shed? Well, the man that wis in charge o the power house could shut off the water. There were a by-pass, they caed it, the weirwall, for when he wanted not so much water goin through the turbines. And it wis a waterway aboot five yards wide and there were usually a big force o water went down there. Well, he could shut that off jist for a bit. And when he shut it off, the fish wis left stranded.

Mainly salmon?

Aye.

You'd often have a salmon for your tea did you?

Oh, aye, aye.

That's very interesting. How important was poaching [in Walkerburn]?

Well, there were a lot o poaching went on. There were some people made their livin from it – quite a substantial sum o money – and others had one for the pot. Because when Ah wis a boy, Ah mean, daist aboot everybody lived off the land, and when the salmon came up. Even, it's been known that the poacher would hing yin on the back door o the police station, ee know, for the policeman! (Mrs Davidson laughs).

Who owned that stretch? Was there just one landowner that owned the stretch?

Aye, it wis the mill. There wis a lot o different methods o catchin salmon. There wis, hand-rods with a long cord, cotton bandin – which came oot the mill, right. This cotton bandin wis used for drivin pulleys. Ee dyed that, aboot fifty yards o that, and then put triple hooks on the end o it, wi a big lead sinker on it, which was made wi an inkwell. Ee poured lead intae an inkwell then ye broke it up and there ee had a big sinker. And ee threw the rake hooks in and ee could see the salmon on a clear day and catch them that way. Ee could also watch the salmon through the day and ee could [set a line] where the fish made their beds tae lay their eggs. And ee could actually see them in the river. And at night a poacher would go in wi a pair o boots and an auld pair o trousers, and wade intae the water wi a strong light and …

Blind them?

Well, they never went away, wi the light. And there ee are, ee wis able tae flick the fish oot the water.

Aye. The light must have attracted them possibly in some way?

Aye, maybe. That's what ee call burnin the water. In the olden days away back in the eighteenth/nineteenth century, I think they used tae burn straw and they could see the fish. However, that wis lightin. And the other way wis they had what ee call cairns where they would build a pier, a wee pier, by throwin stones in, big stones, near the shore. And fish came in there tae rest, so you could put a pot, a net in. Ah seen one the other day when Ah wis up the water. And they had floats. Nowadays they use empty plastic lemonade bottles – we seen them. In my day it wis a bag, and the fish went in there tae rest and ee went down at night and ee pulled them out. And then, as Ah say, there wis a dam. Well, away up the water in the river they built caulds tae keep the water back so's it run down the dam. Well, they come up the cauld. Well, ee stood there wi a huge stick and a cleek aboot that size and ee stood in a row and when the salmon came up tae ee, ee cleekit it. And if there were two o youse cleeked the same salmon, ee used tae toss-up for it. So that wis another way o catchin salmon.

Now you're speaking about all this extremely objectively, of course, and saying one could do this and one could do that! (laughs)

Well, oo wis all brought up tae cleek the salmon because the Walker Burn had salmon up there. Well, when ee wis a wee boy, you got a cleek and you went up the burn.

Was that just a wee burn? I don't know it.

(Mrs Davidson: The Walker Burn jist runs through the village and goes up the hill. It would be aboot that depth and aboot that width.)

Aye, about six feet broad by three feet, aye.

And the salmon, when it wis big, the salmon would come up.

It would be relatively easy to catch them there?

Aye and it wis great fun! It wis fun.

The laddies would enjoy that? So you'd have salmon for your tea quite often in Walkerburn?

Aye. (To Mrs Davidson) Oo've got salmon in the fridge. Have you?

(Mrs Davidson: There might be a bit there.)

I'm not asking if you've got any!

Ah get it give tae me now.

(Mrs Davidson: Aye, well it's fair fishin!) (laughs)

But, I mean, it was obviously very common for poaching to take place among the mill workers in Walkerburn when you were a laddie and throughout your lifetime in the mill?

Uh huh. Aye.

Aye. The mill workers saw that as one of the privileges of living in Walkerburn?

Oh, aye.

So it was some sort of compensation for wages that were often fairly low?

Aye, oh, aye.

And not very reliable, you know, if you had short-time working? Were you yourself ever unemployed?

No. Short-time, never unemployed.

Was that fairly frequent, the short-time?

No. Occasionally. An some o the short-time wis due to power cuts.

In the seventies? Edward Heath's government? The three-day week and all that?
> Aye.
> (Mrs Davidson: Aye, we had three days, aye.)

It wasn't very often that you worked short-time?
> No.

Did the Ballantynes attempt to prosecute [poachers]?
> No. The bailies wis there, mind ye.

Aye. So you had to beware of them?
> Oh, aye, aye. Some o them got fined and some away back in say, the 1930s, some o them got the jail. They were in Saughton Jail ower the heid o it. Ah didnae poach that much.

No, no, no. I didn't mean to put you on the spot.
> Ah would've poached for the pot.

Aye, aye.
> Ah didnae.

Not for selling.
> Or for sendin away, ee ken. Ma uncle wis a policeman in Musselburgh and I might be telt, 'Get your Uncle Wat a fish,' ee ken. Ah used tae get yin for ma Uncle Wat and take it through, somethin like that. But there's a guy in Walkerburn yet, he gave a talk at the Probus Club on his poachin and he's quite wealthy and it's through poachin that he made his money. And he said he believed that he wasnae stealin.

No, no. God's gift to mankind?
> Aye. Well, he believed that.

Well, I can understand that.
> But, Ah love goin up the burns. Ee could go up the burns and fish for trout aboot that size, and Ah still go up yet. And another thing we got wis hares. There wis an abundance o hares, but you can hardly get one now. Shooters used tae have a certain day that they went and shot hares and buried them aa, there were that many. An we used tae go out and get a hare and Ah've still got the recipe yet for hare soup. And we had hare soup when Ah wis a laddie. We got a hare, Ah can clean a hare and make hare soup yet.

Aye. All that's missing are hares!
> Aye, you cannae get yin noo. Ah wis in the rifle club and ye used tae shoot at Pathhead. After Ah come back fae ma Army service, in ma twenties. And oo come down Leithen and Ah've seen us gettin half a dozen hares, either wi a rifle or killin them wi the thingummy. And ye gave them tae that yin and that yin made hare soup. But, ee see, ma mother loved it and ma faither loved it. She'll no look at it! (Mrs Davidson laughs) So now if Ah got a hare and made hare soup, well … (laughs)

Aye, you'd have to eat it yourself! What about wild fruit gathering? Did you do much of that?

Aye, oh, aye, there wis a time that ee went for raspberries an up the hill for blaeberries. An we went tae that hill ower there, tae whit ye caed the nut-wood, and ye got hazelnuts. But half o the folk in Walkerburn widnae ken there were a nut wid up there. Ah tried makin elderberry wine, when Ah wis gatherin it at the roadside. And Ah read the book when Ah come home and they reckoned it's no a good thing gatherin fruit at the roadside because the o the fumes off the cars. Seemingly they go into the fruit. (laughs)

So all these were supplements really? I mean, the mill workers had fairly low wages?
Yes.

But it was possible to supplement your food stocks by gathering wild fruit. And a lot of people, you know when you were a laddie, did that in Walkerburn?
Uh huh, Uh huh. And everybody had a garden an aa, uh huh.
(Mrs Davidson: A lot o folk kept hens.)

For Hume, entry into the world of work came earlier than it did for many of the interviewees. And for potential employers, being on the Education Board evidently had its advantages when you were looking for a new apprentice gardener, as he told Ian.

Did you have any ambitions as a laddie, you know, to become a joiner or an engine-driver or a sailor or … anything like that, that you can remember?
No, no really.

You were interested in sums and woodwork?
Aye, aye. Yes. Aye, Ah would like tae have been a joiner, aye. But the point is that there wis one local joiner, and if he wis needin an apprentice at the time you went, you'd be lucky, and if he wasnae, you could forget aboot it. (laughs) Ah left school when Ah wis thirteen and a half. Ah got offered an exemption fae the school because Mrs Ballantyne wis needin a gardener.

Now, she was the wife of the mill owner was she?
Aye. She wis needin an apprentice gardener.

Was that Stoneyhill?
Uh huh. And she wis on the Education Board. (laughs) So Ah got a job. Ah left, Ah think, in the April. You know, there used tae be April holidays, Christmas holidays … summer. Well, Ah shouldnae have left till the summer holiday and Ah got left in the April holiday. So Ah wisnae fourteen.

Aye. You were two or three months short of fourteen?
Uh huh.

So if the chance had presented itself, would you have liked to remain on at school, even if that had meant going on to Peebles?
No, Ah wis quite happy tae work in the gardens. And the guy that Ah worked wi wis, ken, a local guy. He wis a pal o ma father. So Ah wis quite happy learnin. It wis a nice job. Ah looked after the hens, and Ah shuffled

coal and did gardens and …
[You] did odd jobs aye, as well as the actual gardening?
Uh huh.
Now just one point. Your brother had maybe gone off to the Army just about the time you left school? Would that be so?
Aye, it would be in aboot that time.
Was it that your parents needed the money, you know, that you could bring in by leaving school early?
Oh, well, everybody needed the money in thae days.
Aye. But, Ah mean, was that a primary reason for your not remaining at school? Did your parents ever say to you, 'Now look, son, you're good at your lessons, you're keen. What about trying to get on to Peebles High School?'
No, no. They never pushed iz that way. Ah wis quite happy tae dae the gardens.
Did they leave it to yourself to decide whether or not you were going to leave school and what you were going to do?
Aye. Uh huh. Uh huh.
And, of course, as you already said, there was no vacancy in the one and only joiner's business in the town?
That's right.
Now coming to your job in the gardens then: what were the hours that you worked when you first went?
Well, eight o'clock tae twelve or half-past twelve, would it be, half-past twelve. And then oo got an hour for eer lunch. And then oo worked tae, Ah think it wis tae a quarter tae six at night.
If my arithmetic's right, that's about, what, about eight-and-a-bit hours is it?
Aye. Ah jist worked the mill hours, ee see. Cause Ah got paid through the mill. Ah'm jist tryin tae think. And Ah worked on the Saturday, of course. On a Saturday, tae twelve, Ah think it was.
Till twelve. Four hours on a Saturday?
Four hours on a Saturday, aye.
So that would be somewhere about forty-five hours a week you were working?
Aye.
As a laddie of thirteen and a half, going on fourteen?
Aye.
Now, what about your wages when you first began?
(Laughs) 17s.6d. Ah would be classed as an apprentice, ee see. An apprentice gardener. (laughs) Ah wis diggin gardens and shufflin coal, cause they used tae get coal for their, well, wi havin money, the Ballantynes had spare houses. They would maybe get a wagonload o coal. And the lorry would bring it up and empty it and Ah had tae put it away. Ten ton o coal! Ah wis only, what, thirteen year old. Huh!

Heavy work for a laddie? Had they had a boy before you got the job?
    Aye, they had twae or three apprentices but they were aa goin away tae the Army, you see.
As soon as they were eighteen?
    Uh huh. Uh huh.
How many gardeners were there?
    There were daist the two o us in thae days. Jist me and the boss Tommy Wilson. He wis ages wi ma father. Aye, he wis in the First World War.
That's grand. Now what about holidays? As a laddie of thirteen, going on fourteen, you got a week's paid holiday and New Year's Day and a spring holiday?
    Aye.
What about overtime? Did you ever have to work overtime in the gardens?
    Very seldom. Very seldom. One drawback wis durin the War wis the double summertime. And in the winter, well, for instance, workin in a garden, you had tae wait tae it wis light. An Ah've seen us sittin and waitin tae nine o'clock, goin up there at eight and sit in the greenhouses daist wi the cat in your lap, waitin on it gettin light before ee could start. There were nae lightin facilities. (laughs)
Now what about weather? If it were heavy rain or snow were you expected just to carry on working outside?
    Well, if it wis snow, Ah had tae clean the driveway. And what Ah did, Ah had a wee snaw plough and Ah worked doon the middle. Pushed by hand, right down the driveway. And then that was a path up the middle. And then Ah had a push-board, then Ah pushed the snow right tae the inside, walkin up the pathway and then came back doon the other.
Wide enough for a car to go up and down?
    Uh huh. Aye, it wis.
But if it was heavy rain, you weren't expected to carry on?
    Ah, well, oo had the pottin sheds where oo could work.
Aye. There was always work you could be doing indoors?
    Aye, inside, aye, uh huh.
What do you recollect of relations with Mrs Ballantyne? Was she quite a reasonable employer?
    Oh, aye, you addressed her as Ma'am, you know 'Yes, Ma'am'. You went and got the vegetables but, as Ah say, durin the War eggs wis scarce and Ah looked after her hens and she gave us three eggs a week. It wis bonus. Ah got three eggs.
Did you get on quite well with her?
    Uh huh.
Was she fairly good and considerate as an employer?
    Aye, she wis quite good.

Geography and the built environment

Images 1–12 illustrate the different border communities and their location within the landscape and give a sense of the scale and predominance of the mills within each town.

1. General view of Peebles showing mills, 1896. Ref: DP 230994.
© Courtesy of HES

2. Peebles, showing the Ballantyne's March Street Mills, 1929. Ref: SC 12566620.
© HES (Aerofilms Collection)

3. Peebles with Thorburn's Damdale Mill visible in the top left quarter, 1947
Ref: sc 1268751.
© HES (Aerofilms Collection)

4. Innerleithen, Ballantyne's Waverley Mill, 1947. Ref: sc 01268733.
© HES (Aerofilms Collection)

5. Innerleithen, Waverley Mill, 1968. The gap at the centre of the complex indicates the site of a substantial fire.

© Innerleithen Community Trust

6. Innerleithen, Leithen Mills, 1968.

© Innerleithen Community Trust

7. Innerleithen, St Ronan's Mill, 1968. Often referred to as the top ('tap') mill.
© Innerleithen Community Trust

8. Painting of Caerlee Mill in Innerleithen.
This painting, artist unknown, used to hang in the boardroom at Caerlee Mill.
© Simm, 2021

9. Innerleithen, Caerlee Mill, 1968.
© Innerleithen Community Trust

10. The mill lade at Walkerburn, photograph possibly taken around 1954. Ref: 000-000-043-288.
© The Scotsman Publications Ltd / From the collection at National Museums Scotland

11. Walkerburn, Tweedholm Avenue East, 2009. Ref: DP 061010.
© Crown copyright: HES

12. Walkerburn, Ballantyne's Tweedvale Mill. Ref: SC 426028.
© HES. Reproduced courtesy of J. R. Hume

Border Weave, 1942

Images 13–16, stills from the 1942 film, *Border Weave* (Ref: 0482) show key parts of the mill processes.

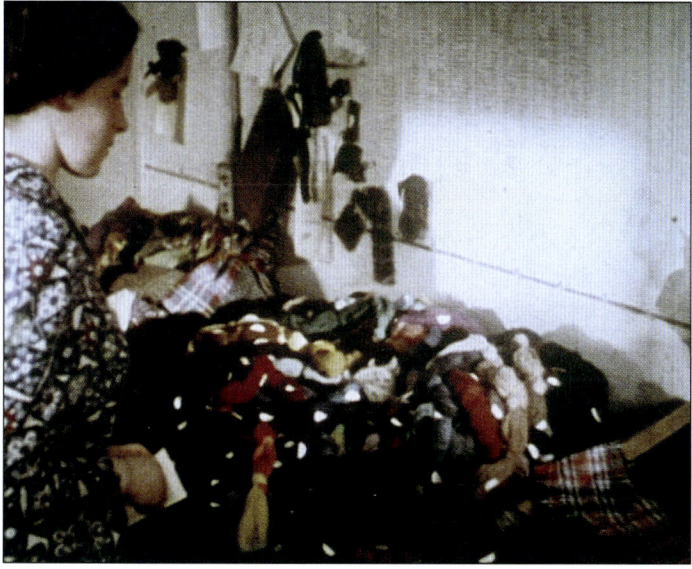

13. The designer picking colours from sample yarns. The samples were then passed to the chemist who mixed the dyestuffs for the dyeing process.

© Scotland's Moving Image Archive

14. The boy seen on the left is an in-giver. This was often the first job a new start would do in the mill.

© Scotland's Moving Image Archive

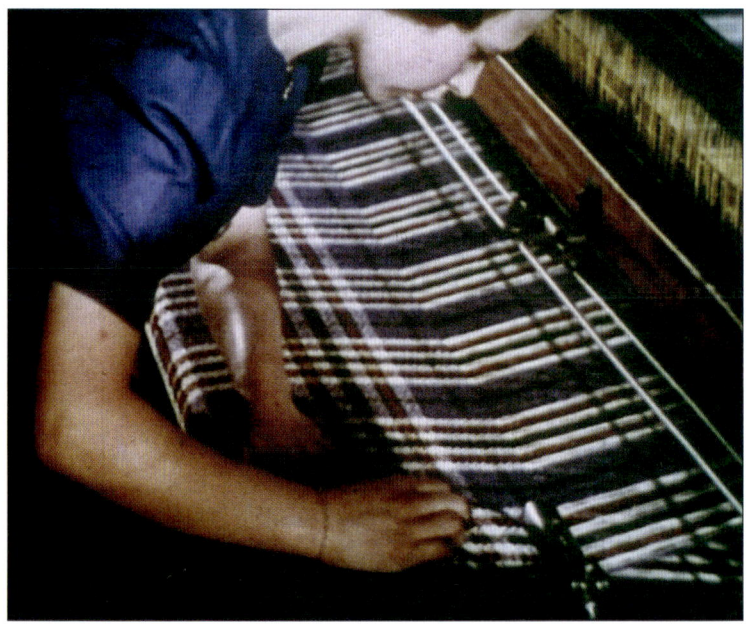

15. A weaver checking the cloth as it is being woven.
© Scotland's Moving Image Archive

16. The finishing department, where the cloth was checked and any irregularities in colour or thread repaired.
© Scotland's Moving Image Archive

Quite often, Ian's interviewees would simply say they had no ambition beyond getting a job when they left school. Not so for John Lunn, who had very definite aspirations.

John Lunn, b. 1936, Innerleithen, childhood aspirations

Now as a laddie did you have any particular ambition? You know, wanting to be an engine driver or a seaman?

No. Ah wanted tae be a farmer. Ah mean, Ah can remember when Ah wis a wee boy – Ah don't know, they wouldnae do it nowadays – ma brother an me bein put on the bus at Innerleithen, changin the bus at Gala and gettin tae Kelso, and ma Granny pickin us up. Ah would only be maybe about six or seven year old. Ah'd a wee case. There werenae aa they rucksacks in these days. Ye packed a wee case and off ye went. That wis me for six or seven weeks.

And you were pottering about on the farm with your grandfather?

Oh, aye, ma grandfather he was the farm manager. And Ah used tae potter about. Help wi the horses. He had an old fellow that drove what they caed the auld horse and Ah suppose he was under orders, but Ah went aboot wi him. Ah'd get sittin in the front o the horse, the cart, ye know, maybe goin for turnips or when they were bringin in the harvest, jist sittin. You thought you were drivin the horse. Ah wouldnae really be, but you thought you were drivin the horse.

Aye, a great thrill for a lad though.

Aye.

And that was how you came to form your ambition?

Tae be a farmer, aye. Even when Ah wis older, when Ah wis at the High School and that, Ah used tae go away down there. And we were very friendly wi a farming family jist about a mile up the road from ma grandmother and I used to work there the whole holidays. In fact, even when Ah started tae work in the mill Ah used to go down at weekends. It wis only a wee croft type farm and they used to wait until the weekend so that Ah could go down and help them with the harvest and that.

Very good. So you had this distinct interest in the land?

Oh, aye. Ah could've got a job on the farm. But Ah would've had tae went tae Kelso. Ma mother wouldnae let us leave home. And Ah tried on the farms roond aboot here but nobody wanted anybody, so Ah finished up in the mill. (sighs)

Because by that time, farm workers were beginning to be replaced by machines?

The tractors. Oh, aye. At Lennel Hill, after the War, all these big boxes arrived and it wis a combine harvester. There were three sons and ma grandfather. An Ah remember this combine, and the three sons and ma grandfather put it together. It jist came in big boxes and aa the instructions. And it had come fae Canada or somewhere. And they all put this together.

Aye. I heard an old farm worker once describe what happened as the Lowland

Clearances, you know, the old days?
　Aye.
When you got the rows of cottages each inhabited by a ploughman and his family. Then they're all empty because there were no jobs for them.

　Oh, aye. Ah mean, when we went tae Lennel Hill they used to get the Irishmen in for the summer. They were at what they caed the bothy. And there was one, Dan. He wis there aa the time. He worked there aa the time. And then the other ones would come across. Different ones would come across for the potatoes or the harvest. And there were a couple o years they had the Italian prisoners in the fields doin the harvest. An the guard stood at the gate wi the gun and that. Ah remember that.

Aye, aye. That would be during the War years?

　That was durin the War years. That's what Ah'm sayin. Ah could go down there for eight weeks, whatever the school holidays was, Ah jist went off.

Aye. You must have felt quite frustrated, when you left school and couldn't get a job on the land?

　Ah was in a way, aye.

Because you were obviously very keenly interested in farm work and being outdoors?

　Uh huh. Ah fell intae the job that Ah eventually did do. Ah've been one o these folk, Ah've jist fallen intae everything, like Ah fell intae goin tae the High School, you know.

Aye. You mean, it was an accident rather than something that you planned?

　Aye. Ah never planned tae go tae the High School. Ah didnae want tae go because none o ma mates were goin. So Ah didnae want tae but, Ah mean, Ah passed, so Ah went. You know, it wis jist a case o ye have tae go and that was it. And Ah would do … Ah wouldnae say, 'Ah'm no doin it!' So Ah did it. When Ah wis fifteen ma parents wanted me to stay on but Ah wis determined that Ah wisnae. An that was when Ah went roond aa the farms lookin for a job. An Ah got a job on a farm doon at Kelso but ma mother wouldnae let me leave home. Ah don't know why because she'd come tae Innerleithen at fourteen! But Ah wasnae tae get tae leave home.

Well, maybe that was why she wouldnae let you do it? Because she'd done it?

　Aye.

Aye. So you left school and did you start straight away in the mill?

　Ah started straight away. Ma father said, 'Well, if you've left the school, you're no doin anything, get yersel round to the mill'. So Ah went round to the mill and Ah got a job in the mill.

While John's parents were keen for him to stay on at school, this was the exception rather than the rule. More often, children were expected to begin their working life as soon as they could. Peter Lavin was acutely aware of this expectation in light of his own family situation. Peter's recollection of being sent for funeral clothes is a poignant reminder that he was still a child in short trousers when he left school to enter the workplace. This insight is echoed later in the interview, when Peter told Ian that his wages went in full, to his mother, who gave him 6d 'pocket money' in return.

Peter Lavin, b. 1922, Peebles, the end of childhood

You didn't sit the Qualifying Exam?
    No. Ye got the choice whether tae stay up there or go up the High School. An I jist thought, well, I'll jist stay where I am because mother wis needin the money and I wis wantin tae get oot when Ah wis fourteen. An I thought if I go up there, I'll probably want to go further on an that, ye know.

Ye didn't feel disappointed in any way, that you couldn't go to the High School?
    Well, later on I think I should have. But at that time, well, ye know, ye're only a laddie, know, an ye think ye're daein the right thing then. But I think masel I should've, an maybe increased a better education for masel. But, you know, you were wantin out an, well, ma family wisnae jist in the best o money, you know.

Cause your father was an invalid really by that time, wasn't he?
    That's right, uh huh.

But you left school presumably in 1936, Mr Lavin? You were fourteen?
    That's right, aye.

And your father died just a year after?
    That's right.

His health hadn't really been good for quite a few years before he died. Is that so?
    Yeah, I think he must've died jist after I wis fourteen. Aye that's right.

Just after you left school or just before you left school?
    No, I think it wis roond aboot the same time because in those days we wore short pants, an ma mum says tae me, 'Ye better go doon tae the Castle Warehoose an get a dark suit wi long trousers for the funeral'. I mind o that, an I had to go an get these, this suit at that place at the back o the Castle Warehoose.

Did that persuade you even more that you should leave school?
    Yes, because, well, we really jist lived from day to day, you know. There werenae much money around. I mean, Christmas, an aa that came an it wis, it would have been as weel as if it hadnae been there, you know. Ye didnae get a lot o things at Christmas time. They'd maybe buy ye a wee toy or maybe gie ye an orange and an apple or something like that, you know. That wid jist say it wis Christmas. But, I mean, ye didnae get computers and things like they get nowadays! (laughs)

If my memory serves me right, you had a younger sister and a younger brother?
    Yeah, aye.

You were the second in the family?
    Uh huh. An, I mean, this wis puttin a burden on to ma mother, you know.

Your mother already had the wee job in the hotel?
   That's right.
Presumably that didnae give her much?
   Oh, no. I mean, she worked in there an I doubt if she got ten bob a week! Terrible!
So you remember your childhood as a fairly straitened time?
   Uh huh.
Not well off?
   Oh no, we werenae what ye could call 'well off', no.

For Walter Scott, working life began while he was still at school and all his earnings went to support the family income. When asked by Ian if he got any pocket money in return for handing over his wage packet, Walter's reply is unequivocal: 'You were gettin yer grub.'

Walter Scott, b.1924, Peebles, jobs around the school day

   We used tae make bogies and aa the rest o it, and barraes and run wi them, ye ken? And then, aye, well, Ah started the High School an Ah got a paper laddie's job, wi Kelly's. That wis ma first job.
And how old would you be then?
   Ah'd be twelve then.
Was this a newsagent in the High Street?
   Up the Old Town. Kelly's wis their name. Ah think Ah went doon at the back o seven an get the barrae, an ye would go fae there tae the LNER station. And ye would wait on the train comin in.
That was at the Innerleithen side of the town, was that right?
   That's right. The train would come in there and ye went to the goods van and the papers wis thrown off. And ye used tae pick up yer papers and then you had tae run wi the barrae, a two-wheeled barrae. You run back up tae the shop. And then ye cairried them in and the wifie in the shop she sorted the papers oot. Ye'd maybe take, say, twenty *Records*, twenty *Expresses*, so many *Scotsmans*. Ye'd a bagfull. Ma roond wis, Ah started it fae the paper shop. Ah came up and did up the Glasgow Road and then Ah came back doon Young Street, St Andrew's Road, Gladstone Place, the cemetery, back doon, up Rosetta Road, March Street, Wemyss Place, Checkland Street, right up tae Eliots Park.
That was quite a big round then?
   Uh huh. Oh, ye covered two or three miles every mornin. And then on a Thursday, well, ye had evening papers as well.
Aye. You delivered in the evening, too? What time did you go back then?
   Well Ah think the train used tae come in half past five, something, tae six. And it wis the same cairry-on again wi the barrae, tae collect them.
And did you have the same round for the evenings?

Mair or less the same. Ye didnae have as many. Hell, that paper bag in the mornins, you could hardly lift it!

So when did you deliver the 'Peebles News'? Was that a separate delivery?

That wis a separate delivery [on a Friday].

As soon as you were out of school?

Ye got oot the school, right doon tae get yer *Peeblesshires*. Uh huh.

So for your morning round, you were down at the shop the back o seven?

Back o seven.

And what time, roughly, would you finish work?

Oh, sometimes Ah wis pushed tae get finished for the school for nine o'clock.

So it would be half-past eight, twenty to nine?

Uh huh but if it wis a wet morning, Ah used tae have tae come hame and maybe get another rig-oot on. Then run to the school.

So you would have to run to school sometimes, did you?

Oh, well, by that time, ye see, Ah had ma bike.

Ah! You went to school on your bike? Were you ever late for school?

Oh, aye a fair number o times, especially if it wis wet.

Aye, because you'd have to get changed before you went off to school?

Aye. They took a dim view o that.

Aye. So you'd be under pressure, as a laddie, covering your round? And then, as soon as you were out of school on a Friday, you rushed to the shop?

That's right.

You didn't go home, you went straight to the shop?

Tae pick up the *Peeblesshires*.

Delivering the Peeblesshire *and the weeklies?*

That's right.

Delivered them, and you'd be finished in time to rush down to the station?

Aye, ye had time tae get hame and get somethin tae eat and then ye were back doon tae go an do the *Evening News*.

Evening News, *aye. And so you'd finish in the evening, delivering* Evening News *about …?*

Seven o'clock.

So you'd be up about quarter to seven, half-past six?

Half-past six or so, aye.

Half-past six. Get your clothes on. Maybe did you get a roll and butter or something before you went out?

Maybe a plate o parritch.

Aye, before you went out. You always had something before you went out?

Oh, ye aye got somethin afore ye got oot, oh, aye.

Aye, your mother would see to that. Because otherwise, you wouldnae have time to eat anything?

Oh, no, no. Ye didnae.

Now what was your pay as a laddie?
>Five shillins.

And that was six days a week delivering?
>Six days a week.

And on the Friday, the very heavy day, you were doing three rounds?
>Three rounds.

Five shillings. And it remained five shillings all the time you did that?
>Aa the time Ah worked there.

And how long did you work there?
>Ah wis there right up until Ah left school. Ah left at fourteen.

So you did that job for about two years?
>Uh huh. In fact, Ah started in here [March Street mills] before Ah wis fourteen. Wi ma birthday no landin tae the seventh o January, in thae days the mill only got one day's holiday. Ye worked Christmas Day. Ye got the first o January. Ye started on the second. So Ah started on the second, on the twistin frames. And here Ah wis sent for to the manager's office. Ah thought, 'Oh, hell, what's happened?' And he explained tae me that Ah would have to go home because Ah wasn't fourteen. So Ah wis sent hame for the rest o the week and started the followin Monday.

You'd be in breach of the Factory Acts! (laughs) That's great. Now just to go back to the job, the newspaper delivery job, when you were a laddie. Did you give your five bob to your mother?
>Uh huh.

Aye. Every week you just gave her the money and then did she give you something back for your pocket money?
>No, no. You were gettin yer grub.

Aye, aye. So you didn't get any pocket money at all as a laddie?
>No, no. Nothin.

You don't ever remember getting any regular weekly pocket money?
>No, no. If Ah wanted tae go to the Empire, tae the picture hoose on a Setterday efternin, Ah had tae hunt for a beer bottle or a jeelie jar or somethin like that.

Cash it in?
>Uh huh.

You could take the bottles to a shop and get a penny or a haepenny return?
>Aye. Uh huh.

So you'd spend a bit of time looking for empty bottles and jars did you?
>Oh, well, when ye seen ony lyin aboot ye wouldnae be lang in stackin them up. And Ah mind there used tae be a Mrs Duncan stayed in Graham Street. Her daughter worked in the baker's, doon the Northgate. And it wis really ma mother landed me wi the ruddy job. On a Saturday mornin – now that wis efter Ah did ma papers – when Ah came back, well, Ah suppose Ah would be

hingin aboot or some damn thing – Ah used tae have tae go tae Mrs Duncan's and she gave me her message line and Ah used tae have tae run the messages. But Ah didnae have the bike then. And she wouldnae say, right, 'Ye go tae the butcher's, ye go tae the next shop and ye go somewhere else'. You went to the butcher's first and then ye came back. And then she gave ye another line. Away again! And then ma last run wis tae go tae the daughter's, whae wis in the baker's shop, doon the Northgate. And Ah'd get her breid and her tattie scones or whitever it wis. And she used tae buy four, Ah think, cream cookies. They'd put them in a box and Ah'd bring them back and Ah got, what, a cream cookie!

Was that your wage?
That wis ma wage.
You didn't get any money?
No, no.
And this was a woman who was a friend of your mother? Was that it?
Well, she stayed in the same kind o square. Ah mean, they spoke to ye. Jist a neighbour, aye, no relation or nothing like that.
Aye. So you were only doing this woman, Mrs Duncan, a favour, really? A big favour? To run her messages?
Uh huh, uh huh.
And the payment for that was one cream cookie?
One cream cookie.
She never slipped you a thruppenny bit or anything?
No, no, no, oh, no.
How long did that take to do these messages, roughly?
Oh, hell, it would take you damned near aboot an hour and a half, two hoors on the Seturday mornin.
What about when you worked on the papers at Christmas time or New Year did you get some tips?
Oh, aye, oh, aye. Ye got a tanner [sixpence] or sometimes a shillin. Very often, maybe an aipple or an orange or somethin like that, ye ken.
Aye, so at Christmas and New Year you got an increase over and above your pay in the form of tips, aye.
Oh, aye, aye.
And did you give all the tips to your mother too? All the money?
Ye handed everything ower.
And again, did she give you anything back?
(Sighs) Ah cannae mind much aboot that. Ah suppose she would dae.

In the final extract Betty Muir, describing herself as shy and 'a kind of loner', explains that she left school just before her fourteenth birthday and immediately applied to go into the mill. Although she would later find her confidence when she went off to do her war service, Betty's intention, on leaving school, was clear.

Betty Muir, b. 1922, Peebles, childhood ambitions and entering the world of work

Now did you have any particular ambitions as a girl, a schoolgirl? Did you want to be a nurse or cook or something like that?

No, no me. Ah cannae remember ever havin any ambitions. Ah wis a wee quiet girl. Ah wis shy, a kind o loner. Ah cannae remember havin ambitions for anything at all.

So it came to the point where you were fourteen and ...?

Yeah, well, Ah wis comin up to fourteen and in those days, well, as Ah say, ye had tae go tae work. And ma father had to apply for a certificate for me to leave school, sayin Ah wis goin to be fourteen in a fortnight's time. And it came up to the Christmas holidays. And if Ah'd went back to school, Ah would've had tae carry on to Easter. But they got this form that they filled in and ye got away frae the school. On the grounds that the money was needed at home.

A kind of exemption?

That's it, an exemption, yeah.

And of course, you wouldnae be fourteen until the January [1935]?

The January, that's right.

Now you left school and tell me what happened then about the job?

Well, we jist went up to the mill and ye had to ask to see Mr Euman. And say you'd come for a job: 'Monday mornin, eight o'clock' – and that wis you.

Did you know how to go about it or did your father say to you or your mother or your friends say to you?

No. It wis jist the family, ye ken ye had tae go an work in the mill. It wis the only thing here unless ye were clever an goin on to the High School to be something. Ma sister, Peggy, who'd been in domestic service for a couple of years, she wis jist in the mill before me. Because when Ah went in, Ah had to do, Ah think it wis six months, on the in-giving. That was where ye put all the individual threads on to the cam that wis to go into the loom to be woven. And Ah remember her boss comin tae me and sayin, 'You'll come in beside your sister an learn the darnin'. And Ah said, 'No, Ah'll no'. Because Ah wis terrified for that man: Jock Miller. And Ah made the excuse that Ah wis left-handed and Ah wouldnae be able to darn, you see. But ye can darn if you're left-handed. But that wis ma excuse then. But it wis jist that Ah didnae want tae go and work under him. Ah wis terrified.

Did you know about him before you went to the mill?

Oh his bark wis worse than his bite. Ah jist knew of him since Ah went intae the mill, there were things that Peggy would come home and say aboot him, ye ken. And when ye went intae his department, ye could hear him shoutin from one end of the flat to the other, ye see. He jist put the fear o death intae me.

Of course as you say, you were a quiet, shy girl?

Yes, this is it, Ah was very quiet and shy.

Yes, yes. That's grand. So there you were. You started work in March Street mill at the age of fourteen.
>Fourteen, yeah.

How did you feel about starting work? Because it's a strange new world. A young girl of fourteen?
>Ah dinnae ken whether Ah would think anything aboot it. Ah jist knew Ah had tae go and work.

Now tell me about the hours? What were the hours of working when you first began?
>Ah think it was eight till half-past five at night.

And did you get a break for your dinner in the middle of the day?
>Aye, yeah, from twelve to one.

And you would come home?
>Home, aye, yes.

Did everybody stop work at twelve o'clock?
>Yeah, aye, there were no shifts or anything in those days. The whole place stopped.

And that was Monday to Friday?
>Saturday mornin as well till twelve or half-past twelve. Ah've a feelin, aye, it wis midday on a Saturday, that's right.

Did you ever work on a Saturday afternoon or Sunday?
>Oh, yes, when the War came, before Ah went to the Services. And ye worked till nine o'clock at night as well.

During the week?
>Durin the week, aye.

How many nights a week would you be working?
>Every night if you wanted to go in, aye. Every night. Oh, it killed you. Ah mean, it wis aa khaki material and it wis heavy. And you had to do as many as you could in, well, the couple o hours that ye worked overtime. Well two and a half hours it would be, half-past five. Six to nine, that's right. Fae six o'clock to nine wis your overtime. And ye had to do as many pieces for tae make a bit.

Now what about the wages when you first began?
>Well, Ah always remember ma first wage wis 6s.10d. when Ah started. And then after six months Ah got a raise and Ah had 7s.4d. for that.

And did you give your wages to your mother?
>Oh, yes. Ye got 6d. back.

To keep you going all week!
>6d. to keep you goin, oh, aye, and it's amazin what you could buy wi that 6d.

What did you buy with the 6d. then?
>Well, Ah had a night at the pictures through the week and a Saturday afternoon.

You went twice a week always?
>Twice a week, aye.

4

The Mills and Mill Owners

This chapter will consider the three Peeblesshire communities at the centre of Ian's fieldwork and focus on the role that the mills and mill owners played in the fortunes of each community.

In Peebles, the main mill owners were the Ballantynes and the Thorburns. The Ballantynes (D. Ballantyne Brothers & Co. Ltd) owned the March Street Mills, while the Thorburn family owned Damcroft, Damdale, Damside and Tweedside Mills. A third owner, Lowe Donald & Co. (later Holland & Sherry) ran a tweed warehouse in town which acted as middle man, getting most of its business from Thorburns. In nearby Innerleithen, the Ballantynes (again, D. Ballantyne Brothers & Co. Ltd) owned Caerlee, Waverley and Leithen Mills and would, in time, also take over St Ronan's Mill (the 'tap' mill), which was owned first by Beckett & Robertson. Meanwhile, in Walkerburn, Henry Ballantyne & Sons Ltd owned Tweedvale Mill (the 'big mill'), and would eventually also take over Dalziel's Tweedholm Mill (known locally as the 'wee mill').

The fact that the Peeblesshire mills were so strongly connected to each other and to the local workforce is integral to the story of the industry within these communities. As fortunes changed due to, for example, changing fashions and innovations in milling technologies, the owners could make use of their size and reach to be flexible – moving processes from one site to another to concentrate resources and become more efficient. This had an inevitable impact on the workforce and workers often found themselves travelling from one community to another to work, often passing workers travelling in the opposite direction. For much of the period under consideration here, the big mill owners were able to support and protect their workforce – albeit often to their own advantage.

The picture which emerges through the interviews is not conclusive and nor does it follow a straightforward narrative. However, taken together, information in the testimonies clearly illustrates that the textile industry in Peeblesshire was always, to a greater or lesser extent, in a state of flux. It is evident that there was a period when the industry in Peeblesshire flourished, with people moving into the area drawn by the promise of plentiful opportunities for employment. It is also true that the Ballantyne family held considerable power and exerted influence in the

Peeblesshire communities, especially Walkerburn which was, in effect, created by the Ballantyne family to house their workforce. However, the interviews also reflect the much more complex and dynamic story of an industry that was always changing and which, by the time Ian made his recordings, was in decline with the mills, which had often changed ownership several times over, being largely closed down or reduced to a fraction of their previous capacity and workforce.

The interviews capture vital and specific memories of much of the history of the mills in Peeblesshire. This includes recollections of ancestors who moved to Peeblesshire for work, some of whom came from areas with their own older weaving traditions. We also hear of the tough inter- and post-war years, when outside forces put many on short-hours within families which were already feeling the economic pressures caused by war. Then there are recollections of the boom years, for both the Border mills and the wider British textile industry. By the 1970s, the heyday seems to have been coming to an end. The mills were bought over and sold on several times before changing fashions, new technologies and the impact of international market forces led to the closure of many of the Peeblesshire mills and the inevitable impact of these changes on the central communities of Peebles, Innerleithen and Walkerburn.

Born in Patna, Ayrshire, in 1906, Philip McGlasson was ninety years old when he was interviewed by Ian in January, 1997. His working life spanned fifty-five years, from 1920 to 1975, with over fifty years at Caerlee Mill in Innerleithen. Philip's father had made the decision to move his growing family from Patna to Innerleithen when Philip was five years old, at a time when the Border mills were booming. By the time he began his working life, aged fourteen, Philip was already the fifth member of his family to go into the mills. Like many of the Peeblesshire interviewees, he left school on the Friday and started in the mill on the Monday. When asked about whether he would have liked a different working life, Philip answered, 'It was just acceptance because ye'd no other priority'.

As well as providing us with some fascinating details about his own working life and changes in the mills during that time, this account places the Innerleithen mills, and Caerlee in particular, at the centre of this account, demonstrating the importance of the mills as the main employer.

In this detailed account, Philip demonstrates the complex relationship between the mills and the mill workers. Through this we can begin to appreciate how closely linked the fortunes of the workforce and management were. As will be seen in the following chapter, this co-dependency could be beneficial to everyone, but it also meant that neither were resilient to the changes which followed the dispersal of the Ballantyne and Thorburn mills to larger, more distant, owners.

Phil McGlasson, b. 1906, interviewed on 24 January 1997

Now as a laddie did you have any particular ambitions? Do you remember thinking before you left school, 'I'd like to be a such-and-such?'

No. Ah went straight intae the mill. Ah left the school on the Friday and Ah wis in the mill on the Monday. Ah was awfu keen on horses.

So did you have any notion to become a vet or a farm worker?

No. I would like tae have owned ma own farm.

Aye, aye. But, I mean, that would scarcely be possible on your dad's wages?

Aye.

You didn't try to get a job working on a farm? Or were you interested in continuing at school?

No. Never.

You didn't want to stay on at school?

No, no, ye see, bein a big family ye just went straight tae the mill, from the school tae the mill.

Did you just accept that when you left school you would almost certainly go into the mill?

It was just acceptance because ye'd no other priority.

(Mrs Meg McGlasson: He could've stayed on but he'd ave had to pay, pay bus fares and everything.)

Right. If you had wanted to stay on at school, could you have stayed on at Leithen or would you have had to go into Peebles?

Peebles.

(Mrs McGlasson: They still do.)

Aye. You had to pay your own fares and things like that.

Aye, aye. So, I mean, that was out the question for your parents?

Uh huh.

Would you have liked to stay on at school?

No. Ah'd nae notion. No.

No, no. You were quite happy to leave school and start work?

Aye, aye. Ah'm vexed for it the day but …

Well, I'm the opposite of you. I could have stayed on but I was desperate to get away and I've never regretted it. (laughs) Because I think you have all sorts of experiences you wouldnae have had at school. However, that's by the way. So you left school on the Friday and you started work on the Monday. Now how did you get the job in the mill? Did you go down and ask yourself?

No. Your parents jist asked if ye were goin tae the mill and ye jist accepted it right away.

Aye. So had your father gone and asked if there was a vacancy?

Aye, ma mother.

Your mother had gone down to the mill?

Aye. Caerlee, it was a tweed mill at that time.

So if you left school when you were fourteen, this would be just after the First World War in 1920 was it?

1920, that's right.

And was that a Ballantyne's mill?

Yes.

Now in that time in 1920, when you started work, what were the mills in Innerleithen?

There was, startin fae the one up near the golf course, was Beckett & Robertson.

Beckett & Robertson?

Uh huh, aye. And it was a spinnin mill. It didn't make any cloth or nothin, jist spinnin. And then there wis Leithen mill. That's at the foot o the Leithen. That wis a mill which started frae scratch in the tweed, ended up in tweed. Waverley mill.

Sorry, was Leithen owned by Ballantyne in 1920?

Yeah, but a different Ballantynes. They were cousins, Ah think. There were Beckett & Robertson, Waverley wis Ballantyne.

But a different Ballantyne from the Leithen Ballantynes?

Aye. And there were Leithen Ballantynes, they were half-cousins or somethin. And there were Caerlee.

Caerlee. Four – so you had four mills?

Aye. And three o them made the tweed and one wis only a spinnin mill – Beckett & Robertson.

Now was Beckett & Robertson a big mill or a small mill, from the point of view of the number of workers?

Oh, there wis only aboot fifteen workers. Aye, it wis a small. It looked big, cause it was aboot three or four storeys. Aye, there were only aboot fifteen.

Now would most of those workers in that mill be men or women?

Ah think there wis only aboot two women there, three weemen, when Ah wis a boy. Aye.

So the spinners up there were mainly men?

Aye, that's right. And they did their own wool sortin. Aye.

Now what about Leithen mill? When you started roughly how many workers would have been employed in Leithen mill?

Oh, Leithen mill, Ah think it had aboot twenty-five looms, Leithen mill. Waverley mill and Caerlee, had aboot … Ah think Caerlee had aboot thirty. Waverley mill, Ah think, there were aboot fifty.

So Waverley was the biggest of the four?

Aye, Waverley was the biggest mill.

Then Leithen and Caerlee were about the same size?

Uh huh.

And the other one, Beckett & Robertson, was really quite small compared to the others?

That's right. Uh huh.
That's great, that's great. So you started in Caerlee?
Uh huh.
Had any of your brothers and sisters worked there before you?
Oh, aye. There were Tiz, there were Bob, Hannah and, for a time, John William – that was the first family.
So when you went there you were the fifth member of the family to go to work in Caerlee. Was that right?
That's right. Uh huh. Frank, he never worked in the mill till, oh, four years before he retired.
So what did he do as a young fellow?
Oh, he was on the baker's van, wi Forsyth.
Aye. So, when you went to Caerlee mill in 1920 what were your hours of work?
Started at eight o'clock in the mornin, and dinner hour from quarter-past twelve till one o' clock. Then from one till half-past five.
You worked on Saturday mornings then?
Yes. Finished at dinner time.
Aye, so that was eight till twelve-fifteen on a Saturday?
Uh huh.
Now can you remember what your first wage was, Mr McGlasson?
Yes. It was twelve shillins a week. But after that year, Ah can always remember, there were something that, ye should've got a rise. But Ah didn't get a rise. Ah didnae get that two shillin a week rise. Ah carried on with twelve shillin, wi the same wage, see, instead o gettin a rise. Whether the wages were reduced or something at that time, whether inflation or whatever it was, but Ah had twelve shillins for two years.
Now you're doing that for about forty-eight hours a week?
That's right. Forty-eight hours.
You were only a laddie of fourteen?
Aye.
So, when you first began, did you find the work tiring?
No. No. No, because, of course, it's all machinery, then. It wasnae laborious, it wasnae laborious work.
It wasn't heavy?
No. It wasnae a case o liftin things, no, no. The hosiery was different. Ye see, it was manpower wi your machine.
Aye. That came later, of course?
Aye.
But when you started in the tweed, Caerlee was a tweed mill when you first began?
Aye, that's right. And there were nae heavy work, really heavy work, there.
So there were about how many workers in Caerlee when you first started, roughly speaking? You thought there were about thirty, twenty-five looms, was it?

Oh, there would be, Ah would say, Ah would say 150 [workers]. Waverley was bigger.

Aye, aye. In Waverley there might have been 200?

Oh, aye, easy. Aye.

And Leithen was about the same as Caerlee?

Uh huh.

About 150 roughly? Roughly, round figures?

Uh huh.

And the wee mill, as you said, was only about fifteen workers?

That's right.

Now of the 150 workers, you know, when you first began, in the early years you were there, how many were men and how many were women? Would it be half and half? Or more men than women?

Well, all the weavers, they were all women. And then ye had the pirn machine. They were all women. The darners, women. Ah think there would be more women than what there were men, aye.

It might have been something like, very roughly, three-fifths women and two-fifths men?

Aye.

You know, if it was 150, that would be, say, about – if my arithmetic is right – about ninety women ... and sixty men ... rather more women than men?

Aye. Aye, because all the weavers wis women. Ye see, o all those weavers, ye maybe had five tuners that tuned the looms. Ken, put the new web in.

And they would be men were they?

Aye.

Were there any women tuners when you first began?

No, no.

(Mrs McGlasson: There never have been.)

When you first went into the mill did you find it a strange, new world, where everything was, you know, a bit puzzling to you as a laddie?

Oh, aye, aye. You'd hear different tales, you know, when you're sittin round the table and things like that.

Aye, you would have some idea of what was involved in the work ...

Aye. That's right.

... before you started there, from the conversation of your elders in the family?

Uh huh. That's right.

But did you find it nonetheless quite a strange world? A world in which you had to learn an awful lot?

Oh, aye. Ah mean tae say, when you went to see them, the threads goin intae the mill, the waulkmill, and seein how it went intae the loom. That was all Dutch tae me. Ah never knew a thing about it! Only what Ah heard. But seein, it's very interestin to see it come fae the wool right tae the loom. It's great.

Now what was the actual work that you did when you first began then, Mr McGlasson?

What they caa in-givin. That's puttin the threads in tae the, what dae ye call the women?

(Mrs McGlasson: Aye, the drawers.)

Aye, drawers. They sat there and ye had aa the threads down between you and the drawer.

So you were sitting facing the drawer?

(Mrs McGlasson: Feeding the needle.)

Separatin the threads, puttin them in. And, by gum, ye had tae move because there were some damn good drawers!

Aye. They worked very quickly did they?

By gum, aye. Of course, they were on piece, they were piece-workers, tae.

So they wouldn't be very patient maybe with a raw laddie?

Oh, no. My God, Ah can remember an old devil called Dick. And of course, Ah'd short trousers on. An Ah'm sittin on the stool under the web. An he's sittin wi his glasses hangin over his nose. (Mrs McGlasson laughs) He wis drawin an Ah must have been lookin away or somethin like that an he gave me a terrible slap across the bare knee. So Ah did that wi ma knee and Ah knocked him off the stool, and his glasses were lyin, Ah remember them lyin on the floor. So Ah jumped oot an Ah never went back tae him. Ah wis feart. Ah never went tae that man again.

So the drawers were both men and women?

Aye, that's right.

So roughly how many drawers would there be?

There was four in Caerlee mill. Aye, four.

And was he the only man of the four?

Aye, that's right.

And he was an old chap?

Aye.

So you never went back to him?

No. Ah wis frightened. (Mrs McGlasson laughs) It was the fright he gave me when he slapped ma knee. Ah jumped an Ah did that wi ma knee an knocked him off his stool. (laughter)

So how long were you doing that then, the in-giving, roughly? About a year maybe?

Aye. Well, Ah'd say about ten month, aye. Then Ah went tae the throstle.

Now tell me what the throstle was then.

It twisted, it twisted the yarn. You know, if it was two-ply, well, sometimes it was a marl, sometimes it was solid.

So what was a marl?

(Mrs McGlasson: A mix.)

Say, a dark grey and a light grey twisted thegither. Or a black and white, and that. That was one o the main colours, wis black and white twisted. That's what they call marl.

And was the throstle a machine?
> Oh, aye, a big, long machine. Uh huh, there was always two [workers] tae a throstle, aye.

So how many threads roughly, could you work on?
> Oh, there would be aboot fifty, fifty turns, aye. That was in Caerlee. An there was an old, old twistin machine.

Aye? Been there for many, many years?
> Yes, uh huh.

And did you find that work quite hard? Demanding?
> Aye, that was, because if ye got bad batches. Maybe yarn that wis brittle and it snapped, ye'd tae gaun right up and put your foot on the trap, ye see, tae stop the spinle goin round and tie the knot again, ye see. And maybe look around and ye'd see another one go. Oh, ye had tae keep goin.

Aye, so that was quite demanding work?
> Aye. A piecer wis the same. That wi twistin the thread, stretchin the thread, ye see, before it went onto the throstle. Uh huh.

So did you do any piecing then before you went to the throstle?
> Aye, Ah did piecin. That was ma last job.

Aye. So it was in-giving, throstle, and then you were a piecer?
> Aye, aye.

Now how long were you working on the throstle then? Roughly? About a year or more than that?
> Aye, because the mill closed, aye, aboot two and a half years after Ah wis in.

About 1922–23?
> Aye, that's right.

Aye. It closed altogether?
> Aye. The mill, aye, the tweeds, uh huh. They broke doon.

So were you unemployed at that stage?
> Eh, no. It wis a Ballantyne mill an Ah wis sent tae Waverley mill for six month till the hosiery started. And then Ah started the hosiery.

You went back to Caerlee?
> Aye. Ah wis sent for, at ten o'clock on the Monday morning, when the machines came into the hosiery. Plain knittin machines. How it started wis, Ballantyne had that much spare yarn, what was it called three times thirty six cut, Cheviot. That wis hard, that hard, hard-wearin. So they bought knittin machines and they started makin stockings in Caerlee for plus-fours. For plus-fours, aye. And then after that we went on tae pullovers, likes o two-and-two rib, five-and-two rib, twelve-and-two and things like that. And then it grew. And then the first frame we got to make pullovers, that was the first frame. And see the size o it now, up in the hosiery. It wis a lot o frames.

The machinery's developed a great deal since you first started there?
> Aye, uh huh. Ye see, ye couldn't put three times thirty-six cuts or twae times

thirty-six cuts on a frame. A frame didnae knit on anything like that. It wis all lambswool or cashmere, mostly cashmere.
So that was a softer wool … that the frames worked?
Aye. The grist wis one-sixteenth and they bocht the first lot from Leithen mill.
Now, just to go back over that. You worked at Caerlee mill for about two and a half years?
Yes.
And then the depression came on?
Uh huh.
And the first ten months, you were working at the in-giving. For about another year, you were working at the throstle, was it?
Uh huh.
And then for the last maybe six or eight months you worked as a piecer?
Aye, jist aboot that, aye.
And then, when the mill closed, you were sent over to Waverley mill?
Doon tae Waverley, aye.
And what were you doing there?
Workin in the yarn store. Uh huh.
Now when the mill closed, Caerlee mill closed, were all the workers given jobs in the Waverley mill?
Well half o the looms wis sent tae Peebles because there were two [types]: there were Hattersleys and Dobcross, an Ah just can't remember whit wis the oldest. But the oldest wis smashed up and the other lot went tae March Street … [and] the workers went up there.
That's the weavers, was it?
The weavers an yarn stores an things like that.
And tuners?
Uh huh.
Aye, they were sent to Peebles?
Aye. Maybe there were be one or two'd be redundant.
But not many as far as you remember?
Not many at the time. Waverley was the biggest loss. That wis a bigger mill, ye see.
Aye, when it closed. But then that was much later on?
Aye.
So you went to Waverley and you were there for about six months?
Uh huh.
And during that time, Ballantyne's were installing the hosiery machines, knitting machines. Is that right?
Aye, that's right.
And as soon as they got them installed you were called back?
Aye, that's right.

And you were put on to work which again was quite different, was it, from what you'd been doing?

Oh, aye. Ah'll tell ye, Ah got stockins to make an Ah wis left on ma own, maybe depending on the chap in front o me showin iz what to do. Ah come in at dinnertime – Ah went tae Caerlee at ten o'clock that mornin, up tae Caerlee. Ah went home for ma dinner and Ah didnae go in in the afternoon.

Why was that?

Because, oh, Ah thought Ah'd never learn!

Aye?

Because naebody seemed tae want tae trouble ye. Ah mean tae say, Ah had tae ask the chap in front for to set the machine up for me. The foreman didnae! Ye had tae depend on somebody else.

One of the other workers?

Aye, and the other workers didnae get nothin for it. So Ah never went in. Ah wis chased back the next mornin.

By?

Ma faither and mother chased us back! (laughs) Anyway Ah started the hard way. Ah happened tae get better and better and better.

It is very discouraging, very difficult, when you change from one job that you're familiar with to something entirely different?

Aye.

So your reaction was perfectly normal. But you weren't allowed to stay out for more than an afternoon?

See, Ah wis never a quick learner. The only thing wrong wi me, Ah wisnae a quick knitter. There were better knitters than me. But Ah always wanted tae dae aathing right. An Ah hardly ever got a garment back. Ah wis always particular. Ah wis always particular.

A perfectionist. So you worked on the stockings for the plus-fours to begin with, Mr McGlasson. Was that right?

Aye.

And then, later on … you got on to pullovers?

Aye.

Once the mill took up pullovers, too?

Uh huh.

And was the Caerlee mill quite successful as a result of switching from tweed to hosiery?

Yes, my goodness! Oh, Heavens! There wis some damn good knitters up there, aye.

So did your hours remain the same once you started on the hosiery?

Aye.

It was still eight till twelve-fifteen and one to five-thirty?

Uh huh. And goin idle. We'd a bad, bad spell in the 1930s. A bad spell.

Oh! That's maybe ten years after you'd gone there?

> Aye, aye. Aye. A bad spell. Ah sometimes used to work one day, for three weeks.

One day in three weeks?

> One day in three weeks. We used to gaun up there: ye were maybe told to come up Monday or every mornin to see if anything come in wi the post. Ah've seen me gettin one garment in a week.

As bad as that?

> Aye.

And was that the case with other workers as well?

> They were all the same.

And did that last for one or two, three, four years?

> Aye, it lasted right up tae 1939.

Till just before the War began?

> Jist. The day that Ah got married Ah wis told to stay off the next week. The day Ah got married, isn't that right, Meg?
>
> (Mrs McGlasson: Of course, that was the beginning of the War and that was a luxury trade, you see.)

So up until, and even after that, things had been pretty bad?

> Uh huh.

A lot of short-time working?

> Ye know, when Ah come to think o it, in 1920, '20, the bad times started, Ah remember the shops used tae be open the Saturday night tae eleven o'clock. And there used tae be five or six o us walkin up and down the High Street. And ye know, there were four of us smokers and we hadnae the price o a packet o Woodbine between us!

And that was only a few coppers wasn't it?

> Aye, 2d. Ye couldn't afford it. Ye had no money in your pocket. And that's true. And nowadays they're stealin, crime, every damn thing. And we tolerated that and there wis nae bother.

So these hard times lasted for many years between the Wars, Mr McGlasson?

> Aye.

Starting in the 1920s – was it maybe after the General Strike that you began to go on short-time? Or was it before then?

> Before then.

Before then. 1922–23?

> Aye.

Not long after the hosiery began?

> That's right. Aye.

So if you started in 1920, by the time you went back to Caerlee it would be 1923, roughly?

> Aye.

And the short-time began soon after that did it?

Uh huh. Oh, Ah've seen the queues from the Memorial Hall right round to Bond Street.

Was that the Labour Exchange?

Aye, the unemployed signin on.

So how many would be signing on then?

By gum, there were lots.

One or two hundred?

Aye.

And did that apply to all the mills in Innerleithen?

Yes.

Did any of the mills close down altogether in the twenties and the thirties?

No, it was a wee bit later, aye.

But a lot of the workers were on short-time, as you were?

Uh huh, aye.

Now when you were on short-time what did you do with yourself? Did you go for walks? Did you go fishing? What did you do?

Well, Ah'll tell ye, Ah wis very lucky in a sense, because Ah could drive a horse because when Ah wis a laddie Ah used tae run aboot wi the contractors, ye see, and things like that. Well, as time went on there were many men idle. Ah was often asked tae go wi the contractor or the Store or anything, tae carry coal the time Ah wis idle, an Ah got asked and Ah wis quite pleased. Every Friday, if ee got a job wi the Store, ye got five shillins for the day.

For the whole day?

Aye, for carrying coal, which Ah wis quite pleased about.

Was that delivering bags of coal into the household and emptying it into the coal cellars or coal boxes?

That's right, aye, aye, aye. Or take a horse down tae Walkerburn tae work wi the County Council. An then shovellin the sand intae the carts an ye jist drivin it away. An Pringle, the contractor from Walkerburn, he wid gie me work, five shillins for a Saturday mornin. Oh, they were good. Ah always could find a job doin one thing or other.

Did you do that sort of thing regularly? They came to you?

Aye. Because they couldnae employ a man, he had tae pay his insurance card thing, ye know?

Aye. It was just an odd job now and then?

Aye, a job. Ken, he would say to me at the whist drive on a Friday night, 'Are ye doing anything the morn, Phil?'

Ah says, 'No'.

He says, 'Will ye take a horse tae Walkerburn and work wi the Coonty?'

Ah says, 'Aye'.

So it was because Innerleithen was a small place?

Yes.

You all knew each other?
> Uh huh.

And you went to whist drives and, you know, folk knew who you were?
> Aye.

And once you'd done the job once or twice and they knew you would make a good job of it, they asked you again?
> Aye.

How did you get an odd job with the Store?
> Wait the noo. Well, Ah'll tell ye. Ma father helped iz tae get that job because Ah wis big and strong then, no like what Ah am the now! Ah wis twelve stone to thirteen stone. Ah wis big. Ah wis strong.

What height were you then?
> Five nine and a half.

Aye. That was quite tall for those days?
> Uh huh. Aye.

And you were a willing worker?
> Oh, aye. Ah wis never lazy.

No. And once you establish a reputation like that people with an odd job to hand out would come and have a word with you?
> Aye.

But in the Store, it was your father, who kept an eye open, did he, for odd jobs for you?
> Aye, aye. Aye. Aye. Well, Ah'll tell ye, Ah went away for, supposed tae be two month – six weeks, to go to The Glen. As an under-butler at Lord Glenconner's house.
> (Mrs McGlasson laughs)

How did you get that job?
> Oh, wait the now. It wis the factor o The Glen, he did all his business wi Dougal Pringle. So there were customers from America got the shootin rights that year. His name was Gurney Munn, ye see. So when he came over tae Dougal Pringle for the messages, ye see, he asked him if he knew a smart man. So Dougal kent that Ah wis goin idle, ye see. So he asked Mr Clark, the managin director, if he could spare me for six weeks. He says, 'Certainly!', ye see, because Ah wis only workin once every three weeks, one day. So Ah got that job. So Ah went over there and wis told where to sleep and it wis above the garage. And the chauffeur wis above the garage, ee see, slept there. And it wis jist across the land tae the house in the mornin. Ma first job was, Ah met the butler. He showed me all the rooms and everything and then he wis goin along the big passage wi doors here, doors there. 'Now,' he says, 'there'll be shoes out here in the mornin and boots'. He says, 'Take them down to the …' what dae ye call it?

The boot room was it?
> Aye. There were a big basket like that and there were polish and brushes and

everythin. That's what the butler telt us aa we're tae dae. And, oh, ma hert dropped, cause Ah says tae masel, 'Ah'm no cleanin somebody else's boots'. So the next mornin Ah got up at seven o'clock. And he told me, of course, that at seven o'clock he expects his cup o tea.

The butler did?

Aye, aye. Anyway, Ah says, now … this is true as Ah'm sittin here … Ah got up that mornin and Ah got aa the shoes intae the baskets. Ah wis gettin £2.10.0. a week and ma keep, mind. It wis a lot o money!

That was quite good pay then?

It was. Of course, the Americans paid that, ye see. And, Ah got the big hamper and put it in. Right, shoes here, boots here, down the stair. And Ah'm standin polishin them and Ah says tae masel, 'You're a silly bugger, cleanin somebody else's shoes'. Now … So Ah put them all back intae the basket. Ah taen them up the stair and Ah says, 'Where the hell …?'

Aye, that was the question I was going to ask you!

(Mrs McGlasson laughs) Aye. Ah says to masel, 'Where the hell did they get thir shoes and where did they get thir …?!' But anyway, Ah put them all back, because Ah wisnae worried aboot gettin the sack or nothin because Ah'd a job tae go back tae, you know. Ah still had ma job, ee see, in the mill.

So, you just put them back wherever …?

Jist, here and there. And the butler, the next mornin, Ah taen his cup o tea in. Ah rapped at his door. He seen the light goin on, ee see, electric light. And Ah went in and put his wee switch on at his bedside. And he had this cuppie and Ah says to masel, 'Hell!' Ah says, 'Ah'm takin a man a cup o tea intae bed!' Ah says, 'He'll no get it the morn!' Ah says tae masel. (Mrs McGlasson laughs) It's true, Ah'm no tellin a lie. The next mornin Ah'm sittin at this table next to the door and the cook looks up at the clock. 'You better take Mr So-and-so a cup o tea.'

Ah says, 'No, he can come for it. He's only across the passage'.

'Oh,' she says, 'the head cook'll be wild'.

Ah says, 'It disnae maitter,' Ah says, 'he's jist across the passage'.

Well, the door opens and he walks in wi his braces hingin ower his hips and he scowled at me and he got his cup o tea and his two biscuits and away through to his ane room. There was never anything more to be said. And the boots at the door. The next mornin they were never out.

So you carried on doing that?

No. Ah carried on not doin it!

Not giving him a cup of tea in bed but cleaning the boots?

Aye. Aye.

And you had that job for six weeks?

Well, when the pipe band came up, ma pal was in the pipe band, ee see. Well, when the pipe band came up there that night, oh, it was like Ah had been a prisoner, you know. Ah wis three or four mile fae hame and yet Ah wis that bloomin lonely.

Homesick?

And naebody would speak tae ye. Nane o them bloomin guys would speak tae ye. The staff were English – head butler, everythin. Jimmy Weir, the postman, taen the letters over to The Glen, ye see, and then Traquair. And he had a bugle. And if the letter wis away up the burns, ken, for a shepherd or whatever it was, they would hear his bugle. Because there was a sub-Post Office at Traquair and they kent, if the bugle blew, there wis somethin in the post office for them. And then he went tae The Glen and they fed his horse at The Glen.

A horse and trap, had he? A horse and trap?

Aye. And he got his dinner. And Ah can always remember givin him his dinner in this hall in the big house and sittin bletherin away. And he always put his butcher meat on the side o his plate. So Ah watched him one day and he took his clean handkerchief out and he put his butcher meat in the handkie and rowed it up and put it in the box. Ah says, 'Jimmy, what are ye daein that for? Is it for the cat?'

'No, it makes me a grand supper when Ah get hame.' (Mrs McGlasson laughs) Aye.

So, he was eating it for his supper instead of his dinner?

That's right, aye. His butcher meat. He ate all the rest. The vegetables and the puddin, aye.

A canny man!

Nae wonder he left money!

So, it sounds as if you really didnae enjoy that experience very much at The Glen?

No. Ah'll tell ye, if Ah'd had a pal, Ah'd ave been there for the six weeks. Cause Ah'd £2.10.0. and ma keep.

Aye, it paid well?

Uh huh. Aye. Ah'll tell ye something, Ah'd two shillins less as what ma faither had per pay. And Ah had ma keep. And yet Ah left.

So, you were there for only the one week was it?

Aye. Ah wis there jist the one week. And on the Saturday Ah went doon, Ah went straight up tae Caerlee mill and told them, if there was a job for iz in the mornin, on the Monday – which funnily there were.

Aye, so you got back in the mill then?

An Ah wis tellin him the reason that Ah left. He laughed! An he chewed tobacco, this manager, ken. And he wis chewin this day and it wis quite a nice day an he wis standin ootside and of course, he jist spat [makes sound of spitting] across the pavement, you know, and he laughed and he laughed and he laughed. Ah wis tellin him the story aboot the shoes and things like that? Anyway Ah wis only there one week. But if Ah had had a pal, Ah'd've been

there aa the time because, guid money, guid food and everything.
Oh, aye ... and you were never unemployed completely? It was always short-time?
That's right. There was always somethin, there'd be somethin.
Aye. Maybe even one day in three weeks or something?
Aye.
Terribly hard times. And these went on for several years between the Wars?
Aye, some times worse than others. Ah've seen us workin overtime, mind, in the hosiery before the War.
Aye, cause it could go up and down depending on demand?
That's right. Aye, aye.
But the short-time working was more common than the overtime?
Oh, aye, aye.
Your father was always employed at the Co-op? He was never on short-time work or anything?
Never idle.
Aye, aye. But they would be in the same position as yourself? They would be working short-time, too?
Aye. But no as much as me. And because ma other brother wis a baker, ye see.
He was never on short-time?
That's right.
Aye. So you had your father's income and Frank's income?
And Cubbie's income. And ma spare income! (laughs)
…
(Mrs McGlasson: No, there was nae jobs wi the mills. The Caerlee wis an offshoot o, what's that big engineering company in Coventry? They used tae make tanks and everything. Well, they took Caerlee mill over and made, what dae ye caa them special cutters. Oh, they were solid, ken, right hard, hard cutters.)
Sort of engineering tools?
Aye. And they sent them tae Coventry.
So that was during the War years?
Aye. That's in ma last years o the War. The mill wis workin normally until war broke oot. And aboot a month after war broke oot they were left wi a skeleton staff at the hosiery.
And they carried on for a year or two?
Aye, they carried on wi stuff from Hawick. Hawick gien them stuff, like jist tae finish it. Millin and borin, things like that.
Then the Coventry engineering people came up, what, about 1943 or '44? Before you were discharged from the Army?
Aye, jist when Ah wis discharged fae the Army.
And they had the use of the building till the end of the War, aye?

That's right, aye.
So what did you do when you came back from the Army?
(Mrs McGlasson: Oh, he wis on sick-leave.)
When Ah came back fae the Army? Oh, Ah didnae work for aboot a year then, later Ah got the job in this factory, [at] Caerlee mill.
The engineering firm. Was this about 1944?
Aye, aye.
And just sort of labouring work, was it? Unskilled work or was it skilled?
No, it wis funny. It wis that machinery, ye know. They set it wi a dial and ye'd tae jist stand and wait till it come near and then cut it off. Oh, it wis right technical stuff, but the machine did aa your job for ee.
You quite enjoyed that work?
Oh, aye. Uh huh.
And you'd be working fairly long hours, Mr McGlasson, were you during the War?
Aye, well, Ah think it wis aboot fifty hours a week.
And was the pay quite good at that?
Aye, it wis quite good.
You worked there until the end of the War?
(Mrs McGlasson: Of course, the hosiery wis closed then.)
So when did the hosiery resume? As soon as the War was over? Or soon after it?
Aye, as soon as the War was over. Because Ah'll tell ye, Ah wis back intae the hosiery then.
Aye. Caerlee resumed as a hosiery mill. And you just went from the Coventry firm into the hosiery? Was that it?
That's right, aye.
It would take them a wee while to remove the engineering machinery?
Oh, aye, aye.
And replace it with the hosiery machines?
(Mrs McGlasson: Aye.)
Had the hosiery machines been stored [in the mill somewhere] during the War?
Aye.
Aye. And then you carried on at Caerlee did you, until you retired?
(Mrs McGlasson: Uh huh.)
Which would be twenty-five years ago?
In '71, Ah retired.
(Mrs McGlasson: Aye. He retired but he got on awfy well wi the hosiery. He was the manager o aa the knitting and things, aye.)
Were you?
Aye. Aa the hand knittin.
So you were there from 1945 until you retired in 1971?
Aye. Uh huh.
But actually you'd been there for fifty years by the time your retired?

Fifty-one years, aye.

Now taking the years between 1945 and 1971 … what was your job in 1945?

In the hosiery? Well, Ah tell ye, Ah wis workin, as Ah say, in the engineers. And the hosiery started and the old foreman at that time was a man called Crozier, ee see. Well, when it opened, he started with three men, Ah think, as they were comin back fae the Army. And then… Well, the engineerin wis jist peterin out then. And Ah started … now, wait the now … Oh, aye, as Ah come back fae the War, he had five workers, this foreman. And then he had another three. And the following Monday there were another five startin. So he complained that he couldnae cope. So he asked for help and the managin director asked him, 'Well, who have ye got tae help ye? Who would you want?'

'Well', he says, 'there's a fellow there, workin in the engineers'. He says, 'Ah would like him'.

So Ah wis sent for and Ah wis tae start the next day. But Ah couldn't start because Ah wis doin a job for a man that wis ill. So [after another week] Ah started as assistant foreman, ye see.

That was quite a step up for you?

Aye. So as time went on they got displeased wi the foreman they had, ee see.

This is Crozier?

Aye. He wis makin a lot o mistakes. Of course, he wis gettin auld. And, of course, time wis meetin up on him. And Ah got his job.

Would that be roughly after a couple of years or so? So, around 1946 you were the foreman?

Aye. Then after that, Ah got the manager's job all in a year, two years after that. That's right. Ah got [Northern] Ireland. Oo opened a place in Ireland.

Whereabout in Ireland?

Coleraine. And then a place in Galashiels. And Ah wis the manager o the hand knittin – no the frames, mind, jist the hand knittin. But it wis a lot o workers across Caerlee, Coleraine and Galashiels.

Oh, that was a demanding job, that?

Ah used tae go tae Ireland aboot five times a year.

Aye. A heavy responsibility?

Aye. But Ah got on fine because the fellae that Ah put in charge [in Coleraine] wis a fellae caed Learmond, and he wis quite a good lad.

You could rely on him?

Aye. And, och, of course, wi Galashiels Ah used tae go down there twice a week.

Aye. That's not so far from here is it? So you did well there then?

Nothing to do with frames. Just hand knitting, aye. There wis around ninety-six knitters in Caerlee. Ah think there were fifty-two hand knitters in Ireland, and Galashiels had twelve.

So that was a heavy increase in your responsibility, then?
 (Mrs McGlasson: Aye.)
 Of course, Ah got on fine wi the manager.
The production manager? What was his name?
 Eh, Bonser. He wis a Hawick man. But Ah hated his guts sometimes because he would gie ye nothing for nothing. He wis a hard man. But he never interfered. Ah put men on overtime, Ah've sacked men, Ah've put them on the sick, Ah've changed the machines, ye ken. Ah stood up for the statements and every damn thing, and he depended on me.
He trusted your judgement?
 Aye. Ah can always remember Ah got intae hot water with him. Ah says, 'Listen', Ah says, 'Ah'll need tae take the men off overtime'.
 He says, 'Why?'
 Ah says, 'Ye hinnae got the orders'. Ye see Ah had aa the sheets for every order, every customer Ah says tae him, 'Ye can dae withoot your overtime'.
 'No.'
 So Ah wis goin, and yin o the Ballantynes, his name wis David, he used tae come intae the cashier's place every afternoon at a certain time. An Ah wis in this pay-day. An Ah withdrew all the pays, hand it out, come back and pick mine up in the cashier's office. And here he's sittin. He says, 'Don't you take a red face, Phil?'
 Ah says, 'Aye, Ah take a red face. Ah'm drawin ma pay'.
 He says, 'Why?'
 Ah says, "Ah didnae get enough!' (laughs) Jist like that! (laughs)
 And David says, 'Your knittin department's costing us a lot of money'.
 Ah says, 'Ah'll tell you how you can save it'.
 He says, 'What?'
 Ah says, 'Put the men off overtime'.
 Damn, the next day, Ah met him in the passage goin towards Bonser's office. So he turns tae me and he shoves me in front o him intae Bonser's office.
 He said, 'Johnnie, Phil tells me you could do without your overtime'.
 'Talkin through his hat!' Just like that.
 Ah said, 'Ah'm no,' Ah said, 'Ye can dae withoot your overtime'.
 He says, 'You're talkin through your hat'.
 So efter Davy went away, he sent for iz.
 He said, 'That wis a terrible thing to say in front o Davy Ballantyne'.
 Ah says, 'Ah'm right', ye see.
 'You're right?'
 Aye, the next day he sent for us.
 He says, 'Aye, you'll have to take them off overtime'. So Ah'd seeven men tae seck.
 Ah said, 'Whae are ye goin tae sack?' Just like that.

'Oh, it's up tae you', he says.

So Ah got rid o the dross. But they were only idle for three weeks. They were aa back.

They were all back again, aye.

He made a mistake because they had plenty orders. Caerlee got the Queen's Award that year.

Did you find that task a difficult one? I mean, you yourself had suffered severely before the War from short-time. And here you were now, you know, elevated to the manager's position, having to turn people off?

Aye, aye, because, ye ken, bein local and in a small toon, ye ken, it wis difficult, very difficult.

So your life after the War, was really very different from your experiences before the War?

Aye.

After the War, you got into a managerial position?

Aye. Well ye see what helped me a lot, tae, when Ah wis in the Army and we were aa local and wi bein an NCO. I wis tellin them they had tae scrub, wash the lavatories oot and things like that. It wis a difficult job. An then efter Ah come back and lookin efter men again, ye see, it helped us an awful lot. The Army helped me an awful lot. No tae be soft or no tae be unfair, because ma father used tae tell me, he says, 'Look, if you're makin a decision with people, before you answer it', he says, 'put yourself in that other's position'. And Ah did that. Ah did that aa ma life. If a fellow complained aboot this or complained aboot that, Ah could tell him Ah wis a piece-worker masel. Ah could tell him or just say to masel, well, he's got a point here.

When you first started in the mill, what about a union? Did you join a union?

Listen, there were no unions at the start.

There was no union at all in 1920, when you went there?

No. No. There was no union. Ah wis in the hosiery, oh, a long time afore they started a union.

Would that be maybe after the 1926 General Strike, or before it, that a union came into Caerlee?

Oh, it wis long after.

So it might have been the 1930s, Mr McGlasson?

Aye. Ah'll tell ye, Bertie Gray will tell ye. Because Bert wis the longest servin union man up there.

But certainly before maybe the early 1930s, your recollection is that there wasn't any union organisation?

No. Ah've never been a member o the union. Ye see, Ah wis never in a union because, well, Ah dinnae think Ah wis ever asked. It wis aa the workers. Ah wis a foreman, ye see. Ah think Ah wis a foreman afore the union sterted.

So you think it was really after the Second War before the union got going?

Och, aye. Ah ken, Ah can't remember ever ony o ma faimly bein in the union.

And was this the case with the other mills in Innerleithen as well, do you think?

Aye.

Aye. The small mill up there, Leithen mill and Waverley, you think they didnae have unions either?

The first time Ah wis ever asked in a union was in that engineerin lot. Because the man says, 'If you're a local man, you'll not get a job,' he says, 'unless you join a union'.

That would be the AEU was it?

That's right. Amalgamated Engineering [Union].

And did you join that?

Yes, Ah had tae.

But then you would come out of that when you left the engineering works?

Aye. That's right.

And you didn't join a textile workers' union?

Because there were nane, bein transferred fae the engineerin tae the hosiery. There were no union until long after the War.

After the War, aye. Gosh, that's quite late then?

Aye.

You don't remember any strikes, for instance, before the War?

No. Ah don't remember. The only strike Ah remember and Ah wisnae in the mill then, that wis after '71

Aye, aye. But there was never a strike at Caerlee in all your fifty-one years there?

No, no.

Now just a final question because I fear I may be tiring you. I'll leave you in peace. I'm very grateful for all your trouble and information. This is just the job. Looking back, you were in the textile industry fifty-one years, looking back, you know, what are your thoughts now, Mr McGlasson?

Well, ma thoughts about the youngsters nowadays and everything. When Ah went back tae Caerlee mill aboot ten years or twelve years since Ah left it, Ah wis horrified to look aboot the state o the floor and everything. The filth that's lyin, old yarn lyin here and what. They've no pride nowadays. They've no pride whatever in their job. Maybe some are. But the majority aren't.

Why do you think that is?

Ah don't know whether it's they're easier worked or the machinery. In the days, ye used tae work yoursel. Ye made your garment and it wis complete and you were fair proud o that garment. You were proud o it. Same as in the olden days, when Ah used tae see the two trains passin – the twenty-past-ten in the mornin, one from Edinburgh and one from Galashiels. And they met in Innerleithen because Innerleithen had a double-sided station. And when one was two to three minutes early, before the up [one] or before the down one came down, they were out wi their thrum and oil can and they were polishin the thingmy. Would ye see that nowadays? And the brass wis shinin like, oh … And the machines in the mill, it wis nicely polished at the weekend and Ah oiled it and everything. Hell, nowadays, it's terrible! They clean the machine but it's no half-cleaned.

So out of the four mills only one, the one that you worked in, has survived? The hosiery mill?

Aye. By gum, and you know this, they've a mill in Bonnyrigg, there are workers gauns there. They put, Ah think it's two, three buses that leaves Caerlee mill every night. Now see aa that money: Caerlee could be far bigger, ken, because they cannae get workers sometimes. Ah seen them advertise just last week.

So though there's only one mill, there are jobs going there that can't be filled?

Aye. Aye, because Bonnyrigg has a big mill, aye.

And they bus the workers from Caerlee?

Aye.

The workers come to Caerlee from Bonnyrigg in some cases?

They come fae Galashiels up, they come from Bonnyrigg and thae places, Dalkeith.

And they bus them in every day?

Yes. That costs a lot o money.

You'd think they would find enough workers in Innerleithen to work in Caerlee?

No. It's often advertised.

Why do you think that is then that people in Innerleithen are apparently unwilling to work in the mill?

Ah don't know. But there should be very, very few workers in Innerleithen idle.

Aye. But it's in the nature of textiles and hosiery isn't it that demand rises and falls, changes of fashion, and this brings unemployment, as you found, and serious short-time working before the War?

Uh huh. But Ah don't like the way they pay them. Ah don't like the way they pay them now because, ye've got some there they go on percentages and everything. And some there, they've got their money made and they could gaun home, the money's there. But they don't give a man the money he makes up there. It's a percentage. The good knitter, helps the bad knitter.

Aye. So you never had any regrets about working in textiles rather than working outside the industry in something else?

No. No, because Ah'll tell ye, if Ah'd had ma rightful position up there, Ah think Ah would've been manager long, long before that. Because … oh, no. And Ah'll tell ye, the foreman, oor managin director, Mr Oddy. Oh, oh, he could sell coals tae Newcastle! He wis great, ye ken. His son, when Ah got ma presentation in Peebles, he had aa the foremen up there an the managers. And he said at ma presentation, he says, 'You know, Phil's name was mentioned every teatime', he says. 'My father in a sense hated his guts', he says 'for the reason he's the only bugger that ever speaks back to me!' Because Ah kent ma job. Ah kent if a thing wis over-milled what the reason was, it wis a bad size or somethin like that. Aye. And Ah jist said to masel, 'Ah hope aa the rest's listenin'. Aye, because it disnae maitter what he said, he wis right. Every time he spoke to me, if Ah thought Ah wis right, Ah jist telt him.

Well that's great. I'm very grateful to you. And thanks for your help too, Mrs McGlasson. But, you see, your memory hasn't needed any spurs because it's amazing what comes back once you start to talk.

Aye.

People you thought you'd forgotten. Incidents come crowding back. So I'm very grateful. You've drawn a very clear picture.

Other Voices

Here, the early days of milling in Innerleithen are recalled by Andrew Burton.

Andrew Brunton, b. 1928, milling in Innerleithen

And Caerlee was always hosiery?

No, no. Ah dinnae ken when the hosiery would start but it wis a spinnin mill when ma grandfaither used tae work there away afore the War. Ah dinnae ken what wis aa involved in Caerlee. Then, efter they sterted the hosiery, that wis money-makin. So it became a hosiery mill.

And it has remained so to this day, aye?

Right. Uh huh.

Aye. But it wasnae always so?

No, no.

In the more remote past it had been a spinning mill?

Ye ken, Ah cannae give ye much history, but the Caerlee mill wis built by a Traquair blacksmith [Alexander Brodie] who'd went tae London an made money. He built that mill up there.

So was that the first mill in Innerleithen? The oldest mill?

No, Ah dinnae think it would be the oldest mill.
(Mrs Doreen Brunton: Are ye talkin aboot Caerlee?)
Aye.
(Mrs Brunton: That wis the first mill in Innerleithen.)
An at one time, a lot o the weavin wis done in the hooses, ye see. Ye ken, before the mills taen ower.

At another point in the interview, Andrew talked about the power of the Leithen Water and the dam system which made the area such a successful one for industry.

And Caerlee was the hosiery mill?
    Uh huh.
And there was a wee mill up the Leithen Road? And that was called?
    That wis a spinnin mill an aa. That wis, eh, Robertson's, Ah think that they caed it. Ye see, we used tae talk aboot the tap mill. We jist aye caed it the tap mill.
The tap mill. It wasn't a Ballantyne's mill, that one?
    No, no. It wisnae, no, no.
All the other mills in Innerleithen were owned by Ballantyne's?
    Uh huh.
Waverley, Leithen and Caerlee? They were all Ballantyne's?
    Uh huh.
And only the wee one, the tap mill, Robertson and what's-his-name, were separate from that, aye?
    Aye, uh huh, uh huh. There was another wee mill ower there but it was never workin in ma time. It wis a silk mill. Aa these mills were powered off the dam. What you might caa a lade, ken. From the Tweed. They were aa belt driven then, ye see. Ye ken, years ago they were aa belt driven. And efter the War, they aa got electric an it wis aa electric motors an that. But before that, they were nearly aa belt driven. So, an it wis aa workin wi turbines and water wheel things, ye ken. So they were aa right doon tae aboot a mile oot o the toon there, up the road, the Leithen wis diverted wi gates intae this dam. It runs now, ye ken, but it's no used tae the extent it used tae be. An that tap mill wis the first yin. An then the hosiery wis run off o that. An then efter that wis Smaill's, the printers. An efter that, there wis Jimmy Stewart's sawmill. An efter that wis Hogg and Robertson's. Oh, that silk mill would be driven there tae. That wis between aboot Hogg and Robertson's and Smaill's.
Aye. What was Hogg and Robertson's?
    Eh, engineers. An efter Hogg and Robertson's wis Leithen mill. An then it went intae the Tweed efter that.
So they were all on the Leithen Water?
    They were all on that dam, they were aa driven by the water off that dam. An it wisnae a big dam. The dam at Walkerburn … it carried a lot o water. But that dam aboot maybe eight foot across jist, an it drove aa thae industries in the toon.

Robert Sanderson shared his memories of the Thorburn family, who owned the Damdale mill.

Robert Sanderson, b.1929, the Thorburn family
Now who was the head of the firm when you first started at Damdale?
    Hunter Thorburn was, he wis the big chief, yeah.

He was the managing director, was he? Did he live in Peebles?
> Yes he did, aye, aye, aye. Up Bonnington Road. Greystones, they call it, aye. It's still there to this day. His father wis Sir Michael Thorburn, who was at Glenormiston, you know, the big house between Peebles and Innerleithen. Glenormiston Estate. Sir Michael, that was his father. He wis the original one. Ah don't know if he wis the founder but the old chap that used tae work wi me used tae talk about Sir Michael, you know. Old Sir Michael, he wis a shareholder in the LNER railway and that. He even got a halt at Glenormiston, so that he could get off the train there, you know. (laughs)

Those were the days, eh? You would never meet Sir Michael? Presumably he was dead long ago?
> He must have been, yeah, he must've been dead.

Have I got it right that there was a Colonel Thorburn?
> Hunter Thorburn. He was the Colonel. W. H. Thorburn – W. Hunter Thorburn, aye. He was the welfare officer or that during the War, you know. People used tae come and see him when Ah wis there in '46 and that. They used tae come about welfare things, you know, connected wi hubbies servin in the Army and things like that, you know.

Aye. Yes, yes. He was quite a notable local figure, wasn't he, Thorburn?
> He was then, that's right. Yeah, yeah, uh huh.

He was quite a dominant influence?
> Yeah, he was, aye.

Now do you know anything about the politics of these mill owners? I mean, Thorburn would, let me guess, be a prominent Conservative?
> Ah would imagine so, aye.

But you didn't yourself have any connection with him in that way?
> No, no. He must've died in the 1950s, Ah would think.

While you were away doing your National Service?
> No. After Ah came back, because he was still there well into the fifties. Yeah, Ah can remember him fine, yeah.

And was he succeeded by his son as managing director?
> His nephew, Ah would think. His son was in the business, Alastair Thorburn. But the other Hunter Thorburn, David Hunter Thorburn he became the managing director then. He wis one o the Rosetta Thorburns. His father was 'Millie' Thorburn, that's what they called him.

Now when you say Rosetta Thorburns, does that mean they lived over in that side of Peebles?
> At Rosetta, yes. Where the big caravan park is now at Rosetta, the big houses up there. So he wis brought up in that house, yes, aye. They were quite separate families, that's right.

Big shots within Peebles? I mean, you were aware of the name Thorburn?
> Oh, yes, aye. The mills were always Thorburn's and Ballantyne's, you know.

THE MILLS AND MILL OWNERS

Was it the case that workers tended to remain either with Ballantyne or with Thorburn's?
>Ah suppose they did.

There wasn't much crossing over?
>No, there wasnae much comin and goin that Ah can recollect, no, no. I was the first one in our family that worked in Thorburn's, you know. Everybody else had worked in Ballantyne's

You weren't regarded as a traitor? (laughs)
>No, no, no, no.

Was there rivalry between the mills?
>No really. Not to any great extent.

I mean, there would be some commercial rivalry? Were they making similar sorts of clothing?
>Ah suppose they would be. But Ballantyne's was always that bit bigger, you know. There'd be more people there and, you know, after the War, there were over 500 worked there for a while, you know.

Then they had mills at Innerleithen, too?
>That's right. They werenae weavin mills, you know. They were yarn and that as well in Innerleithen.

In Innerleithen, aye. They had this division of labour didn't they?
>Aye. The likes o Peebles wis the cloth place.

But it was rare, was it, for workers from March Street to come and work in the Thorburn mills, while they were still there?
>Very. Ah think maybe there wis an odd one, you know, that maybe left, had a row aboot something and … but there werenae many. It wisnae a regular thing.

People, once they started at March Street or at Damdale or Tweedside.
>They seemed to stay. That's right.

That was the tradition?
>That's right. Yes, they did. Aye, yes, yes, oh, aye.

The following extract from Eric Pearce explores the Ballantyne connection more fully, enabling us to understand how they fostered a paternalistic relationship between themselves and their workers: a situation which would change drastically when new owners took over in later years.

Eric Pearce, b. 1927, the Ballantyne family, Walkerburn and change over time

Yes. That's grand. Walkerburn was more or less built by the Ballantynes wasn't it?
>It definitely was, because I think in 1854 they opened a mill and then they had to provide accommodation for the workers, and they started building houses. There was very little private housing. Just the mill owners built their

mansions up on the hillside. And some of the better off, let's say mill managers and so forth, built private houses up what's now known as High Cottages, that area.

They were the managers' houses up there?

They were mainly the manager and sort of really doctors and anybody in that particular class. But all the workers were more or less housed in the valley, round about here. And then, I don't know when the first council houses were built.

It would be after the First World War, I suppose?

Yes, I think it was even just prior to the Second War, because it was in the thirties, I think, they just built the first council houses along the avenue there.

Presumably there was virtually nothing at Walkerburn before the Ballantynes opened the mill here?

No. It was just a farm. There was a farm down at the burn, Gaberson Farm. And I think the mill owners had scouted around some time to check what was a good area to start up in and discovered that this was an ideal spot for the water supply, which was the main item of the mill, which also provided the power, of course.

And the Ballantynes came out from Galashiels to found the mill here?

They came from Galashiels. Because Galashiels was getting flooded with small mills and I think they wanted to expand. And the Ballantyne family was pretty big at that time and I think there was no scope for the sons of the owners up at Galashiels. So they came here and built the first mill. And then even he himself had four or five sons.

This was Henry, was it?

This was Henry Ballantyne, yes. He built the mill, got the lade built, which provided the power to the waterwheel and supplied all the power to the machinery in the mill – pretty basic nowadays but it was quite effective at the time.

It would be quite an advanced mill, of course?

It would have to be, being the new mill. Of course, in the old days, it was so many levels. Nowadays everything's on the ground level. But in these days, you had first floor, second floor, third floor.

And they were called flats, was that the term?

Flats, yes. You'd the spinning flat and the carding flat. The heavier the machinery, the lower down in the building it became.

So the mill as built in the middle of the nineteenth century had three floors did it?

Yes, some of them had, uh huh. Various buildings that were just ground level, but the main part of the mill was at least three floors.

THE MILLS AND MILL OWNERS

Hume Davidson outlined something of the extent of the Ballantyne influence, particularly in Walkerburn.

Hume Davidson, b. 1928, the Ballantyne family, Walkerburn

It wis aboot '52, Ah think, when we moved intae the new houses. There wis aaready one or two houses in Walkerburn that had the bath and the runnin water, mind. There werenae many wi electricity. You see, they reckoned yin o the reasons wis, they reckoned the Ballantynes had shares in the gas company. An aa thir big hooses there, they had one, two, three, four, Ah think there were five big houses up the hill. They were all masters of the mill.

Aye. All Ballantyne family?
All Ballantyne family. And they had their own wee generators. You heard them going purpurpurpurpur! So they had their electricity then.

The sound of Walkerburn in your youth?!
Aye.

So they had the electricity but they werenae prepared to install it for their workers?
An Ah think the wey oo got electricity, would be because the mill decided tae convert tae electricity rather than make their own. They had different ways o gettin electricity: the water and then the gas engine and the Tangye engine. They'd two different engines plus turbines and the hill job tae make their electricity. So Ah think they decided tae, well because, you see, things would be gettin difficult tae get because they would be aa direct current, opposed tae alternating current.

Aye, DC/AC?
Aye. The machinery would be a help then.

They'd have to bring themselves up to date?
Aye.

Bob Anderson also recalled how powerful the Ballantynes were and reflected on the impact that this had on the workforce and the community in Innerleithen.

Bob Anderson, b. 1931, the Ballantyne family, Innerleithen

But Dawson's had a reputation, or have a reputation today as pretty ruthless employers?
Oh, aye, aye, that's right, aye, uh huh.

You didn't find that in the earlier days with Ballantynes?
No. But the Ballantyne's. Ee see, they were a funny firm the Ballantyne's. If anybody did onything wrong they phoned up the rest o the mills and [that person] couldnae get a job in Peeblesshire.

[They were] blacklisted?
Oh, aye.

Because originally, as I understand it, there were two different families of Ballantynes?
Aye, that's right. There were aa Ballantynes at Walkerburn. And aa

Ballantynes at Peebles.
And each of them owned a mill in Innerleithen?
Aye, but Ah think they were, were they no cousins or somethin?
They were cousins, aye, but then at some later stage they all amalgamated?
Aye, they were always on the same board at the finish up, Ah think, aye, aye. But that's what they din.
Now that was in your time in the mill?
That wis in ma time, aye, aye. And no only that, there were firms wanted tae come in here after the War: there were Weston's Biscuits. Ee see the big food stores down at the station there? Have ee ever been doon there? Weston's Biscuits wanted tae take them over after the War. But the Ballantynes wis on the town committee, and they says, 'Oh, oo've no got enough workers'.
They were a really powerful family, weren't they?
Oh, powerful, oh, aye.
Now politically they were what – Tories or Liberals?
Oh, they'd be Tories likely, (laughs) aye, Ah think sae.
I mean – correct if I'm wrong – I dinnae think of either Peebles or Innerleithen as being, you know, particularly politically active?
We're no politically minded at aa. Same as religion and aa oo're no like them in the west and thae places.
No, no, no, because there's strong class conflict [there], or there has been historically? But not down here?
No, no, no, no, no, no.
I mean, presumably the Labour Party here is fairly weak?
Aye, it wis aa Liberal.
Aye, Liberals and Tories?
Aye, that's right, aye.
But you think the Ballantynes were Tories rather than Liberals?
Ah think, Ah think they wid be, aye. I've nae idea, but I think they wid be, because they were aa for theirsel! (laughs) Ken.
Aye. How did you find them as employers? You know, did you find that they were approachable or remote or …?
The thing wis. Ye see, at that time oo wis only allowed tae make, say, 5s.9d. an hoor, like when oo wis workin night shift oo could make oor pay in four nights. And, Ah mean, the last night o that we didnae need tae work, because oo'd made oor pay. But if ee put in extrae they cut the statements. Well, there were twenty-six o us on night shift. That wis twenty-six days work they were lossin every week, because oo couldnae make any more.
Aye, you just had to work a four day week at the time?
That's right, aye, aye.
You just didn't turn out on the last night?
Well, oo turned oot aaright, but oo didnae dae much work.

You didn't do much work.
>If somebody wis maybe doon on their pay a wee bit oo knitted a jersey for them. Ye ken, oo jist aa worked thegither.

Aye, aye, I see, aye.
>Aye. But it wis a shame really. Ah felt it wis a shame, because there could have been that much mair production if they'd allowed us tae make that wee bit mair. But they widnae dae it.

They wouldn't do it.
>No, no.

Did you find they were a pretty rigid firm?
>Aye, they were rigid in a certain extent, aye, oh, aye.

Of course, the union was fairly weak wasn't it?
>Aye it wisnae very guid, no, no. Ah'll gie ye an instance. Ah wis in the office aboot somethin, and the union man sterted tae speak and the manager says, 'That's enough o you'.

So he just had to close his mouth?
>That's it, aye, aye.

Was that because quite a few of the workers weren't in the union?
>No. There were a lot o workers in the union then.

Most of them were in?
>But, but Ah think they were aa feared for the bosses really – feared for their jobs. Ah think that's what it was.

Aye. Of course if the firm operated a blacklist...
>This is it.

...you'd have to be careful?
>Aye, aye.

Because it wouldnae be easy to get alternative work in and about Innerleithen?
>Oh, no, oh, no, no, no, no. But that's what Ah think. They were that strong then, the firms.

Can you remember anybody at work who was blacklisted in that way and who had real difficulty in getting a job?
>No. Ah cannae jist really mind o that. But Ah ken that's what went on, aye, aye. Uh huh. They jist phoned up somebody, phoned up another mill and says, 'Dinnae employ that yin', ken.

And, of course because they seem to have dominated the area.
>Well, they dominated everythin, because they had the toon, they were in the town council.

Aye, there were always Ballantynes on the town council?
>Oh, aye, aye. They had the hearsay o everything – buildin hooses or factories or the council had the say. Ee see, they were aa landowners, ee ken, they were aa landowners.

Aye, aye. So ye couldn't necessarily get a job on a farm if you wanted to?

> Well, this is it.
>
> *You know, if you were blacklisted in the mill?*
>
> Ye widnae get a job, no, no.
>
> *No, no. Their influence permeated everywhere?*
>
> Oh, it spread aa oot, aye, it spread aa ower the county, aye.
>
> *But that's no longer the case now?*
>
> No, oh, no, no, no.
>
> *Ballantyne's influence has diminished?*
>
> They're aa retired now anyway, aye. But it's aa the multiples, the likes o Dawson's and Laidlaw & Fairgrieve.

Hume Davidson also shared his thoughts on local politics and the influence that the Ballantynes exerted in the local community.

Hume Davidson, b. 1928, Walkerburn politics and the role of the Ballantynes in community life

> This is a Liberal place. It has been for a long time. And David Steel aye comes tae oor coffee mornin. And aa thae auld dears wis up tae see David Steel. (laughs)
>
> *Aye. So the tradition of Walkerburn has been that the mill workers were Liberal voters anyway, rather than Conservative?*
>
> Aye, they were either Liberal or Labour.
>
> *Labour, aye, aye. But the Ballantynes may or may not have been Conservative or Liberal?*
>
> Ah didnae ken their politics, no.
>
> *You don't remember your parents speaking about that aspect of things or seeing meetings addressed by the Ballantynes or whatever?*
>
> Ah aye mind that the … if you wis a property owner, you got more votes, you got another vote? Was it the candid vote or somethin they caed it?
>
> *Aye, well, it was the plural vote.*[11]
>
> Aye. They got an extra vote if they were a property owner.
>
> *But your parents weren't politically active? Your father wasn't in any party?*
>
> No.
>
> *You didn't have political discussions at home?*
>
> No. No. He wis a Labour man, but—
>
> *He wasn't a member of the Labour Party?*
>
> No. No.
>
> *And was it your impression as a laddie that the mill workers were generally Labour voters?*

---

11 The right to vote more than once in a General Election based upon residence, property ownership and university affiliation. The plural vote was abolished by the Representation of the People Act 1948.

Aye. Uh huh.

But the Liberal tradition was still quite strong in Walkerburn?

Aye.

Maybe among professional people like the local teachers?

That's right, aye. And some o the workers, some, the women, especially (Mrs Davidson: Uh huh.)

But what I wondered was whether, since this is a kind of mill village where the Ballantynes were obviously quite a dominating, certainly a very powerful, influence, in what ways did this show itself in village life? Was there a lot of deference towards the Ballantynes when you were a laddie before the War or even just after the War. You know, if you saw the Ballantynes, a member of the family, walking down the road or coming down in the car, did you stand and salute or doff your cap or anything like that at all?

No, no. No, no,no, no. You'd maybe dae that to your schule teacher. (laughs)

On the other hand, was there any sense of animosity among mill workers towards the Ballantynes?

Ah think there'd be a wee bit sometime. But, Ah mean, as Ah say, lookin back, they were good tae the village, when ee think on it.

Aye, aye. I mean, you didn't get the extremes, where people sort of bowed and scraped in the public road when they saw a Ballantyne passing by?

Oh, no.

And on the other hand, you didn't get people shaking their fist and saying, 'Oh, away you go, you Ballantyne so-and-so!'

No, no, no.

There wasn't much in the way of demonstration of political loyalties or personal feelings, that you remember?

No, no.

Were there any other facilities, social, sporting facilities, maybe educational prizes, that sort of thing, that the Ballantynes provided in Walkerburn? Besides the tennis courts?

Well, you see that club doon there – Henry Ballantyne Memorial Club. That's the name o it. And it wis actually, when ma uncle referred to it, it wis a library, a public library for the village.

(Mrs Davidson: But the Ballantynes gave them that. They gave them the whole buildin.)

Aye, oh, aye. It belonged to the village. And there were a couple o snooker tables in it when Ah wis a laddie. And there were no licence tae the mid-fifties, Ah would say, the late fifties before it got a licence. And that wis Ballantyne's an aa, ee see.

That was a donation to the village?

Aye.

There wasn't anything like Ballantyne's bursaries?

No. But what Ah can mind o is King George V's Silver Jubilee. That was a party run up at Stoneyhill. And Ah actually got a medal for runnin the race when Ah wis six year auld or somethin. And Ah think the Ballantynes would mair or less run that. And then when the King [George V] died, there wis then the Coronation for the present King [George VI] and that was another party. And Ah would think the Ballantynes would run that. So onything like that, the Ballantynes would organise Ah think you feel it now. The village feels it now, that you've no the Ballantynes tae turn tae.

None of the Ballantynes live here any longer?

There's one, Jeremy. He lives in a house just outside Walkerburn, on the hill, just at the thirties. That's Jeremy Ballantyne.

He's the last of the family with a Walkerburn connection?

Yes. Uh huh.

(Mrs Davidson: The Ballantynes didnae let any other trade into the village. As things became empty and, Ah mean, they knocked doon a lot o buildings there raither than let somebody else in. So that when they went there was nothing left in the village.)

Nothing left. This was after the War they wouldn't let anybody else in? What about traders? Did they have any objection, or did they themselves run any shops in Walkerburn. You know, any food shops or dress shops?

No. But oo had a canteen.

In the mill?

In the mill. And during the War it wis made intae a British Restaurant.

Open to the public?

So it was open to the public. The big Union Jack on the door. So they were all over ... if you was in Edinburgh, you could go to a British Restaurant and get a meal for a reasonable [amount] ... well, they had one here. And some o the vegetables that Ah grew, Ah took doon tae the British Restaurant, ye see. So the Ballantynes helped oot, and the head cook was a Ballantyne. Aye, Miss Alison, and she was a very good woman.

Uh huh. Was she married?

She was single. Alison would be a daughter o J. K.

Aye, Alison Ballantyne. And she was head cook in the canteen?

Aye. And she actually – Ah forget the name o it – she adopted a lightship. It wasnae a lighthouse it was a lightship. And every year she collected money or presents. Aa the workers in Walkerburn adopted this lightship. So she was at the bottom o that an aa, Alison.

That was very unusual that she'd be the cook in the mill, if she was the daughter of the mill owner?

Aye.

She must have undergone a course of training at some time?

(Mrs Davidson: Aye, Moray House, Ah think. And aa the school children went to the mill canteen. Like, they didnae get their school dinners at the school. The school dinners afore they made dinners at the school, they came

to the canteen. After Ah went to the mill Ah would go tae the canteen.)
Did you? You normally went to the canteen?
   Aye. And you got quite a big dinner.
Aye. Was that cheaper then, eating at the canteen than coming home?
   Aye. Ah think so.
Because you could easily have come home?
   Aye. But, as Ah say ma mother would maybe be workin then, ee see.
Of course, aye. Well, that's very interesting. What about the relations between the Ballantynes and the Walkerburn Co-operative Society? I mean, was there any sense in which the Ballantynes would have seen the Co-operative Society as some kind of rival body that they couldn't control?
   No, Ah don't think so.
   (Mrs Davidson: Well, Ah think they would let them into the village anyway. Cause they're aa the Store hooses as you go fae where the Walker Burn is, I mean, you go up the Peebles Road, the first lot o houses you come to, they all were the Store houses.)
Ah! So the Store owned houses as well as the Council and Ballantynes and Beattie?
   (Mrs Davidson: Uh huh. At one time. And thae buildins, the biggest half o them are aa been bought, or else the Mackays, them that has the chemical works in the village now, they've bought the rest o the Store houses.)
So [if they were built in 1863] that was within a decade of the foundation of the first mill – in 1854, you said?
   Uh huh, uh huh.
I know that in Midlothian, where I used to work, the Earl, the Marquis of Dalkeith and his manager of the Lady Victoria Pit, they owned all the shops in Newtongrange and Rosewell, the two principal mining villages, and they wouldn't allow other traders, vans or shops, to come in there.
   I see.
I think there was only one exception in Newtongrange: there was an Italian who had a shop.
   Uh huh.
They even put up posts in the street to prevent traders getting in and all that sort of thing.
   Oh?
Now from what you're saying, it doesn't sound as if you had that kind of experience in Walkerburn?
   No that Ah can mind o.
…
What you were saying, Mrs Davidson – thanks for that, we didn't get recorded with changing the tape – was that the original Co-operative Society shop was at the end of the road here, Jubilee Road.
   (Mrs Davidson: Uh huh.)

And it jutted out into the street that runs down the hill there?
   Aye.
   (Mrs Davidson: Uh huh. Well there's a wee house jist as you come doon the steps there and that was the first Co-operative. Because ma friend used tae live in it. And one day she saw this man up on the dyke ootside her house and he had a camera and she thought, 'What's he doing?' And she says the next thing he wis away roond the other side o the hoose and he says,
   'Oh, it's aaright. I'm only taking photies. It's the centenary o the Co-op and they're wanting photies o the first'.
   And she says, 'How wis the Co-op in here?'
   He says, 'This is where the very first shop was built before they built their ane bit'.) (laughter)
   (Mr Davidson laughs) Ah couldnae mind that.

Well, you see, you know, the principle, I mean, you've got here a family, the Ballantynes, that really were quite powerful. There were numbers of sons and brothers and they had mills founded here, Innerleithen and Peebles, Galashiels, and all the rest?
   Aye, that's right.
And then into Walkerburn, which was really their village?
   Uh huh.
They founded the mill, they, from what you're saying, they built the village didn't they?
   Aye.
… comes the Walkerburn Co-operative Society, nine years after the opening of the first mill? Now what I'm wondering is, what were the relations between the Co-op Society and the Ballantyne family? Did the Ballantynes see them as intruders, whom they couldn't control? Or was the Co-operative Society in some way, rather like, you know, as in Midlothian, where the Rosewell Co-op was very much the creature of the Marquess of Lothian?
   Uh huh, Uh huh.
Was the Walkerburn Co-operative Society controlled by the Ballantyne family in some way? Because Co-operative Societies by and large were very democratic societies, as you know …
   Uh huh.
… that were controlled by their members, the shareholders?
   (Mrs Davidson: Uh huh.)
   Oh, it was a good, it was a good Co-op here. They reckon it was one o the biggest dividends in the country: 3s.6d in the pound.
Oh, that was good. St Cuthbert's was 3s.6d., and I think that was quite exceptional.
   Aye, aye.
   (Mrs Davidson: And, Ah mean, they built a dozen houses and they built aa they shops.)
   Aye, oh, aye. Aye, that wis aa the Store: beyond the farm on the left-hand side wis aa the Co-operative.

Aye. What I'm wondering, you know, is what – I don't know if you remember your parents discussing this point or having any recollection of it yourself – what was the relationship between the Ballantyne family, as the local mill owners and dominating influence in the village, and the Walkerburn Co-operative Society?

(Mrs Davidson: Well, the Ballantynes used the Store jist the same as what we used it.)

Aye, aye. But you see what I mean? Did they control the Store in any way?

Ah don't think so.

(Mrs Davidson: Ah dinnae think so.)

It was quite independent of them?

Aye. Oh, aye.

It seems slightly surprising they allowed it to be set up?

Aye.

You know, if they couldn't control it?

Uh huh. Oh, well.

(Mrs Davidson: They must've allowed it to come in because, Ah mean, you know, when you think back.)

Ah dinnae think they had ony influence in it at aa.

Any control, no, no, no. I wonder what happened to the records of the Walkerburn Co-operative Society?

Ah dinnae ken.

(laughs) To be pursued! Well, that's great. Now you're being deprived of your nourishment, Mr Davidson, there. You're working too hard.

No. (laughs)

In this extract, Anthony French describes Peebles in the 1930s, when the mills were 'the biggest thing in the town'.

Anthony French, b. 1929, the importance of the mills

No, no. Ma Auntie Ina, oh, she'd be fifty year in the mill. She wis a weaver. Oh, aye. She wis one o the old hands.

So there was a kind of family tradition then, even though your father and your grandfather hadn't been in [the mill], your grandfather's sister [was]?

That's right. Well, of course, in thae days, in the thirties or whatever it was, the mills wis the biggest thing in the town, wasn't it? The main employer. I mean, ye'd three or four mills then, know what Ah mean? Ye had two o Thorburn's, one Ballantyne's and Lowe Donald's.

Lowe Donald's? Where was that then?

That wis along where Gateway, Somerfield's is. It's now Holland & Sherry.

Aye. But Lowe Donald was a producing mill?

That's right. That's right.

Because Holland & Sherry are not producing mills, are they?

They are now.

They are now? Is that very recent then?

Well, you see, Ah don't know, but when Ah wis with Thorburn's in the sixties, they, Lowe Donald's, which wis known as Lowe Donald's then, LD & Co., and they used tae get a lot o stuff fae Thorburn's. I think they bring it all in fae England now, don't they?

I don't know. My understanding from what one or two other people have said, is that Holland & Sherry don't, or didn't, make cloth. They simply acted as middlemen, you know?

That's right. That's what they are.

They weren't mills in the sense that Thorburn's and Ballantyne's were?

That's right.

(Mrs Wilma French: No, well, no, Ah suppose not.)

They do sell the cloth although they don't actually make it?

That's right. They were the middlemen. Maybe for Japan or whatever the case may be. Or America.

So Lowe Donald's were their predecessors?

Uh huh. Uh huh. Uh huh.

Aye. Maybe just a change o name or ownership?

Well, ye see, the Lowe Donald's, it wis the Thorburns that run the Low Donald's and it wis Thorburns that had the mills. And they were aa cousins or brothers, whatever there wis. There wis Walter, there wis Sir Ronald, there wis 'Sirs' amongst them all. Of course, Thorburn was a famous name for the mills in Peebles, for top-quality cloth.

Here, Betty Muir provides an insight into community allegiances to either the Ballantynes or the Thorburns.

Betty Muir, b. 1922

Aye. I was asking about Thorburn's and Ballantyne's, and you were saying that you thought there was a bit of rivalry between the two?

Ah think so, aye. Ah don't know what it was but it was always Ballantyne's for me. Whether it wis because Ah wis sent there when Ah wis fourteen to start, it wisnae to Thorburn's. Ah don't know what the difference would be really. It wis exactly the same mill doin the same things. But Ah never liked Thorburn's. Ah mean, it wis aboot four stories high. Whether it wis the buildin that Ah wis against, Ah don't know.

Whereas Ballantyne's was just a single storey was it?

Aye, that's right.

This next extract comes from Anthony French, who worked for both the Ballantynes and the Thorburns and provides an interesting comparison for us to consider.

Anthony French, b. 1929

You left the railways in 1959, went to Tweedside, worked in Tweedside – that was the Thorburn mill?

Uh huh.

Till it went on fire in 1965?

Uh huh.

You remained there for a few months maybe, because the wool department wasn't affected. Then you went to Damdale and you were there about a year. Then you went to March Street and then about 1970, you left March Street and went into the building trade?

That's right.

So when you went back into the mill in 1959 at Tweedside, did you notice any differences between working for Thorburn's at Tweedside and your former employment with Ballantyne's at March Street?

Well, ye see, Ah wis in an entirely different place. Where Ah wis in the finishin at Ballantyne's, Ah wis in the opposite end in Thorburn's.

Right at the beginning of the process?

Right at the beginning, insteed o bein at the end at Ballantyne's.

You were sorting the wool?

That's right. It wis in the wool. Well, oo wis supplyin the wool for them tae turn it intae yarn. Ye understand?

Yes. And how did you find that kind of work? Did that appeal to you? Did you find it interesting?

It wis a good job. It wis a good job. It wis a good mill. And there wis only three o us. Ken whit Ah mean?

Three wool-sorters?

Well, Ah wisnae a wool-sorter. But eh, there wis no sortin in those days. Aa the wool came sorted.

Ah, right.

The wool came from Gala or whitever it wis. There wis no sortin in these days.

So what exactly did you do then?

Well, they supplied the batches that went tae the throstles or wherever it wis. And that's whit aa came fae the wool store tae there, tae the yarn, tae the spinnin, etc., etc. We jist supplied aa that.

Aye, so that's what you were doing. And there were three of you doing that?

Three o us, uh huh.

And can you remember what hours you worked when you started at Tweedside?

Ah think, was it half-seven? Ah think it would be.

(Mrs French: Quarter-to-eight.)

Quarter-to-eight, maybe, half-seven, quarter-to-eight till half-past five.

Half-past five. And five days a week?

Five days a week.

Did you work Saturday mornings?

If it wis necessary but no aa the time.

Aye. But then it was a five day week, was it?

Five day week.

And it wasn't shift work?

No, no. But Ah've seen us on the Saturday mornin an comin in overtime at nights.

Now tell me about the Tweedside mill. I mean, first of all, how many workers when you went there, or while you were there '59 to '65, roughly how many workers were employed there at Tweedside mill?

Ah would have to say anything between forty and fifty.

So it was much smaller than March Street?

Oh, aye! See, when I'd be in March Street in 1940-whatever it wis, there'd be anything up tae three or four hundred workers in thae days. Renwick would tell ye that as well. And now they're down tae a quarter o that.

Aye. Now of the forty or fifty workers at Tweedside when you went there, or, you know, who were there during the six years or so that you were there, what proportion, roughly, would be women and what proportion men?

No, there wis more men than women.

Was that a difference from March Street?

March Street, would there be more women as men?

(Mrs French: Aye, because, well, there wis more darnin, wasn't there?)

Aye.

(Mrs French: There wis more darners and birlers and that, uh huh.)

Aye. So more men than women at Thorburn's, at Tweedside?

And more women than men at March Street.

At March Street, aye. And that was a striking difference? The numbers were different?

Uh huh.

Because at Tweedside they were much smaller than March Street?

Yes, uh huh.

And the balance of the sexes were different as well. Was there any other difference you noticed, when you went to ... or, you know, the longer you were there, the more you noticed, between Tweedside mill and March Street mill? Maybe the atmosphere, friendliness?

The atmosphere wis better at Tweedside. Aye.

In what sense then? Was it more friendly or relaxed there?

Well, ... Ah think they were more friendly and, as Ah say, when there's only three o ye in the wool store, ye shouldnae have any problem wi three. It's

different wi maybe aboot twenty or thirty. You're always goin tae get the odd one or two. But no, no problems at Tweedside. It wis a good mill.
What were relations between the management and the workers at Tweedside?
Management wis good. Management wis good.
Uh huh. Efficient, competent, were they?
Good. Good managers.
Sympathetic to the workers?
Ah would say so.
Aye. Was that more or less so or much the same as at March Street?
No, no. Ah would've said Thorburn's at Tweedside wis a better manager [than] wis at March Street, but different breed again maybe.
Aye. Now, the manager when you'd gone to March Street was Mr Euman, was it?
Joe. Joe Euman.
Aye. It was he who had given you the job?
Uh huh.
Aye. Now who was the manager at Tweedside, when you went there?
Clem Bonson, Clem Bonser. Peebles born and bred. His father had a shop right across fae where Ah wis born in the Northgate. Bonser, the cooked meat shop.
Aye, right. So you think it was partly the difference in the personalities and the attitudes between Mr Euman and Mr Bonser, accounted for the difference in the atmosphere?
Ah would've thought so, aye. Ah would've thought so.
But there was altogether a better, happier atmosphere in Tweedside than there had been in March Street.
Ah would say so.
I mean, that was, you know, I can quite understand it's your impression and recollection and maybe other people would find something different, you know? But that was your feeling when you went there?
Uh huh. Uh huh.
You enjoyed working at Tweedside more than you had done or seemed to?
At March Street, aye.
Aye. That's grand. And then you worked on there until the fire. What caused the fire?
We do not know for certain but we feel, or it's our belief, that someone came out of the spinnin shed and struck up a cigarette prior to hittin the main door. And he'd maybe light his cigarette and throw the match down. And they feel it might've been somethin that jist caught oil or somethin.
Aye, it began as simply as that?
Oh, aye.
I suppose there were always these hazards in the mill?
Oh, aye.
Cause you're dealing with very combustible materials? Oils?

Plus the fact, there wisnae the Health and Safety regulations then.
No. Was smoking prohibited in the mill?
No, no, no, no, no, no, no.
No. Were there certain areas where it was allowed?
Oh, there wis nae strictness in smokin then.
No. Surprising, isn't it, you know, given that a fire could start so easily?
But when ye think o the oil that wis runnin aboot on the flair. And the floorboards were jist solid grease. And it wis all over in hours at that mill when it went up in flames. Aboot five o'clock?
(Mrs French: That's right.)
It would be an old building, was it?
Aye.
(Mrs French: Uh huh.)
They were frightened o the whole church goin as well. If there'd been a wind that night, they feel the whole church would've went.
It was quite an old building?
Aye, oh, aye, aye. An old one but a good one.
Aye. Well, that was a shame because it meant the forty, fifty, sixty workers lost their jobs?
(Mrs French: That's right.)
At the drop of a match literally?
That's right. That's right.
It must have come as quite a shock to you?
Oh, it did. An then, of course, when we had a meetin with the owners of the mill, the Thorburns, they were goin tae build us the finest mill that money would buy. They were goin away tae get machinery at Germany an they were gonnae do this, they were gonnae do that. And they finished up taking everything down tae Blackrock at Huddersfield.
Do you know why that was?
Ah think they got a good chance o that mill doon there for a song. Ah think there wis somethin in it.
So you, yourself, and your forty or fifty fellow workers, moved from Tweedside immediately after the fire?
No, we were still there.
You stayed on there, aye.
We stayed on.
Was it just the three of you that stayed on?
Uh huh. Uh huh.
But nobody else?
No, because the whole mill wis away.
Aye, apart from your particular section?
That wis burnt to a frizzle! It wis only our side that wis aaright.

It must've seemed a bit strange, just the three of you?
Uh huh. The wool store.
Just working away there. But then you werenae very far from Damdale?
Oh, no problem at aa. No problems. The motor used tae jist come ower an take the wool away.
You didn't feel cut-off or isolated with just the three of you? No?
No, no.
And then after a few weeks or months, you went from Tweedside to Damdale?
To Damdale, uh huh.
Did you mind doing that?
No, no, no, no.
Again you were joining the main body?
You wis jist joinin the Thorburn's group again.
Aye, the main body of workers. How many workers were there at Damdale, when you went there? Fifty, sixty, a hundred?
There'd be more. There'd be more. Ah'd be more inclined tae say eighty tae a hundred.
Aye. So it was considerably bigger than Tweedside?
Oh, aye, aye, aye.

The complexity of the relationship between the mill workers and mill owners had implications across all aspects of work and community life. One example is that of unions and union membership and negotiations as Robert Gray explained to Ian in this discussion which looked at the reach of the Ballantyne empire and local political affiliations.

Robert Gray, b.1926, industrial relations

Well, Ah know that there was no union activity within the mill prior to the War.
Now, sorry, is this just the Caerlee mill or any of the Innerleithen mills?
Ah well, Ah don't think there was any sort o union in any of the mills.
Any of the mills. And at that time there were four mills, is that right?
That's right, yeah.
Waverley, Caerlee?
Uh huh.
Leithen. And was it called the small mill was it, the one up the top o the water there?
Aye, Beckett & Robertson's?
Beckett & Robertson's, aye.
Aye. But, you see, although we had the mills they aa belonged the same people. They were all Ballantyne, with the exception of Beckett & Robertson's.
So was it the same Ballantyne who owned the other three? Or was the family divided

into cousinships at that time?

Well, the Waverley mill, which is still over there, Caerlee and the Caerlee knittin mill belonged the Ballantynes, the Peebles Ballantynes.

That's … is that David, David Ballantyne?

Aye, David Ballantyne, Henry Ballantyne. But they were young men then, you know. It was their father's. But Leithen mill belonged the Ballantynes o Walkerburn. But the Ballantynes o Walkerburn and the Ballantynes o Peebles are cousins, as far as Ah can make out.

Aye. And the whole lot came together, did they not at one time?

They did, aye, eventually, aye. That was much later.

That was much later, after the War, aye?

Oh, aye, a long, long time. Oh, a long, long time after the War.

Aye. Maybe in the seventies or the sixties?

Oh, aye. Long after that.

…

The Ballantynes always done their own wage negotiations. So whether they saw the trade union as a way [of thinking] – 'All right then, we've got to talk to somebody. We're as well talkin to them'.

Aye. And in your own experience did you find that they were reasonable, when it came to negotiations?

Reasonable to a degree that they paid very, very slightly more than the trade rate. Very, very slightly more.

But, I mean, you never found that they were hard-faced, grasping employers, that tried to screw down or grind the faces of the poor?

Oh, Ah'm sorry but as a trade union official, Ah view all employers that way! (laughs) Ye never get any more out an employer than what he wants to give you!

Aye, but you know what it is, there are some that are much, much meaner than others?

Oh, yes, yes, Ah know that, aye. Ah've dealt wi quite a few o them in ma day as well. But, Ah mean, no Ah wouldnae say they ever wanted to see their workers' noses in the ground. But they liked their pound o flesh. You know, they liked their pound o flesh.

Did you come to know any of the Ballantynes fairly well personally as a result of negotiations?

Yes, aye, that ye couldnae avoid bein sort o local and aa the rest o it, yes.

They lived locally, of course, didn't they?

Well, there was one o them lived in Innerleithen here. He was the one that Ah would say that Ah knew, eh, best – he was Company Secretary. He was called David Ballantyne.

And what was the house in which he lived?

'The Pines', up St Ronan's Terrace.

And there were one or two lived in Walkerburn were there not?

Well, they were cousins. The other Ballantyne that was up there was Douglas Ballantyne. And Henry, of course.

Aye. So, as you say, they had a pretty dominating influence locally?

Oh, yes. Henry Ballantyne, he was the king-pin really. Ah mean, that, if you could convince him, that was it. He convinced the rest.

Was he the managing director?

He was chairman, managing director, he was everything!

Aye, the big white chief. Now politically, were the Ballantynes by tradition Liberals or Tories?

Well, away back they were Liberals. They used to support, eh, Sir Donald Maclean, was it? And at some time, some time during the years they changed from Liberal [to Conservative]. Oh, they were great Liberals at one time, the Ballantynes, aye. The Peebles Ballantynes. Ah don't know what the Walkerburn ones were. But certainly the ones at Innerleithen and Peebles, they were great Liberals at one time.

Aye. Ah cannae for the life o me remember if Donald Maclean was a Lloyd George Liberal or an Asquithite.

Uh huh. Ah can't remember that.

I can't remember. But if he were a Lloyd George Liberal, it's possible that was when the Ballantynes changed.

Yes.

You know how the Liberals were split?

Yes, yes. That's right, aye. Certainly they've been Conservative since the Second World War if not for quite a long time before it.

Aye, aye. That's probably what it was. Now socially also there was presumably a lot of deference expressed by ordinary people in Innerleithen, Peebles, Walkerburn toward the Ballantynes? They were the great source of power, employment?

That's right. Oh, there was a certain element, you know, that would touch the cap to them, you know, when they passed and aa this but, but mind you, a lot o that died out after the Second World War because of what people had seen, you know, the majority o men, anyway. Ah mean, and a lot o women, had seen a different part o the world and were put intae a different sort o sphere altogether when they were taken away from the likes o Innerleithen and sent away somewhere else. They'd seen a lot o different things.

I wonder too, unfortunately we cannae ask people who were there at the time because they're all away now, but I wonder, too, if that wasn't the case to some extent after the First World War? I mean, men who'd been away in the trenches for four years.

That's right.

They presumably are not just going to sit down and touch their caps?

No, no, Ah would think they'd probably get a bit o reaction to that as well. But certainly, Ah would say, after the Second World War an awfy lot o that went. There was still an element that thought they were, you know, 'Oh, they're providin us with a job', and aa the rest o it and this, that and the next thing … But there was also quite a lot o people realised what was goin on, that they, the Ballantynes were havin a damn good livin out the sweat and aa the rest o it of the workin people in the valley here.

The situation in Innerleithen … was there a strong support for the Labour Party or Labour governments? Was there a strong tradition of Liberalism, Radicalism, Liberal-Radicalism, sort of Gladstonian Liberalism? Or were most ordinary working people Tories, working-class Tories, in Innerleithen?

Ah would think that to answer that Ah would say that most of them were working-class Tories. (laughs) And a helluva lot o them are to this day! But no, there's definitely not a strong sort o Labour tradition in Innerleithen, no. Not even in Peebles either. Ah would think really, mind you, that Ah would say that, you know, David Steel bein the MP for such a long time and aa the rest o it, that Ah think the majority o people are sort o Liberal Democrats nowadays.

Eric Pearce talks about how the relationship between the workers and mill owners changed over time, away from a paternalistic one to one more influenced by external factors.

Eric Pearce, b. 1927, the mills and change over time

The picture I'm forming in my mind as you tell me this, Eric, is that for roughly the first half of your working life, say, from 1942 when you first went into the mill until about 1968, that's, say, for the sake of ease, twenty-five, twenty-six years, things were relatively stable in the mill and in the textile world? You know, you were in the same building, though in different parts of it obviously, doing different jobs. But there was a certain continuity and stability there? And then somewhere maybe from the early, middle 1960s leading up to this change in 1968, there followed a great deal of instability, at any rate, of ownership and management? Would that be roughly the case?

That's definitely true, yes. The David Ballantyne's mill at Peebles, March Street mills, was owned, well, the main owner was Henry Ballantyne, he was obviously a descendant of the original Henry Ballantyne. And he sold out to a company and made a vast amount of money.

This was the Worsteds, Scottish Worsteds?

No. It was … I'd need to go back to my book and look it all up. It's all in the book. But it was the SUITS, S-U-I-T-S, that was an abbreviation for some Scottish Universal something-or-other. And he sold out to them and then eventually they sold out to Dawson and they made a profit on selling out to Dawson, and he was left holding this sum of money and I think he bought himself back into the mill at Walkerburn.

This is Henry Ballantyne?

This is Henry Ballantyne, he bought the shares from … let's say the parts of the Ballantyne family that weren't involved in the actual manufacturing but were dissatisfied with the way it was being run. So they sold out to him and he got controlling interest and he came down and installed himself in the boardroom at Walkerburn. And then eventually he managed to buy back his own firm at Peebles again.

When did he come down to Walkerburn?

He must have came down just prior to, let's say '67 or …

Just before you were transferred to Peebles?

Yes. Uh huh. And he took over then.

So his taking over at Peebles meant that was when the office was transferred more or less was it?

Yes. They bought it back in again.

How did you feel about the transfer? I mean, you'd always worked in Walkerburn, you'd lived in Walkerburn since you were a boy?

Well, what we did lose was … funnily enough, it was like one big family. I mean, anything that happened in the village, the Ballantynes attended to it. I mean, our local summer festival, everything that went on, the Ballantynes just used to send their squad of joiners or things and they would put up the decorations. They would do everything. They took a great interest in the welfare of the village. Anything that happened in the village, you could just go to the Ballantynes and say, 'We're wanting to do this or wanting to do that', and they would support it.

Quite generous patrons of village activities?

They were very good. I mean, I suppose the houses, the rented houses, weren't very big and the wages weren't very big, but the outlay for everything that you had to do wasn't very big. So everyone seemed to have a reasonable lifestyle under the Ballantynes in the old days.

It sounds to me, forgive the word, it sounds very paternalistic, Eric?

Yes.

The mill owners were also leading figures in much of the village life outside of the mill work? Was that the position?

Very much so. I mean, I suppose it's something like New Lanark and Port Sunlight where they built their factories and their houses and everything was controlled by the owners. There was no problems. Anything that needed done, you could always get it done through the mill workers and the mill tradesmen, let's say. All that sort of changed after they started amalgamating and takeovers and so forth.

It must have been a very unsettling time for Walkerburn people who'd been accustomed to a very sort of set regime?

Uh huh.

They had certain expectations the Ballantynes would do this, look after them in this way and that way and the other. And then suddenly in the sixties it was all changing?

Was that the position?
>That was the position, yes. And the mills were still functioning but what they did, they cut out a lot of the production. Some of the jobs, like the weaving and so forth, were all transferred to Peebles. And a lot of the machinery was. Then they started splitting the company into different divisions. You know, there was a spinning division and a weaving division and a retail division. They'd a lot of shops all over the country at that particular time, selling various garments and so forth.

Were they just Ballantyne's shops? Were they just named Ballantyne's?
>No, they weren't Ballantyne shops. They were Highland Home Industries and that type of thing. They were owned by Ballantyne's and they were all run from various offices in the factory. And then they were all moved to Peebles as well.

Were there changes taking place in the economy of the textile industry in the 1960s?
>Oh, I think all the small firms that was in the textile industry throughout the Borders discovered that they just couldn't survive unless they amalgamated or were bought out. But a lot of the firms that were bought out were closed down. I mean when we were trading as Scottish Worsteds and Woollens, by this time we'd actually taken over George Roberts at Selkirk, William Brown's at Galashiels, Simpson and Fairbairn's at Earlston, Wilson & Glenny at Hawick, Henry Ballantyne at Walkerburn and David Ballantyne at Peebles. We were invoicing under about five different names, because these firms still had various good, let's say, contacts abroad but their mills were closed down and we were manufacturing the stuff here. In Walkerburn and Peebles, and selling it still under these trade names, until eventually it got to such a state that they had to scrap the whole lot and rejig it and they now trade as one company, Robert Noble. When I left Peebles, we were trading as Roberts, Noble and William Brown, which had a very big market in Japan so they didn't want to change that one.

William Brown was the old Galashiels company?
>An old Galashiels firm, yes.

Which had long since been closed?
>Exactly, yes. Aye.

Did you find, you know, those years you were up at Peebles less satisfying, less fulfilling on the whole than your Walkerburn years?
>Yes, that's definitely true. And as computerisation came in, of course, there were less and less bodies. I mean, when I went up there, there must have been about twenty people in the one little office. And I think by the time we finished there was about me and three girls. Everything was on computers and it was quite a sort of demanding job. There was a lot of pressure. You had to keep working late nights and so forth.

So you feel that the second half of your time in the mills was really pretty unsettling, an unstable period?

Yes. Definitely a bit more stressful.

Did you feel really quite glad to retire when that point came?

There's no doubt about it. I think the last few years prior to retirement I really was looking forward to it. You know, it couldn't come quick enough really. The job changed entirely. The demands were a bit more excessive and there was no real job satisfaction latterly.

That was a shame. You spent your life in the mills, half a century?

Yes. And you were part of the Dawson regime, which is very demanding. Dawson work on the principle that if something's not paying after so many years it's scrapped. So you always had this sort of thing hanging over you. You didn't know whether they would just close the place down or not because they'd that many strings in their bow that if one wasn't sort of financially viable for them, they didn't keep it on very long.

Because they have mills throughout the United Kingdom, is that right?

They have, in Bradford and elsewhere. Of course they own Ballantyne's Sportswear, Cashmere at Innerleithen, and Pringle's at Hawick, all these – a lot of knitwears, and they own a lot of big companies.

You must have felt pretty vulnerable in the latter years that you were employed then at Peebles?

Yes, you could see the upper management were struggling the whole time. They were really the worried people. I mean, we were sort of the level below. We were just hoping that things would keep going on because there was such a lot of changes, you know in personnel. There'd be managing directors getting golden handshakes and paid off and new ones coming in.

Very, very great instability compared with earlier years?

Quite unsettling, quite unsettling, yes.

And the old sense of paternalism presumably, you know with the family firm, the Ballantynes or the Thorburns, whoever it may be – that had gone? So you were transferred up to Peebles with quite a few of your colleagues in '68?

Yes, and they ran this mill as a spinning mill only, as part of the Laidlaw & Fairgrieve concern at Galashiels, which was also in the Dawson group. And then I think Laidlaw & Fairgrieve also had a mill at Selkirk and Dalkeith and Walkerburn. And I think what happened was, the workers came back from their summer holidays one year, and they were assembled in the main canteen and the manager got up and said, 'I've got to tell you this mill's closing at the end of the week'. Some were transferred to various mills in Galashiels and so forth but 170 I think, were put out of work just at a stroke.

And some of these presumably were men and women who'd worked in the mill for quite a number of years. Maybe all their working lives?

All their working lives, yes.

Was it the older ones who didn't get jobs, on the whole? Or was it a mixture of ages?

Yes, it was mainly the older ones.
So the ones who'd been working longest, found themselves without jobs in many cases?
Yes, there are still people who have never worked since that particular thing.
When was that, Eric? You went up to Peebles in '68?
I'm just trying to think how many years back now it is. It's quite a good few years. At least fifteen years or more.
About the middle or early eighties? '82, '85, something like that? Don't worry, I can find the date. The mill was closed down as abruptly as that? There was no inkling before the holidays that that was likely to happen?
That's right. None at all. They were just sort of thrown on the scrap heap. And there was a lot of activity locally. They held sessions up in the local hall where various organisations came and spoke to them about various jobs and so forth. And they started computer classes up there as well, I think, and various training courses. It went on for some time and then it gradually just drifted away.
Aye. At the time the Walkerburn mill was closed, Eric, what other sources of employment near or in Walkerburn were there?
There was a small chemical works in the village.
Which was quite independent of the mill?
Oh, yes, quite independent of the mill, Rathburn Chemicals. And they employed quite a few workers but not a great deal – I mean, it wouldn't be in to the twenties. Less than twenty.
So they wouldn't have many vacancies?
No, there were no vacancies. A few people left here and went up to Innerleithen and eventually got jobs there. Some got jobs at Peebles.
In the mills mainly?
In mills mainly, yes.
But there must have been a pool of people who were left without jobs?
Oh, yes, I think there was. It lasted for some time. You know, it gradually whittled away as people eventually maybe got jobs elsewhere. But they were scattered all over the place eventually if they wanted to work. But a lot of people just gave up the thought of working, some of the older element.
They felt they were too old easily to get another job?
Uh huh. Well, you know if you go for a job it's 'Sorry, you're too old'.
And was there also some emigration from the village after the mill closed? People moved out altogether?
Well, certainly not abroad.
No, I mean, you know, out?
There could've been, yes, there could've been.
Moved out to Galashiels or moved up to live in Peebles or …?
Uh huh. There always was a changeover. There were always people moving out and in the village, yes.

THE MILLS AND MILL OWNERS

You were saying that, at its height, quite some decades ago maybe, the population of Walkerburn had been about 1200?

Yes, about the turn of the century, I think, aye.

But, I mean, it wasn't that there was a sharp decline in population in the year or two or three after the mill closed?

No.

The population had been declining?

No, it more or less stayed the same. I think actually at the moment the population's starting to increase again. There seem to be a lot of young families being moved into the village. At one time the school was in danger of being closed because it didn't have enough pupils. But now it's well over the closure figure.

I don't know Walkerburn at all well, Eric, please keep me right on this – but my impression, you know, just coming along the main road and walking down the wee road to visit you this morning, an awful lot has died in the village. Shops seem to have closed. Well, I don't know if they were ever flourishing, but they were once there.

Uh huh.

And there was a Walkerburn Co-operative Society as well?

Yes. Uh huh. Walkerburn had quite a vast amount of shops at one time. You know.

Would this be when you were a young man or even later on when you were older?

Yes, when I came to Walkerburn first of all, before the War, I mean, there'd be about four sweet shops in the village. There was a chemist's, a jeweller's and of course the Co-op had the grocery, the fleshing, the bakery, the millinery, the drapery. They had every department that's known available. And there was various shops all over the place. There was two chip shops, one at each end of the village, and there was a tailor's.

Newsagent?

The Post Office was a general store and newsagent's. There seemed to be quite a lot of shops and they've all gradually closed down. The Co-op closed their main branch and moved into that shop you were on about as you came down the hill. That was their shop there for a while.

That's very small though isn't it, a very small place?

It's got quite a big back area. But it was a sort of self-service place. It seemed to work quite well.

But that's closed altogether now?

That closed down and the manager was moved up to Innerleithen and he runs the Innerleithen branch now, I think.

What is the Co-op in this area then? Is that the Borders?

Yes, it's Borders Co-op.

There have been a whole lot of amalgamations there too, of course?

Uh huh.

Innerleithen Co-op has gone too presumably into this other organisation?
   They're part of the Borders, yes. Uh huh.
Peebles as well?
   Peebles don't have a Co-op at all now.
My impression – it may be wrong – is that the Co-op was centred on Galashiels. It was the old Galashiels or Borders Co-operative Society that took in the smaller ones here. Is that right?
   It did eventually, yes. Uh huh. Walkerburn of course was entirely self-supporting as a Co-operative for years. I mean, it was one of the big occasions of the year when the people went to collect their six-monthly or yearly dividend, was it? They paid a very big dividend here at one time. It would be about four or five shillings in the pound. That really was amazing!
And was it that the Co-op closed after the mill closed?
   No. The Co-op was declining prior to that.
Now at the time that you were transferred to Peebles how many workers roughly were left in the mill at Walkerburn, in '68?
   Well, they changed it over from a weaving mill to a spinning mill and the number would drop quite drastically, I imagine, to about 200-odd. And then gradually, as I say, up to the time when they closed, there was only 170 workers in there.
Whereas in the earlier days, as you mentioned, there were you reckon about 400 workers normally?
   More than double that, yes.
During and after the War?
   Uh huh. Because you had all the other sort of facilities from weaving onwards, you know. The weaving, the darning, the finishing – these are a lot of processes that involved a lot of other workers. But that particular side of the business was transferred to Peebles.

The reach of the Ballantynes in the Peeblesshire textile industry meant that they were, initially at least, agile, able to be flexible in response to when changes in fashion or technology required it. In this extract, Betty Muir recalls how, as a fourteen-year-old girl in 1936, she remembered the workers coming to Walkerburn to work for Ballantyne's from Galashiels and Innerleithen.

Betty Muir, b. 1922, travelling for work

Was that common that Peebles folk went to Innerleithen to work or Innerleithen folk travelled to Peebles?
   When Ah wis in the mill at first, there were women came up frae Galashiels tae work in our mill, Ballantyne's. Ah can remember them as plain as anything. Especially when Ah wis that wee, while on the picking. An Ah can always remember this Cis Grossart wis her name. She wis ginger-headed.

Oh, bright, red, gingery hair. And on a Saturday morning she used to always bring a bar o Cadbury's Dairy Milk chocolate. A thin bar it was in these days, and that's what we had wi oor cup of tea on the Saturday mornin. These Gala women aa brought this up tae the young yins.

Oh, they brought one for you, the girls?

Aye, the young girls that wis there. There were four of us. And that's what ye had wi your cup of tea on the Saturday mornin.

Now how did they come?

The train. We had the train at that time.

So they would have to pay their own fares?

Ah don't know whether they got a travellin allowance or no but they travelled as far afield as Gala. And then we had aa the Innerleithen girls as well. And yet they could have went tae Walkerburn, because they had the Walkerburn mill wi darnin shed. But they seemed to prefer Ballantyne's.

That was a lot nearer to Innerleithen, Walkerburn?

Oh yes, aye. Jist a couple o miles doon the road.

Aye, they could almost walk there?

Aye.

But there were quite a few girls from Innerleithen?

Oh, yes.

And some women from Galashiels as well? And that was before the War?

Yeah.

But did you find that so much after the War?

Well, there wis still quite a lot o the Innerleithen yins. The Gala ones aa faded away. But the Innerleithen yins were still there when Ah left, one or two – no a great deal because a lot o them in the meantime retired. They were aa older women and they aa retired.

And were there many men or girls, women, who went from Peebles to Innerleithen or Walkerburn, do you know?

Ah've no idea. Ma sister, Marion, before she came back into the mill, she applied for a job at the hosiery and she tried it doon there but she didnae like the work, so she left. And that wis when she came back into the mill again.

Hosiery was a very different business, wasn't it, from the tweed?

Aye, she said that.

You never fancied that yourself?

No, no, no. Marion said that. She hadnae the patience to pick it up. She said it wis different entirely to what we were used to.

It would be more limited was it?

Aye, Ah think so, Ah think so. A wee bit mair pernickety as well.

And there were hosiery mills in Innerleithen and Walkerburn?

Oh, no, Ah don't think there wis hosiery, Ah think it wis jist the tweed mill at Walkerburn.

Just tweed there, but it was hosiery as well as tweed at Innerleithen?
    Yes, yeah.
Was Innerleithen, in your working life, a more important or a less important textile town than Peebles?
    Oh, less, aye, they werenae big places that they had at all.
Smaller factories?
    Aye, smaller, aye, yeah. And then they ended up wi jist havin the spinnin machines doon at Innerleithen. When they took them oot o Ballantyne's here, that's where they put them doon at Innerleithen. And then they started jist gatherin a few girls together for the darnin and we used to send the pieces down from oor mill down to them. We were jist like a wee subsidiary, the Tweedside.
So Peebles was more important?
    Oh aye, it's the main one, aye.
There was more employment in Peebles than there ever was in Innerleithen or Walkerburn?
    Yeah, yeah, oh, aye, aye.
Walkerburn was the smallest of them all?
    Of them all, that's right. They were all Ballantyne's, they all belonged to the Ballantynes.
Thorburn's had mills in Peebles but not Innerleithen?
    No, no.
And not Walkerburn?
    No.
And in Galashiels?
    No. Jist that one in Peebles.
Aye. Whereas Ballantyne's were a much bigger mill because they had, they still have, I think, something in, it's either Bonnyrigg or Dalkeith. Bonnyrigg, I think. They have a Ballantyne's Sportswear.
    Oh, well, that'll be tae dae wi Innerleithen if it's sportswear.
Aye, aye, but it's all the same family?
    The same family, oh yes. Although they're all out of it now, the Ballantynes.
They've been bought out, aye?
    Yeah. Ah dinnae ken, Ah think there's only Mr David left anyway. Oh, and Mr Douglas. Ah see him whiles, comin up the High Street.

The following extracts provide more detail about the Thorburns.

Effie Anderson, b. 1925, Thorburns

    Oh. Thorburn's went in for quality, no quantity.
Was that the difference between the two firms?
    Ah would say.

Thorburn's aimed for quality, whereas Ballantyne's were more interested in quantity?
  Aye.
Did you ever work for Thorburn's?
  No.
No. You heard from other workers, was that it?
  Oh, aye.
But, I mean, was it commonly understood among mill workers in Peebles, that Thorburn's produced better quality cloth?
  Oh, Ah would say so.
Aye. I mean, that's always been your understanding?
  Aye. Have ye no spoke tae anybody else?
Aye. But nobody else has made that point.
  Have they no?

Robert Sanderson told Ian about the size of the mills and their workforce, the different processes and how individual tasks were often assigned, particularly to male or female workers.

Robert Sanderson, b. 1929, Thorburn's in Peebles

Now tell me about the … because you're the first person I've had the pleasure of meeting in Peebles who worked for Thorburn's. All the others I've spoken to thus far worked in March Street mill.
  March Street, yeah.
There were two Thorburn mills in Peebles, is that right? Damdale and …?
  Tweedside. Uh huh, uh huh.
Now when you started there at the age of sixteen, roughly how many people altogether – office staff and workers – were employed at Damdale?
  That would be a problem.
If I plucked a figure out the air and said 200, would that be too many?
  Ah would've thought that would've been a bit too many. Although there must've been a good 150/160 Ah would've thought, because looms were only you know, one tae a loom and things like that, you know. Not like nowadays. And there were a lot o darners and shaders and that, you know, on the women's side.
So if there were about 150 folk employed at Damdale – again this is an unfair question – do you know roughly how many would have been employed at that time, when you were sixteen, at Tweedside? Would it be more or less?
  No, no, much less. It wis a cardin and spinnin mill. You know, the wool came in as wool and it wis carded and spun and came out as yarn. But that wis, you know, the only processes there. So Ah would think, fifty tae sixty. Ah don't think there'd be many more than that.
As few as that. So the two mills together, somewhere about 200?

Ah would think so. Ah would think so.
Aye. Now at Damdale – another difficult question: what would be, roughly, the breakdown of men and women workers? You know, maybe two-thirds men and a third women? Or two-thirds women, half women, very roughly?
Ah would've thought there'd be more women than men.
Maybe three-fifths women, two-fifths men? Something like that?
Ah would think something like that would be nearer it, you know, because darnin, shadin, birlin, you know, were all women. And quite a few weavers were women, you know.
There were certain jobs, I gather, that were done by women only?
That's right.
Certain jobs that tended to be done by men only?
By men, if they were heavy.
And some jobs that were, you got men and women?
Yeah, that's right, aye. But on the weavin they would be men and women. Although most of the weavers would be women. And what they called tuners, you know, the men who set up the looms, would all be men, you know, who do liftin and …
You never got women doing that job?
No, no.
What was the distinction? Was it if it was heavy work or very skilled work, it was done by men?
More heavy work, Ah would think, you know. The likes o the tuners were the ones that set up the looms, you know, put the cards and that on them.
And that was quite heavy work?
Aye, and also carried in the beams, you know, which went in as warp before they put the weft across in the loom, you know.
Women never did that work?
No. That would be heavy, that wis heavy work. And they're actually what you'd call engineers of the loom, you know, the tuners.
So that was a very skilled job?
That's right. They had the ticket that told them what was the pattern and everything. You know, that wis their job, tae set it up an get it goin. Yeah, but as Ah say, that wis all men that did that. Ah think in Thorburn's time, most of the weavers would be women, you know. There wis a few maybe men.
When you first went there?
Yeah.
When you were there from the age of sixteen to eighteen?
Aye, that's right, yes.
And, as far as you were aware, had that been the case for many years past?
Oh, Ah would say so. Aye, Ah would say so.
That most of the weavers were women?

Would be women, that's right.
Whereas all the tuners were men?
They were all men. But likes o, ye had maybe one tuner to six looms, or something like that, you know. Ye had fewer tuners than ye had weavers, you know, aye.
Oh, yes, yes. And roughly how many looms were there, when you first started there at Damside?
There were two flats, there were two flats o looms, so twenty, aye, Ah would have thought there must've been between sixty and eighty, something like that, Ah would have thought. There were two flats o them, you know, on both sides. So there must've been something like that. Ah would've thought there'd maybe be between fifteen and twenty on each side, you know. So it would be between sixty and eighty, Ah would say. Quite sizeable. They were aa Hattersleys that they had, they were all Hattersleys.
That was the name of the machine?
Aye.
Quite up-to-date machines at that time?
At that stage, Ah suppose they were, yeah.

As Bob Anderson told Ian, the tradition of mill workers travelling for work extended beyond the Border mill communities. Bob's father had taken the family to Kilmarnock during some lean years, before he moved back to Innerleithen and from there travelled between the Peeblesshire communities wherever the work was moved to.

Bob Anderson, b. 1931, travelling for work

Now you started school in Kilmarnock?
Uh huh. Glencairn. That was the name o the school, Glencairn
And you started when you were five?
Yes. Aye.
You hadn't been long in Kilmarnock when you went to school?
No, no.
Did you feel a wee bit at sea in Kilmarnock? You know, a wee laddie with a Borders accent?
Aye, well, there were a lot o Border folk there, ee see. Fae roond aboot here.
So your dad was not alone in moving?
No, no, no, no. There were quite a few families moved there at that time.
Aye. Maybe that's how he came to be there?
That's right, aye.
One of his workmates or one of his neighbours had already gone, aye?
Uh huh. Aye. There wis quite a few moved because there were no work here, ee see. You see, ma father, when Ah was a wee laddie, he was only workin one

week in thirteen. An he cycled tae Peebles tae save the fare.
Aye, to March Street?
   Aye, aye.
And, of course, though it's not too far and it's a reasonably flat road, you've got prevailing headwinds?
   That's right. Aye, aye, aye.
It's not so bad coming back in the evening, you know, with a bit of wind like this?
   Uh huh. Uh huh. And yet before, when he worked at Walkerburn, they started at six in the mornin and they walked. And they walked home at night at six o'clock.
So he must have been up at half-past four?
   Aye.
What a long day?
   Aye. Oh, aye.
And then he would just drop asleep after he got his dinner?
   Well, this is it. Aye, that's right.
It's a long day. And he would just walk down the road to Walkerburn?
   Well, they were a company. Ye see accordin tae what ma father said, there were a crowd met at the top o the street in the mornin and they all walked tae Walkerburn. Uh huh.
Aye. Sometimes, I think, they walked along the riverside?
   Aye. Uh huh. Aye.
But sometimes they walked down the road. I think they preferred the road?
   That's right. Aye, aye.
   …
   Ma father's occupation was a tuner in the March Street mills in Peebles.
So he had lived in Innerleithen?
   Aa his days.
Aye. But travelled to Peebles?
   Aye. Travelled to Peebles. And he also walked to Walkerburn in his younger days.
Aye. He started work in Walkerburn?
   Yes, that's right. And then they brought the weaving looms up tae Leithen mill, which is knocked doon now. And then they moved the looms up tae Peebles, tae March Street.
Aye. That was just before the War?
   That wis afore the War. Aye, a good bit afore the War. Uh huh.
But your father belonged to Innerleithen, too?
   Yes. Aye. Ma father, ma family, and ma mother's family, aye.
And just remind me, he was in Walkerburn, the Leithen mills and March Street. So he was in all three towns?
   That's right.

Would that be fairly unusual for somebody?
> No, because Ah think most of the weavers and that at one time were at Walkerburn, ye see. And this up here was just the spinnin. Well, when they shifted the weavin up tae Leithen mill, he was in Leithen mill. Then at the hinder end, they shifted it aa tae Peebles cause it was a bigger mill. It was aa the same company, ee see. It was aa Ballantyne's.

Of course, there were two separate lots of Ballantynes weren't there?
> That's right, aye. Of course, when Ah worked in there, the likes o Leithen mill an the Waverley, they were Ballantyne's mills. But they also supplied us wi the yarn for the hosieries, ee see. Lambswool and cashmere, ee see.

From Walter Scott we get this account of the Ballantyne empire beyond Peeblesshire.

Walter Scott, b. 1924, Ballantyne mills in Forfar and the Vale of Leven

> Ah wis only back hame maybe aboot a year, then Ah went away tae Forfar. Ah wis there six months or so. And then Ah came back. Well, ye see, Ah wis better off there again because Ah wis gettin dig money and that when Ah wis away. So Ah wis aaright. And then Ah came back fae there and then Ah wis only back aboot six month again, and we sent looms away through tae Dumbartonshire, tae the Renton. And Ah wis sent through there. So Ah wis away there aboot three and a half year.

Were you? Living in Vale of Leven?
> Aye.

And did you live in Renton itself, Alexandria?
> Aye. First Ah stayed in Bonhill. And then Ah came doon tae the Renton and Ah stayed there in digs. And there again, it wis only a wee box bed Ah had. Well, in Bonhill, we had a bedroom. But at Renton Ah jist had a wee box-room off the sittin room. And there were nae bath in that hoose, and Ah used tae go intae Dumbarton and go tae the public baths there and have a bath.

Aye. Now all these factories in Forfar and in the Vale of Leven were owned by Ballantyne's were they?
> Well, they must have rented the places oot because it wis aa the mill stuff that we were weavin and that through there.

Aye. But, I mean, the Forfar factory belonged to Ballantyne's?
> Aye.

It was a Ballantyne's factory in Forfar. And it was a Ballantyne's factory in Renton?
> That's right.

Aye, aye. So it was really quite an extensive firm was it?
> Oh, aye, aye.

Did they have factories anywhere else besides Peebles, Innerleithen, Forfar and Renton?
> No, no that Ah ken o.

No. These were the four?
    Aye.
When had they moved up to Forfar and out to Renton, then? Was that before the War?
    No. That wis aa after the War. Aye. They were expandin then, aye.

One way that the mill owners addressed the need for more manpower was to provide hostel accommodation for young women workers.

Robert Sanderson, b. 1929, the Peebles hostel

When you were a lad, there would be 700 or 800 mill workers? As you say, 500 at March Street and maybe 200 at Thorburn's.
    March Street had over 500. Thorburn's as well in the 1940s. They had a hostel at what was called The Mount. It wis a big house.
Where was that then?
    You know where Dalcushie Hotel is? Dalcushie and Kingsmuir Hotels? It's sort o between them, on that high road. It actually looks down on Peebles.
From Edinburgh?
    Up that end. If you go over Tweed Bridge, you know, where the clock is. Dalcushie sits up on the hill lookin down.
On the south side of the river?
    That's right, and high up. That's where The Mount was. It's where all these new houses are now. That's in that sort o estate on that side. But that wis a hostel. There were over twenty girls stayed there.
And where did they come from then?
    Some came from Dunfermline and some came from Lanarkshire and that.
Aye. This was in the forties?
    That's right, yeah. When Ah worked in the office, because Ah used tae often get the job of goin up there if somebody had arrived, you know, and had got a job. Ah'd tae take them up and show them where The Mount was, you know. And they stayed up there. There wis two women looked after this hostel.
    And there must've been about seven or eight of them that married Peebles people, you know. And some are still here. But there wis aboot twenty girls stayed in The Mount at that time.
And that had been in somebody's big villa?
    That's right, it wis a big house and they took it over.
You know, can I just ask you about The Mount, did each girl have a room to herself?
    That's right, yes.
It wasnae a dormitory business?
    No, Ah think they must have had rooms and that. Maybe two shared in some cases and that, aye, aye. But that's right.
Yes. And that was when, really, Thorburn's was at maximum production then?

THE MILLS AND MILL OWNERS

That's right. Jist after, they had tae bring them in because they couldnae get enough locals, yeah.
And did all those girls work in Damdale?
Yes.
None in Tweedside?
No, they were all maybe, darners or weavers or that, you know. But, aye, they all worked there, yeah, yeah. But a lot o them worked there for years, you know. Some o them were even still workin when they were transferred to March Street and that, and were there till they retired. Aye. Yeah.
So the demand for workers, if there's a great demand for the goods and the firm has to bring workers in, as you say from Lanarkshire and Dunfermline and elsewhere, did you find that wages were rising fairly steadily?
Aye. Generally you got a rise, you know. It wasnae like it is nowadays, where everybody expects one every year, sort o thing. It didnae happen like that then.

Nearby, Walkerburn also provided hostel accommodation for young women workers, as Eric Pearce told Ian.

Eric Pearce, b. 1927, the Walkerburn hostel

It was originally built by one of the early mill owners as a hostel, to bring in workers from other areas because there weren't enough locally.
Did it have a particular name?
Barn Walls it was called. Barn Walls Hostel or something. But it was mainly filled with young women. There'd be quite an intake of young women because women were really greatly in demand and there weren't enough locally.

Hume Davidson provided this further detail about the Walkerburn hostel in this account of mill housing in Walkerburn.

Hume Davidson, b. 1928, Walkerburn hostel

No. I'm with you. Tweedholm was the wee mill.
And Jubilee wis a wee bridge over the dam, we caa it the dam. And it wis a cuttin doon tae the station. And that wis known as the Jubilee. It wis made in Queen Victoria's Jubilee in, there you are, 1887. Ma faither wis the first bairn tae gin ower there. So eventually, Jubilee Road … Dalziel's Brae got called Jubilee Road. But that's where the Jubilee was. (laughs)
Aye, that's the original, aye.
Uh huh, that wis the original.
That's very clear, though. Now when were these houses, that you're living in, built? Do you know?
They would, they would be built, Ah would imagine, in the 1860s. Ah would

185

imagine, for the workers. And eventually they built a hostel for workers, incomin workers, too. It's an old folks' flat, now.

And what was that called? Did it have a name?

No. Ah think we jist called it the hostel, Ah think.

And how many roughly would it house?

Phew, Ah don't know. It wid be twenty-odds, Ah would imagine.

(Mrs Davidson: Once they had finished it wi the hostel, they turned it intae the offices.)

Oh, aye, it's been a few things. It's been a Youth Hostel.

(Mrs Davidson: Then, then they turned it intae old folks' homes.)

The Polish sojers wis in there durin the War, you know.

Aye. But originally it was built as a hostel?

It was built for a hostel for their in-comin workers.

In-coming workers, aye. And that would be built, again would that be in the 1860s, 1870s?

No.

(Mrs Davidson: The 1880s Ah would say.)

Because the men used tae say aa that area that Ah'm tellin you aboot, where the hostel was an that, was called the strawberry field. It wis a field (laughs) before they come.

Aye. So men that you remember, they could remember it as an open field, aye?

Uh huh.

In the hostel was it just women workers? Or were there families or men and women? Or did it vary from time to time?

Ah don't know. Ah think it would be women mainly. There were a Miss Somebody that looked efter it.

(Mrs Davidson: Aye, Ah think it wis aa women.)

Ah think it would be aa women that wis in there.

Aye, aye, girls, mill girls, young women?

Uh huh. Aye.

Mainly unmarried women?

Uh huh.

Uh huh. But you can remember women being there can you yourself?

No.

No. Before your time? Before your memory?

Aye, and jist told aboot it. What Ah mind o it wis, well, durin the War, thirties. Ah jist minded durin the War o the Poles bein in there.

Aye. You can't remember the mill workers, women mill workers, being sort of turned out to make way for the Poles?

No. No, Ah cannae. Ah cannae.

So it may be that it was empty for a year or two?

Maybe, maybe.

In this next selection, we hear from a number of contributors who told Ian more about their experience of working in the mills during decades of change.

This first extract is from John Lunn, whose career began at Waverley and whose experiences included changing mill ownership, working in different mills and responding and thriving through innovation and change.

John Lunn, b. 1936, change over time
Can I ask when you started in Waverley mills roughly how many workers were employed in those mills?

Oh, there were, there would be over a hundred in the Waverley at that time.

Was the Waverley the biggest of the four Innerleithen mills?

It wis the biggest o the three spinnin mills. But what they called the hosiery.

Caerlee?

Caerlee was the biggest employer. They had the most workers, aye.

Leithen mills was about the same size as the Waverley?

Leithen mills was, no, Leithen mills was about maybe half the size o Waverley. And the top mill wis, oh, Ah think it only had about twenty folk or something, aye.

Aye. So there'd be maybe fifty, sixty, seventy at Leithen mills?

Aye … maybe 120 at Waverley.

120, when it was busy?

Uh huh.

And Caerlee maybe 150–160?

Oh, there'd be more than that. A couple o hundred anyway, aye.

Aye, aye. And the other one was just a wee mill?

And the top mill had about twenty or thirty folk in it, if it had that.

Now what sort of folk, I mean, was there a distinctive kind of Innerleithen person, man or woman, who worked in the wee mill? Were they older workers?

Oh, they were aa old. They caed it the pensioners mill! There were folk worked up there until they were in their eighties.

Really?

Aye.

And this is when you were a lad?

Oh, when Ah wis a lad. Ah used tae sometimes go up there. In those days, the mills didnae have their own engineers. And there wis an engineerin firm jist round the corner, called Hogg & Robertson's. And the man that run it was a Mr Thomson. And he took a great interest in iz as well. Ah've aye had a lot o sponsors, if you like. And John Thomson aye took a great interest in me. And he [would come] doon tae the mill tae dae a wee job or that, or if when you were an apprentice, you were told, 'Take these wheels up and get them welded' or 'Get that bracket welded'. So Ah used tae go up there and Ah could blether tae anybody, like Ah'm now, ye see.

But you were interested in these things?

Aye, Ah wis interested. And John used tae take a great interest in iz. Even in later years, John aye had a great interest. And when Ah wis supposed tae be workin in the Waverley, John used tae take me away up tae the top mill. We used tae walk up and walk doon. So, Ah mean, Ah wis away for aboot half a day (laughs) tae see what wis up in the top mill. An Ah must've been quite good at ma job because a lot o the times he took us up, he wis takin us up so that Ah wis actually goin up there, even as a boy, aboot sixteen or seventeen, Ah wis goin up there tae solve some o their problems.

And these were carding problems?

Cardin problems, aye.

So was it an old-fashioned kind of mill up there?

It was. It was really old-fashioned. It was spinnin only. They'd no dyein or anything like that. Ah think they had four cards or five cards and some spinnin.

And what were they producing?

Ah don't know. Ah used tae go up there quite regular, and Ah never saw anybody workin yet! (laughs)

Really? Aye, very easy-osy?

It wis easy-osy, oh, really easy-osy. But it wis different in the Waverley. Ye had tae work in the Waverley.

Aye. Now at Beckett & Robertson, were they producing yarn for a particular purpose?

Tae be fair, they were one o the ones that wis intae the knitwear first. They produced knitwear yarns. They had a family connection. The Hutchesons were connected. One brother ran the spinnin mill up here but the other brother was a director in one o the knitwear firms. Ah think it wis Braemar or one o them in Hawick. And they had the connection and, of course, they got this knitwear work. In those days, the Waverley didnae do knittin yarn. We supplied March Street mill completely wi yarn for what they called the Sportex cloth and tweeds. And it wis in later years, when Ah wis jist aboot ready tae go tae Gala, when Ah wis aboot twenty, that they started tae make the knitwear yarn. But tae be fair, what we caed the top mill, had been makin knitwear yarn for quite a long time.

But the Caerlee mill had been hosiery?

An it wis hosiery. Originally the Ballantynes had three mills. When Ah say Ballantynes, the Ballantyne brothers, because it wis actually Henry Ballantyne that had Leithen mill. Henry Ballantyne had Walkerburn mill and Leithen mill. But the Ballantyne brothers had three mills. They had March Street mill, they had Waverley mill and they had Caerlee mill. And originally they were all what they called vertical mills, in that they all, they had spinnin right through tae weavin.

The whole business, aye?

The whole business, right up tae aboot 1936/1937. And that's what Ah say, ma father started at Waverley but then in 1936 or '37, he wis sent tae March Street because they took aa the weavin out o the two mills in Innerleithen and they sent aa the weavin up tae Peebles. And they brought aa the cardin machines and spinnin out o Caerlee and out o Peebles and they brought them all down tae Waverley.

Aye. That's great. So that was the situation in Innerleithen?

So Ballantynes brought aa these together before ma time. Before the War.

Just at the time you were being born in fact?

Uhuh. So they then turned Waverley intae a completely spinning mill; March Street intae a cloth-makin mill. And they had their ambitions of havin a knitwear factory in a small way, up there at Caerlee. And their idea was to expand it, which they did. But, of course they started tae expand it and the War came along and it wis turned intae various things.

Polish troops billeted there?

There were troops and they had engineerin. There were one or two people that came tae Innerleithen because they were doin the engineerin work. They brought lathes and everything. Ah mean, don't ask me, Ah wis jist a wee boy. But there were folk came fae Glasgow and they were doin engineerin work – hush-hush – in that place. And by the time the War started tae sort o die out, if ye like, it went back tae textiles. There were always a wee bit but nothin much in it. It wis mainly engineerin an that, that wis in it durin the War. An they reopened it up as a blouse factory. An the folk went in and they made blouses. This wis the start o the nylon. And for many years they made blouses. Ma mother she wis requisitioned durin the War. The big stores an that, ye'll hae seen them. An the trains used tae bring in the goodies intae these stores.

These were food stores?

Food stores. An ma mother wis requisitioned ontae that job. When the trains came in, she had tae go away and work, ye know, take the stuff fae the trains and wheelin the barrows. But when she wis decommissioned fae that, she started tae work as a machinist. She wis quite a good sewer, obviously. She wis brought up in service so she'd tae do sewin and everything. So she got a job as a machinist makin blouses. And then after two or three years, they stopped doin that and they reverted completely back to knitwear.

Aye. That was before you, just before you started work?

Jist aboot when Ah started.

The late forties or early fifties?

Aye. Durin the late forties it wis a blouse-makin factory, makin blouses.

As late as that?

Uh huh, uh huh. Cause ma mother didnae start workin up there until about 1945 or '46. And she wis one o the first that went to make the blouses because they were lookin for machinists and she could machine. Eventually the blousin went out and they went back on tae the high cashmere. They decided tae stick to the cashmere. And then they built the mill up on cashmere. And that wis when Ah wis sayin, when jist before Ah left Ballantyne's here tae go tae Laidlaw & Fairgrieve's, they decided that they would make their own cashmere yarn. And we converted four o the machines in the Waverley from makin the tweed yarns tae makin the cashmere yarns, and tae supply the cashmere. And what happened wis, it wis actually an exchange in a roundabout way. They made it intae two mills, if you like. Ah wis left, along wi the son o the cricketer, we were left on the woollen side, which was the big side and the four sets that had been converted, they brought a carder up from Gala tae look after them.

…

Ah went tae Gala in 1956 and Ah went tae Selkirk in '63.

Aye. And you were the assistant manager?

Assistant carder.

Assistant carder, aye, all the time you were there?

Aye. And then Ah went tae Selkirk as the cardin manager. They had changed the titles: instead o bein a foreman carder, you were a cardin manager.

Now can I ask, why did you decide to move from Gala to Selkirk?

Ah wis transferred. It was the same firm.

The same firm.

Laidlaw & Fairgrieve's. Although it was called Brown & Allan's, but it was Laidlaw & Fairgrieve's. By this time it was part o the Dawson group. Fairgrieve sold out and it was the start o the Dawson group. Dawson's was Todd & Duncan's and there were a firm called Dawson's who made tops and imported cashmere in Bradford. And they wanted to take Todd & Duncan's over. And Alan Smith, Sir Alan as he is now, decided that he wasnae goin tae be taken over, so he did a reverse takeover and he took over Dawson's. But he became the head man, if you like. And then their next acquisition was actually Laidlaw & Fairgrieve's. So that was really the start o the Dawson empire, if you like.

So that would be, sorry, the early sixties then?

That was, Ah think that wis 1959.

'59, just a couple of years after you had gone to Gala?

Aye. About three year after Ah went, aye.

They were taken over by Dawson?

By Dawson's. So by this time we were part o Dawson's. Laidlaw & Fairgrieve's, when Ah went, consisted o Laidlaw & Fairgrieve's and Brown Allan's, which is the mill in Selkirk. And then there was this takeover by Dawson's, as it then was Todd & Duncan's.

So they just had one mill in Gala and one in Selkirk?

And they decided tae build a new factory up at Dalkeith. So the chap who was the cardin manager at Selkirk got a job as a sort o technical chap, tae help tae build this factory at Dalkeith. An Ah got his job at Selkirk. So Ah wis transferred tae Selkirk.

And that was '63?

That was '63. And in '65, when they had this factory built, or late '64 or early '65, when they had this factory built and half-runnin up at Dalkeith, Ah went up tae Dalkeith tae run it.

Quite a few changes in a short period for you then?

Aye.

Now when you went to work in Selkirk did you also go to live there?

No, no, Ah travelled. Well, by this time Ah wis married and Ah had a house in Gala.

When did you get married?

'62.

Aye. So just before you went to Selkirk. Do you mind if I ask, was your wife a mill worker, too?

She worked in what was called Gladstone's, the shrinker's, in the office. In Gala.

And what brought you back to Waverley then? Was the job at Dalkeith done by then? It was finished?

No, no. Nowadays they would call it 'head-hunting'. In those days, a lot o folk were. But ma father was still at Waverley mill and by this time, the Waverley, the Ballantyne dynasty, wis finished as such. And it wis Baird's that owned the mill, William Baird.

Dawson, Dawson hadn't yet entered?

No. Ah wis workin for Dawson's, if you like, under the Laidlaw & Fairgrieve's guise. But Ballantyne's had sold out in about '64 or '65. They sold out tae the old Sir Hugh Fraser – SUITS.

Why did Ballantynes sell out?

Well, it wis the old story o the families were gettin spread and spread and spread. And some o them were wantin money and there were some gettin money that, you know, well: 'Why are they gettin money? They've never worked in the mills. They've never done anything.' But it wis their father or their grandfather, ye know, and …

Sons of the fathers!

And ye know, like some o them that wis there, like Douglas had four or five sons. David had five, eh, three daughters. Henry had three daughters and a son. And the son wasnae interested in the mill. The daughters were aa married, ye know. What does the money come from? So they sold out, and then of course Sir Hugh Fraser got intae trouble over trying to take one of the newspapers over or something like that. So tae get money an that, he sold the

Ballantyne part to William Baird's, Bairdtex. And they put in a managing director. And they wis lookin for a manager. They decided they were goin tae have two managers in the mill. Again, they were tryin tae get intae this knitwear business because before Ah had left there, they had set up the cashmere side. But the other side supplied completely March Street mills wi their yarn. Now when Bairdtex took them over, they didn't want March Street. So they sold March Street back to the Ballantynes. So that became a Ballantyne mill again. And Waverley and the hosiery stayed as Bairdtex, William Baird. And they decided that they wanted tae get intae the knitwear firm, business – fine lambswool and Shetland again, supplyin the Midlands trade wi this bulk for M&S and people like that. You know, the jerseys. Baird's had decided this is what they wanted tae do and they wanted somebody that knew the trade. So Ah'd seen the job advertised an Ah wisnae botherin about it. An there wis one night ma father phoned an ma father never phoned. It wis aye ma mother that phoned. Margaret says, 'That's your dad on the phone'.
'Ma dad? What's he wantin? He never speaks on the phone.'
'Well, it's him that's on the phone. He wants tae speak tae you.'
He says, 'Have ye seen this job that's advertised at the mill?'
Ah says, 'Aye'.
He says, 'Have ye put in for it?'
Ah says, 'No'.
'Oh, well,' he says, 'Ah think ye should put in for it'.
Ah says, 'Ah dinnae ken aboot it. Ah've got tae think aboot it'.
'Ah think ye should put in for it,' he says.
So, Ah cannae mind what day o the week it was. Anyway he phoned back on the Friday night. Ah never did anything about it, and he phoned on the Friday night and he says, 'What are ye doin the morn?'
Ah says, 'Nothin'. How?'
He says, 'Mr Rae', he wis the manager there, 'would like to see you. Can ye come doon? Ah've telt him that ye could come'.
Ah says, 'But Ah didnae put in for it'.
'No, no, but he wants tae see ye. Ye've tae come doon. Can ye come doon and see him at ten o'clock?'
So, 'Och, aye, Ah'll come doon'.
'Right, Ah've telt him you'll be there.' (laughs)
So Ah come doon on the Saturday mornin and saw this Mr Rae and a Mr [H…], and Jimmy Howie wis there and, 'Oh!' he says, 'You've got tae come back!' Jimmy, you know, [wis always] one o these ambitious types. He always hung about the Ballantynes and that. If Robert Rae or they were there, Jimmy wis aye there. Ah suppose that wis where ye were supposed tae be if ye were a manager. And of course, Jimmy wis there on the Saturday mornin. He would know they were interviewin folk and he was probably told tae be

there, so that he could then give his opinion. And, 'Oh, ye want tae come back'.

Ah says, 'Ah dinnae ken aboot this, Jimmy'. Ah says, 'Ah've got quite a good job where Ah am'.

'Oh, no. You come back. You tell Robert and you tell Mr Rae, you want the job. You tell him!'

And so this was before Ah went in. The first person Ah saw wis Jimmy. (laughs) Jimmy wis aye hingin aboot. And so he gave me this patter. And so intae the interview. Ah went away, came back oot and spoke tae Jimmy again and then Ah went and come roond tae ma mother's of course. Now that Ah wis this length Ah jist went round there. And the next thing was on the Monday mornin Ah got a phone call: 'When can ye hand your notice in?' Ah says, 'Well, ye've no even telt iz what the pay is'.

'Oh, we'll give ye so-and-so.'

Well, this was an awfy lot mair than what Ah wis gettin, so Ah jist went, 'Right, Ah'll hand ma notice in and Ah'll stert in a month'. So Ah jist went intae the mill at Dalkeith and handed ma notice in. That wis it. Nothin in writin, nae nothin, jist that wis it. Ah never got anything in writin. And when Ah started on the Monday the only thing that Ah ever got was Ah wis given a copy o a letter that had been circulated roond the management before Ah arrived, sayin that Ah wis comin and that Ah would be in charge. And if Robert Rae wasn't there, Ah wis next in line tae the managin director.

So you were in charge of the whole mill then?

Ah wis in charge o the whole mill, jist straight off.

Waverley, aye. And what age were you then?

Thirty-two.

Uh huh. That was quite young was it? There wouldn't be many managers younger than that?

No.

So by that time you'd worked just over half your life in the mills, various mills – first Innerleithen, then Gala, Selkirk and Dalkeith?

Ye see, this is what Ah wis sayin away back. It wis like ma school days. Ah wis never ambitious. Ah mean, Ah didnae put in for the job. Ah didnae. The only job Ah ever put in for wis the job when Ah went tae Gala. Ah wis transferred tae Selkirk, Ah wis transferred tae Dalkeith an Ah wis more or less, what would you say, forced …

Aye, head-hunted, as it were?

Aye, tae come back tae Innerleithen. Oh, it wis a good move for me. Ah mean, Ah wis quite happy tae come back. Ah felt more at home and it wis a much better job. But, at the time, Ah wisnae intendin tae move.

Did you feel it was less strenuous?

Well, it wis a big step, it wis a big step up. Ah mean, Ah wis workin aa the hoors o the day and night at Dalkeith. And here wis somebody comin along oot o the blue, wis offerin us a job that Ah didnae even have tae dirty ma hands in.

Aye. It was a purely managerial job?

Purely managerial. The top man next tae the managing director. Jist oot o the blue and he wis givin iz about fifty per cent rise in ma wages, withoot even puttin pen tae paper.

Well, that was a tribute to yourself especially, you know, since you were still just a young fellow?

So Ah actually went away fae here and Ah come back … Ah left here as an apprentice and Ah actually came back tae be in charge. And when Ah came back and Ah walked through the mill, it wis jist like turnin the clock back. Virtually everybody was still there. That's what Ah'm sayin, they were quite young when Ah was a boy. Ah didnae think they were young but they were still they must have been quite young, the folk that wis workin there.

Late thirties, forties?

Because here Ah was, Ah came back and everybody, virtually everybody that was on the cardin and the spinnin and the windin was still aa workin there in the mill. It wis jist like Ah walked oot in the mornin and come back at night. It wis jist exactly like that. There wis maybe about half a dozen faces that wisnae there and half a dozen other new faces. Everybody else wis still the same.

Nothing much changed?

The only difference was Ah wis at the top instead o the bottom.

Aye. But much of the machinery had changed had it?

No, everything wis jist [the same]. An it wis jist like walkin in in the mornin and walkin back at night in a different job. As if Ah'd jist aged overnight.

Aye. And that's already nearly, well, it's nearly thirty years ago since you came back?

It is, aye.

So you remained as manager?

No, no. Ah got made redundant in 1990. But Ah wis manager for twenty-odd years. Ah saw a lot o changes in that time.

Yeah. Now were these changes mainly in the ownership and management of the mill? Or were there technical changes as well?

Big technical changes as well.

Would you care to tell me about the technical changes?

Well, when Ah come back, it wis … there were old spinnin frames and cards. And jist … that was in 1968, beginnin o April '68 Ah came back. And late November '69 Baird's decided they were goin oot o textiles, or oot o the spinnin side, and they sold the mill tae Dawson's. So Ah then became a Dawson employee again. Only eighteen months or so after leavin them. They werenae really interested in the spinnin mill. So after about three months they decided that they were jist goin tae close the doors. So the firm closed its doors.

This was the Waverley that was closed?

This was the Waverley. They jist decided tae close the doors. So everybody wis made redundant. But they said that anybody could buy the mill. But in the meantime, again somebody had heard it wis closin and they phoned up and they asked iz if Ah would like a job. And this wis in Lancashire.

So you got the offer of a job in Lancashire?

Well, they were lookin for carders and managers, so they said. So him and I, a chap called Phil Schofield, who wis the carder there at this time and Ah wis the manager, we decided we'll go down and have a look, see what they've got tae offer. Nothin tae lose, because we were losin our jobs anyway. So when we got there, here were all the directors o this thing.

Where was this about?

In Shaw, in Lancashire. A firm called Clough Mill. So we went down and they started tae ask us about ourselves. And then Ah started tae talk, talk aboot the mill. The result was, we got there about ten o'clock in the mornin, we left about four o'clock in the afternoon, and on the Monday mornin, when Ah got back, Robert Rae says tae me, 'You know, they've been somebody on the phone enquirin about buyin the mill'.

Ah says, 'Who is it?'

He says, 'A Mr Foulkes'. He says 'Ah believe you were talkin to him on Saturday'.

But the trade that they were in was making yarns for curtains and fabrics. And it was all acrylic. So here wis a mill that was runnin fine cashmere and fine lambswool and there were somebody wantin tae run acrylic on the same machines. An Ah told them that ye could do it. So, Ah got a job wi them. And Ah went doon there and Ah stayed for aboot a week or a fortnight in digs. And then Ah wis moved back up tae Waverley. And so we then started the process of convertin all our machines tae run acrylic and man-made fibres, from cashmere. So that wis quite a hard task. So that wis a lot o technical changes. And at that point, when Mr Foulkes, senior, was livin, he had quite a lot o ambitious ideas. And he spent quite a bit o money. February 1970, they officially took over. An so then, we changed aa the machines over, we had tae put new card wire on and various other things, tae make it run on the acrylic. And we got it up and we got it runnin and we got big productions out o it and, oh, they were quite happy. And they were that happy on it, that in 1974 there wis a new process came out, which is open-end spinnin, which is like chalk and cheese compared tae what we'd been doin before. The yarn instead o havin great, big cardin machines, ye used tae have a wee, short cardin machine, and it wis made intae a sliver, and it came out the sliver and that sliver actually goes intae a machine as a big, thick sliver and it came out the machine as the finished yarn ready tae send tae the customer. So we cut four or five processes out. And when we got these machines runnin, which nobody had ever seen before and they'd never run on acrylics, so we'd to do aa the work – no me personally, but Ah wis in charge o it, Ah'd tae make a lot o decisions – we were able when we'd been employin somewhere like 120 people to produce twenty ton o yarn a week, we were then able with six people to produce twenty-six ton o yarn. So that wis an innovation on its own. And at that point we were makin a lot o money. And we then started what they called the 'fancy yarn department'. And we got machines in where the rollers stopped and started. And ye could take three or four yarns and ye put them thegither and ye get big bouclé bits and lumps. And we put in these machines at the same time and they were high labour intensive. So the folk then had tae be trained fae what they'd been doin before, tae run these machines. And we had tae learn how tae do the yarns. Suddenly, overnight, we had tae become yarn designers and technical folk on machines that nobody had ever run before. And in actual fact, the number o employees went up. We went fae jist over 100 tae up tae 200. At one point, we'd 240.

Gosh, that was a huge increase.

Aye. Because at that time everything was boomin, and although we put in this new spinnin plant, they were gettin so many sales that we still kept the old spinnin plant runnin on a limited basis, but we still kept it runnin tae keep goin on the overspill. And in the meantime we put in this fancy twistin department tae try and take up the labour and make money, of course. And there wis these machines and we'd tae keep all these. And eventually the trade fell, and we stopped the original spinnin. In fact, we demolished the mill, where the original spinnin was. And, the old men kept goin and the fancy yarns. And then there was another machine brought out, which they called the hollow spindle spinner, where the thread came up through the middle o the spindle instead o bein on the outside o the spindle. And we got three o these – again nobody had ever seen them before – straight fae the drawin board intae the Waverley. And the folk, at this point the folk used tae come up fae the Tech, tae see it – aa the lecturers and everything.

To see it. So you really were in the vanguard?

Oh, we were away in the vanguard. And then, Ah don't know what happened. Mr Foulkes, his son came intae the business, one thing led tae another and eventually the business sort o went down. But at one point, when the father wis full o ambition, it wis all go.

Great boom obviously?

It was boomin. And he wis makin a lot o money. That wis in 1970 they took over and then Robert Rae got another job in Selkirk and he left in '73 and Ah become sole charge o the factory in Innerleithen in 1973. An Ah wis in complete charge o the factory right up until 1990. Well, various things happened and they eventually made me redundant.

How did you feel about that? Were you really broken-hearted?

No!

You weren't shattered or devastated?

No, no. My attitude was, oh, Ah'll get a job somewhere. An Ah did. Ah got a chance o two jobs and Ah took one in Kilwinning. Again it wis innovative. Back tae Dawson's – it wis part o the Dawson group. And they were wantin tae start what they called semi-worsted. Ah went through and Ah had an interview and again Ah went through, Ah think it wis the Wednesday or Thursday, and Ah went. Ah says, 'Can Ah see the plant?'

He says, 'No. Ah can let ye see where it's goin and let ye see some o the machinery'.

And he took us up intae this attic and here wis a whole load o machines lyin jist in heaps. Ah says, 'It's no new?'

He says, 'No, it's second hand'.

Ah says, 'So who's buildin it?'

He says, 'Well, you could help tae build it'. He says, 'We'll get in an engineer'.

Fair enough! So Ah got home on the Thursday night and the Friday mornin there wis a letter, 'Could Ah start on the Monday?' So Ah went there and here wis this big pile o machines and an old engineer that had worked in a brickworks. He'd never been in a factory before. And between the two o us, we built aa this machinery up and got it runnin.

How long did that take?

Well, tae get the machinery, the spinnin frames were put up by a fitter. But the windin and the cardin and everything, we put them all up. And even the spinnin, they only put the basics up and the old engineer and I did aa the rest. Ah went through there at the beginnin o October and we made oor first yarn the week before Christmas.

That was quick work?

Aye. But we built it up and Ah wis there for four years. But it never really took off. And eventually they closed the mill. It wis nothin tae do wi the semi-worsted. Blackwood Brothers, which is part o Dawson's they'd one at Cumnock, one at Kilmarnock and one in Kilwinning. Ah wis in the Kilwinning one. And they decided that they were only going to have two factories. They decided tae close the Kilwinning one, so they put a notice up, lookin for voluntary redundancies. So Ah jist thought, 'Och, Ah'll take this. Get me back home'. So Ah put ma name in for it. And they said,

'Oh, no, you're no gettin it, because we want you to come up to the Kilmarnock factory and work'.

Ah says, 'Na, na. Ah dinnae fancy workin in Kilmarnock'. So Ah got ma redundancy and came back. Sort o early retirement, if you like. Ah wis only fifty-nine. Ah didnae do anything for aboot eighteen months. And then at the end o last year, Ah saw this job in the Job Centre and Ah gave the fellow a ring. And he says, 'Oh, aye, start on Monday if you like'. So Ah started, sixty-year-old, Ah got a job in Selkirk.

Aye, aye. So which mill is that then?
Gardiner's.

And what are you doing there?
Carder again. Back tae basics.

(Laughs) The wheel's turned full circle? You're enjoying that?
Och, aye, it's quite good.

Looking back, I'll keep one eye on the clock, and I'm delighted to hear rain on your window because this justifies me bringing my brolly. I've been trampin about all day.
Aye. So when do you get your bus, like?

It's quarter-to. And is it about twenty-five ... my watch is a wee bit fast.
It's twenty-five past now.

Robert Sanderson provided this further reflection on the dynamic nature of mill work.

Robert Sanderson, b. 1929, change over time

Before the Second World War, 1936, '37, '38, sometime around then, they had a reorganisation, where they – if I've got it right – was it the one process was sent down to Innerleithen and those who were doing the other process in Innerleithen were sent up to Peebles? So you got one mill in Peebles doing nothing but X and the mill in Innerleithen doing nothing but Y.
Ah see, yeah. Certainly the spinnin and that wis shifted back down to Waverley.

So the weaving came up here from Innerleithen? Was there any sense of rivalry among the workers in the two companies that you can recall?
Not really, no, no. Ah think everybody wis quite content in their own place.

There was never cat-calling? 'Och away, you work for Ballantyne's!'
No, no really, no.

Even the jocular sort?
No, Ah never, no, Ah must say, Ah can never recollect that happening, no.

Well, that's great. Now as far as you know, had Thorburn's always had the two mills in Peebles, you know, from the first time that they opened?
Yes, as far as Ah know, they always had the two anyway ... in fact, Ah don't know. There wis a third one, which Ah don't know if they ever had it, you know. It wis actually next door to Damdale. It wis called Damcroft.

Ah! That was before your time?
Oh, aye, aye.

Do you know when Damside mill was built roughly? Was it a very old building?

>It was, aye. Ah reckon it must've been nearly a hundred years when it wis knocked down in '68 there.

And it had closed by then had it?

>Yes, aye. Aye, cause Ah wis one o the first ones that shifted when they amalgamated with March Street and that wis 1968, June. So Ah think it would be about the end o that year that they knocked it down.

And what about Tweedside?

>Tweedside got burned down in 1965. That wis a fire that, you know, it went up in about an hour, aye.

What caused the fire, do you know?

>Jist some sparks off some machine or something, they reckon. But you know, the floors are saturated wi that oil, you know, for mixin the wool and that. And it pppttttoooaaa – and it jist went up, aye.

Couldn't be saved?

>Oh, no, no, no.

That would be a terrible blow to the workers?

>Oh, aye, it wis. That's right

To find they were unemployed?

>Because they all got shifted to Selkirk and Innerleithen and that, you know, a lot o them.

Not to Thorburn's though? Thorburn's didn't have any other mills?

>There wis a connection at that time with Selkirk, you know. But Thorburn's, Ah think, by that time had become Roberts, Thorburn & Noble. They were an amalgamation with George Roberts at Selkirk and Robert Noble at Hawick, you know. And they were a kind o joint thing there.

Aye. So workers found employment? I mean, there wasn't anybody left unemployed, as far as you know?

>No, no, no. Ah don't think anybody got paid off. But some landed at, you know, at different places. Some came to March Street, came to Damdale at that time as well.

Yes. Quite awkward for those who had to travel?

>Yeah, there wis quite a few obviously. The ones who did spinnin and cardin, they all got— they had all to travel to Selkirk.

How did they get there? Did the firm provide transport?

>Ah don't think so, no. Some o them had cars and that.

Because there wouldnae be any direct bus service there? It would be hopeless?

>No. That's right, aye.

Hume Davidson recalls his own experience of change from his working life in Walkerburn and Peebles.

Hume Davidson, b. 1928, changes in ownership and technology

Which was the larger of the two mills: Tweedvale or Tweedholm?
(Mrs Davidson: Of course, then they were baith the same mill.)
And they renovated it and they made the whole lot a weavin shed for the whole mill. They went thegither before the War. But ee see Dobcross wis the make o a loom. And there were Dobcross in the wee mill and there were Hattersley, that wis the other make o loom, wis in the big mill. Oo caed that the wee mill and the big mill. So they still kept some o the Dobcross, so there were two lots o tuners and two lots o type o weavers. Of course, a lot o them could do them both. But, as Ah say, Ah went to the pattern shop and Ah always remember the fire. Innerleithen Fire Brigade wondered how the best place tae run their hoses. So Ah directed them through the canteen, through ma pattern shop, tae put oot the fire. And aa their blinkin hoses wis leakin and ma pattern shop wis aboot a foot deep in water. And onything that ye'd left ower that weekend, well, there were shuttles lyin on the floor. Well, a shuttle efter it wis wet wis hopeless – it swelled. And they had tae be exactly the same for tae fit the metal boxes in the looms. And even ma shoes, people's shoes and everything wis aa ruined. It wasnae the fire that ruined them it wis the water! (laughs)
(Mrs Davidson: The far end [was] never touched.)
People come in anyway for tae clean up and then eventually they got things goin again.
It would be quite some time. A matter of months rather than weeks?
It wid be quite a while. Because they rebuilt the bit that got burnt and they made it intae a dye-house, ee see, and willae [willow] house. And it wis a modern, ee see. Ah suppose insurance would cover a lot. And the thing is, you were riskin your life tae try and put somethin out and you find oot efter that they're goin tae be in pocket. Ye know what Ah mean? (laughs)
Was there any indication at the time of what had caused the fire?
No. Ah think heat and wool.
Aye. Kind of internal combustion?
…
So anyway as Ah wis workin in the pattern shop, the Ballantynes at Peebles took over the mill. See, this mill wis individual. It wis Ballantyne's o Walkerburn. However, they were dyin off and Ballantyne's o Peebles took it on.
Aye. And when roughly would that be then?
It would be aboot '77–'78?
Maybe two or three years after the fire?
So they decided … well, they had a pattern shop here and a pattern shop at

Peebles, weavin here. And they decided tae make it all one. And eventually we wis shipped tae Peebles.

Nobody lost their jobs?

No. Provided ee'd travel to Peebles. Ee wis offered free transport, so ee didnae get redundancy because they were offering ee free transport wi the same job and the same wage. There wis one girl fought against it and she got her redundancy, sayin that – and it wis true – she wis a non-smoker and you went up in a van in the morning and jist aboot everybody smoked. So she went tae a tribunal and she won her case. But, Ah mean, well, Ah wisnae near ready for retirement. Ah needed a job anyway. So ee got the same job up at Peebles.

And, sorry to interrupt, it was a van, was it, provided by the firm, that took the workers to Peebles?

Aye. It wis yin o thae vans wi seven seats up each side. Aboot a dozen o ee sittin in it. Ah sometimes drove it. The van wis loaded tae start wi and then gradually they got less and less. But Ah worked up there tae. Ah done the same job at Peebles as Ah did here in the pattern shop. And Ah done it for quite a while. Myra worked there an aa. And she done a job caed the stake warpin that she wis tellin ye aboot. And eventually they got in a machine caed the Hergeth. A German machine. And it done Myra's job. If ee wid like to know how it worked, it wis a bank wi yarn on it. And it come through a grid wi things like that. There were ten levers and the lever put up the yarn you wis wantin, the colour. And there were a belt wi a hook on it took it roond this big cylinder. And there were belts and it aa moved along. So it wrapped the yarn round this cylinder. And then after it wis finished you had tae put a clamp on it. The clamp wis tethered tae two belts and they went round the machine slow. And ee tied the other end in bunches to a canvas on the cylinder and pressed the button and the yarn came off. It's jist like windin yarn round your hand like that, and then cuttin it, right? And then wound it intae a wee ball. Well, that's roughly what it was. And then after it was intae the cylinder, ee put it on tae a beam for tae go intae the loom. So that done away wi Myra's job. So Ah got taught how to do that and, of course, wi the one machine it had tae be goin all the time. So Ah wis put on tae shifts. So luckily Ah had a car, so there wis three, sometimes three o us on it and we would do three eight-hour shifts or two twelve-hour shifts. It would depend. Eventually they got two machines, but that wasnae tae a later date. It wis, it wis if you had a black job and a white job, and it wis the settins wis the same, ee had tae tie them thegither. And as Ah told you, ma grandfather used tae tie wi the hand. Well, they had machine for that, so we had to learn that. So if you wis a warp – that's a Hergeth warper – ee had tae be able tae tie wi the tyin machine, too. Of course, in a pattern shop ee've got your busy spells and ee've got your spring, summer and, ee know, aa the different styles. And in a pattern shop, ee had your lull, then you got your busy time. So they decided tae learn ye something other than the Hergeths. So they called it 'multi-skilled operator', ee see. So Ah got sent through to the weavin shed and the weavin up at Peebles wis a wee bit different fae what it wis in there. It wis, there were Swiss looms called Sulzer. So Ah got learnt the weavin. So and then eventually they got German looms in called Dornier, the same as the Dornier planes durin the War. And so Ah wis a multi-skilled operator. So ee got moved aboot a wee bit. (laughs) So Ah done that tae eventually Ah retired. Ah could've kept on because one o ma workmates, he wis a pattern weaver and he worked tae he wis seventy.

Well beyond retirement age?

Aye. Because, ee see, he wis a pattern weaver and there no such a thing now. You can hardly get them, pattern weavers. So, but Ah decided tae retire when Ah wis sixty-five, and Ah learnt a young fellow ma job and then after Ah learnt him Ah got put into the yarn store for tae do odd jobs and get him ready and then Ah retired.

So that was it?

That was it, aye.

That's great. You've a very clear memory and clear recollection of these things. Because it's so long ago and so many other things intervene?

The following extracts provide more detail about change beyond the big mill families. As this first extract demonstrates, the move away from family ownership was often unsettling and disruptive.

Margaret Gray, b. 1933, changing ownership in the mills

(Mr Robert Gray: A big lot o the changes came to the local factory due to change of ownership. The factories here that have changed hands in ma lifetime, aboot what, four, five times. And ye realise that with every change of management, ye get a change, different ideas how you should run the place. And Ah mean, at Ballantyne's when they run them completely on their own, they seemed to be sort o quite happily, sort o, driftin along, gettin their money – right. They could make their money and that was it. But then once ye get taken over wi people, ye know, if ye make X this year, ye make Y the next again year. And, ye know, it screws things up.)

The old sense of continuity was going?

(Mr Gray: That led to an awfy lot o dissatisfaction in the factories.)

I'll tell you. It jist came to me, really, what Ah wis thinkin about wis that the people that came, ye widnae have resented them [in the past]. An Ah've got to say ye resented them, because they hadn't a clue what they were talkin about.

These were managers?

Yes. They knew nothing about the job.

Where did they come from?

Ye got them frae Uniroyal – makin tyres, makin tyres.

Not even the same industry?

(Mr Gray: No.)

They hadn't a clue, hadn't a clue!

So these were people ... Ballantyne's sold out to whom first?

(Mr Gray: Ballantyne's first of all sold out to what they cry SUITS, Scottish and Universal Investment Trust, which was Sir Hugh Fraser's outfit. Sir Hugh Fraser then sold his share, I think it was probably fifty-two per cent share, to the Baird group. Ballantyne's then bought certain parts of their empire, as I'll put it, back and formed a company by the name of Scottish Worsted and Woollens. And then the Dawson group took over Scottish Worsted and Woollens, ye know.)

And all this was in a fairly short time?

(Mr Gray: It was in a fairly short space of time, yes.)

At times ye didnae know who the hell ye were workin for.

And managers were changed with each change of owner?

(Mr Gray: Management changes, attitude changes and everything.)

Ah mean, they would walk through the shop floor and they would never look right or left or say good morning or anything, which, it doesnae take much to say good morning, ye know.

Especially again in a small town like Innerleithen, where everybody, or most people, knew most other people?

Yes, yeah, uh huh. They looked upon you as if ye were dirt at times. As Ah say, ye wis jist a number.

(Mr Gray: This outfit that came that Margaret mentioned earlier, Uniroyal, you know. They came aboot 1969. They worked in some place in Edinburgh. And from the managing director down, right through, he brought with him about, what, fifteen other people, didn't he? And he put them aa into strategic places.)

So Uniroyal actually owned the mill at one time?

(Mr Gray: No, no. They came here. They were employed by whoever owned it at that time, to come here and modernise the industry.)

The whizz kids of management?

Whizz kids, aye, yes.

(Mr Gray: Whiz kids, aye, but professional management as it were.)

And that managing director once told me, when Ah wis challengin him aboot it, ye're no dealin with just an ordinary thing here, ye're dealin with a company that have, ye know, a sort o reputation for a very high standard of quality an everything else. He told me, he said, 'Look, it doesn't matter a damn,' he says, 'what ye make in this world'. He said, 'If you make cashmere garments, if you make golf balls, if you make tyres or you make sausages, it's all the same!' So, you know, what is the answer to that?

Nuff said, enough said. So you felt you'd had enough?

Yes, uh huh, yes. A lot o people left Ballantyne's hosiery and came to Murray Allan's as they got bigger. And they advertised more jobs. And we used to speculate in Murray Allan's about who'd be comin for this job, you know?

Aye, like throwing bits of breadcrumbs to the birds to see what kind of bird turned up to take it?

Yes. In fact, it didnae go down well in the hosiery that people were leaving to go to Murray Allan's.

(Mr Gray: No because it was aa vastly experienced people that were leaving.) Ah mean they had trained these people, ye know, and they were highly trained. Highly trained and they were leaving to go to another [mill].

Now tell me a wee bit about Murray Allan. Were they an Innerleithen crowd?

He was a local chap, yes, aye.

And he worked in Ballantyne's at one stage as well?

Yes, uh huh, uh huh.

And just set himself up?

He wis a designer, wasn't he? He wis actually a plumber to trade, yes, aye. And then he went into the designin and then he started up in Galashiels actually, on his own. And then he moved up to Innerleithen and he got very highly skilled workers to work for him, ye know.

And he was making hosiery items himself?

Jist exactly the same.

Aye, but with his own designers?

Yes, uh huh, uh huh.

(Mr Gray: Only, to add to that, by this time, to a much higher quality because he maintained the old, sort o traditional standards.)

He probably had seen what was happening in Caerlee, of course, that there was a decline?

Uh huh.

(Mr Gray: He saw the decline.)

He saw the decline, yes, that's right, yes.

And he stepped in. Now where was his place about then?

On the High Street, the old Masonic Hall, which used to be the picture house.

When you went there in 1975, roughly how many workers were employed at Murray Allan?

There was quite a lot o knitters. Aboot forty-ish? Forty-ish, fifty-ish, roond aboot there, aye, roughly, yes.

And from what you're saying, Mrs Gray, the numbers were going up fairly steadily as business took off?

Yes, uh huh.

And people, of course, were coming from Caerlee because they were fed up, as you had been?

THE MILLS AND MILL OWNERS

    That's right, yes.
Did it go on growing then until, you know, you yourself retired?
    Oh, yes, uh huh, yes, aye.
In that time it maybe went up to what, about a hundred?
    Over a hundred.
    (Mr Gray: There's over a hundred there now.)
    Over a hundred, yes, aye, there's over a hundred.
And that was pretty well starting from scratch?
    From scratch. But, you see, he didnae really need to train anybody.
They were all trained.
    They were aa trained, uh huh, yes.
And did you join Murray Allan's at a fairly early stage in that firm or had he been going for a few years?
    Maybe aboot three, four years, round aboot that, yes, aye. But he wis down in Galashiels, you see, and then he moved up tae Innerleithen. Ah joined him when he moved up intae the new premises that he had there, yes, aye.
So you did the same work essentially, passing there, and you carried on doing that until you retired.
    Yes, until Ah retired.
And that was three years ago?
    Three years ago, well, it's almost four, almost four, yes, aye.
It's a tremendous record of work then?
    Yes, aye, yeah.
And did Murray Allan pay standard rates or slightly above?
    Jist slightly above, slightly above, aye. But then it's the same as everywhere else. Ah think he got disillusioned. An then that wis taken over and it's now owned by the Japanese.
Since you retired?
    When Ah wis there it wis owned by the Japanese, before Ah left.
Just shortly before you left?
    Couple of years or something, aye, yes.
What happened to Murray Allan then?
    He died, aye.
And then it was taken over? Or it was taken over before he died?
    Now. It would be taken over before he died, because he went to live in the Isle of Man, yes.
He sounds as if he'd made quite a considerable amount?
    Oh he made, oh, aye, yeah.
    (Mr Gray: It wasnae the Japanese that took over directly from Murray Allan.)
    No, no, no. We'd aboot two takeovers before the Japanese, yes. The London boys and then there was somebody else.
    (Mr Gray: The London boys, what did ye cry them, Neil Bevin and Mike

Litchfield. Aye they took over.)

Mike Litchfield, aye, yeah, that's right.

A familiar tale in the local textile industry, then, takeovers?

Yes, aye, yes, yes.

But that wasn't too long before you retired yourself at least, that Murray Allan gave up?

No, aboot ten years.

Oh, ten years. As long as that?

Aye, it would be aboot that, Ah would think. Aye, Ah would safely say round aboot that.

In your last decade there you were under a series of new owners?

Yes, aye, aye, he got out and sold it and he went to live in the Isle of Man.

Did you find that much the same happened once these new owners and managers came in as had happened to you?

Uh huh.

It was the same story repeated on maybe a smaller scale …?

Yes, uh huh, on a smaller scale, uh huh.

… as what had happened at Caerlee?

Yes. The pressure was put on ye, although the quality was still better as it was in the Ballantyne's Sportswear.

But it declined a bit compared with Murray Allan's heyday?

It declined a bit, yes, uh huh, yes, uh huh.

How did you feel about that?

Ah didnae like it, no. Because if anything came back it fell on to you, because there was a way they could tell who passed it and in fact I got to the stage where, there was two or three o us and I used to keep a book with what they said was aaright tae go. Because they used to say, 'Oh that's aaright'. Then it come back. But they would deny all knowledge o sayin that they had said it wis to go.

I find it more and more difficult to understand that.

Yes. So it made you quite devious, too, didn't it?

Managers are paid to take responsibility but in my experience, it seems like very few of them are willing to take the responsibility. They will blame their underlings.

That's right, yes, that's right.

(Mr Gray: They put the responsibility on to someone else.)

Aye. Aye, it got to the stage that we got fed up wi it, so it had to be done and that was it.

So it sounds as if by the time you came to your retirement you were not too sad to go?

No, no. Ah think, really, by the time you come retiring age, you're wantin to go anyway though. So that was it.

But that was a shame that that's happened to you twice over, you know?

Aye, but Ah suppose that's what happens.

Aye, that's what happens. It certainly has happened in the textile industry?

Yes, aye, yes, yeah.
I don't imagine textiles are alone in that.
No, I don't think so, uh huh.

For Betty Muir too, the move away from family ownership in the mills led to a frustration with falling standards of workmanship and the uncaring attitude of the new owners to their workforce.

Betty Muir, b. 1922, decline in standards

So you went back into the mill, March Street again after your war service?
Yeah.
And did you notice any changes in the mill or in working procedures or anything?
It jist seemed to be goin on jist the same as when Ah had left.
Just the same. Nothing drastic had happened? No higher degree of mechanisation?
No, no, no.
Not a huge number of workers brought in or anything like that?
No, no, no. Aa the new machinery came efter that when they started getting aa the new looms, new types o looms, which Ah dinnae ken much aboot. But they did get different types. And different kinds o pirn machines, bob machines, more automatic things, you know, that you jist stood and watched and if an end broke, ye jist tied it.
So you went back and you became a darner after the War?
A darner, aye.
And you carried on doing that for quite a few years?
Quite a few years, aye. Ah wis tryin to remember who wis ma boss. But anyway he retired and this young fellae came from Galashiels, Brian Donaldson. And he wanted somebody to help him. Ah wis put in beside him to be what they caed a chargehand, to help him oot, especially wi paperwork.
He was a kind of undermanager was he?
No, he wis the foreman actually o the darners. But he had lots o other paperwork that he couldna do [as well as] give out the work, because there would be aboot sixty darners – sixty women in the flat.
As many as that?
Oh, aye, there wis a lot. And that took up most o your day. So he wanted somebody to help to do that. So that wis when he learnt me to count up, how to work oot the tickets for them, that they got for to darn. Everything wis put down on a paper, aa the broken bits and knots that hadnae been lifted and that. And they got paid so much for doin aa these bits. And he showed me how to count aa this up. That wis jist on a slide rule at that time. It wis later when we got the wee automatic machines in for countin up. And he learned me to do that so's he could get away and do aa the other big paperwork. And then eventually they got in computers and started up a computer room. So

he got the job, so that wis when they put me in charge o the whole shebang! So Ah got another girl under me for to help, cause there wis a lot o paperwork forbye – givin out the work to the workers and doin the pay books and things like that. There wis lots o other work behind that ye had to do. And ye needed somebody else really to help ye out. But Ah enjoyed it. But Ah didnae enjoy when Ah had tae argy-bargy wi the bosses, when they wanted maybe ye to slip back. There were some things on the darnin, if you understand, that you could let go. Nobody would see them. Unless ye had a trained eye, ye couldnae see these threads were missin. And some o them, when the time-study men came in, they wanted aa this missed. But Ah wisnae for this because wir biggest dealer then wis a French firm for Sportex. That wis men's suitin. And they were our biggest suppliers o work in Ballantyne's mill at that time. And they wanted it done on their pieces, and Ah said no because they liked everything perfect. Bit these time-study men came in and tae me that wis the ruination o that mill.

Really?

Yeah, they started sayin 'Let this go, let that go, let another go'. So the standard fell, and of course the orders for Sportex started to go downhill. And tae me, that's jist my feeling aboot it. It wis them that ruined it.

There was a big demand for Sportex?

Oh, yes, aye.

And Sportex was just the name of the cloth?

The cloth. The firm, Ah think. Sportex. Ah canna tell ye much aboot the French firm really, but Sportex was the name that wis put on the cloth.

Sorry, Sportex was the name of the French firm?

Firm, yeah, aye.

Oh, I'm with you. I thought Sportex was the name of that particular kind of cloth?

Aye, well their name wis put on the material, doon the sides, aye.

Aye, that was their name. Yeah, I'm with you now, yes, yes, I'm with you now.

And ye had tae be very careful with it aa.

You would find that pretty frustrating?

It wis, aye.

That you, as a trained worker, an experienced worker, were not being heard.

Aye, an they wouldnae listen to you, aye.

And these were fellows that would be Johnny-come-latelys?

Aye, jist time-study, aye. One o them became a director o the firm and the younger o the two, he's still in there as a director as well, as far as Ah know. And they knew nothing aboot it. Oh aye, we had some quite big barnies wi them but they jist wouldnae listen.

So it was a conflict between people like yourselves, who were skilled workers and were keen to get the standards as high as possible and these characters, who were after maybe quicker profits?

Aye, aye, yeah, let this go and let that go and get it away quicker.
…
Oh aye. That wis one o the reasons, when the mill started to go downhill and they said there were goin to be redundancies, well, Ah wis comin up to sixty at that time. And Ah wis goin tae be askin for early retirement. And when Ah heard there were goin tae be redundancies, Ah told the boss that wis put above me by that time, 'Put my name at the top o the list,' Ah says. 'Ah want tae go'.

But he said no.

Ah said, 'Yes,' Ah says, 'Ah'm goin'. Ah says, 'There's nobody pays the slightest bit o attention tae me here and Ah'm fed up wi it. Ah'm wantin to go'.

So that wis when Ah retired.

That was a shame that you should have felt obliged to retire in these circumstances because by then, you'd been working in the mill for what …?

Oh, aye. Well, it would be forty, forty-six years, aye, aye.

Forty-five, forty-six years. That was a shame to end your working life with that sense of frustration?

Aye. And do you know this, the day that Ah left not one o them came and said goodbye to me?

The management?

The management. And Ah stayed on extra times wi Peter Lavin, tryin tae help him wi some o the things he wis needin to know. And they never came near me and said, 'Cheerio, hope ye have a nice retirement'.

That's dreadful! Was that common in the mill?

No, no really. They used to send for you to the office and …

Have a wee presentation, which would be the normal thing.

Aye. Oh no. There was always a presentation. Ah told the girls no. Ah said, 'And Ah mean no'. Ah says, 'If Ah find oot that ye have got something,' Ah says, 'it'll stay in the mill'. Ah says, 'Ah won't take it. Cause Ah respect it from the workers'.

You mean from your fellow workers, aye?

Aye. Oh, management, you never got anything there unless you were fifty years, and you got your clock then if you were fifty years.

Did women get clocks?

Aye, everybody got a clock.

That was the standard presentation?

And £50. Ah think ye got £50 as well. A pound for every year you'd worked.

What about an occupational pension? Was there such a thing?

Oh, yes, aye, they had wee pensions, aye.

Just quite small?

Quite small, aye, oh, aye.

Were they index-linked? You know, were they linked to the cost of living?

    Ah couldnae tell ye because Ah didnae get one, because that wis aa stopped before Ah finished.

Oh I see. There was a scheme but it came to an end?

    There was, aye.

It didn't last very long?

    But it wasnae much. It wis only aboot thirty shillings or somethin like that.

So you don't at the moment have an occupational pension?

    No, Ah've only got ma pension, that's aa.

After working forty-six years in the mill?

    Years, aye. But it really hurt me, that. Ah wis hurt that they never came and Ah worked hard for them. And Ah got a lot o their work oot, which they wouldnae hae.

You were trying to keep the standards up?

    Aye, aye. It really hurt me that they never came to say goodbye.

That was terrible.

    And Peter Lavin could tell ye that. Ah wis wi him. Ah steyed wi him aboot another hour, when Ah should've been away because there were a lot o things that he didnae understand. And Ah says, it's terrible tryin tae gie ye aa this in an hour! He got flung in at the deep end. Aye, he did. He really did. But I enjoyed ma years that Ah worked there. Ah really did.

You found it a satisfying job?

    Aye, oh aye, aye.

And it was excellent materials that you were producing?

    Oh, yeah. That's right. When Ah'd finished doin whatever Ah wis doin, ye ken, and checkin it aa tae see that everything wis done, it wis a great feelin tae think that ye'd got that piece perfect again.

You'd created something, aye?

    Aye, aye. Ah mean, because it was invisible mending. Ye couldnae see where ye'd worked. Well, there were some, ken, there were some people that they were forever gettin told off. They were tight, what you called tight darners. They would pull their thread through too far and of course the minute it struck the water it would burst. And then it would have to come back frae the clean and then get aa redone again, which wis a waste o time. Jist for the lack o doin like that, ye used to have to do like that along the back o the bit ye had drawn in.

Pull your forefinger along it, aye?

    Along it. Jist tae ease it off. And a lot o them widnae dae that. As soon as they got the thread in, that wis it.

They were in too much of a hurry?

    Too much of a hurry.

Was that because they were on piece-rates?

    Piece-work, aye, tae get it off and get another one on. But then when they got their piece back to go over it again, they didnae get paid for it, so it wis a waste o time in the first place.

A waste of time. Frustrating?

And then of course, they fought for that after a while and then they had tae get paid time for any pieces that they got back.

While Betty Muir saw the drawbacks of moving away from family-based ownership in the mills, Robert Gray provides a different perspective. Here he reflects on the lack of investment which, had it been provided, he felt could have helped the industry thrive during the crucial post-Second World War period.

Robert Gray, b. 1926, decline in investment

On the whole, when you came back from the Army in the late forties, the fifties, sixties, these were the prosperous times. A sort of golden age almost [in the mills]?

But even in that prosperous time, there was still certain periods where there was a shortage o work because, as you say, because of fashion trends. And the textile industry is one o the most vulnerable industries goin for, you know, if anything happens, it seems to strike the textile industry first, you know. It's unreal. It's too dependent upon fashion, Ah suppose. And that, particularly the sportswear up there, of course. Well, they were always sort o aboot ninety per cent dependent on cashmere comin from China and Tibet.

Sorry, was this the Caerlee?

Yes, aye. You know, a lot depended on the price o it, what price they were payin for it, what was available.

These would be supply problems? Or if your customers are changing their attitudes to fashions and trends and so on?

It's always very, very difficult in the textile industry. Because they've got to judge aboot, sort o, maybe, three, four month ahead, what fashion's goin to be three or four month ahead. And they have got to get their designs and their samples out and aa the rest o it. And Ah mean, it's a hit or a miss, really. Ah mean, ye can get it dead right and ye can get it dead wrong.

Someone told me, forgive me, I've seen so many people recently, but someone told me – and it seems incredible – but, of course, you can understand how it happened – a major change was that in Scandinavia, where I think it was the March Street mill had provided seat coverings for cars to keep folk warm in the cold Scandinavian winters.

Uh huh, uh huh. All that trade was lost when the car heaters were introduced or were included.

(Mrs Margaret Gray: Yes, aye.)

And the Finns and the Swedes no longer needed this sort of thick tweed covering!

That's right …

You know, a simple thing like that over which you couldnae, sitting here, you couldnae begin to imagine would've happened. But it did happen! And it affected folks' jobs.

(Mrs Gray: Yeah, yeah.)

So in your time working in the mills and as a full-time official in the union you've obviously seen a whole lot of changes? The cumulative effect though, was that, as you said a few minutes ago, textiles have been badly run down in the Borders?

Textiles were badly run down because that, for donkey's years, they worked on the same machines as they had done away back in the past, you know. There wasn't the investment put into the industry that should've been put into the industry. Ah'm no sayin that that happens today because, Ah mean, that, as far as Ah've seen in the Borders mills at the present day, or up until Ah retired, there has been quite a lot of investment. But there was a period of time from just after the sort o Second World War up until about, say, oh, the late-fifties, sixties, that investment just wasnae there. And that was the boom time of the industry.

Why was there not investment?

There was too much money bein taken out, because they were more or less family-owned, family-based. And the money was bein taken out the industry. The industry that, you know, they didnae give back.

It's above all the Ballantynes you have in mind?

Well, they done it here. But they're not the only ones. Ah mean, ye can see it up and down the Borders.

Aye. Thorburn's as well?

Yeah, Thorburn's as well. Aye. Thorburn's, of course, they were bought over by the Ballantynes. Thorburn's never invested a lot.

It was a smaller concern than Ballantyne's?

It was a much smaller concern, yes, aye.

Now that's another – thanks – that's another aspect, of course, that you must've seen in your own working life, ownership and control in the mills? Originally it was very much in Innerleithen, Walkerburn and Peebles very much Ballantynes and Thorburns. The only exception to that was the wee mill up the Becket & [Robertson].

Oh, it was eventually bought over by the Ballantynes as well.

Ballantynes. But before they bought it, they had separate owners, the wee mill?

Hutcheson.

The wee mill was the exception. All the other mills in Innerleithen, Walkerburn and Peebles, were owned either by Thorburn, who only had a couple of them.

Thorburn and Ballantyne, yeah.

But Ballantynes, you know, the various clans and families, were the big owners in these parts?

That's right. They were. They owned everything, that, you know. They owned everything, they were on the councils, they could control things and, you know, that was that.

Now how did you find the Ballantynes, from the point of view of trade union organisation? Were they very, very resistant to allowing organisation within the mills?

They allowed organisation within the mills, that they allowed collectors to go round collectin, you know. They never objected.

No. They didn't try to keep the unions out?

They didnae, they didnae try to put ye down or anything like that, no, no.

Why do you think that was, because they seemed to be very much nineteenth century paternalistic mill owners? One would have expected that they resisted?

Yes, Ah know, you would have expected that they would have resisted any sort o form o that. But Ah don't know. Ye see, the Ballantynes, well, in recent years, up until it was aa changed, you know, the Ballantynes went out the business – no out the business but they were never members o any sort o group to ma knowledge anyway. They were never members o any group of employers for wage negotiations or anything like that. They done them all themselves.

This next extract, from Duncan Murray, illustrates one of the more unfair consequences of changing ownership.

Duncan Murray, b. 1918, effects of changing ownerships

Now, you went back in about June or July 1945, and resumed your pre-war job as journeyman dyer. How long did you work in the mill? Till you retired?

Yes.

March Street mill? You didn't work in any other mill?

Oh, no, no, no. Ah started there, Ah served ma apprenticeship in March Street mill. It wis only after Fraser – they came into the mill. They sold out to Baird.

That's House of Fraser?

House of Fraser. And Baird came in after that. They sold out to Baird. And then Dawson, Dawson International, they came in. Now Henry Ballantyne sold the mill and got in the mill at Walkerburn. And then he bought back that part o the mill there.

At March Street?

At March Street. Well, by that time, we had the dye-house there. And when he bought back the mill Baird wanted to keep the dye-house cause they needed that. So we were dyein for Baird with no dye-hoose. But they'd a dye-hoose in the mill at Walkerburn. So he kept that. So anyway, they were buildin a new dye-house at Innerleithen, Waverley mill, and that wis the Dawson group. So Ah transferred frae there down to Innerleithen.

So you were an employee of Baird at that time?

Ah wis an employee of Baird.

And you left Baird and went to work for Dawson?

Well, Dawson had taken over Baird.

When roughly did you go to Innerleithen, then? What year was that?

That would be 1970.

So you were at March Street from '45, when you came back from the War, to 1970?
  Aye, right up tae '70 but changed over frae Ballantyne's tae Fraser.
The House of Fraser took over Ballantyne's when? In 1947, '49–'50?
  Much later than that. Must have been well into the sixties.
So there was a very rapid change of ownership?
  Yes, oh, yes.
Fraser just a year or two, and then Baird…
  And then Baird.
… just a year or two, and then Dawson?
  That's right, yes. So anyway Ah landed down there, and the managing director o Dawson International he said that everything would be all right down there. They wouldnae close. Six months – and they closed the dye-hoose and that wis me finished.
'70, aye, so you were only there six months?
  Aye, Henry Ballantyne phoned iz to say, oh, aye, they were needin a dyer at the dye-hoose at Walkerburn. Would Ah be prepared tae go there. Well, that wis me out of a job, so Ah said yes. Oh, yes, if they needed a dyer down there. So Ah went down there.
Did you travel daily from Peebles?
  I travelled, yes by car. Aye, so Ah travelled by car. So Ah arrived at Walkerburn. And, oh, aye, Dawson eventually bought the mill at Walkerburn. Ballantyne's gave up the mill at Walkerburn and Dawson bought that. So I wis back wi Dawson, and Dawson closed the mill – closed the dye-hoose first.
When was that?
  Ah'd be aboot sixty-two or sixty-three.
So you'd been there about ten years when Dawson took it over?
  Aye. Well, anyway they closed the dye-hoose because they had a bigger dye-hoose at Selkirk, ye see. So that wis that. So the other dyer that wis along wi me down there that wis him out of a job and that wis me out of a job again. And Ah thought, 'Well, this is it'. But before that Ah got a message to say that they were a job [at Walkerburn], if Ah wanted to go down. Ye see, they still had the mill. It wis jist the dye-hoose they had closed then.
Aye, right, right. A job, but not in the dye-house?
  So they gave iz a job on the cardin machines. So Ah finished ma time on the cardin machines down there. Ah had three years there.
Three years. You retired when you were sixty-five?
  When Ah wis sixty-five. The policy at that time, ye had to retire at sixty-five because o the unemployment. So that wis that. So Ah retired then, and of course that wis me finished. Ah mean Ah never left the Ballantyne's, but Ah finished up wi nothing. Ken, ye're supposed tae have fifty years. Afore ye got anything at all, ye had tae be there fifty years. Ah lost aa that. No through any o my doin.

Changes of ownership over which you had no control whatever?
   Ah'd no control at all.
Did you have an occupational pension? You know, was there any pension scheme?
   There was a pension scheme, aye, but Ah lost out on that as well. Now one wis the Ballantyne. Now that wis transferred to Fraser, transferred to Baird, transferred to Dawson. And when Dawson closed the mill down there, that wis the end o that. Finished.
Sorry, when he closed the mill at Walkerburn?
   Innerleithen. The dye-hoose there. That wis me first and then Ah went back to Walkerburn. But anyway that wis it, that. So you could either freeze it or take the lump sum, less the tax. They were goin tae take the tax off. So Ah froze it. So Ah went to Walkerburn wi the Ballantynes after that. And they started another yin, ye see, so Ah started again. So …
You lost out there?
   Ah lost out there because, when they did away wi the dye-hoose there, that was the end o that. And it wis Dawson. So Ah lost that yin. Ah wisnae goin tae get much out o that. They said, 'Now ye either freeze it or take out a lump sum' – which wis nothing at aa. So Ah said, 'Ah'll freeze it again'. So Ah have a wee bit. Ah have aboot £10 a week over and above ma pension.
After fifty years?
   Aye. Oh, Ah must say Ah wisnae very pleased.
No, I should think not!
   And one o the Ballantynes, I retired, it wis in March. May, Ah met him and he wis goin on about it and Ah told him. Ah says, 'Ah didnae think much o the set-up and that now and how they did aa that'.
   'Oh,' he says, 'you wis one o the unlucky ones'.
   Ye see, it jist depends on your luck! (laughs)
You certainly were unlucky.
   Aye.
And after your experience in the War that's the thanks you get?
   Aye, Oh, that's whit ye get, oh, aye.
So you must have a certain amount of bitterness about it?
   Oh, yes. Oh Ah didn't think they did iz very well at all. Cause Ah used to do a lot o workin nights and overtime and that. And at one time, we got paid for overtime and latterly we didnae.
Now you became a foreman at what stage then? Was it soon after the War?
   Soon after the War. As soon as Ah come back. Oh, well, George Paterson, he wis the dyer. He wis still there. He would be maybe another five years. Ah went back there as the assistant dyer and he died.
About 1950 roughly?
   It would be about that. And Ah wis asked if Ah would take on the job and Ah said Ah would.

And you were foreman from that point right up until ... you retired in 1983, was it, roughly?

Aye, yes, aye.

So about thirty years you were a foreman dyer?

Yes, aye.

From 1950 until about 1980?

Yes.

That's thirty years and that was the thanks you got?

Aye, aye.

5

Life in the Mills

Having explored several aspects of life in the mill communities outwith the mill working environment, including domestic and community life and the impact of war, it is clear how economics, gender and the power of the big mill families meant that many of the interviewees followed a predictable trajectory into the mill. Often they followed other family members and remained loyal to the mill their parents or siblings (sometimes grandparents) were already connected to. The impact of two significant factors – changes in ownership and technology – are to the fore in this chapter.

Changes in ownership meant a move away from a paternalistic managerial style to one more focussed on profits and, in pursuit of this, near constant technological innovation. A film held by the National Library of Scotland film archive (*Border Weave*, 1942, Ref NLS0482) observes that while weaving has existed for thousands of years, the means of production changed remarkably over time. Innovation in the manufacturing process is evident throughout the interviews Ian made with the Peeblesshire workers. The working life trajectory for Ian's interviewees remained the same, but the means of production, the place of work and the products being produced, were seemingly ever-changing.

This chapter will look more closely at life within the mill and across the milling industry – in both cloth weaving and hosiery production. The focus is very much on detailed descriptions of different parts of the mill process and how these changed over time. As well as exploring different parts of the mill processes, we will also consider other aspects of working life, some of which have been touched on in preceding chapters. Industrial relations and health and safety were significant points of discussion in the interviews Ian conducted and examples are included here. There is no doubt that the mill environment could be dangerous, yet the interviewees seemed to be largely unconcerned about this as they related to Ian their own recollections of accidents within the mill. In other areas, such as career progression, pay, pensions and policies regarding returning to work after marriage, the gender bias is clear in the experience of older interviewees. There is also evidence of positive change in the accounts of more recent experiences. Girls often started at the in-giving and boys at the bar-filling. Progression thereafter depended on a number of factors and sometimes included a degree of individual choice, although the level of choice appears to have been weighted in favour of the boys. From this collection of interviews, it seems boys were more likely to do external work or embark on formal apprenticeship training. This seems to have been dictated by the opportunities given to them and the complexity of the job they were preparing for. As a general rule, we can also note that jobs which were more physically demanding were done only by men.

This first extended extract, from Ian's interview with James Howitt, helps to set the scene for this chapter and for the shorter extracts that follow.

Born in 1911, James Howitt first joined Lowe Donald when he left school, aged fifteen, in 1926. The following January he left there and went to work at Ballantyne's March Street mill. Of Lowe Donald he recalls, the workers had a reputation for being the 'the best dressed men and the lowest paid men in Peebles'.

As well as explaining the processes of wool sorting and carding, which James describes as the most important part of the milling process, we also learn about his wartime experience. Exempted from active service, James was involved with aircraft monitoring and provides an insight into the experience of war 'at home'. This account also highlights a number of issues which are pertinent such as the centralisation of Ballantyne resources during the boom years; changing production during the Second World War; improving health and safety and the impact and pace of changing ownership in the later part of his working life.

James Howitt, b. 1911, Interviewed 21 February 1997

Now how long did you remain at the High School?
    Until I was fifteen.
So you stayed there a year longer than the leaving age at that time?
    Yes. But Ah was very foolish, actually. Ah left the High School because all ma closest pals had left and got jobs. And Ah said, 'Well, I'm going tae', That's how Ah went intae Lowe Donald's.
Aye. Were your parents trying to persuade you to remain at school maybe?
    They did, actually. But …
You'd made your mind up?
    Well, they saw Ah wasn't happy about it. Actually, it turned out, it turned out aaright. Ah wis only the nine months at Lowe Donald's. And Ah started at 7s.6d. a week.
How did you get the job there? Did you go along and ask to be taken on?
    Yes. Yes. Ah went up … Actually, one o ma closest friend's father, was a manager of Lowe Donald's. Dyer, his name was. And they lived just down a bit from where we lived and the son and I were very friendly. And it was through him. Ah was never out their house, you know.
What was your friend's name? First name?
    James. Jim Dyer. He died in a motorbike accident.

Oh, dear. Did you have that job before you actually left school? Or did you leave school and then go?

No, no. Oh, yes! Before Ah left school. Ah got the job and then left school.

And then left school, aye. So you left school on the Friday and started on the Monday?

Uh huh.

And what were the hours at Lowe Donald's?

Oh, Ah think it was half-past eight to five o'clock, Ah think. An hour for lunch. Aye.

And you would go home did you?

Oh, yes.

Did you work on Saturday mornings?

No. Not in Lowe Donald's.

That was unusual in those days? Most people worked on Saturday morning, Ah would've thought.

Well, we didn't work a Saturday morning.

Do you remember if you had any holidays in that job?

Oh, yes, we always got a week in the summer time.

Was that paid?

Yes.

So conditions were quite good then?

Oh, yes. Oh, they weren't too bad.

Compared … I mean, we're talking about 1926?

That's right. Ah started in the mill the 10th of January 1927 after being in Lowe Donald since Easter 1926, when Ah turned fifteen.

Now just let me ask, what did you actually do in Lowe Donald as a laddie?

Oh, in the office. I was the office boy.

So you were a sort of gofer, were you?

A gofer, that's right. Ah took the telegrams and stuff like that. Ye see, Lowe Donald's bought their cloth from all sorts of people: worsteds from England and Harris cloths from Harris and, of course all the people that we bought the cloth from in Lowe Donald's, all their addressed envelopes, Ah had tae look after all the envelopes.

These were orders?

Aye.

And these were being sent out for the cloth, aye.

That's right. And look after the stamps and that sort of thing.

You took the letters down for posting and things like that?

That's right. That's correct.

Now the workers, the employees at Lowe Donald's, were they mainly textile workers or were they mainly clerical workers, office workers?

Oh, they were mainly textile workers. And they handled tweed.

So once the cloth came in what did they actually do with it?

Well, they cut it to order, you know.
So they were cutters really?
Most o them were cutters, yes.
They weren't tailors like your father had been?
No, no, no, no. They weren't tailors, no.
And the cloth was then sent where? To tailors, was it? Tailoring shops?
Well, it was sent out aye, to shops. Aye. Oh, yes. Oh, all over the world. And Lowe Donald's had places in Brazil.
Aye. So they were essentially middle-men, were they?
Aye. That's right. They were a warehouse.
Warehousemen, aye. Was that the sub-title? Lowe Donald, Warehousemen?
That's right.
Did you find that interesting work?
I didn't. Not from the office point of view. Had Ah been in the actual textile side of it. But it was the office side of it Ah wis doin.
And you didn't find that so interesting?
Oh, no, no.
Now the wage at that time, was that a sort of average, normal wage for a laddie of your years?
No. Ah think it was probably a little low. Because they used to say that Lowe Donald's employees were the best dressed men and the lowest paid men in Peebles. Because they got their cloth cheap, very cheap – beautiful blue serges. Ah had a Harris coat that cost me … the coat length cost me 7s.6d. (laughs) It wis real Harris, you know, the real Harris.
So you didn't really find satisfaction in that job?
No. But you didnae have to linger there too long before you got into the mill?
Now how did you get into the March Street mill then?
Well, again, ma mother was very friendly with a family called Dalgleish. And Adam Dalgleish was the wool foreman, the wool-store foreman in March Street mills. And through him, through ma mother, Ah got apprenticed as a wool sorter. So Ah was really in the textile business then, which was a very highly skilled job.
Right. So you were delighted to move from Lowe Donald into this job?
Oh, yes. And ma pay rose from 7s.6d. to ten shillings. And Ah thought Ah wis king o the castle!
Aye. Cause a half-a-crown was a lot in those days?
Oh, a lot o money then.
When you got the pay for Lowe Donald, did you hand it over to your mother?
Yes.
And she gave you some pocket money?
That's right. Exactly.

And how much did you get pocket money?
> Oh, Ah couldnae tell you that, maybe … About a shilling, Ah think, aye. Aye.

And then the same when you went to March Street? You gave your pay packet to your mother and she gave you something to yourself?
> That's right. That's right.

So you started there at ten shillings a week, which was an increase of twenty-five per cent in your wages?
> That's right. Ah wis in Heaven then! (laughs)

Aye. And what hours did you work there?
> Eight o'clock in the morning to half-past five at night.

So that was a considerably longer day?
> Oh, yes.

And did you work there on Saturday mornings?
> Yes. Ah worked then on Saturday mornings.

From eight o'clock until twelve was it?
> Twelve, Ah think, aye.

So that's something like forty-eight or forty-nine hours a week, I think, roughly?
> That would be right.

Tell me about the actual work of wool sorting. Was it a formal apprenticeship that you entered into?
> Oh, yes.

Did you sign an indenture?[12]
> Yes. Four years. Of course it's a very highly skilled job. And, we, well, Ballantyne's, of course, they were what they called a vertical unit. They made their cloth right from the fleece, right up to the finished article.

Everything was done there?
> Everything, right up. And we had about four, eight, we'd eight full-time wool sorters, eight, and one apprentice. I was the apprentice. Then when I got further up, went into ma second year, we took on another apprentice.

That hadn't happened before? There'd only been one in the past?
> That's right.

So that was a sign of expansion, was it?
> It probably was, yes.

It was just the two of you, two apprentices, all the time you were there? They didn't take on a third one, while you were still an apprentice?
> No. They took a third one after I left. That's right.

After you'd gone, aye. So it sounds as if things were expanding in those years?
> Yes, that's right. That's right. Then, of course the mills were changing then,

---

12 Formal agreements between a master and apprentice stipulating that a less experienced person would be taught the skills required to become a tradesman.

too. You see, March Street was a vertical unit: they'd wool sorters, carding, spinning, all the different processes right up to the finished article out the door. Then they had a mill … two mills in Innerleithen: Caerlee mill, who had spinning, carding and spinning; Waverley mill, who were a weaving mill to start with and then they put in four sets of carding machines and they became carding and spinning and then so much weaving and darning. Then they decided to centralise everything and they made Waverley a complete spinning mill. Took all the weaving and darning, cairted that up tae Peebles.

Roughly when would that be, Mr Howitt? Was that a good few years after you started?

Oh, yes. It would be in the 1930s.

Maybe ten years after you had started?

Oh, yes.

You would be well out of your apprenticeship by the time that happened?

Oh, aye. Because my apprenticeship, the last year of my apprenticeship, they asked me if Ah would go on to the shading – that's when they took on another apprentice – to go onto the shading, which was matching the colours, you know, with the dye. And it was quite, quite a skilled job, too. So Ah finished ma last year between the shading and the wool sorting.

Ye see, normally Ah would've passed from the wool sort, from the wool sorting, Ah would've become a full-time wool-sorter and it wis paid piece-work. But Ah never went on to piece-work. Ah got on to this shading. And then at the end of that they came and asked me how Ah would like to go down to Waverley mills. The carder down there, the carding engineer, was getting past his sell-by date, you know. And he'd be an old man. And they wanted somebody. They had somebody there but they weren't pleased with what he was doing. Of course, 'Oh, yes. Aye. Ah'll go. Ah'll take it on'. So Ah became a carder, went to be a carding engineer.

Just to establish roughly the order in which things happened. You started in March Street in January 1927?

'27. Uh huh.

And you were into your final year of your apprenticeship …

That's right.

… when you moved partly into the shading side of the business?

'32 … it was '32, that Ah went down.

Immediately you finished that, you completed your apprenticeship, more or less?

That's right. That's right.

You didn't work on at March Street for two or three years after your apprenticeship?

No … no, no.

So it was '32. And that would be before the centralisation of the three mills took place?

That's right. At that time there was carding and spinning in both places.

So you were only a young lad of nineteen when you went down to Waverley?

That's correct.

LIFE IN THE MILLS

Now what I was going to say, if you care to tell me just a wee bit of what you remember about March Street. At the time that you started there or while you were an apprentice, roughly how many employees would there be in March Street?

Oh, there must have been anyway, Ah would imagine, 600.

As many as that?

Oh, Ah think so.

It was quite a big mill?

Oh, well, of course, you see, they'd everything. They'd all the processes. Aye. Ah would say there must have been about 600.

Now among the wool sorters, were there any women wool sorters?

No. All men. All men.

You know, just listening to other people who worked in the mills, I formed the impression, which I hope is correct, that there were certain jobs and trades and tasks that men did and others that women did?

Uh huh.

And there were some, but not very many, where you got both men and women. I mean, before the Second World War?

That's right.

I think, I get the impression that since then, things may have changed? You know, whereas before, you would only get men doing certain tasks, nowadays maybe you've got some women?

That's right.

But in, you know, when you were a young fellow, wool sorters – that was a job exclusively for men?

Absolutely exclusively. Because there was some quite heavy workin, quite heavy work connected to the wool sortin.

Now tell me a bit about wool sorting then, if you would, please. What did you actually do?

Well, you'd different types. (clock chimes) Ye had Cheviot wools coming in as fleeces. And, they were rolled up, you know And they were rolled up in a certain manner that the tail always went to that end, you see. And they were on a table. Under the table was a compartment. Behind you there was boxes – a large one, middle-sized one and a smaller one. Those were for the different sorts. Now at one time we could take fourteen different sorts off one fleece – fourteen different sorts!

Now, forgive my ignorance, but when you say a sort, you mean quality of wool?

Yes. Quality, colour and ... yes.

Length?

Well, you know how the hind end of a fleece, the sheep is always dirty. That went under the table and was probably thrown out.

Thrown out, aye. There was no use for that?

And then the coarser types, the main sort went over the table to the end, where there was a big … it wasnae a compartment, it was jist put on the floor at the end. The biggest of the boxes behind you took the second main sort. Well, it was all numbered, of course. It was all done by so many cuts, you know: thirty-six cut, forty – that wis the higher the number, the finer the wool. And that's how you sorted it all.

Now how, again forgive my ignorance, how did you actually sort the wool? Was it done by hand?

Oh, yes. Oh, yes, oh, aye.

You felt it and you could tell, after a time, how fine?

Aye. And sight, of course, sight. Sight. I mean, you could see the … Well the fleece was like that, see. Along the skirt – it was called skirts. Along there was the coarser bit, you see.

The outer edge, as it were?

The outer edge. And then you came to the tail, which was …

The rough stuff?

Rough stuff.

That was rejected?

That wis rejected. And the skirt, you could use the skirt for certain types. And then you had the breast. That was the good stuff.

The finest wool?

And the back. That was the finest wool. So you had to have a knowledge of where the different sorts were.

Of course. And that would only come with time and experience?

Oh, yes. Definitely.

But you were under the instruction of the journeyman were you, as an apprentice?

Well, that Mr Dalgleish, who was the foreman, he came round every day and inspected all your boxes. And if you had a wee bit coarse stuff among your fine stuff, you were told about it. Or you could be out doing something else, like unloading wagons – we used to, sometimes we had fifteen wagons in a day.

Now, when you say wagons, was that lorries, not railway wagons?

Oh, no, railway wagons. We'd a railway side entry came right in. Ah've seen up to fifteen wagons a day and those had to be emptied and stored away.

Aye. It was the wool sorters that emptied them was it?

Yes. And, of course, you were paid time for that. You see, it was always piece-work the wool sorters were on. But you got time-work for emptying the wagons. Well, you might be away emptying a wagon and he would go round your boxes. You'd come back and there'd be a whole pile o stuff on your table! (laughs)

Aye, that he wasnae pleased with?

And if there was too much, you were told about it.

Now did he do that just for the apprentice?

Oh, no. No, no. He did it for the journeymen, too. Oh, yes. Oh, yes. Oh, heavens, aye. Everybody got it.

And as an apprentice were you under his instruction only? Or under the instruction of the journeymen around you?

No, under his instruction only, really. He more or less … You wis left to yourself. But you could go along and get the advice.

Aye. You could watch your journeymen at work?

Yes. There was one old chap next to me. He was very good.

That was maybe why you were put next to him was it? Because he was helpful?

It probably was.

He'd keep an eye on the younger people?

Some of the younger ones. Younger men.

Because it must have been very strange to you when you first went in? You hadn't done work like that before?

Aye, but you didn't feel it. It was very, very interesting, you know.

Aye, aye. But what I mean is, you know, you were sort of plunged in at the deep end really?

Oh, yes. But you werenae long in learning, you know.

That's great. So you found that work really interesting?

Oh, very.

And you learned quickly?

Oh, yes. You're not long in learnin. And then, of course during that time, I visited the Technical College, Galashiels on day release.

Oh, that was unusual in those days was it?

No, no. No. That was quite normal.

Aye. A lot of young lads had to go in the evenings to classes?

Uh huh.

But you went during the day?

I went during the day. One day a week.

Aye. And it was the whole day you were away?

The whole day, aye.

And Ballantyne's paid your fare?

Yes, that's right. That's right.

You learned about all the processes?

Aye. You got right from the very start – wool sorting, you know.

So you attended that day release class for four years?

Yes, yes.

Was it a service bus you got down?

No, the train. We got special tickets.

Aye. Ballantyne's would attend to that, aye.

That's right.

Were there quite a few apprentices went down from the mill?

Oh, yes, aye. Because, you see, there were apprentices in all the departments.
Yes. Weaving, spinning and all the carding?
Weaving, spinning, aye, and dyeing.
So there might have been what, maybe about ten, a dozen of you, going down to Galashiels?
Aye, there'd be that.
A dozen anyway?
Yes. Yes, aye.
And were they all boys or were there any girls among them when you went?
No, no girls. Not when Ah went. No.
No, no. Apprenticeships at that time tended to be for boys rather than girls?
That's right, aye. The only girls that I know were in the darning.
(Mrs Howitt offers tea)
So you enjoyed the day release classes?
Oh, yes. Oh, yes. Oh, Ah learned quite a lot. And, of course, … Ah did very well there. Ah passed all ma first-class certificates for City and Guilds. Ah did very well there.
So you completed your apprenticeship and then you were asked to go down to Waverley on the carding?
To help out on the carding.

…

It was a long day for a laddie of eighteen or nineteen. Do you remember feeling tired at the end of the day?
No.
So you cycled down six miles and worked, really virtually twelve hours, and then you cycled back six miles often against a headwind at night?
That's right.
But you didn't feel exhausted?
No, no. On the contrary. On the contrary. Ah would get ma tea, washed, shaved maybe, if Ah did shave, off to the golf course and do eighteen holes of golf. (laughs)
You must have been fit! Aye, you must have been fit.

…

That's great. Now tell me then what you were actually doing in the Waverley mill? What was the nature of the work?
Well, a carding engineer … This is very difficult to explain this.
But I'm sure you'll do it. (laughter)
Well, carding is a preparatory process for spinning. And a carding machine consists of a series of rollers. The main roller, called a swift, is about fifty inches in diameter and it's covered with … well, the easiest way to explain it, it's a cloth with spikes or very, very fine teeth. And round about that cylinder there are eight smaller, eight-inch diameter rollers, called workers. They're

also covered with this card clothing, this clothing with the teeth in it. And they're facing in opposite directions. So the two tease the wool out, you see. It's like a comb. Then there's a little, a smaller one still that works alongside the worker. It's called a stripper. That strips the wool off the worker and lays it back on to the swift. Hence you get mixing of different wools, if there's different wools, if there's different colours, you get mixing. And, finally, there's another one, another roller, called the doffer.

That's D-O-F-F-E-R?

Well, you know, to doff your cap, means to take off? Well, that is also covered with the spikes and … The swift lays its layer of carded wool on to the doffer, which takes it through and it's eventually taken off there and goes through another process. Now that's what a carding machine is.

Right. Well, that's clearly explained.

Now, a set of carding machines, usually consists of four units, built, as I've told you, each one, each one with a finer set of card clothing so that you get a complete range. And yet it's continuous. You've got different connections between each section, which, it's continuous. Eventually, it comes to the last part, which is called the condenser. It comes off the last doffer in the form of a very, very fine web. And it goes into this condenser, which is a series of tapes like that.

Criss-cross.

Criss-cross. And the web goes through there and each tape cuts its own width into a ribbon like that. Those ribbons go through a set of leather rubbers, which are reciprocating like that. (Mr Howitt makes rubbing noise with his palms) And rubs the ribbon into a round but no twist. Those are wound on to a bobbin, of which you can have a set of four or a set of six. The more bobbins, the more sets, the finer the yarn, right? Those are wound on to the bobbin and are ready for the spinning. Those bobbins are taken away on to the spinning. So that's the carding process. It's a combing out, mixing process.

Aye, which prepares it for the spinning?

Prepares it for the spinning. That's what it is.

It goes forward to the spinners on the bobbins?

Goes forward, that's right. It's usually, well, there are different types of spinning again. But the main spinning when I went down, was mule spinning. That's, eh, it's a development of the old spinning jenny, where they used to work it by hand. And there are 360 spindles. Well, each bobbin coming from the carding machine has thirty ends, see. So thirty intae 360: that's the number of ends. Where the mule, the spinning mule – it's all mechanical, of course. It's got a delivery. It's got drafting, where, coming from that to that, it's drafted out. I stretch it, you see.

Aye, aye, from thicker to a thinner.

And at the same time, there's a small amount of twist goes on to help the drafting process. And then from there, the third part is full twist, full twist. That's all controlled by the spinner himself.

Right. And this provides you with a fairly strong yarn?

So that's it. Now I've always said that carding and spinning, carding especially, is the most important part of yarn, of the whole textile trade. Because if you have bad yarn, you've bad cloth.

Aye, there's no way you can improve the quality.

That's right. So it's a very, very important job. And it's got to be very, very carefully watched.

So that was your task in the Waverley as carding engineer?

That was … yes.

To make sure everything went well?

I went down to learn. Well, an apprenticeship for a carding engineer is four years. Ah was there for two years and the old man died.

He was the foreman was he?

He was the foreman. He died. So they sent for me to go up to the office at Peebles and see the boss. He asked me if Ah was willing to carry on. I said, 'Oh, yes. I'm willing to carry on,' Ah says, 'I'll do my best, anyway'. Ah says, 'If Ah don't make out,' Ah says, 'can I come back to my own job?'

'Oh, yes, oh, certainly, certainly.'

That's to say, they were asking you to become the foreman?

That's right.

Aye. That was quite an honour for you then?

Aye.

After only two years?

Well, it was to take over, you see. I said, 'All right'. Well, again, I was very fortunate. There was an old chap there. He was terrific. He was just a carding-machine attendant but he was a chargehand. And he knew the thing from A to Z. And Ah learned the job in no time at all.

Aye. It didn't really take four years to learn it? You had substantially learned it in two years?

That's right.

Otherwise they wouldnae have asked you to become the foreman?

That's right.

So at that stage you were only twenty-one or twenty-two?

That's right.

And you became a foreman, and a carding engineer?

That's right. Ah became the youngest foreman at twenty-one. That's right.

That was very unusual? Because presumably even if you had completed the four year's apprenticeship, a few years might have passed in the ordinary course of events before you became a foreman?

Oh, yes, definitely. No question. That's right.

So that was very young indeed?

That's right. So that's how I finished up there.

Aye. And how many carders were there in the Waverley mill then?

You mean carding engineers?

Aye, carding because carding engineers were separate from the carders? Your job as carding engineer was to look after the machinery? That was all?

That's right. That's right.

So there was just the two of you? The old foreman, who died, and yourself as apprentice?

That's right.

And then when he died you took over his job?

That's right.

But there was also this other fellow, the chargehand was he? Or was he a chargehand carder?

Oh, he wis. But he died, too.

He died too, aye. So there were really just the two of you? The old chap, who died?

Uh huh. And Ah wis left maself after that.

Yourself. Aye. I mean, there were journeymen carding engineers? It was just the old foreman, who died?

That's right. And then, of course, through time, I appointed a chargehand of my own. A young chap. And that was it.

That was it. Good. That's excellent. Thanks very much. Now just one or two other things that occur to me. In the March Street mills, when you first went there – this question arises from what you were saying about the old foreman who died – were there workers, either in March Street or in the Waverley mills, who were there beyond the normal age of retirement? Say, sixty-five. You know, were there some quite old people, men or women, when you started? Or in your early years in the mills? Did they all retire sharp at sixty or sixty-five? Or did some of them go on?

No. Some of them went on, aye. Quite a few of them went on, in fact.

This old foreman, who died, for instance. I gathered that he was maybe more than sixty-five was he, when he died?

Oh, no, Ah don't know.

Or was it just that you were a young fellow, so anybody who was over thirty seemed old to you?

That's right, aye.

But you can't remember any workers who were maybe in their seventies or maybe their eighties, in the mills?

No, not really. Ah don't think Ah don't recollect any as old as that.

They tended to retire when they were sixty-five or later sixties maybe, aye?

That's right. There weren't so very many lived to that, to seventy, in those days.

Aye, aye, that's right, the expectation of life has increased a lot.

229

No. Ah can't think of any.

Now another question. Again it's not easy, it's a long time ago – but even just a rough idea. When you were in March Street – you were there roughly four years before you came down to Waverley – what would the proportion of men and women in the mill be? Was it far more men? Or was it fifty/fifty, men and women?

Ah would say it was about … Ah would say about fifty/fifty. Because most, all your weavers were women, all your darners were women. (clock chimes) And there were quite a number of those. Aye, it would be about fifty/fifty.

And you were there for two or three years before the centralisation took place?

That's right.

So in those few years, I know it's a long time ago, and it was only two or three years before things changed radically.

That's right. Ah think there'd be more, Ah think there'd be more women than men in the Waverley.

More women than men?

Aye. Because you only had four sets of carding machines and two, four, six, eight, ten – ten pairs of mules. And there were only … aye, that's right. But you had a lot o darners. A lot o darners then. And it was all women weavers.

Aye. So that was a difference between March Street and …?

That's right.

But on the whole they were about fifty/fifty in March Street? But in Waverley there were rather more women than men?

Ah would say so.

In those early years?

That's right.

Things may have changed after the centralisation?

Oh, they changed after that. That's right.

That's great. That's fine. Now another question that occurs to me. When you were an apprentice in March Street what, generally, was the sort of atmosphere in the mill? What were the relations between the workers and management? You know, was it friendly? Was it hostile? Were managers and directors unapproachable or were they coming round and, you know, sort of friendly relationships?

No. Ah think they had a very good rapport. Very good. Ballantyne's were excellent people, excellent people to work. Ah never saw a bad manager.

No, no. They were all efficient and approachable?

Yes, they were always very helpful.

It wasnae … You know, nowadays a lot of people find that management is breathing heavily down their necks all the time?

Yes. Too much of that.

And it's intimidation and … I don't just mean in textile mills, I mean, speaking generally, you know?

That's right.

But you never found that?
 No. No, Ah never found that, no.
Was that the case also in Waverley?
 That's right, yes. Oh, aye.
Aye. Now were the Ballantynes, that was D. Ballantyne, who owned March Street mills and Waverley? There were several brothers, was it?
 That's right.
They were the directors?
 That's right. They were the directors.
And then underneath them, you had managers in the various departments?
 That's right. That's correct.
And then underneath them you had the foremen and forewomen?
 That's right.
Were there any forewomen in March Street, when you were there as an apprentice?
 No, Ah don't think so.
No. The foremen were men?
 Aye, because even in the darning shed it was a man.
Things have maybe been changed a bit there in more recent times?
 That's right.
And it was the same at Waverley, that one or more of the Ballantynes, maybe, was in the mill was he as director?
 Ah, but he wasn't resident there, no.
No. He just came down from Peebles?
 That's right. He came down maybe every day or something like that.
And then under him, sub-managers, foremen and so on?
 That's right, foremen.
Were there any forewomen at Waverley, when you ...?
 No, no. No, they were all men.
Aye. That's great. Now another point that occurs to me, as an apprentice were you a member of a trade union? Or could you have joined a trade union indeed? Because some apprentices ... in some trades, apprentices werenae allowed to join the union?
 Ah never was a member. No.
No. Was there a union in March Street? As far as you know?
 Oh, yes. Oh, yes.
Which union was that, then?
 Eh, Textile, eh, what was it ... Dyers and Textile?
The National Union of Dyers and Bleachers?[13]
 And then it became, it became ... That's right. Then it became the Transport and General Workers. Mind you, when I went in there first, there was no

---

13 The National Union of Dyers, Bleachers and Textile Workers was formed in 1936, amalgamating with the Transport and General Workers Union in 1982.

union. Ah don't think there was any union when I went in at first.
In March Street, no. That's what I was trying to ascertain, aye.
That's right. Ah don't think so. Ah think union was a dirty word in those days. No. No, Ah never was.
In some industries, I don't know about textiles, but in some industries, apprentices weren't allowed to join unions, you know. And then when you came down to Waverley mills, was the position much the same there? The union wasn't very active or maybe didn't exist at all?
It was beginning to get pretty active then, oh, yes [in the early thirties] Ah never was a member of a union.
No. Did anybody ever ask you to join?
No. Of course, Ah was a foreman right from the start.
Yes. You were unusual. You went from apprenticeship straight to being a foreman?
Ah was kind o unique as far as that was concerned.
Aye. That's great. So you were there for about three or four or five years at Waverley and then the company centralised things, rationalised things?
That's right. That's right.
And just tell me what happened? There was a bit of exchanging of spinning and weaving?
Well, they had four sets of carding machines at March Street. They'd four sets at Caerlee, carding machines. And they had four sets at Waverley. So they took, as Ah said, they took all the darning and all the weaving and finishing away from Waverley and brought all the carding and spinning and sent it to March Street. Brought all the carding, the four sets of carding machines and the four sets of carding machines from Caerlee – that was eight. And the four, the four that were already at Waverley. And that was all the carding machines: twelve sets.
So, as it were, to an ignoramus like me, the early, the initial, the preliminary, the first processes, that's the carding and the spinning, were centralised at Waverley?
That's right. And the wool sorting. They still had wool sorting. And there was wool sorting came down from Peebles, too.
Aye. And then the later stages of the process were centralised at March Street mills: the weaving, the darning, the dyeing, was it?
Dyeing was up there.
Aye. That was shifted from Waverley mills?
That's right.
Now was Caerlee still a tweed mill at that time in the thirties? It hadn't become a hosiery mill?
Well, it was, eh, the hosiery actually started in March Street mills, in a small corner of the weaving shed.
Was that when you were an apprentice? Or was it before you went there? Or after you'd been there for some time?

Ha, ha! Now I'm not very sure about that.
I had the impression that Caerlee began hosiery somewhere in the 1920s. Maybe just about the time that you were starting at March Street?
Aye. Of course, aye, that's right. You're quite right.
But they still had carding machines at Caerlee?
Oh, they still had, aye. It was a separate thing altogether.
And they were put into the Waverley. That's great. Now you were saying, too, that naturally the workers had to move from Peebles to Innerleithen?
That's right. Yes, yes.
And from Innerleithen to Peebles. Did that mean that some workers came down permanently to live in Innerleithen? Or was it simply that the vast majority just travelled back and forth?
Well, Ah think the majority at that time travelled backward and forwards on buses. They got special workers' tickets. And they had to pay for those themselves. But they got special fares, special concession fares.
But even so it was quite, I suppose, quite an extra bit of outlay?
That's right. That's right.
I take it nobody was sent from Caerlee up to Peebles?
No.
No. It was from the Waverley to March Street?
That's right.
And from March Street to the Waverley?
That's right.
So taking the Waverley first, roughly how many workers who had been employed there were transferred to Peebles? Would it be a hundred? Two hundred? It's so long ago today. We're talking really about sixty years ago.
Well, in the carding flat, that would be what … two, four, eight, ten. There'd be twelve in the carding flat. And another maybe, two, four, six, eight, ten, twelve, fourteen, twenty, twenty-four, thirty, forty-two, fifty. Oh, Ah would say maybe about a hundred.
Aye. Aye. Somewhere between maybe sixty/seventy and a hundred? Roughly speaking?
Aye. Maybe a hundred is just too many.
Yeah. Maybe seventy, eighty, ninety?
That's right.
And they were transferred with their work from Waverley to Peebles? And was there a similar number transferred from Peebles down to Waverley?
That's right.
You know, somewhere between fifty and a hundred workers, aye?
Aye, aye.
That's great. That's excellent. Now presumably, am I right in thinking that most of the people employed at the Waverley mill, who were transferred to Peebles, would be women? Because they were working on the weaving and darning side?

That's right. That's right.
Whereas conversely most of the workers coming from Peebles to Waverley were men?
Were men. That's right.
So there you were. You'd been working in the Waverley for maybe three or four years when this transfer, this centralisation took place?
That's right.
It was somewhere, I think, about 1937, if I've got it right, '37/'38, not long before the War?
That's right.
By which time you'd been in the Waverley for three, four, five years?
That's right, that's right.
Now in your own case when did you come to live in Innerleithen? Was it at that stage?
1939.
So that was a year or two after the transfer, the centralisation had taken place, before you yourself came to live?
That's right. That's right … before the outbreak o war. That's right, because we were married in 1939.
An unfortunate time to choose to get married! (laughs)
Aye. (laughs) And again, of course, Ah was fortunate there because when they brought the carding machines down, the foreman at March Street [Jim Brown], he came down with it. And, of course, he was senior to me then. He was senior to me. Well, when war broke out, Ah went up, got ma papers. Ah was called up and Ah went to put in an application to join the Navy. (laughs) When Ah got there, oh, Ah took various tests and the last one Ah got was, they got a stool. And Ah'd tae jump up and down on this stool. And he went away and left me. Ah wis puggled! (laughs) And he came back, he said, 'That's enough, Mr Howitt.' He says, 'I believe you come from Innerleithen?'
Ah says, 'That's right'.
He says, 'How's the fishing down there?'
'Oh,' Ah says, 'it's all right'.
He says, 'Well,' he says, 'we don't need you'.
'Oh?'
'No,' he says, 'you've to go back to your job'.
Well, it turned out we were doing, making khaki and RAF stuff, for the Army, and we were going full blast, working night and day. And this old fellow, [Jim Brown], that came down from Peebles, couldn't handle it. (clock chimes) It wis too much for him.
Aye. He was quite elderly was he into his sixties, maybe?
Probably more than that, aye. Anyway – reserved occupation.
So Ballantyne's must have put in a word for you when you were called up?
Oh, aye, (laughs) because the chairman of the company, Mr Henry

Ballantyne, he was exempted. The other brothers, they were called up, but he was exempted. And he was given the command of the ATC, the local ATC – Air Training Corps. And, of course, Ah got landed in for that. (laughs) Ah was a pilot officer. Then rose to flying officer. Ah'd a commission.

Uh huh. Had you flown before the War? Had you been interested in aviation?

Oh, Ah'd flown. Only in one o those circuses. Ah got a free flight for guessing the height of an aeroplane when it passed over, which was held up in a field away up above Peebles. Ah got a free flight. It came right down over Innerleithen. (laughs)

You weren't attracted to going into the Air Force, then, instead of the Navy?

Well, funnily enough, that was another point. When Ah came back into the mill. Every firm had to have a lookout.

Aye, fire-watching?

Fire-watching, aircraft. And I became very interested in aircraft recognition. In fact, I became an expert in it. It was in the ATC. Oh, the Observer Corps, yes. We were connected to that. But Ah wasn't connected to it officially. It was just for the mill. I had a little tower there, where Ah kept all my binoculars and all the what-do-you-call-it. In fact, Ah was there the night o the Clydebank bombing. it was a moonlight night. And you could see the Dorniers flyin across the moon that night.

Aye. They flew over this way?

Uh huh. But they weren't right over the town. They were away down there [tae the] south. They come up the west coast. Followed the Tweed.

So they must have crossed the North Sea to about Berwick then, you think?

They must have. Oh, it was a terrible night, that night in Clydebank.

Aye, it was two, a couple of nights, I think, wasn't it? Two or three nights?

So Ah actually became very interested in that. And, well, Ah was made pilot officer and we were attached to East Fortune aerodrome. And, oh, Ah got quite a lot of flying to do and all kinds of things.

You found that interesting?

Oh, very, very.

…

Now at the time that you came to Waverley mills in 1931–32, how many mills were there in Innerleithen?

Well, there was Caerlee, Waverley, Leithen mills – just the three.

And was there not a wee one, Beckett & Robertson?

Oh, that's right. Yes. That's right.

Now Caerlee and the Waverley were owned by David Ballantyne and Son? Was that right?

That's right.

Who owned Leithen mills?

In my time, Hutcheson. People called Hutcheson.

They were the owners when you went down?
> That's right. And [Ballantyne's] took it over.

Aye. And who owned Beckett & Robertson?
> Well, there's a house just outside Innerleithen, when you come in: Taynuilt. Well, that used to be called Red Roofs at one time. And Robertson, he built that house and he was going to marry one of the Ballantynes. That Robertson was the Robertson of Beckett & Robertson. Ah don't know who the Beckett was.

Aye. Beckett & Robertson. That was a quite a small mill?
> Just a small mill.

Were you ever in it?
> Yes. We bought, we took it over.

What did you know about the mill before you took it over? Was it pretty out of date?
> It was doing fine yarns, cashmere. They were doing cashmere yarns, but not very well.

It was quite small? A small number of workers? And, I gather, many of them were sort of elderly people?
> Oh, aye. It was a sort o home from home. That's the type o place it was.

(Laughs) They hadnae kept up to date with machinery or techniques?
> No. No, no.

And when did that Beckett & Robertson mill close then, roughly speaking? Would it be after, a good bit after the Second World War?
> (Clock chimes) Aye. That's right. That's right. We closed it down.

Aye. 1970s? Sixties/seventies, maybe? Uh huh. And there were just a small number of workers?
> Oh, aye. It was just very few.

Twenty, thirty, forty?
> Ah don't think there'd be as many as that. Ah think there'd be about twenty. A couple o dozen maybe, something like that.

And what about Leithen mills? How many workers roughly were employed there, when you came to work in Waverley?
> Maybe round about a hundred.

And did they produce a fine type of …?
> Cashmere. Then we started making cashmere.

And when were the Leithen mills closed down then? That would be in much more recent times?
> Oh, that was more recently, aye, yes.

Maybe ten, fifteen years ago, something like that?
> That's right. That's right.

They were part of Ballantyne's, aye. Now in Peebles, when you went to March Street mill, how many other mills were there in Peebles? You know, when you were a lad?
> Oh, just the two, Ah think. Thorburn's and …

Would Thorburn not have two mills?

>Aye, they'd a spinning mill and a weaving mill. It was … Their units were separate. The spinning mill was down at … Where the swimming pool is. Aye. That's where the spinning mill was. It had a fire, a terrible fire.

Was it the case that workers in the March Street mills tended to remain there all their working days. And likewise, Thorburn's?

>Oh, Ah would say so.

Rather than people moving back and forth quite a lot?

>Ah would says so, yes. You might have got an odd, an odd one or two, you know. Ah think more would go from Thorburn's to Ballantyne's than vice-versa.

Were you ever inclined to move?

>Never even thought about it.

So the War came on and you were still foreman carding engineer in the Waverley? And did you remain foreman carding engineer right through the War?

>Yeah.

Aye. Right through the War. And you were busy, as you were saying, with your ATC work and so on. That must have taken up a fair bit of your time?

>Oh, yes. But, most of that, of course, was at nights. We went down to East Fortune quite a lot at weekends.

It would just be an occasional day during working hours?

>That's right.

That's fine. And anything else about the War that you remember? You were keenly interested in aeroplane observation and spotted the Dorniers going up to Clydebank. Any other incidents you remember from the …?

>Well, Ah remember the bombs being dropped in Peebles.

Were there?

>Aye. Incendiary bombs.

Oh? Was that at the same time as the Clydebank raids?

>Well, it was a plane supposed to be returning from that.

Just off-loading its bombs?

>It wasn't right over the town, fortunately. It was Venlaw Hill?

So nobody was injured or killed?

>No. No.

Fortunately. And these were the only bombs dropped in the area were they?

>That's the only ones that I can think of.

Were there any changes in the mills or their production as a result of the War? You mentioned you were very busy at the beginning of the War, making khaki and Air Force uniforms?

>Oh, that went on all though the War. That's why I was brought back. Because Ah was called out sometimes at two and three o'clock in the mornin. That material that went round the cylinders. If it broke it caused an awful

mess. Machinery wis broken. It had to be re-clothed and that wis another job of mine that Ah picked up. They used to get specialists to come and put this stuff on. They usually came from Yorkshire. And Ah learned from them how to do it and Ah put it on masel.

Aye, aye. This was the stuff that went round the cylinder, aye?

Aye. Uh huh. Ah wis on call twenty-four hours a day.

And were you often called out in the middle of the night?

Oh, not too much. But Ah had to be prepared to go.

Now was the main production at the Waverley mill then during the War; uniforms for the Services?

Oh, most of it, yes – there were huge batches. There were big 3000 pound batches.

And it was always khaki and Air Force blue?

That's right.

You didn't produce anything for the Navy?

No. Ah can't remember doing anything for the Navy, no. We did a lot of Air Force. And, of course, we did both officer stuff, the fine stuff.

And did the mill take on extra workers during the War? Or were some workers away and weren't replaced?

That's when women came into it a bit. A lot o women came into the mill then.

To replace the men who were away in the Services?

And then there was some pretty old men, you know.

Aye, that carried on beyond normal retirement age?

Carried on, that's right. That's right.

But women came in and were learning the jobs that previously had been done by men?

Aye, that's right. Especially on the spinning part of it, which was. Carding was a pretty dangerous job. And, ye got a few women but not very many.

But not many, no, no. So that raises another question about occupational hazards. Were there dangers from the machinery on the carding side?

Oh, very much so. Oh, very much so.

Did you yourself ever get injured?

No, no.

No. You were fortunate there. Do you remember anybody else being injured?

Oh, yes. Oh, gosh, aye.

So it was quite a common occurrence?

It was very bad, some very bad injuries. Ah remember some very bad injuries.

Tell me about one or two you remember, please?

Well, there was one fellow, this tape condenser I was telling you about, there were two big steel rollers. And they had grooves in them, you see. And he went to … Ah don't know what the devil he was doing, but he went to clean a piece of fluff off a roller. And his overalls got caught. And it was pulling him into, between those rollers. And Ah came along at the time luckily, and pulled the belt off and stopped the machine.

He wasn't injured?

Oh, he took a bit out his …

Out his side there?

Took a chunk out o there.

It would be extremely painful? Out of his side, out of his chest?

It was, very.

It was lucky you came along.

And then another one, another one, the first part of the carding machine was a … they called it the licker-in. And that's it. That's what it did. It went through two little rollers with heavy spikes on them. Not as fine as the carding. And then there was a bigger roller, about this size. About nine inches diameter. That was the licker-in. And it was covered and it was very, very dangerous. And if you went, you know, try to take a bit o stuff off it – stupid! And this fellow, it took his pinkie right off.

Aye. But there were others as well?

Oh, there was quite a lot o that.

So it wasn't an uncommon thing for accidents?

No. See the trouble was that there wasn't nearly enough precautions taken in those days. They became very, very strict after that.

After the War?

After the War.

So the machinery was sort of open, in the sense that you could put a hand in. But after the War it became more shut-in, did it? Fenced around?

Because there was far too many accidents, you see. That was the trouble. Ah remember a fellow losing his hand in the scouring house, between the squeeze rollers. You know, the end of the scouring machine. That was up in March Street, though.

So injuries that took place were generally in the initial processes like carding and the scouring, but not so much in weaving or spinning? It was more in the heavy end?

That's right.

And therefore it would be the men, apart from the war years, when some of these jobs were being done by women?

That's right.

Was there any sort of medical service within the mill to deal with that?

Well, every department had a First Aid attendant, you know.

Now, did you get Poles coming in to work in the mills after the War?

Yes. Oh, aye. Quite a few.

Were these fellows who'd maybe worked in textile mills in Poland before the War?

Ah don't think so. An awful lot of them were farm workers.

But they proved quite good workers in the mill?

Oh, very good. You see, an awful lot o those Poles, they were brought up, they had different jobs. They were trained in different things. There was one there, he was a mill engineer, he was a watchmaker. In fact, he started a watchmaker's business after he left the mill. He could put his hand to anything. He'd actually trained in each of those jobs. And quite a lot of them were like that.

Like that, aye. But they were good workers?

Oh, very. Very good workers.

Aye. There were quite a few of them came into Waverley after the end of the War?

Oh, yes. Oh, we got a lot.

Maybe twenty, thirty?

That's right.

These were fellows who'd been billeted in Innerleithen?

In there. Aye, that's right.

Or maybe some of them had married local girls by then?

They did. Aye, aye. Oh, aye.

So there are quite a few families in Innerleithen even now are there, whose father is or was – because some of them may be dead now – Polish?

That's right, aye. Polish names, aye.

But they've integrated? There was never any difficulty of integration?

No, never. Never. No, they got on very well.

So the War was over, you carried on still as the foreman carding engineer in the Waverley mill, and did that remain the case until you retired, Mr Howitt? Or did you change jobs or responsibilities some time after the War?

Well, Ah changed responsibility, yes. Ah became manager.

Of the whole Waverley mill?

Yeah.

Aye. When was that then?

Dates! (laughs) Oh, it was after the War.

Maybe the sixties?

Aye, maybe. It would be about then.

Aye. If you think maybe, you know, the Korean War broke out in 1951, didn't it? 1950 rather, the Korean War. Now that maybe affected production at the mill? Maybe you got more orders for khaki again, because there was a kind of remilitarisation?

Ah don't think so.

And did you retire at sixty-five?

No. What happened was that Ballantyne's were taken over by the House of Fraser.

When was that roughly?

Oh, dear. You know, Ah'm hopeless with dates. House of Fraser took over, but the Ballantyne's ran the mill. Then House of Fraser took over a printing firm called Odhams. And what did they do? Sold us out to William Baird,

LIFE IN THE MILLS

Holding Company. William Baird came in and they did alterations. Brought in time and motion people and all sorts o things. And then in turn gave it over to our greatest rivals, Todd & Duncan or Dawson [International] who closed the Waverley down.

Did they?

Aye.

Aye? When was that then roughly? That was while you were still there?

Oh, yes.

You were manager at the time?

I was manager. They closed the Waverley down. The reason was always said that they were the great cashmere people, you see – Todd & Duncan of Kinross. And, they supplied the sportswear, Ballantyne Sportswear, who was a Ballantyne firm, with cashmere. We started to make cashmere, and were making a very good job of it. (laughs) And he was losing his orders. I don't know whether you should put that in or not! So they reckon he bought the Ballantyne Sportswear [from Baird], so that he could get hold of Waverley. And he closed Waverley.

In order to close it down presumably, aye? As a competitor?

And funny, actually I was caretaker manager there after they bought it.

Roughly how long were you caretaker? Was it a matter of weeks or …?

Not for very long for he started sending work, lambswool work, which he couldn't handle. Wouldnae give us cashmere, of course. He started giving it to us, to do work for them, which is a silly thing after closing the place down. So we never looked back after that.

So it was partially reopened within a very short time?

Oh, very short.

And then fully back in production?

Oh, aye. And then it was eventually taken over again by Clough, who are Yorkshire. But they weren't woollen. They were artificial, they were synthetic.

Aye. Man-made fibres?

It was all synthetic – man-made fibres. But we were able to do the same work as they were doing but a different style of work altogether. But we could do it on our own machines. And that started that.

So it's man-made fibres in the Waverley now? It's not wool at all?

That's right. Oh it's only a ghost place from what it used to be.

How many workers are employed there now roughly?

Ah think there's only about thirty or forty. There were about 300 when I was there.

But you, you survived all these changes in ownership?

Oh, aye. I survived them all. (laughs) Aye.

Aye. So that was a period of really remarkable change in a fairly short time, wasn't it?

Yes, yes, it was.

241

Baird's, Dawson International?
    Oh, aye.
None of them lasted very long?
    It was a tragedy that, it really was.
It must have been very upsetting for you?
    Oh, terrible.
Because by then you'd worked in Waverley mill for about thirty years?
    That's right.
I mean, this was all happening in the sixties and seventies?
    That's right. Oh, the closing down just knocked the stuffing out of everybody. Luckily, it didn't last very long.
No, no. Then people managed to get back and get their jobs back again?
    That's right. Ah, well, there was quite a, quite a few that hadnae got jobs, you see. There was no jobs.
No jobs, no. It must have been a serious loss?
    Because there was nowhere else to go. But, oh, it was a great relief when they came back.
So an industry which throughout virtually the whole of your working life, had really been fairly stable, from the point of view that it was the Ballantyne's and they were there?
    That's right.
And there was, you know, inevitably times of short-time working, no doubt, but on the whole, from the time that you had entered, as a laddie of fifteen at March Street and then your years in Waverley you personally never suffered unemployment?
    No.
You had a wee bit short-time working now and again? Was that the case?
    That's right.
But on the whole the mills were pretty busy throughout your working life?
    Oh, yes.
And then in the latter years of your working life, Mr Howitt, the position was that ownership changed several times over and everything became a bit uncertain?
    That's right.
And that culminated in the closure of the Waverley mills?
    That's right.
Though that only lasted a short time? Was it weeks or months it was closed entirely?
    Phew! It never really was closed because there was quite a lot, there was quite a bit of orders still to put out. And, as Ah say we did keep some o the staff and got rid of all the outstanding batches. And by that time, Dawson started sending us work.
So it never really closed entirely? There was always some work going on?
    Never really closed entirely. Always somebody there.
But a lot of the workers were paid off?

No, well, not very many.
So it was a threat that proved to be on paper rather than reality?
That's right.
Aye. Most of the workers kept their jobs?
That's right. Ah mean, Ah got redundancy money. Ah got redundancy money but Ah never was off.
No, no. You managed to keep going, aye.
Well, they kept me on.
So you retired in your later sixties.
Ah would be about seventy.
So you've been retired about sixteen years?
That's right.
You retired somewhere about 1980?
It would be about then. That's right.
It would be about then, aye. And by that time, things had got back on an even keel? Clough's had taken over had they? And you enjoyed the work?
Oh, yes. I enjoyed every minute of it.
Hard work?
Well, Ah never found it hard. I mean, when you enjoy your work, you don't find it hard. The only time, as Ah say, was during the War, having to get out at all hours of the morning. But that wasn't a long phase.
No. And it didn't happen every night. Just occasionally?
It didnae happen every night. Oh, no. Oh, Ah could never have done it.
And then did you find the later years, when the ownership was changing so rapidly and often, did you find that a strenuous time? A worrying time?
Maybe, yes. At the back of ma mind, yes. You wondered, well, what's going to happen next, you know. But it never happened, you know. Ah was fortunate in that respect.
Aye. You managed to survive all these changes and remain as the manager throughout?
Yes. Well, of course, there's such a thing as making it survive, too, you know. I mean, I put myself out to make the job mine. (laughs)
Aye. But sometimes, you know, the forces in charge are too powerful to be resisted?
Oh, yes, oh, yes. The only shaky period that Ah was ... when Baird's people brought in the time and motion people. Because they brought in people that, well, time and motion, their theories on time and motion weren't what Ah would've called time and motion. Everything was speed. Now in the carding, in the carding especially you can't rush things. You can't speed things. You've got to go at its own level. Because it's a very, very complex job. It's a very tricky job. You've got to watch ... all the time. And that's why I started, I started a quality control system of ma own.
Was this before the time and motion people came in, that you started that?
No, it was after. Because they were, as Ah say, everything was, 'Get it out! Get

the stuff out!' They counted on the output. Well, but you've sometimes got to be slow to be quick.

And of course, you were interested in the quality as much as …?

Exactly, that's right.

The quality, you felt, was going to suffer?

That's right. That's why I got quality control.

Because Ballantyne's had a reputation for the high quality of its goods?

This is it. They gave me every back-up there.

But it sounds like the old story where, you know, the owners are desperate to get the maximum and the quality is threatened with a decline?

Aye. Well, you see, the Ballantynes were never like that.

No, no. But the Bairds were obviously?

Oh, aye. I mean, the Bairds they weren't a textile firm. They were an engineering firm. They're a holding company.

Is this Baird's, the old steelmakers in the west of Scotland was it?

Aye, William Baird.

William Baird, aye. Steel masters, aye. So, presumably, the time and motion study must have led to a bit of an upset among the workers in the factory did it?

Oh, it did. Oh, very much so. They would come and stand over them, you know. I mean, nobody likes anybody standing over you.

And that was very much against the tradition of what had happened in the past was it?

That's right. Oh, yes. Oh, yes. Very much so. And it was going to affect the wages.

Aye. So was there a bit of industrial trouble at that time?

Oh, yes. That's when there was trouble with the unions and that sort of thing.

Now any final thoughts then about your days in the mills that we havenae touched on? Any aspects we might have missed?

Well, no. They were happy days then.

What do you think of the position now? You know, is it a happier world now so far as the mills are concerned or a sadder world?

No, no, no. Well, the mills as such are no longer there. It's the same all over the country. Look at Galashiels. I mean, they had about twenty or thirty mills at one time. I think there's only about three left.

Very sad.

Oh, it's terrible.

17. Inside one of the Walkerburn mills in the 1950s. Ref: 000-000-044-501-C.
© The Scotsman Publications Ltd / From the collection at National Museums Scotland

18. An Intarsia knitting machine in Caerlee Mill, 2013. This photograph was taken by Ross McGinn shortly after the mill closed its doors on production.

© Innerleithen Community Trust

19. HM Queen Elizabeth II visiting Caerlee Mill, 1966, when the Border mills were world-leading manufacturers.
© Innerleithen Community Trust

20. Caerlee managing director, Arthur Oddy, who made a number of trips to America to encourage overseas sales.
© Simm, 2021

21. Advertisements like this one reflect both the popularity and high status of the Border mills products.
© Simm, 2021

Workers and the working environment

22. Waverley Mill workers, *c.*1955.
© Innerleithen Community Trust

23. The typing pool and friends, Caerlee Mill (*c.*1960): Margaret Nicholson, Sylvia Thomson, Madge McCallum, Norma Greig, Rita McDonald, Barbara Ballantyne, Nettie Watson, Chrissie Fraser, Georgie Park.

© Simm, 2021

24. The pressing department, Caerlee Mill.
© Simm, 2021

25. Workers in the passing department, Caerlee Mill (*c.* 2005): Mary Gray, Helen McLeod, Maureen Allan, Janice Park, Margaret Cockburn, Sandra Lammie, Pat Hunter, Linda McPherson, Elma Wallace, Charlotte Muir, Rachel Muckersie, Sharon Runciman, Lynne McDonald, Margaret Redpath, Ann McCracken.

Courtesy of Rose Johnstone

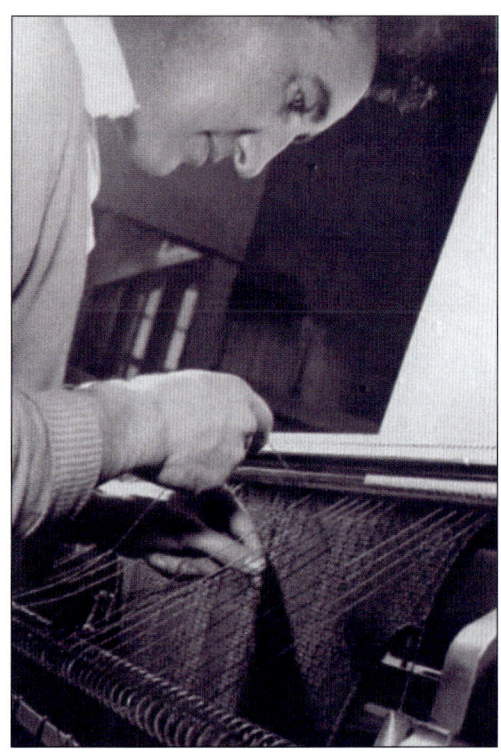

26. Dod McGinn working at a hand-knitting machine, Caerlee Mill.
© Simm, 2021

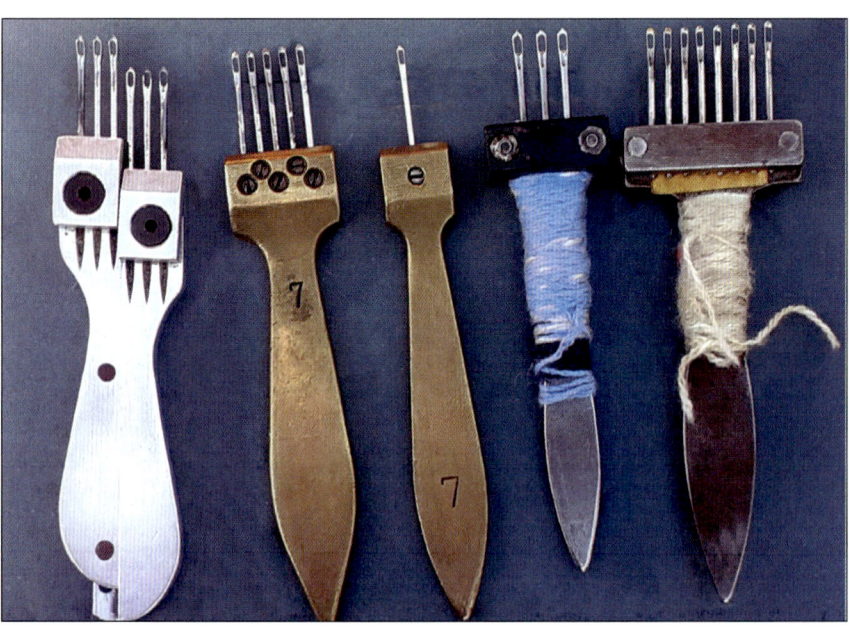

27. 'Ticklers' (these ones belonging to Douglas Barnett) were used for guiding threads in hand knitting.
Photograph: Fraser Simm

28. Peter Anderson in the Caerlee Mill yarn store.

© Simm, 2021

29. Louise Coulson finalising an Intarsia design for production, Caerlee Mill.

© Simm, 2021

30. Pat Laurie at a ribbing machine, Caerlee Mill.

© Simm, 2021

31. Janice Dodds operating a buttonholing machine, Caerlee Mill.

© Simm, 2021

32. At the end of a shift at Caerlee Mill, *c.* 1980.

Photograph: Fraser Simm

Other Voices

We now hear from workers in other mills. Robert Sanderson went to work in the office at Damdale, a mill owned by the Thorburn family, when he was sixteen. He was well supported in his apprenticeship in manufacturing, spending a year in different parts of the mill before going on to work in the pattern department as he told Ian in this extract.

Robert Sanderson, b.1929, Thorburn's Damdale mill, Peebles

Now when you left school then, what was your first job?
> Ah went tae work in the mill and Ah worked in the office at Damdale. Thorburn's. Ah worked in the office for the two years before Ah went tae the Air Force.

Now how, can I ask, how did you get that job?
> There wis a vacancy and Ah applied for it and Ah got the job at that time. Ma aunt heard about it on the grapevine and Ah went down to see about it.

Did your aunt work in Damdale, too, at that time?
> This was the aunt that didnae work, that heard about it. No, the other aunt that worked in the mill, she worked in March Street.

Now, so you started work when you were sixteen?
> Yes.

Just tell me what you were doing in the office?
> Office boy, you know, collecting the mail, doin all the filing and answering the phone, things like that.

Did you find that interesting?
> It was quite, aye, Ah didnae dislike it, you know. They offered me this job in the pattern room, to look after the pattern room, when Ah came back. You know, before Ah went away [to National Service], they said, because the chap that did the pattern room, he wis bein promoted to look after the warehouse. And they offered me that for when Ah came back. Aye.

That was quite early promotion for you then?
> Yeah, it was, aye. Ah worked in all the departments in the mill for about a year when Ah came back, you know. To get the experience. Ah did a bit even at Tweedside, which was the old spinnin mill. Ah worked there for a bit and Ah did all these before Ah landed in the pattern room. So Ah wis in the pattern room then at the back-end of 1950, Ah suppose, Ah started there.

Now when you started in Damdale you were sixteen. Can you remember what your wages were to begin with?
> It wis thirty something shillins, but would it be thirty-two or thirty-six?

[And, your working week] would be about forty-three hours a week?
> It would be something like that.

That's nine to five and nine till twelve or so on a Saturday. Something like that?
> Aye, that's right, it would be, yeah.

Did you find the hours long as a laddie, sixteen, seventeen?
>At first Ah think ye did. You know, after comin frae school, Ah think ye found it up tae five o' clock. Although you were often busy, you know, the last hour, gettin mail ready to go away and things like that. We often had tae take stuff across to the station for the train and aa that carry-on, you know.

Did you attend evening classes at all before you went to do your National Service?
>Ah did, Ah did for a bit. But Ah packed it in. Ah didnae like it. They wanted me to do commercial studies, you know, and that. Bookkeeping and things like that. A wee bit o that, typin and that.

So you work away in the office, just learning office skills really, until you went off to do your National Service?
>Yes, that's right, yes, uh huh.

Now in your own case, as an office worker, before you went off to National Service, were you ever asked to do overtime?
>No, no. Bein staff, ye didnae get overtime.

You didn't get paid for overtime?
>No, no.

Before you went to the Services what were your holidays?
>Ah think the mill got a week in August or the end o July, whenever it was, but the office ones, we got a couple of weeks, Ah think.

Did you get paid for those holidays?
>Yes, yes, aye.

You got paid. Right from the day you started?
>Yes. Two weeks holiday. We worked on Christmas Day, uh huh. And we got, Ah think, two days at New Year, aye. They had what they caad the October holiday and the May holiday, which is now a week in most cases, you know, but it was a day then.

Aye. And was that a purely local Peebles holiday?
>That's right.

Aye, aye. Two weeks a year, two days at New Year and a day in the Spring and a day in the autumn?
>Uh huh, aye, yeah, a day in the autumn and two days at New Year.

And you got paid for all these?
>Yes, oh, aye, ye got paid for them all, aye. Latterly, you know we didnae have a week in April, we had three in the summer, you know, latterly. Then we had a week in October. And we'd virtually a fortnight at Christmas, you know, aye.

So that was a huge improvement on your holidays?
>Oh, aye, tremendous improvement. That's right, yes.

As an office worker do you ever remember being put on short-time?
>No. Ah've never, ever been on short-time, aa the years that Ah worked. Never, never, never.

Do you remember some of the process workers, the weavers, spinners, tuners and others at Damdale in your time there, were they ever on short-time?

Ah think some of the weavers maybe were at times. Ah think sometimes they were sent home, you know, if they didnae have a job for them. And they'd be sent for when they had a job, you know. Ah don't remember that much happenin then but Ah know it did happen, you know. And then likewise other times when they would be workin overtime, you know, at a busy time.

Was overtime maybe more common than the short-time [in Damdale]?

Ah would say so, then, yes.

Now just tell me what you remember, please, about the various departments [in Damdale] that you went into when you came back?

Well, Ah first went tae Tweedside originally, you know, and Ah worked in the wool store for a bit, you know, which is where the raw wool comes in.

Where did the raw wool come from?

Most of it would be bought through agents, you know, in this country, you know, down in Yorkshire. It mostly came up from Yorkshire. Obviously some of it was New Zealand wool, maybe Australian wool.

And were there grades of fineness and coarseness?

Ah suppose there was, aye. Not that, you know, Ah would know much about it. And then after that it went to the cardin machines, you know, which takes it from wool intae a thread, which is a pretty soft thread, you know. And then it goes to the spinnin, where it's spun tae make it a firmer, you know, more pliable handler thread.

Is it mixed with anything at that stage?

It's mixed with oil originally, and that. Oh, there's various tricks, Ah think, that the spinners maybe use. Some oils and that on it, you know, to make sure that it's not gonnae break. But that wis the three processes there.

Were all these done at Tweedside at that time?

They were all done at Tweedside, aye, aye.

And then once the yarn was ready, it was brought over was it to Damdale?

It was brought over to Damdale for the various processes there.

And what were the processes there, as you experienced it?

Well, there wis the dyein, the dye-house wis there, where the …

Was that the first stage after the yarn came over?

Yes, or sometimes the wool would be dyed. Ah think the wool was sometimes dyed raw as well. And then it landed in the yarn store and there were various processes from there, you know, where it wis maybe on the twistin machines or that, you know, if it wis made intae two-ply or three-ply. And then, of course it had to be warped after that.

What did warping involve?

That's the long thread, you know, before they put the weft across it. The warp mills, which is a great big wheel, you know, and it's run round this great, big wheel in the width of the cloth, you know. And that's the warp mill. And it's put there on to a beam off the warp mill, which is the beam that goes intae the loom latterly. Then it comes from the warp mill to what they caa the drawers, who slay it through another machine. Ah cannae remember the name of it, but they have to draw it through so they're settin it up for the weft to go through, you know. It's drawn and then it's ready for the loom after that. And it's into the loom and the weft is put through it then. But the drawer has aa these, what they call cams on the back o this and these cams are aa programmed to lift up and down, you know, so that one thread's above the other and that, you know, so that the weft thread can pass between them, you know, to make the cloth.

Yes, yes. Aye. And you would find all this interesting?

Oh, very, aye, oh, aye. Ah did about a month in each [department], you know, roughly.

So that would take the better part of a year?

Ah, wis there a good year, aye. In fact I wis longer at the other end, when it got down to the darnin and shadin side. Cause one o the foremen there wis off ill for a long time. And Ah wis there a bit longer, helpin out there.

And what was your own position at this time? Were you described as an apprentice or …?

Ah suppose so. Ah wis, yeah, Ah wis more or less that. Ah wis jist an apprentice in the manufacturin. Ah wis jist learnin a bit about the manufacturin to see, you know, what went on and that.

And was your experience, the experience that other young people also underwent?

No, no. It wis peculiar to me. Other ones came in, you know, tae do one department and that. That wis goin tae be their job, you know and that wis them stuck there.

So, your experience was unusual, was it?

Oh, aye, very, very. Oh, aye. Ah've never known anybody else that did that, no, no, no. They jist wanted to make sure that, you know, that Ah knew a bit about [the different processes] before Ah went up to the pattern room

That was presumably because they could see that you were a lad with potential?

Well, and bein this, the young boss comin in, you know, this young Hunter Thorburn probably wanted his ideas intae it, you know. It wis him that wanted me to do that.

But, I mean, you must have been seen as a young lad with potential?

Possibly. They certainly wanted me to learn, you know, what was goin on.

Aye. But you found all this very interesting?

Oh, aye, very, aye, yeah, yeah.

There must have been a huge number and range of cloths, qualities and colours and all the rest of it?

Oh, aye, that's right, yeah, that's right, yeah, yeah.

And was that regarded as a very good cloth?

Aye, it wis good cloth, yes, oh, aye, yes. We used tae sell a lot tae all over the world, you know. A lot in America and that, America and Europe, Germany, places like that. They'd a lot o home trade ones as well. Hepworth's [tailors], people like that they did a lot of for.

Did you have anything at any stage to do with the export of the cloth?

Not at that stage but later on Ah had an enormous lot to do wi exportin cloth, aye.

So once you'd completed your year of going round and studying the various processes …

Yeah, Ah worked in the pattern room after that which wis sendin patterns, you know, out to all over the world. We had agents in about every country, you know, in these days. But aye. But Ah did the patterns, oh, till '63.

And you were sending patterns out?

That's right. And then a lot o people ordered lengths of what they had bought, you know, as a pattern, you know. And we had tae send out, you know, sample lengths. We did all that as well.

You found that interesting?

Oh, aye, yeah. That wis … aye, aye. Because Ah worked away up there maself, you know.

Yes. You were quite content to do this pattern work? That was what you wanted to do?

Oh, aye, yeah, oh, aye, yes, aye, Ah quite enjoyed that. And then, of course, Ah went on to cloth after that, you know, doin full pieces rather than small bits.

Samples, aye?

Yeah, yeah, that's right.

And again you're sending out the full pieces through the world, as it were?

Full piece, oh, aye, tae everywhere, all over the world, aye.

So there was a strong and steady demand in those years?

Uh huh.

You came back from National Service in 1950. Can you remember what your wages were once you came back from National Service?

Ah cannae remember. When Ah left there in '68 it wis aboot, Ah wis on aboot seventeen pounds a week or something like that.

And how did that compare with other folks' wages in the mills, as far as you know? I mean, were you one of the highest paid workers?

Possibly Ah'd be higher than some o them anyway, depending on if some of them would be on shifts or on extra overtime.

Piece-work and so on?

Maybe they might have been on more, aye.

Ahead of detailing the experience of workers in the Ballantyne mills, an account from Myra Little provides a good overview of different tasks within the milling process at Gibson & Lumgair.

Myra Little, b. 1936, working for Gibson & Lumgair

Tell me about the jobs that men did first, Mrs Little. What jobs were they?

Well, the men done the preparin o the yarn and things like that. When it comes in raw. And it's tae get washed and it's tae get washed and teased. And it had tae get washed and dyed. And then it has tae go in through the teasin machine for tae break it all up. Then it gaun tae the spinners.

Now before it goes to the spinners, were most of the employees men? You know, in these early stages of the process?

They were aa men. Even most of the spinners were men.

Were there any women spinners at all?

Ah cannae mind o women spinners where Ah worked.

No, no. Not in Gibson & Lumgair?

No. There could've been, but Ah cannae mind o seein them.

Almost all the workers up to the end of the spinning stage, were men?

Were men.

Now, on the weaving side, were they mainly women or mainly men?

They were mainly women.

Mainly women in the weaving.

They were mainly women in the weavin.

There were some men weavers were there?

There wis tuners. The tuners, them that set the looms up and thing, they were all men. The tuners were all men … nae women tuners.

No. But most of the weavers, or all the weavers, were women?

Ah'd say that aa the weavers in Gibson's were women at that present time.

And then the later processes: that would be the darning, checking, dispatch?

Aye. What Gibson's did have wis men lookers. And they were … You've got your web and your loom and you've got your leafs. And the men used tae come round every morning and check. They'd put aa the leafs down, they'd pull one up and they knew by the pattern. And they'd check it all along tae see that all the threads were there and in the right bit. Then they'd put that one down, pull another one up and they checked that. These were men. The men checkers.

Aye. Now what about the other processes? There'd be darning was there?

Darners were aa women. They were aa women. Men, men were in charge.

Aye, the foreman or chargehands were all men?

Aye. They're men.

Were there any women chargehands in your day that you can recall?

At Walkerburn, yes. But not at Selkirk, no, not that Ah can think o at Gibson & Lumgair's.

No, no. Right. And then the next process was what?

The passin and the darning. Darning and passin. And they were aa women. Again they'd aa be under the same sort o foreman, the darners, the passers, the markers. The markers came first. They pulled the web over and they could see by the light on the mat where an end wis broken and where a wrong thread wis in and things like that.

How did they mark it?

With chalk. They marked where it started and where it finished. And at the sides they marked where maybe the weft had broken. If it wis the warp they marked that way, and the weft the other way they marked.

Horizontally for the weft and vertically for the warp, aye?

Aye, aye, and that went to the darners. And they darned it. And then it went to the washers. And that wis men. They were aa men that washed it and hung it up for tae condition it. And then it went to what we used to call the press shop. The cloth wis put on this big press that came over a thing and you put a bit o material – cardboard wis it? A bit o this white cloth, material and then a bit o cardboard on the top. And they rolled it aa doon and they pressed it and left it like that overnight. And then it went to the clean darners after that. In case anything had been missed, it went tae the clean darners and passers.

A double-check, as it were?

Aye, it wis double-checked, aye.

And then it was the dispatch section was it after that?

In the dispatch bit. Then it got aa folded up or rolled down tae beams. Some o it wis rolled and some o it wis left full width on bales. Jist bits o cardboard, ye ken which you've seen in the tailor's shops.

Yes, aye, aye, tailor's lengths, as it were? Now were most of the workers at that stage women or men or were they just about half and half?

Men in the packin, but women in the clean darnin and thing. They were half and half. You could say the men done the heavy work and the women done the lighter jobs in thae days, aye. The men done aa the carryin and things like that. It wis heavy work, it wis very heavy work. You were tired at night. But you never thought aboot that. It wis jist life. It wis hard work keepin your magazines filled and everything like that.

There wasnae time just to sit about and fold your arms?

You never, you never got a minute. Oh, no! No way! Goodness, if you were seen daein that they'd have shot you! They'd have shot you!

(Laughs) So your recollection is that there was quite a strong discipline, work discipline, at Gibson & Lumgair?

Oh, aye. Uh huh. At Gibson & Lumgair's, we stopped one o'clock every Friday and the machines were cleaned. You went to the storeroom and the man gave you two paintbrushes, two dusters, and a jar o paraffin.

To clean the machine that you were working on?

Aye. The whole mill stopped at ma bit on a Friday at one o'clock. That wis immediately after your dinner break. And the machines were stripped and cleaned. Every Friday without fail. You had tae take aa your wee bits out and clean aa your thing, and you had paintbrushes for tae clean aa your spindles o

your machine and thing.
How long did that take, Mrs Little?
That took the whole afternoon.

Myra also shared information about the dangers of working in the mill:

So working conditions in terms of cleanliness and convenience, were quite good?
Oh, it wis good. Very good. Very good. Gibson & Lumgair wis one o the good mills for work in actually.
Now what about safety? Do you remember any accidents?
Oh, safety wis very good. Well, let's face it, Ah mean we were in the windin. The weavin wis jist behind our machines and thing. Ah think every factory got shuttles flyin out and things like that and thing. Ah got ma fingers caught in ma pirn machine goin back and forrit some day but, Ah mean, it wis only maself. It wis ma own blame that Ah done it.
That was when you first started at the age of sixteen?
Aye, aye, aye.
Was it quite easy to get fingers or [a] hand caught in the machines?
Oh, aye, it wis easy. It wis easy. It wis easy for the yarn tae burn your fingers.
Were burns to fingers quite common among the girls?
Oh, aye. Ken, like a yarn burn, ye ken. Aye, because if you held your yarn like that and let it run fast through your fingers, Ah mean, it did take a friction skin burn. But then a lot o them had, like, wee finger shields. They gave you finger shields.
The management gave you these, aye?
Aye. Uh huh. Uh huh. The darners had them made o leather. But the ones that we had were sort o bone. They were … They wouldnae be plastic in thae days.
Bakelite maybe?
Aye. Sort o somethin like that.
Something like that. A hard, a hard substance, aye?
It wis jist a thing like that, that slid over your finger.
Like a finger stool, aye.
Aye. It wis jist a wee short thing because when you started up your pirn, you used tae push the pirn on. You'd tae put a bit o wool round first the spindle, push your pirn on and hank it over the wee bit windin thing. And then you held it up like that to make sure that it started right and, Ah mean, it did burn your fingers.
Yes. So it was really just down from the first joint of your finger to the tip that it covered?
Aye, aye.

Ian asked all his interviewees about union membership and industrial relations and there is a section dedicated to this later in this chapter. For the moment, we can hear again from Myra on union membership within Gibson & Lumgair.

Now can I ask about trade unions? You had not been in a union in Woolies [Woolworths]. Did you join a union in Gibson & Lumgair?
Ah must've been in the union in Gibson's. Ah've an awfy feelin for years it wis sort o compulsory. You jist automatically went intae it.
More or less a closed shop was it, in Gibson & Lumgair?
Aye. Ah'm sure it wis a closed shop in Gibson & Lumgair's. It came off your wages.
Do you remember what union it was, Mrs Little?
It would be the Bleachers and Dyers.
Were you active in the union, as a young girl I mean?
No, no.
Do you remember if there was much activity by the union in the mill? You know, did they hold meetings, even if you yourself didn't go to them?
No really because Ah'll tell you at that age you werenae really that interested.
No, no. You don't have much recollection of union activity?
No, no.
Do you remember anybody maybe you worked beside who was active in the union, was very keen on the union?
No really.
Was there a shop steward within Gibson & Lumgair that maybe you went to if you had a particular problem?
Yes, but he wis in the weavin side, ken. Each department had a sort o shop steward. But the weavers and the winders and the throstle ones were aa sort o maybe under the same one.
Aye. And that was a man in your recollection?
That wis a man.
But you don't remember a lot of meetings or activities?
No, no.
Were you ever on strike in Gibson & Lumgair, you know, as a young girl?
No, no. But, Ah mean, that wis only until 1954. Ah got married, you see.

The Ballantyne mills: Waverley and March Street

Most of the interviewees had spent all or most of their working lives in the Ballantyne mills – across both the cloth weaving and hosiery. In this next set of extracts cloth weaving production and processes across the Ballantyne mills are described in detail. This includes: cloth sorting, scouring, dyeing, carding, spooling and spinning, weaving, darning, finishing and distribution.

In this first extract, Margaret Melrose – who was one of Ian's oldest interviewees – explains that she left school at fourteen with no expectation but to go, 'jist intae the mill'. Margaret followed a fairly typical trajectory for a girl. She went first to the in-giving, then the pirn machine and then completed her training as a weaver.

Margaret Melrose, b. 1907, Waverley mill

Ah wis quite satisfied wi the mill.

You never thought of becoming a nurse or a teacher or a postwoman?

No. Ah once said to ma mother Ah would like tae be a nurse. She says, 'Woman, if ye gin oot that door,' she says, 'ye'll no come back again!' (laughs) That wis when Oo wis on the dole.

Oh, aye. So did your mother not want you to become a nurse?

No, no. She didnae want us tae leave the hoose.

She was worried if you went away from home, was that what it was?

Uh huh. Ah dinnae ken if it wis that or no but that's what she said.

Aye, 'You'll not be back in again'. Were you interested in becoming a nurse yourself?

No, no.

Not really? Was that just something you said?

It wis jist something. The lassies were aa wantin tae get different jobs because oo wis aa on the dole. There were one or two went away tae America then. Uh huh.

Aye. Your sister who went to America, what had she done for a living?

She wis a weaver. She died oot there in the flu epidemic o 1918. Ah think she bade wi cousins in Boston. And Ah think she wis the only yin that died.

That was a big step for her to take wasn't it? To go to America?

Uh huh.

Because she'd still be quite a young woman then, when she went?

Aye. Uh huh.

Do you remember her going?

Yes. Ah remember goin to the station wi her, seein her away. Ma mother went tae Glescae wi her for tae see her on the boat.

What age would your sister be then, when she went?

Oh, she'd be aboot twenty, Ah would think.

It was a big step for a young girl to take?

Uh huh. Aye, in thae days.

And what did your other sisters do when they came to work?

Well, ma sister, one o them wis a darner and the other, she wis what they call a drawer.

Aye. Both in the mill?

Aye.

Aye. So you all worked in the mill? All the girls, aye?

Uh huh.

So, you worked in the Waverley Mills from leaving school [in 1922] until you got married ten years later, at twenty-four?
>Uh huh. Ma first job wis what they call in-giving. That wis for the warpin for tae get the bits ready for the weavin. Ah think Ah wis a year and a half, Ah think. An Ah got on tae the pirn machine. An Ah wasn't long. Ah think Ah wis a year on the pirn machine, then Ah got on to the weavin. An that wis me.

Aye. So you did the weaving until you got married?
>Aye, that's right.

You became a weaver?
>Uh huh.

That's great. Now what about the wages? What was your wage when you began work?
>Thirteen shillins [a week].

And that would be for those hours, which were probably about you probably worked about forty-eight hours a week?
>Aye. It would be forty-eight then. Uh huh.

And did you feel at the time or did people feel that was quite a good wage for a girl?
>Naebody argued, no, no.

Did you give all your wages to your mother?
>Aye, that's right.

And did she give you something back for pocket money?
>Uh huh.

How much did she give you back, Mrs Melrose?
>A couple o bob.

Aye. As much as that?
>Aye. (laughs)

So was there some sort of training for young girls like yourself, when you went into the mill? There was a kind of recognised series of jobs that you did, you know?
>No. Well, the likes o the in-givin, ye got shifted off o that. But the pirn machine, you could stay on it if you wanted.

Aye. All the young girls started with the in-giving? Was that it?
>Aye, aye.

Then after that you might go on to the pirn?
>The pirn machine or the bobbin machine. There were a bobbin machine, what we called a bobbin machine.

And did it depend on whether there was a vacancy in these other jobs, where you went?
>Ah think so, uh huh.

Aye. And then you could either stay where you were, once you were on the bobbin machine or the pirn machine?
>That's right.

Or you could do as you did, Mrs Melrose, and move on to spinning or weaving?
>No spinnin. The men did the spinnin. But then there were the darners, the darners and the shaders and different things.

Aye. Packers and so on? Now, very roughly, when you first began, you were only fourteen, roughly what proportion would be men and what proportion women? Would it be half men, and half women, or two-thirds women, one-third men?

Well, Ah think there'd be more women.

There might have been, say there were 140 workers altogether or 150. So maybe ninety women and sixty men?

There were more women because the bobbin winders were aa women. They had boys on the in-givin but no very much. An the pirn-winders wis women. The darners an the shaders an aa them wis all women.

The weavers, were they a mixture of men and women?

No. They were a weemin.

All women, aye?

But the men wis the tuners.

Tuners? And the piecers and the spinners?

Aye. The dyers wis men.

Men, aye. The sort of heavy jobs were done by the men?

Uh huh.

What about the packers and the despatchers?

Well, Ah think they were mostly men. There werenae women in there then, no.

But there were definitely more women than men, when you began?

Tae me there were, onyway, uh huh.

And did you find that you were soon earning more than the thirteen shillings a week that you started with? You know, once you got away from the in-giving?

Uh huh. On the pirn machine ye got more wages.

So by the time you got married, when you were twenty-four, 1932, can you remember what your wage was at that time?

Oh, Ah could make fae thirty shillings to £2. £2 whiles.

That was quite a good wage?

It was a good wage then. After Ah wis married, ye couldnae get intae Waverley. They didn't take married women.

Aye. As soon as you married, you had to leave?

Uh huh. But Ah got back for Ah think it wis six month. They were busy. And then Ah wis paid off and Ah got a chance o a job at Thorburn's in Peebles. An Ah went up there.

Aye. So, do you mind if I ask, was your husband an Innerleithen fellow?

Aye.

Aye. And he worked in the mill?

He wis in the washin, washin the cloth.

And he had always worked in the mill, too?

That's right.

So you met in the mill?

Uh huh. And they closed down the weaving bit part, doon in the Waverley and he didnae get shifted tae Peebles. They shifted some o them tae Peebles but he wasn't shifted. And he wis three year on the dole. This wis after Ah got married. And Ah got intae Thorburn's then at Damdale.
Aye. When your husband was on the dole?
Uh huh.
Was there a special bus to take workers from Innerleithen to Peebles?
Aye, that's right. Thorburn's paid your bus fare. That was 6d., 6d. on the bus.
That was a long day for you?
Aye. Ah wis aye rushin at the last minute! (laughs)
You wouldn't get home till about six o'clock, from leaving home at six-thirty in the morning, would you?
That's right.
Were you quite tired?
Ye didnae think nothing o it when ye wis young.
…
Ah wis jist oot the mill, oot the Waverley aboot a year, Ah think, and Ah got the chance [of work]. An Ah wis back for jist aboot six month. They didnae usually take ee back but they were a wee bit busy an Ah got in. But Ah wis paid off again an then Ah went tae Thorburn's an they didnae pay off married women.
So you weren't really without a job for very long at all?
No, no.
Until after the War, when you had your son?
Uh huh.
And you gave up your job then?
Aye. For five years. Then Ah got into the hosiery.
Once your son went to school?
Aye.
Did you find there was a big change between working in the Caerlee hosiery mill and the Damdale and Waverley?
Well, it wisnae so hard work.
Ah. hosiery was easier?
Aye. But it wis still a staunin job an Ah'd aye sair feet! (laughs)
Aye. So what did you do in the hosiery mill?
Well, at first Ah did what they call bindin. And then Ah did skirts. That's them at the bottom. An then fae the skirts Ah went tae the garments. They got aa washed an ee'd tae put them aa onto their tickets, ee see – the right size and that. An then Ah got on tae what they caad the rippin oot. That wis a sittin job. That wis the last job Ah wis on.
Now what did ripping out involve then? What did you do when you were doing that?
Well, it's these skirts. There are different persons makes them, ee see. And

there's these stitchin, ee've tae rip and get the stitches ready for them tae put on for tae join them up.

Join them up into the jersey itself, aye?

Uh huh. Uh huh.

Did you enjoy that work?

Aye, Ah quite liked it.

Aye. Did you prefer the hosiery work to your old job in the weaving?

Oh, yes. Ah wis paid off the hosiery. They were slack and they paid us off. An Ah went back to the weavin at Walkerburn and, oh, no, Ah didnae like it!

It was hard work?

Hard work. They were heavy looms. You could make guid wages but – no!

Did you find that Thorburn's was quite a good employer?

Yes. Uh huh. Very nice. A nice place to work.

The following extract from John Lunn provides a detailed account of both Waverley and March Street mills and includes a full description of the carding process. John's training included a year of 'going through the mill' so that he had an understanding of each part of the milling process. Ballantyne's also supported him in his studies towards City & Guilds qualifications which he gained through day release. John's account also includes information about his time with Laidlaw & Fairgrieve, where he found a company that was run along very different lines to a Ballantyne mill.

John Lunn, b. 1936, carder

Aye. So you left school and did you start straight away in the mill?

Ah started straight away. Ma father said, 'Well, if you've left the school, you're no doin anything, get yersel round to the mill'. So Ah went round to the mill and Ah got a job in the mill.

You just went round and asked?

Aye.

There was no advertised vacancy, anything like that?

Oh, no. Ye jist went. In those days, ye jist went. Aa the locals jist went tae whatever mill we wanted tae work in. So Ah jist went roond tae where ma father was and asked if there was a job.

Which was Caerlee, was it?

No, this was Waverley.

Waverley, Waverley, aye, uh huh. And you got a job?

I got a job. Ah jist started the next week.

So what was your first job? What were you doing?

Well, Ah don't know if you've interviewed him but there's a chap called Jimmy Howie. Well, he wis the manager o the mill at the time. And, of course he knew me. Well, he knew ma father and he knew me vaguely. Ah wis a wee boy and he had been on the games committee. And Ah suppose ye know we have our local festival?

Aye.

Well, Ah'd been two or three times in what they caed the 'goonies', the monks. So Jimmy knew that Ah obviously wisnae a stupid wee boy and offered iz an apprenticeship. But at that time he didnae know what the apprenticeship wis tae be. So Ah went in and Ah worked in the cardin and Ah wis in the cardin for a bit, two or three month. And then Ah went intae spinnin and then Ah went tae March Street mills wi the same company.

Peebles, aye.

And Ah was up at March Street for about seven month and Ah worked in aa the various departments up there. Then Ah wis taken back in and Ah wis reinterviewed.

In the Waverley?

In Waverley. And Ah wis actually asked what job Ah would like.

You must have done very well then as a beginner?

Whether Ah wanted tae be a tuner or what and Ah said, well, again, bein no that ambitious, Ah thought, well, Ah'm no gonnae travel tae Peebles, so Ah'll jist plump for the cardin in Innerleithen and it's on the doorstep. And that's how Ah started out as a carder. And the fact that my grandfather had been a carder as well.

Thanks very much. That's great. Now tell me – I'm an ignoramus – tell me what was involved – or tell me what jobs you did to begin with, before you actually got on to the carding?

Well, Ah worked in the wool store. Ah went right through the mill. Ah started off and Ah worked in the cardin for a bit. And then … they had this scheme. Ballantyne's were quite progressive in their own way.

As employers?

As employers. And they had this scheme where everybody had tae know everybody else's jobs. And actually, it wis somethin like a six-week scheme and the girls used tae come doon fae March Street. There werenae many girls in the Waverley but they had weavin and they had darnin and everythin. Darnin wis a trade. And the girls that wis goin tae learn the darnin, they had tae learn the whole bit so that they could say, 'Oh, there's somethin wrong wi the yarn', and they knew what they were talkin about in a way – maybe no technically, but they knew all the bits. And it usually jist consisted o aboot a six-week thing. Ah don't know why but mine's went on for nearly a year! And Ah started in the wool store wi the wool sorters. The wool in those days came intae the mill unsorted, straight fae the farms.

Now was the wool brought in exclusively from farms round about here or the Borders?

Some came … no, from all over the world. But it still came in what they called 'unsorted'. And there wis four wool sorters in the mill in those days.

All men?

All men. And they opened the fleece up on the bench and they pulled off the bits intae aa the different qualities. And they threw it intae the bins.

Was it, sorry to interrupt, as I say, just keep in mind that I'm a total ignoramus and all this fascinates me. Were there particular fleeces?

For different qualities.

For different qualities.

Aye.

Now for instance, if you got local fleeces from the Borders, the Cheviots and Black Face?

Aye, that would be for suitins, jackets like what you've got.

Aye. So that would be sort of rougher?

The Black Face didnae come into it. We didnae bother wi the Black Face because Black Face wis more for carpets and things like that. But the Cheviots, the wee Cheviot sheep and that, the fleeces would come in fae them. And we got fleeces, a lot fae New Zealand. Came fae all over.

What kind of sheep were they? Cheviots?

No. They would be Merinos and Corriedales and Texels and that sort o thing. And when the fleeces come in, they were jist like a fleece.

Aye, just as it had been rolled up?

And they jist put it on the bench and they took all the greasy, dirty stuff off. That went intae one bin. And then they worked their way intae the centre until they got the finest qualities and it all went intae the different bins.

And this was just done by hand?

By hand, by feel.

By touch?

Aye, aye. Aye. It's still done by feel.

That would take a while to learn?

Oh, aye. I didnae learn it. Ah mean, Ah only wis there for two or three weeks. But the men that were there, you know, they could pick up a bit o wool and they could tell ye what fleece.

With their eyes shut!

Aye, what it was.

A great skill?

Uh huh.

Just to do it, a great skill.

Aye. Obviously Ah jist learned tae take the bits off the side. You know, the dirty bits, the scrag and that.

But then you were only there of course as a beginner, a learner?

Oh, Ah wis jist tae get an idea.

Aye, aye. So you did that roughly how long?

Ah wis in that for maybe about a month. And then Ah had two or three days in the blendin and that.

So tell me about blending? What did you do?

Well, the blendin is where they bring all the different wools together and different colours tae make up a blend and a shade.

This is using the yarn?

That's ... No, usin the wool.

The wool itself, aye?

The wool. The wool then went away tae be dyed. The dye-house wis at Peebles. And the plan was tae build a dye-house at Innerleithen but at that time it wis never done. It wis done years later, in later years. So the wool came intae Innerleithen and it wis all sorted out and it wis scoured in the scourin-house, a two-lane scourin-house, which wis jist bowls where the wool went through, it wis jist taken through wi like rakes. And out on the dryer at the end. It went from there: if it wis tae be used as white it was kept, if it wis tae be dyed it wis sent up tae Peebles wi the colour it wis tae be. And then we had the shade-matcher, who passed the shades.

This was a man?

A man. In those days most o these jobs were done by men.

Aye. The preliminary processes?

Aye, aye. And then the manager or the wool-store man, ye had the different qualities and again, tae get your yarn right ye didn't jist use one wool. You'd tae get the right feel so you'd a mixture o wools. And you'd have a lot o mixtures o colours because you had to match your colours as well. So when the dyed wool come back it wis all shaded intae whatever colours ye needed for your mixture, so that you got your heather mixture and everything. So you'd to learn a bit about that, your proportions, and how you worked out your proportions.

A lot to learn?

There was a lot to learn. And then the blendin wis where all the big machines opened the wool out and blended it together primary mixin, if you like, and openin. And at the same time, wi havin been scoured, you had to put your oil back on and water, tae make sure that it would run in subsequent processes.

That would be a matter of fine judgement again?

Ah, well, it is nowadays. But in those days it wis supposed tae be but it wis only put on wi a waterin-can. (laughs) So many waterin-cans! But, Ah mean, it wis quite precise. Ah suppose it wis jist about as precise as what the machines are now because if the man measured it out properly, he wis puttin in the right amount.

Aye, aye. And you would find all that very interesting as a laddie?

Oh, aye. A lot to learn, aye.

Had you been in a textile mill before?

Only when Ah went doon tae see ma grandfather. And Ah seen the big machines but as Ah say, he retired when Ah wis only aboot nine. So any memories Ah had wis before Ah wis nine year old.

Just a wee laddie. You wouldn't understand the processes. And then from the blending?
>From the blendin it went tae the cardin.

And did you go to the carding?
>Aye. Ah went tae the cardin. Ah wis only in the these other departments jist tae sort o learn.

A few weeks?
>A few weeks, jist tae learn. Ah wis about four; six weeks wis the normal. Ye used tae have about a week, dependin on what the process was, ye used tae have about a week or a couple o days, you know, a couple o days ye could learn or ye saw what was happenin.

Aye, get an idea?
>You'd jist get an idea and then moved on. Ah don't know whether Ah wis picked for it. There were other boys that did it as well. An then went tae cardin and Ah went tae spinnin. Ah wis in the spinnin for a wee bit.

How long did you spend in the carding at that stage?
>Well Ah had actually been in the cardin tae start with. An Ah'd been there for maybe aboot a couple o months before Ah started tae do this. Before Ah started tae go what they called 'through the mill'.

Aye, aye, right. So you already had an idea of the carding?
>Aye. They come and they said, 'We want you to go through the mill. Ee've tae learn the rest o the trades'. And then Ah went on tae the spinnin for a wee bit. And then, as Ah say, Ah went tae March Street, worked in the wools, in the yarn store.

And how long were you up in March Street?
>Ah wis up in March Street for about six month.

Six months, aye. Saw the whole process by then?
>Saw the whole process when Ah wis at March Street.

The better part of a year, by the time you came back to Innerleithen?
>By the time Ah came back it was nearly a year.

And it was at that stage that you went into carding?
>Ah went intae cardin full-time, permanent. Cardin.

And that was your decision?
>That was ma decision at that point. Actually we had a personnel manageress. Ah mean, as Ah say, Ballantyne's were a quite progressive firm.

Was that not common in other firms, as far as you were aware?
>No. Not round about here. They had their own personnel department. In fact, it hadn't been long started. Ah think the lady was really startin out tae get everything structured.

Aye, aye. This would be in the early fifties?
>This was in 1951. '51/'52. It was a lady called Miss Dewar and Jimmy Howie was involved, as Ah say. He was the manager. And, you know, Ah wis taken in and, 'Now, you want to be a carder? You've made your mind up? You

wouldnae like to have one o the other jobs?'
You got a choice?
Aye, Ah got a choice for some reason.
Now that's great. Just before we come to your work as a carder, what about the hours? When you first started in the mill what were your hours?
We started at quarter to eight in the mornin. We'd a three-quarters of an hour lunchtime and we finished at half-past five at night.
So that would be …?
A nine hour day.
Aye. So you worked there for about five years at Waverley mill?
At Waverley, aye.
And you left when you were twenty. You started when you were fifteen?
Uh huh.
Straight from school. And what was the firm you went to work for in Galashiels?
Laidlaw & Fairgrieve's.
Aye. And again carding?
As a carder. Ah went as assistant manager – assistant foreman carder.
Oh, that was a considerable promotion for you then, whereas you'd only …?
Aye. That's why Ah got ma big rise in ma wages.
Aye. You were only twenty years old. Now you were saying that you'd gone to college when you were about, was it sixteen?
When Ah wis sixteen.
Sixteen. And were you there for four years?
Ah went for four years.
And what did that involve? Was there day release or something?
It was day release Ah went for, aye. One day a week.
That was unusual at that time?
It was, aye.
So again was that another reflection that Ballantyne's were quite progressive?
Well, no, that wis the college that started this. Originally some o the folk that were a wee bit older than me went to night classes. But then the college changed about 1952 and they started doing the same course durin the day. And there wis quite a class o boys an that. Again it wis mainly boys. Aa the boys, everybody that wis in ma class at the college, and that wis in the old Technical College. At Galashiels, where the tax office and that is now and the social security office.
And you got the whole day off?
Ye got the whole day off fae the mill. Ye got paid but ye had tae pay your own bus fare. What happened wis, ye'd tae pay your own bus fare, but if you passed your exams at the end o the year, ye got your bus fare back. So that was like a bonus.
From Ballantyne's?

From Ballantyne's.
That was an incentive?
Aye. That wis an incentive.
That would be quite a sizeable sum of money?
Aye, oh, aye.
Because you'd be paying, what … 2s. a day or something like that?
Oh, it wasnae as much as that.
1s. and something?
1s. and something a day return.
But still, over a thirty-five-week term?
Oh, when ye come back at the, aye, at the end o the year, when ye got it back.
£2 or £3, aye. Quite a useful sum of money?
Uh huh. But if ye didnae pass your exams ye didnae get it. And ye didnae get back tae college the next year.
No, no. So that was it.
There were no two bites at the cherry though.
You knew where you stood. But you didn't have any difficulty there?
Oh, no.
You carried on for four years before you moved on?
Four years, aye.
And you enjoyed that?
Oh, aye.
So what was the course there then?
Well, Ah took what they called yarn manufacture, which wis jist again general manufacturin. You know, how yarn wis made, where the wool came from, types o wool, quality control. Jist general.
Aye. You'd find the course interesting did you?
Oh, aye.
Aye. Especially since the other four days a week you were working at the job?
You're working in the mill, uh huh. Aye, Ah enjoyed that. An there were the two courses. You could either sit the certificated course or the practical course. The practical course, Ah think, wis only two years. An Ah went for the certificated course. But no havin got any certificates at school, Ah had tae go for an interview. Ah wasnae tae get on the course.
Aye. Because you didn't have any Highers?
Ah didnae have any Highers or Lowers.
You didn't have Lowers either, no.
An this Miss Dewar, who was the personnel officer, must have spoken to the college because when Ah went down to register, Ah wis told Ah wis doin the practical course. An then Ah wis sent back the next day, wi a flea in ma ear, and told tae get registered for the right course. So Ah had tae go for an interview. An they had tae get a reference fae the school and Ah wis allowed on it,

although Ah didnae have the qualifications tae go on it.
Well, that was a tribute to yourself again.
And they said that they would give me six month to see how Ah got on.
Probationary period?
Aye.
But you coped and you managed all right?
Coped – Ah came out top o the class.
Excellent! Well, you obviously had that native ability, which you'd shown in your schooldays, too?
Uh huh. Ah got, well, Ah got four certificates: one for each year. And every one o them wis first class.
Very good. Aye. And of course, that would encourage you to do more …
Aye.
… when you were clearly doing so well? So the certificates were in what?
What they called the City and Guilds of London.
You did very well then. So you're armed with all these certificates?
Oh, aye.
And your practical knowledge. And by the age of twenty, twenty-one, you decide to move down to Galashiels for …?
Yeah. Well, this job, this job came up at Gala and ma grandfather says … Ye see, ma grandfather wis retired but he stayed in the High Street and Ah used tae see him every day, ye see. Both him and ma granny, they stayed in the High Street and Ah used tae see them every day. Ah bumped into them or Ah went tae see them. If Ah wis short o a bob or two Ah went tae see them. They'd aye plenty money! They werenae rich but they'd aye plenty money compared tae ma father and mother like. An if ye were wantin chip money or fish money or somethin like that, ye went and saw your granny. A source o income, as grannies were supposed tae be, Ah suppose! (laughs)
Aye, indulgent.
Aye. And he says tae me, 'Have ye seen the job at Gala?'
And Ah said, 'No'.
He says, 'You want tae get yoursel doon there'.
So Ah took his advice and Ah put in for this job. Well, Ah'd jist finished at the college on ma day release. But Ah knew Ah'd passed the exams, so Ah put in an Ah hadnae ma certificate by then but Ah told them Ah had passed and that. Went in and had an interview and Ah wis jist offered the job on the spot.
Very good.
It was, Ah don't know if you know him, Sir – he's now Sir Russell Fairgrieve.
Oh, yes … he was an MP wasn't he for a time?
An MP, that's right. He interviewed me. It was still a family firm, of course. It was the Fairgrieves that run it. Then, of course, Ah got aa this patter about,

'You're too young', and aa this. But he offered us the job on the spot.
Aye. Very good.
And then that caused a row up here when Ah came to hand in ma notice.
Aye. Because they would take the view that they had borne the cost of your training?
That's right.
Well, you'd got the job in Galashiels and you got this big increase in your pay.
Aye.
And you're still only twenty years old?
Uh huh.
And that was over £7 a week?
Aye.
So even with your 7s.2d. bus fare or your six day pass you were still relatively quids in?
Ah was, aye.
Almost twice as much as what you made in Waverley mills?
Uh huh.
Now just to come back to precisely what carding involved? And then we'll come to Gala.
Aye. Well a cardin machine is a big machine – it consists o rollers. And they're covered in card clothin, which is jist like clothes brushes or hair brushes but fine, very fine and very, very sharp. And the wool is fed in, in precise amounts and goes through these rollers. The wires in them are facin opposite directions and it combs it out, if you like, brushes it out, mingles it, levels it. Ye have various bits within the machine for doin that as well. When it comes tae the end, you have what ye call your condenser, where you have various ways of doin it, although mainly now it's all wi leather tapes. But in the old days there wis different ways o doin it: rings wi divisions in between – and these picked up the fibre and made them intae individual ends. And then they go through what they call a set o rubbers, leathers. Nowadays it's plastic type rubbers but in the old days it wis leather. These are oscillatin sideways as well as forward and they make the yarn intae a thread but without any twist in it, just a soft thread. And then it goes from there, built ontae a spool, what they call a bobbin, and then it goes from there tae the spinnin, where the twist is put in.
Aye. That's great.
So it's really the machine that makes your yarn. If your yarn isnae made in your cardin machine you'll never make it, you know. The spinnin only puts the twist in and that. It's the basic process of everything.
Thanks very much. An excellent, clear definition. Great.
…
Well, goin back tae Waverley, when Ah started in there it wis all done by a big steam engine …
As late as 1951?
As late as 1954. When Ah wis there, they took the steam engine out and they

put in motors. We'd a line-shaft. Everything wis driven off a big complex o line-shafts and ropes went all round about.

This is in the steam engine days?

In the steam engine days. And the first thing they did was they went tae electricity but they didn't put electricity on tae individual machines. They put … where the big rope wis, what they called the big rope come in, they jist left the big pulleys on and they put a motor down on the ground next tae it and they still drove the line-shaft.

Aye. And that was the case for two or three years? Three or four years?

That would be about 1953 or '54, that they took out the steam engine.

And then the line-shaft was driven by electricity?

For quite a long time after that. Individual motors didnae come until much later in the textiles.

So, well into the sixties before you got individual motors?

Uh huh. Aye. And when Ah went tae Laidlaw & Fairgrieve's, they had a power line as well but it wasn't steam, it was water.

Gosh, even further back technically?

Aye. Technically, it wis water-powered.

That's a point that occurs to me, you know, what changes, what differences did you find, when you went to Laidlaw & Fairgrieve? That's one of them.

Well, we'd been on to power on … but jist still line-shafts. When Ah went tae Laidlaw & Fairgrieve's, compared tae Waverley, it wis old-fashioned. It wis a big mill but it wis old-fashioned.

How many workers roughly when you went there?

Oh, about fifty or sixty. But they only worked the day shift. And some o the machines were quite modern but the methods, compared tae Waverley. That's what Ah'm sayin, the Ballantynes in their way were very progressive. Goin intae Laidlaw & Fairgrieve's wis like a mixture o Waverley mill and the top mill. There were old men there. When Ah went, there were really old men. And tae me, they were really, really old!

Well over sixty?

Oh, one … There were two brothers there and Ah'm talkin in 1956 and thir fellows had played football for, Ah think it wis Hearts. One o them had played for Hearts or Hibs in the 1890s! (laughs) And they were still workin in the sixties. So, Ah mean you can add sixty-odd years, seventy years on tae when they played the football! They were in their eighties!

They must have been.

Their sons, their sons and their grandsons were workin in the mill as well.

What was their name?

Nicoll. The family … in fact they were great cricketers. Ye still see the name in the cricket. And there wis another fellow. But what had happened was, the story came out. They used to sit and read papers. An Ah used tae say, 'Ye wouldnae get away wi that in the Waverley'. Ah mean, Ah'd been brought up tae work.

During working hours, aye.

We'd been brought up tae work, although Ah wouldnae say it wis hard work. Ye werenae allowed tae sit about. If ye wanted tae smoke or anythin like that in the Waverley, ye had tae go tae the canteen. And there were two managers. Jimmy Howie wis the spinnin manager and Sandy Fleming wis the overall manager. And tae get tae the canteen or that, ye had tae walk past Sandy's office. Now if you were more than ten minutes, somebody wis sent out and asked what ye were doin in the canteen.

Because you were only supposed to be there for ten minutes?

And if ye walked past Sandy's office and he saw ye and he saw ye goin intae the canteen and ye'd see him lookin at his watch – it wasnae your time tae be there. He would rattle on the windae and ask ye where ye were goin. But when Ah went tae Laidlaw, they used tae sit at the front o the machines and read the papers. Ah mean, ye accepted that ye worked. Ah mean, you could find places tae dodge, if ye werenae doin much. But if ye were seen hidin away somewhere, ye were called in and ye got a warnin.

There was a sense of accepting the firm's discipline?

A sense that ye had tae work, aye. Ye were there tae work and ye were supposed tae be workin. Ah mean, if Ah wis in the cardin and Sandy or Jimmy walked through and Ah wis away bletherin tae somebody: 'What are you doin up here? Get back to your own bit'. You know, ye were brought up tae that. But when Ah went tae Laidlaw & Fairgrieve's Ah wondered when Russell Fairgrieve interviewed me, and he kept sayin, 'And what speed do you run your machines? And what sort of production do you get?' He wis interested. And when Ah went there, Ah could see why, because here were aa thir old men and they were aa jist sittin about and the machines were jist creepin. The machines in the Waverley, we had them goin quite fast in those days anyway – as Ah realised later. Ah didnae know this when Ah wis servin ma time. Except, Ah knew the top mill wasnae as fast An Ah thought, 'Och, that must be a unique place!' But here Ah went tae Laidlaw & Fairgrieve's and it was sort o a halfway house, if you like. It wasnae quite as bad as the top mill but it was a sort o halfway house. (laughs) An there, Fairgrieve had said tae me, 'Ah'm wantin young blood in'. He says, 'Ah feel that the firm is no progressin and Ah'm lookin for young folk'. And he says, 'Ah cannae get much younger than you'. So when Ah went there, as Ah say, here wis aa thir old men and they sat aboot, they chowed baccie and they spat all over ye.

You weren't accustomed to that in the Waverley?

Ye werenae allowed tae smoke at the Waverley. Ah mean, it wis it wis like goin intae a holiday camp.

Had there been any tobacco chewers in the Waverley?

No. I'd never seen ony there. When Ah look back, it was mainly younger folk that worked in the Waverley. Ah mean, a lot o the folk, Ah thought they were old, some o them are still livin yet. And they were aa sort o ma father's generation. They were only, like, twenty, thirty year older than I. So they were sort o forty, maybe fifty.

Aye. Middle-aged?

Aye. Ye hadnae really old men. And suddenly Ah went intae a mill and it wis aa old men.

And they really were old. If they played for Hearts in the 1890s?

Aye.

As you say, they must have been in their eighties?

Aye, aye. In the Waverley, we'd three men watchin six machines. Here Ah went and there were two men watchin one machine. And it wis only goin half the speed o the ones that wis at the Waverley. Oh! It wis like steppin back intae an ark. So after Ah wis there, he got me back up and he said he was wantin tae modernise the mill. And he wanted me as a young chap to be involved in it and do a lot o work – which Ah did. And when Ah went there in '56 and Ah wis transferred out again in '63. And by the time Ah left it wis a really modern factory. We put in aa new machines, new condensers where the yarn wis made. When Ah went they sometimes only produced about 5000 lbs a week. When Ah left we were producin 20,000, 30,000 lbs.

That's in weight?

In weight. In yarn, aye. So we went in the five or six years that Ah wis there, we put the production up aboot ten times. Russell Fairgrieve's father wis still the chairman.

What was his first name?

Old Alec. Ah said tae Russell one day, 'Ye know, we're never gettin off the bit. You keep pushin us for production'. Ah says, 'Look at them,' Ah says, 'they're sittin there readin papers,' Ah says, 'and you never say a word tae them'.

'Oh,' he says, 'Ye know, they fought through the War wi ma father, ye know, and he doesn't like tae see them troubled'.

That's interesting. The First War?

The First War. His father wis a colonel or something like that: KOSB. And these were his men.

Aye, aye. A sense of loyalty?

One o them was his batman. The other ones had been fightin, ye know, they'd went through the War together. So they were never goin tae get paid off. They took their time and they were there until they decided that they were goin tae pack up workin. And gradually we brought younger folk in and we did away with the older ones. The older ones retired. And it took aboot two or three years. But as the younger ones came in they were told, 'Ye watch three machines' – or whatever it was. And they jist, ye know, they got the extra money for doin it. And that's what drove the older ones out because the younger ones were comin in and they were getting a couple o pound or £3 a week more. And they would say, 'Oh, Ah'm not getting that amount'.

'Well, you'll have tae watch the machines.'

'Oh, Ah cannae do that!'

'Well, your no gettin the money.'

You know. And eventually they jist went. And the mill changed.

So the workforce went up from about – was it about fifty workers when you first went?

Aye. And it went up. In fact now I think they employ about 200 or something like that.

Aye. So it would be up to maybe about a hundred, by the time you left?

Well over a hundred.

And again, very roughly, I realise that it's not an easy question to answer, the division of the sexes? More men than women?

Well, when Ah went tae Laidlaw & Fairgrieve's, Ah think there wis only about four women worked in it. There were one or two in the office, a couple in the office. But in the factory itself it wis aa men. There were only aboot three or four women. By the time Ah left there were a lot o women. We actually had women on the cardin machines. It wasnae ma doin but they got a consultancy in. A wee chap came in and, well he decided [that]. Ah worked alongside him and we did a lot o time-studies and everything. And, in fact, we put a twilight shift on. Russell was one o these fellows, he hadnae an awfu lot o interest in the mill as such. But he was a great salesman. And he always had more work than he could do; cope wi. And he jist kept pushin and eventually we'd night shift on and then we put a twilight shift on. And the management decided, that the twilight shift would be women.

That would be two to ten, was it?

Well, what it was … they worked in Gala. It wis half-past seven tae half-past four. And it was half-past four tae ten o'clock at night they had this twilight shift. And they decided that that would be all women. Now the carders and the spinners, no the people that watched the machines but the actual carders like maself, we had tae work because they didnae bring in other carders. So we carried on workin overtime. So, Ah mean, Ah used tae go down there in the mornin and work tae aboot eight or nine o'clock at night.

From half-past seven in the morning?

Aye. And then the night shift chap come in and took over with the chap who did the night shift.

You'd be exhausted were you not?

Och, aye, but Ah wis young. …

So you went to Selkirk. You were there for two years and you were the carding manager there?

Aye. Uh huh.

Now what contrasts or what similarities were there?

Well when Ah was at Laidlaw & Fairgrieve's at Gala they had decided they would go intae the lambswool and Shetland trade. And, as Ah say, Russell Fairgrieve was a great salesman. He could get as much work as he could do in this Shetland and we adapted the machines to do the Shetland work. And obviously put the production up tae get it as cheap as it could be, etc.

Now what was distinctive about Shetland work and lambswool?

Well, it wis knitwear. When Ah went it wis all weavin again, as had been the Waverley.

Tweed?

Tweed. We made yarns on commission for various firms all over Scotland, all over Britain. It was jist what they called the commission spinners. And they jist made yarn for whoever wanted it. But it was all tweed yarn. It was all for weavin. And Russell saw this openin, as had the Ballantynes, that knitwear was goin tae be the big thing. So he decided that he would go intae lambswool and Shetland for knitwear, rather than the weavin. And we adapted aa the machines. That wis ma job really. Ah jist spent ma time movin machinery about, puttin bits on.

Sorry, this is in Gala mill?

This is in the Gala mill.

In your latter years there?

In ma latter years. Jist movin machinery about and puttin new bits on, gettin them runnin. Mainly mechanical, you know, engineerin, if you like. Forbye, Ah had tae run the mill as well in ma spare time, in the flat, ye know, and did aa these sort o things. But the mill at Selkirk had always done cashmere knittin for years. It was a much slower process. It had been intae the knitwear and this was what Russell was wantin tae be intae all over. But when Ah wis at Selkirk it wis cashmere, fine cashmere.

You would welcome maybe that change? It was always another experience?

Oh, aye. Ah mean in those days Ah wis never in one job very long. Cause even, as Ah say, when Ah wis at Gala we were always changin. There were always a new machine comin in. The time-study man was there. Ye'd six months o that and then ye'd six months o maybe puttin machines in. So, the job varied.

A great variety, which you would welcome?

A great variety, aye, aye. And then when Ah went tae Selkirk, as Ah say, it wis all cashmere. They did cashmere and the pace was much, much slower. It was like again – no steppin back in time, because they were aa modern machines – but the pace was like steppin back in time.

Now how many workers employed roughly at Selkirk?

Well, at that point, there wasn't that many. But they were in the process o buildin a dye-house and blendin plant, which put it up quite a bit. But when

Ah went, there was probably about sixty or seventy. Ah think that, it went … when the dye-hoose, which was separate really, but that employed aboot another twenty or thirty people eventually, a big dye-house.

Aye. So by the time you left two years later there might have been about a hundred workers altogether? Something like that?

Aye. Between the two bits. Uh huh.

Aye. And again the balance of sexes?

Well, there were more women in the mill at Selkirk, for some reason.

More women than there had been at Gala? Which would not be difficult! (laughs)

No. There would probably be aboot a forty/sixty mix. We actually had girls workin in the cardin and everything, and there were a lot more girls.

So women, speaking broadly, were beginning to penetrate, where they hadnae been before.

Aye, aye.

Was that because there was a shortage of male labour?

It wis startin tae be. Ah don't know where they were goin, because the electronic factories hadnae really started then. But the mills were aa busy. At that time there wis really a boom, really a boom, right in the middle of the early sixties, the late fifties, early sixties. The mills were really boomin then. They were puttin in new machinery all over the place. Things were movin. Ah wis there for a couple o years and then, as Ah say, Ah went up tae Dalkeith.

And how did you find that, because that was a brand new factory?

That was a brand new factory. That wis again built for the hosiery. An it wis really an extension o the Gala factory – that type o trade, where we were doin fine lambswool and Shetland for knitwear. Aye.

So were conditions very different at Dalkeith?

Oh, they were different. They were different folk and everything.

Because they wouldn't have a tradition of textiles there?

No. There was a lot o ex-miners and miners wives and, well …

Aye, who had to be trained presumably?

Had to be trained. From scratch. Oh, they were good, they were good folk. But, Ah mean, they had no tradition, ye know. But you could train them up quite well. It wis hard work. That wis the hardest work Ah ever did.

Was it?

Oh, aye. Two years. Ah went there in 1965 and Ah left in 1968 and Ah would say that wis the three hardest years Ah ever worked.

Was that because the workers were new and inexperienced?

The workers were raw. And what Laidlaw & Fairgrieve's or Dawson's or whoever made the decision, decided [was] that they werenae goin tae even employ [any experienced staff], other than the actual foreman, the spinner and the carder. That wis the only people, that wis maself and a chap fae Gala. The rest were aa Dalkeith.

Local folk?
>So when you wanted a shift carder, somebody tae run the machines, from day one it wis three shifts. An a lot o women on the machines. In fact, all the watchers, all the spinners, all the carders, all the cardin-machine operators, were aa women. An they got on motor mechanics and boys that had served their time in the pits as engineers and ye had tae train them up. Now OK, if a machine, if a wheel fell off, they could put the wheel back on. But if anything else went wrong – it wis a night and day job for me.

So you were on twenty-four hour call then?
>Ah was, virtually.

Where did you live at that time?
>Well for the first seven month or eight month Ah wis still in Gala. And it wis the winter. Ah must've started up there at late '64, actually. And Ah travelled a winter from Gala. And the worst one was Ah come back over Fala Hill one night and Ah went back up the next mornin and when Ah got tae Middleton Moor, Middleton Toll, Ah met a police car. And he says, 'Where have you come fae?'
>
>And Ah says, 'Gala'.
>
>He says, 'Dae ye no ken the road's been blocked for twenty-four hours?'
>
>Ah says, 'Well, Ah went home last night an aa!'

(Laughs) This is the A7?
>The A7.

Aye, Middleton Moor's a desolate place at the best o times?
>Aye. And he says, 'That road's been blocked since six o'clock, yesterday'.

But you got through? (laughs)
>Ah got through. Ah'd a big Vauxhall Victor in those days. Ah remember that night, because Ah'd went up in the mornin, Ah left Gala at seven o'clock the mornin before that. And Ah went up and it started tae snow and Ah didnae finish workin until nine o'clock at night. And of course it wis late on when Ah went back home.

But nobody had told you?
>Nobody had told me. Ah jist went up and doon.

Of course, it would be dark when you went to work?
>And dark when Ah come back. When Ah went home at night it was a blindin snow storm.

It could be very fierce!
>An that wis when Ah decided, 'Ah'll have tae get a house'. So Ah got a house in Loanhead. We moved up to Loanhead in the June '65.

That was quite a considerable change for you and your wife because you'd always lived in the Borders?
>Aye. But Loanhead wisnae that far away.

We now hear from Margret Lavin, who started as an in-giver and then served a three-year apprenticeship to become a drawer. Once qualified as a drawer, Margaret then taught her own apprentices: both boys or girls. As she told Ian, this was piecework, so each worker was paid according to how much work they completed. Men and women were paid at the same rates, so there was pay parity across genders. However, as Margaret explained to Ian, your wage fluctuated depending on a number of factors, particularly the quality of cloth you were working with.

Margaret Lavin, b. 1919, working life in the mill

So, you left the school then, when you were fourteen, so that would be maybe the summer of 1934? You'd be about fourteen and a half by the time you left?
    Uh huh, uh huh.
And did you get a job right away?
    Yes.
Tell me, how did you get a job? Did you apply for it or did you see a vacancy or …?
    No, no. Ye jist went up to the mill an they said, 'Start on Monday'.
And that's what you did? You just went up?
    Uh huh, uh huh.
Did some of your friends maybe go with you?
    Yes, uh huh.
There were quite a few of you?
    'Jist start on Monday.'
And tell me what mill was that again, Miss Lavin?
    March Street.
Ballantyne's, aye. So what did you do when you first started in the mill?
    Well, it was what they called in-giving and ye gave the threads intae the drawer, who drew them through to make the pattern for the weaver.
And was that just the ordinary sort of work that a girl of fourteen would do?
    That's what everybody went into, that.
All the girls started with that?
    Uh huh.
Can you remember what your hours of work were? When did you start in the morning?
    Was it eight o'clock? Eight tae half-past five.
And did you get a break for your dinner?
    About three-quarters of an hour.
And then you came home for your dinner did you?
    Uh huh.
Did the mill have a hooter or …?
    Yes, uh huh. It blew at one o'clock. And if ye weren't there, ye got locked out. (laughs)
So what happened then? You had a reduction in your wages, did you, at the end of the week?

Well, Ah wis never locked out. (laughs)
No. But suppose, for those that were locked out, what happened to them?
Oh, well they would lose their wages. They would be off all afternoon.
If you weren't in promptly, you were locked out!
That's right, aye, aye, that's right.
Is that so? Now what about the morning? Suppose you didn't get there promptly for eight o'clock?
You were locked out. (laughs)
For the day? Or the morning? Was that the day?
(Peter Lavin, brother: Ye come back at lunch time.)
Aye, so it was for the morning? And if you were locked out at one o'clock, you were locked out for the afternoon?
That's right.
But nobody was locked out for the whole day?
No.
No, no. That seems a bit drastic!
(laughs) Oh, well.
And you personally were never locked out?
No. (laughs)
Never. No, you were always punctual. Do you know of anybody who was locked out?
Ma father, because he wis asthmatic. And Ah know on one occasion that he wis locked out.
Cause he just couldn't get there in time?
Uh huh.
So he suffered the loss of a morning's or afternoon's pay?
That's right, aye, uh huh.
And that would have been quite a big loss, wouldn't it?
Oh, aye.
Now tell me about your wages when you started? How much were you paid?
Eight shillings. Then when you were in six months you got 6d. a rise. An then it went on tae 9d. a rise. (laughs)
Now once you'd been there another year, how much was the increase? You know, you got 6d. after six months.
Well you'd get moved into another job. That wis jist temporary. Ye got moved into another job.
Right. What age would you be when you got moved on from the in-giving?
Maybe fifteen and a half or so.
Aye. When you'd been there about a year or eighteen months?
Aye, uh huh.
And what was the job that you were moved to do?
Well, Ah stayed in the same department and became a drawer. But Ah had to serve an apprenticeship – three year apprenticeship.

(Minnie Lavin, sister: And ye had tae pay for that.)
You had to pay?
    Aye.
You had to put down a sum of money?
    Aye, for tae be a drawer. An ye had tae be proposed and seconded.
And who proposed and seconded you then? Was it other workers?
    Uh huh. Jist other people in the department.
Now at the time that you started work there, Miss Lavin, when you were fourteen, roughly how many workers would there be in the mill?
    Three hundred and odds, 360 or something.
Well over 300 workers in the March Street mill?
    Uh huh.
Tell me what did the March Street mill do? Did it do everything? Weaving, hand-spinning?
    No, not spinning. Spinning was done at Innerleithen. But March Street did the drawin and the weavin an the darnin an finishin.
Right. But the earlier parts of the processes?
    Was done at Innerleithen, Innerleithen mill.
Innerleithen. What was the mill called there?
    Waverley.
Waverley Mill. And that was owned by Ballantyne's too?
    Uh huh.
Right. So what did the apprenticeship then consist of?
    Well, ye jist had tae learn the different patterns and that. By the time the three years wis up, ye were quite ready tae start and make your own pay.
Right. Now how did you learn? Was there somebody who taught you or did you just watch other workers?
    Jist had to watch other people. Ah sat beside a drawer.
You sat beside a drawer and just watched?
    Uh huh, uh huh.
And you had some chance, of course, to try the work yourself?
    Oh yes, uh huh.
But you didn't go to classes, for instance?
    Oh, no.
And were you attached to some particular worker, some particular drawer?
    Yes, uh huh.
There was one person that you were attached to was it? What was her name?
    Well, that was before she wis married. It wis Betty Clyde. (laughs)
And she sort of took you under her wing, did she? (laughter) And taught you how to do the drawing? Was that how it worked?
    Yes, uh huh, that's it.
Aye. And was it difficult to learn?

LIFE IN THE MILLS

Aye, it wis difficult to start with. A lot o countin and different things, uh huh.
You would have to, again just tell me because I know nothing about the processes, you know, what exactly did you have to do, when you were learning to be a drawer?

Well, when you start you're an in-giver. Well, you're at this side of what was called a cam. And they had tae give ye it, you put a hook through what was called a heddle. H-E-D-D-L-E. And they put the thread on to the hook and you drew it through. But then you had to do it in different patterns and watch a pattern an. It's very complicated tae.

Were you sometimes a bit worried that you were making mistakes?

Oh, aye.

It must have been very easy to make a mistake?

It was, uh huh, uh huh. But ye had to concentrate.

But Betty Clyde was patient and helpful, was she?

Ah wouldn't say so. (laughs loudly) No, she certainly wasn't. (laughs)

So what did she do?

Shout and swear and kick! (laughs)

Kick you as well? Oh, dear! So life couldnae have been very pleasant for you?

Ye jist got used tae it. It wis jist a case of gettin used tae it.

Aye. You were a shy, young girl when you started, I take it?

Oh, aye.

I mean, you'd never been in a textile mill before, had you?

No, no.

So you must have been a bit upset if here was somebody shouting and swearing at you? A bit bad-tempered and impatient?

Aye. (laughs)

(Peter Lavin: It wis a way o life then. When you went into the mill, it didn't matter what department you were in, there would be somebody there who'd knock ye about, you know.)

Was that so?

(Peter Lavin: Aye. Oh, there was lots of it.)

That's interesting. We'll come to that. So there was a bit of physical work as well? People shoving you and kicking you, as well as …?

Well, ye see ye were sittin facin one another. And it wouldnae be as wide as this. But if you missed her hook, when she put her hook through and you missed it. (laughs)

You were sitting closely enough to be kicked on the shin?

Aye, uh huh.

It would be quite painful! And I mean, it wasnae a playful kick?

Oh, no. (laughs)

Well, that was a different form of learning from Peebles High School?

(Laughs) But that didn't happen very often. Cause, you see, the drawer, which Ah eventually became, you had to make your own pay. It wis piece-

work. An of course they needed their in-giver to be quick.
It's understandable if, you know, the senior woman …
　　It wis their livelihood.
How long did it take, Miss Lavin, to get the hang of it?
　　Well, ye were three years' apprenticeship.
So it was quite a long apprenticeship.
　　Uh huh.
Did you sign indentures?
　　Yes, uh huh.
So it was a formal apprenticeship to become a drawer?
　　Uh huh, uh huh.
And that was quite a skilled job then?
　　Uh huh.
Was that a job done only by women?
　　Oh, no, there were men doin it as well.
Roughly how many drawers were there in the March Street mill?
　　Well, Ah wis in the pattern department and there would be aboot six, Ah think.
And were there other drawers in other departments?
　　There wis other drawers in the big flat where the weavin wis takin place. This wis the pattern department that Ah wis in.
And how many other drawers would there be in the other department then – roughly? Not as many as that?
　　No, it would be aboot six, seven.
About half a dozen. So in the mill, there were only about a dozen drawers altogether?
　　Uh huh.
So that was really quite a skilled job?
　　Uh huh.
Was that a job that you wanted to do?
　　Ah wanted to do it once Ah got into the mill.
Was there some other job, that if you hadn't begun as a drawer, you could or would have done?
　　Oh, Ah could've been a weaver or anything like that.
Aye. There were several jobs, once you got through the first few months that you could have tried to get?
　　Aye, uh huh.
But you opted to become a drawer?
　　Uh huh.
Why was that? Because the money was better?
　　Oh, the money wasnae any better. It wis jist that Ah liked the job.
So after your three year apprenticeship finished, you duly became a drawer. Did you then have an apprentice of your own?

Uh huh.
Aye. Did you kick that apprentice?
No, Ah don't think so! (laughs)
I'm sure you're too much of a lady. Nor swear or shout! Was it a young girl that you had?
Ah had girls and Ah had boys.
Was there equal pay? Or it was piece-work?
Aye, it wis piece-work.
Were the women better and quicker at drawing than the men?
No, no.
So you would find that in the mill, men and women drawers, who were earning roughly the same amount of money? It wasn't the case that the men were getting paid extra?
No, no. No it was the same. It was piece-work.
The same rate, aye. And the amount paid, of course, would vary from time to time?
Aye, but every week it was different.
What determined the changes then every week?
Well, it depended on what kind of work ye got.
So tell me, there were some particular kinds of work maybe, that were better paid than others?
Uh huh.
Tell me about the best paid work? What was that?
Aye, the worsted work.
That was the best paid? And was that common, the worsted, or was it uncommon?
Quite common.
Could you work from one year to the other sometimes on worsted? Or would that be uncommon?
Oh, no. No, ye had to take your share.
Aye. Was it shared out in some way?
Uh huh.
There was so much worsted and so much what else?
Aye.
What was the other kind of work?
Well, there wis Sportex and different kinds of yarn.
And they were paid at different rates?
Uh huh.
But the worsted was the best paid. And then after that?
Well the finer the jobs, the finer the yarn was, as it went down.
The finer the yarn the higher the rate of payment?
Uh huh.
And as it became coarser you got rather less money?
Aye, aye.
Can you remember roughly what your weekly pay would be?
Oh, well, it would be aboot £2 something or £3 something.

Was that quite a good wage?
  Well, it was quite a good wage in these days.
Because you would then be roughly about seventeen or eighteen?
  Uh huh.
And it would be under £3 some weeks but maybe other weeks just a wee bit over three pound?
  Aye, aye, jist roond aboot the £2 and £3.
That would be quite a good wage for a girl of your age?
  Aye.
Before the War, say, in 1936/37. Just about the time your father died.
  Uh huh.
Now when your father died, did your mother return to work?
  Uh huh.
What did she do?
  Across the road from where we stayed there was a big house. It's a residential place now. But the ladies ran it like, as a hotel. And she helped there.
Just sort of general duties?
  Aye.
Now, I was asking about when you were paid; it wasn't a Saturday, it was a Tuesday when you first began? But it was always a weekly pay?
  Yes.
Now, when you got your pay, you know, when you first started at the mill, did you give your pay packet to your mother?
  Yes.
And she gave you a wee bit of pocket money?
  Uh huh.
Can you remember how much pocket money you got as a lassie?
  About 9d., a shillin or somethin. (laughter)
Your mother kept the bulk of your wage?
  Aye.
Now what could you do in Peebles, when you were fourteen or fifteen, with 6d. or 9d. a week? What did you do?
  Pictures. (laughs)

Betty Muir also remembered how her wage would fluctuate depending on the quality of the cloth she was working with. Betty started at the in-giving and was moved on to different parts of the process and describes her work as a penciller, on the birling and the picking. She was then able to train as a darner, which she enjoyed much more.

Betty Muir, b. 1922, working processes in the mill

Tell me the various processes that went on in the March Street mills, please. You know, from the beginning. As I understand, it was a weaving mill?

Well, when Ah started in it they also had the spinning. But that's where they spun the yarn on the long machines that went back and forwards like that. That wis there then and it came frae the spinnin on to what they caa the throstle, where Peter Lavin worked. And they put it on to there. And then that went to the looms, where it was set up for to weave. And that was where you started in the mill, on the in-givin, where you put these threads through the cams for it all to be drawn through. And then they put it through what they caed a slay. And then it went intae the loom then. And of course ye had your bobbin machines and your pirn machines for tae get the pirns to weave with. They were different machines entirely. And then it came intae where we were, intae the darnin, where it went tae what ye caed – where Ah started makin ma wages – on the birling. This wis where ye pulled the cloth across a table and ye rubbed and ye felt for aa the knots in the material and ye lifted aa the knots up. Some ye had to open, so as they could be crossed and didnae leave a mark on the material. Then ye had tae put them up over rollers and look through them to see if you'd left any. And then they went on to the next bit, on to the darnin, which Ah took up in later years. And ye darned in any broken ends or faults. Sometimes ye had a thread out from end to end, sixty yards o material. Took quite a bit o doin, the darnin. So Ah learnt the darnin later on.

That was quite a skilled job?

Oh, yes, aye. Ye had to serve a three years' apprenticeship. When ma sister went intae the mill from comin out the cleanin job she had to serve three years. And ye served two years learnin and the woman that wis learnin ye, ye got part o her wage. Whatever she made that week, ye got two-thirds o her wage for your wage, which was good. And then after that third year wis up, ye went on for yourself and made your own wage. And it wis the same that job that Ah did first, the birling. When Ah went on there this woman learnt me. And Ah remember when she told me Ah wis goin on Ah got aboot three weeks and then she said, 'Now ye'll go on it and make your own wage'. She says, 'Now see that book,' She says, 'if ye fill that page with numbers,' she says, 'ye'll make £2'. And that's a good wage. So that wis ma first wage. It wis £2.5.6.

And what age would you be then?

Oh, Ah'd only be sixteen, aye, jist sixteen, when Ah did that.

That was a good wage for a girl of that age at that time?

Oh, aye, aye. But Ah worked, Ah always remember workin like a navvy that first week. And that wis what Ah had, £2.5.6. Ah thought this wis great. But the next week Ah got a comedown because Ah had some harder pieces tae work with and Ah couldnae take them off as quick. So ma pay came doon

below the £2. But it wis quite a hard job really.
You were on piece-rates?
Piece-rates.
So you started at the age of fourteen and to begin with, just remind me, you were doing what?
What ye called the in-giving. And that wis the threads, one at a time on a broad piece o cloth that came from the loom.
And was that the normal sort of work that young girls of fourteen started on?
Everybody had tae start there, aye. From there, well, by the time ye got an idea o what wis going on in the mill. And if ye took a fancy to something, ye asked tae get a shift when somebody else came in frae the school. You were moved on, ye see.
That could be usually maybe a few months?
Six months, something like that. Three months, six months, aye, depending who wis comin in.
It would just depend on vacancies, how skilled and keen you were?
And who wis in before ye and that. And Ah wanted to learn to be a penciller, what they caed a penciller.
What was that then?
That wis further on intae the clean department, after the pieces had aa been scoured, washed and dried. And it wis some bits that would come up light and they should've been darker. And ye went over them wi these wax crayons and different coloured pencils and that. Ye covered up aa the flaws mair or less that you could see, before it wis properly finished.
What attracted you to that work?
Ah don't know, but whether it wis … Ah liked the girls that worked on there and Ah had a lot to do wi them at break times. And Ah used tae come in and stand and watch them. And Ah used to think, 'Oh, Ah would like to do that'. So when Ah got a move Ah got moved intae that shed, but Ah wis put on to what they called the picking. And that wis the most borin job in the mill.
Oh, dear, what was that?
It wis jist like aa the dark pieces, the likes o that, if there were maybe wee white bits, wee white threads or wee white specks on them, ye had to sit wi a pair o tweezers and pick them oot.
Oh, that would be monotonous?
Oh, it wis a monotonous job.
Was that piece-work?
Yeah, piece-work as well, aye.
So you had to work quickly, too, to make a wage?
Oh, aye, and, oh, it wis borin that. And when Ah wis on that job, the boss frae next door came and he wanted two people tae help him out on the birling. And that wis when Ah got put onto the birling. And Ah never got back. We

were promised tae get back in there because they knew Ah wanted to go on the shadin and they were waitin until Ah could go on. But Ah never got on. Ah got put on the birlin and that wis where Ah stuck. Because Ah went fae the birlin tae bein a darner. They became short o darners, so ma boss came and asked me if I would like to learn. He says, 'Ah know you do a bit o darnin'. Well, ma sister had learned me at home, you know, and the different lifts that's in the darnin, ye know, with the different designs and they had aa different lifts. And he said, 'Ah know that ye can darn a plain thing'. He says, 'But if ye get a wee bit training would ye go on?' So Ah said yes, because it wis better money. So Ah learnt to be a darner, so Ah got on to the darnin and that wis better wages. And I enjoyed that better than the birlin. The birlin wis a bit monotonous as well.

So you were relatively happy on the darning?

Oh, aye, Ah liked darnin, aye, yeah.

Now of the workers in the mill roughly how many would be women and how many men? Was it half and half, you know, in the early years when you started? You started in 1936 so up to the War?

No, Ah think there'd be maybe slightly mair weemen than men.

Three-fifths women, two-fifths men, something like that, very roughly? It would fluctuate a wee bit no doubt?

Aye, something like that, yeah, yeah, aye, cause it wis nearly aa women that wis on the weavin, on the machines, aye. It wis aa women in oor shed and the clean side it wis aa women. It would jist be, what, aboot half a dozen men that wis in the scourin hoose where they washed the things. And there wis only the dryin machine, two knottin machines. That's where the knots that we had raised in the birlin, they went through this machine and it cut them off. And then there wis other two at this side. Aboot half a dozen men in there as well. And the men on the throstle, the warp mills, and the yarn store. That wis aboot aa – and the tuners for the looms. Aye, the biggest percentage wis women in the mill.

Women, aye, uh huh. And were they women of all ages?

All ages, yes.

Including married women?

Oh, yes, aye. When Ah went in, Ah wis put on wi Susan Watt, and, well, she'd be old tae me, she'd be in her fifties, startin in her fifties when Ah went in.

And they were married women as well as unmarried?

Oh, yes, aye, yes, aye.

Was it common in Peebles before the War for married women to go back to work in the mill after they got married?

Oh, Ah think so, aye, it wis, aye.

You know, in many places and many other jobs as soon as a woman got married, before the War, she ceased to go out to work and stayed and looked after the house. But that wasn't so much the case in Peebles?

Ah don't think so. Ah cannae remember.

Aye, textile places were different weren't they?

Different, aye.

I think in Dundee it was really quite difficult for men to get jobs. It was the women that went out and the men stayed at home and looked after the house.

Aye, yes, yes. Oh, no, we had quite a lot of married women. Because eventually I wis boss in the darnin shed, I eventually took that on. And Ah had a lot o married women workin under me.

In this next account, Walter Scott describes his trepidation when he was sent to mill manager Joe Euman's home to ask about a job at March Street. He was told simply to 'start Monday'. His first job was on the twisting frames and this account focuses particularly on the twisting and tuning processes.

Walter Scott, b. 1924, twisting and tuning processes

That's great. So you didn't have any ambitions, you know, to be a fireman or an engine-driver when you were a laddie?

No, no, no.

You didn't want to stay on at school?

No.

No. And presumably your parents would expect you to leave as soon as you could?

Soon as Ah could an get a job. That's right.

Was your father working at the time you left school?

Ah think he was. Ah think he was.

Now your father's experience presumably was not uncommon among mill workers in Peebles when you were a boy? That's to say, it wasnae just your father who was unemployed? There were a lot of mill workers unemployed?

That's right.

How many mills were there in Peebles when you were a lad?

Well, there wis Ballantyne's, there wis Thorburn's big mill and then ye had Thorburn's Tweedside.

Right. So that was March Street mills, Ballantyne's, and then there was Tweedside. That was the bigger of the two Thorburn mills, was it?

Well, it wis actually … Thorburn's at Damdale, where the housin scheme is now, wis more or less the weavin, ware-room an aa that side o it. Tweedside wis cardin and spinnin. So once it was carded and spun and made intae yarn, it wis shipped up tae the big mill and they made it intae tweed.

Aye, aye. And you would be familiar with all this sort of work and talk, through your father being a mill worker?

That's right.

You'd be familiar with some of the terms. It's a long time ago, can you remember, did

you just expect to start work in a mill, when you were a laddie, you know, at school?
More or less. Ken, had ma fither been a brickie or a joiner or somethin like that, then it might have been different. But it wis mair or less all kind o mill talk. Same wi ma grandfaither wis in the mill, ma auntie wis in the mill. Both ma aunties wis in the mill. Yin wis a weaver. Ma father's sisters – An Ah mean, when they came to the hoose, they talked aboot mills – how they were daen, what work they were doin. So you grew up wi it.

So how did you get the job? Did you apply for it? Was there a vacancy advertised somewhere?
No, no, no. Ah went tae the mill manager, which wis Joe Euman, Ah went an chapped on his door.

Was that the usual way of looking for a job when people left school? Or was that something maybe your parents had urged you to do?
Well, Ah think maybe ma faither had said tae me, ken. It wis thon, the twae half doors, ye ken? They had an inside door. And Ah mind, Ah wis dead bloody scared, ye ken! Ah chapped the door. Joe Euman wis, oh, hell, he wis aboot six fit six and built like a tank. Oh, a big man. An he chowed baccy, ye ken and he would spit, ye ken. Christ!

Aye. Was that common practice among mill workers at that time, chewing tobacco?
Aye, in the aulder men, aye. They chowed. Then of course he asked whae a wis, ye see. And Ah explained whae Ah wis and, well, ma fither wisnae workin in March Street. He wis in Thorburn's. But Ah says, 'Ma grandfather works in the ware-room now'.

He was still working, your grandfather?
Oh, aye, he wis still workin. And Ah says, 'Ma twae aunties work in the mill, ma auntie Meg and ma auntie Jenny'.
'Oh, Ah ken ye fine, aye. Start on Monday.'

Was it important to be known then to the manager when you were applying for a job?
Ah think so. Ah think he carried a bit o weight.

Aye. And especially if members of your family were already employed in the mill?
That's right, that cairried a bit o weight.

So you got the job. Tell me what you did then, when you first began?
Well Ah started in the mill on the twistin frames. That wis … ye had twae bobbins and ye twist comin doon ower the machine, through rollers, on tae a spindle that turns, an ye have two threads twisted intae one, which makes a stronger thread. So Ah wis on that fae Ah came intae the mill in 1938, and Ah wis on that till jist at the start o the War, the 9th September 1939. And the young chaps that wis in on the tunin side, they were goin away to the War, and they were advertisin for a tuner, a man for the dye-hoose and one for the design office. And Ah wisnae botherin aboot it. Ah wis quite happy where Ah wis. But the foreman, Jimmy Birnie fae Innerleithen, he came and approached me and asked me if Ah wouldnae be interested in one o the jobs. And Ah

says, 'Well,' Ah says, 'Ah dinnae ken'. Ah says, 'Ah'd need tae ask ma fither first'. Ye jist wouldnae pack in yer job like that. So Ah came hame and asked and, well, ma old man asked ma auntie Meg what a tuner's job was like. And she said, 'Oh, it's quite a good job, ken'. So Ah came back and Ah seen Jimmy Birnie and telt him. So aboot a fortnight efter that Ah started in the tunin. An Ah wis there till Ah wis called up [in 1942]. And Ah wis there tae the feenish and then Ah came back. And Ah wis pit on as a kind o improver. Like, a tuner in there then had twelve looms each. And Ah wis pit on as an improver an Ah had six looms. Plus, Ah had tae help anither tuner. And then eventually Ah got a full section o ma own, twelve looms. And then Ah came on tae, aye, Ah'd be aboot a year then, and then Ah came on tae the full tuner's wage efter that. And the mill, aye, there wis quite a lot o work right enough. There wis single-loom weavers then. And if a weaver got her piece oot while the tuner wis lookin at that job, she jist couldnae stand and hing aboot. She had tae clock oot and go hame. She stopped. And then once you had that job in ready for her tae weave again, the apprentice could jump on tae his bike and he would gin oot and tell her tae come back in.

Now there might be an interval then of what, an hour or two hours or an afternoon?
Oh, sometimes. Sometimes if there wisnae a job ready for her she would maybe be off a day. Half a day.

Short-time working really?
Aye, aye

But as soon as she was finished, she was paid off, as it were?
That's right. Aye. Well, ye see, in thae days they were a on piece-work. So it didnae pay tae hing aboot. And the sooner she got oot then back in, away it went again.

Aye. But that was in the nature of the mill work that there was a good deal of short-time working, in a sense that, you weren't just kept on the payroll?
Oh, no, oh, no.

As soon as you'd finished a particular piece of work you were paid off in effect, though it might only be for an hour or two or at the most a day?
Aye.

Then you were brought back in?
Oh, sometimes it'd be mair. It all depended on the work.

Yes. It could be two or three days?
Aye. Oh, aye.

And this was after the War?
This was after the War. Aye, they were aa on piece-work. And, Ah mean, the harder the tuner worked and got thae jobs back in, the better the weaver's pey wis, the better the tuner's pey wis.

What hours did you have as a laddie of fourteen, just starting?
When Ah started in the mill, now did Ah work fae, Ah think it wis eight

o'clock start and ye had, was it three-quarters o an hour for yer dinner and ye finished at, was it half-past five? Somewhere aboot that. And when Ah started at the mill, when Ah came intae the mill at first, Ah had 7s.3d. And ye worked a Saturday mornin tae a quarter past twelve.

And that would be, if my arithmetic is right, that would be somewhere about fifty-one hours a week? But once you reduce that by three-quarters of an hour for your dinner that would bring it down to about forty-seven, forty-eight hours a week? Something like that?

That's right. That's whit ye worked. Roughly aboot forty-eight hours a week.
Did you get any breaks, tea-breaks in the morning or the afternoon?
Ah think ye got ten minutes in the morning.

Ian also asked Walter about any rivalries between the workers from different mills.

Was there any, or do you remember at any time before the War, any sense of, you know, sort of friendly rivalry or competition among the workers or between the workers in the March Street mills and in the Thorburn mills?

Ah cannae say Ah ever recall ony rivalry, no. No. Ah cannae say onything aboot that then. But, ye see, after Thorburn's wis closin doon it would be, efter the Tweedside mill went on fire. That wis burnt tae the ground. They more or less wis closin doon. Well, Ballantyne's then more or less took ower Thorburn's. And the majority o the workers came here intae March Street. And there used tae be, well, it used tae bother them when they were sayin 'Oh, we didnae dae it this way in Thorburn's'.
'No,' we used tae say, 'no, that's why the bloody thing closed doon! You buggers'.

Aye, just sort of teasing?
Teasin, aye.
There was never any nastiness, I take it, nothing like that?
Oh, no, no, no, no. Ah mean, there's a lot o the chaps in there yet that wis in Thorburn's, ye ken. Och, no, they were aa jist yin faimly.
Most of the workers in your recollection were members of the union but the union was pretty weak. It had to do pretty much as Ballantyne's and Thorburn's – presumably the same at Thorburn's – said?
Aye, as they said. That's right.
And wage increases were pretty small?
Nowadays, of course, they're aa on set wages, ken. Some o them come in there and hing up their bloody coat and that's it. Haud their hand oot at the end o the week.
They're no longer on piece-rates?
They're no on piece-rate, no, which, personally, masel, Ah think is a mistake.

But that's the way it goes nowadays.

When did this change take place then, from the piece-rates to the time rates, roughly speaking?

Well … a wee while efter the War. When they started tae dae away wi the auld Hattersley looms and then ye got Dobcross in. And then they got rid o them and ye were on automatics. And now ye've got Sulzer and Dornier looms. An instead o one weaver watchin one loom, ye've one weaver maybe watchin four, sometimes six.

So it's been since about the 1950s that the change has come from piece-rate payments to time rates?

That's right.

Are there any workers at all in the mill on piece-rates?

No.

Nobody at all?

Nobody at all now. They're aa the set wage.

That's a big change then? Because when you began first most of the workers were on piece-rates? And you personally regret that?

Ah do. Ah aye found that ye were better off on piece-work. Aye.

Although keen to go into the mill, Effie Anderson was initially persuaded to go into service, aged fourteen. Eventually though, at sixteen, she got her wish and started at March Street where, because she was a bit older, she started on the bobbin machine rather than the in-giving. Effie's account also includes details of health and safety considerations within the mill when she worked there. She also talks about the end of her working life, before she was made redundant in 1971.

Effie Anderson, b. 1925, health and safety in the mills

Now what about mother. What did your mother do?

Ma mother worked in the auld mill. Tweedside.

Tweedside, what did she do there?

Now as far as Ah ken she worked on the 'jeanies'?

Jeanies?

Things that went back and forrit.

Oh, the jennies, spinning jennies?

That'll be jennies! (laughs)

She called them the jeanies! Good, that's fine. And she did that, she was doing that before you were born?

Oh, aye.

From when she left school maybe?

Ah wid imagine so, Ah dinnae ken though.

…

When Ah wis twenty-two Ah left the mill tae get married and Ah went tae

Fife. And Ah wis only married six and a half years when ma husband was killed.

Oh, dear. I'm sorry to hear that.

And it never entered ma head tae come back here. But Ah had an aunt and an uncle that worked in Tweedside mill. And it wis ma aunt that said to me, 'Why dae you no come back to Peebles and ye'll get yer job back in the mill?' Ah had made Kelty ma home. Ah had met new friends. However that's what Ah done. Ah came back to Peebles in 1955 and Ah wis only back a week when Ah got ma job back in the mill. One wee boy wis at the school and the other one, well, ma mother looked after him till he wis age for the school.

…

When Ah went in tae the mill Ah didnae go on tae the in-gien. Ah wis put right on tae the bobbin-machine because Ah wis sixteen. Ah wisnae fourteen. And Ah think wis it two weeks ye got to learn? And Ah wis put on ma own time. An Ah made £1. And Ah thought, if a make £1 every week this'll be great! (laughs)

Well, it almost trebled your wages! And that would be, that would be about 1938? Just before the War, was it that you started in the mill? You were sixteen?

Aye. Ah've got masel kind o raivelled here. When Ah left that private school Ah went to the County Hotel for a wee while. Not for long. Ah wis waitress and cleanin. And that's when war broke oot, when Ah worked in the County.

Now just to go back to the beginning at the mill again, you went into the mill because your friends were already there.

Uh huh.

And can you remember, did they encourage you to get a job in the mill?

Oh, aye. They were always saying, 'Get a job in the mill'. So Ah went up tae the front office and saw Joe Euman and Ah asked him if there wis any chance o gettin a job.

And he took you on right away then?

Uh huh. I started on ten shillins. And then, when Ah wis put onto ma own time Ah made £1. Ah thought this was magic! And it fluctuated. Ye maybe made a wee bit over the £1. Some weeks if ye'd had bad work it wis a wee bit under the £1.

But on average it was £1?

Aye.

Which was almost three times as much as you'd been getting in your previous jobs?

Uh huh. (laughs)

And again did you give that wage to your mother each week?

Aye, but ye got maybe half-a-croon or 3s. back. (laughs)

So you were definitely better off?

Uh huh. (laughs)

And you were doing that for roughly about a year and then you were paid off?

That's right. And Ah went to the forestry and Ah wis there for aboot nine month, maybe ten month. And then the mills. They said that if we wanted tae come back, we could come back.

Right. So you went back at once?

We went back.

You didn't prefer to remain with the forestry?

No. Ah liked the mill. And then Ah stayed on the bobbin machine for a wee while and Ah asked for a move to the weavin. And Ah went on to the weavin. Ah went on to the pirn machine first. And then Ah went on to the weavin and Ah liked the weavin.

Aye. Was that the job that you preferred in the mill?

The weavin, aye.

Had some of your friends been working in weaving?

That's right.

They had … Maybe they said things that made you feel you'd like to have a go?

Aye, aye, probably, probably. And ye had a guid boss: Bert Milne.

Bert Milne? Uh huh. Was he a Peebles man?

Aye. He wis the foreman in the weavin flat. He wis a great guy.

Now, in the first couple of years or so you were there, roughly what proportion of women workers, what proportion of men workers, would there have been?

I would say more women than men. Ah would say mair than half onywey wis women.

Some of the men maybe had been called up of course, by the time you started?

That's true. That's true.

Aye, aye. Now when you started were there any women who were in senior jobs? Any forewomen, for instance, or women foremen?

No, it wis all men, Ah think.

You don't remember any women in positions of seniority? There were no women managers or anything? Assistant managers?

No, no.

But there were particular jobs that women did and other jobs that men did?

That's right.

What were the jobs then that women were doing, on the whole?

Windin, weavin, darners.

Were there any women dyers?

No.

No. That was a man's job?

Uh huh.

Why was that, do you think?

Ah don't know.

Was that heavy work?

Ah suppose it was. Ma son wis in the scourin hoose when he left the school.

And ma other son wis a joiner. He done his time in the mill.

There were a few tradesmen as well? Joiners, engineers, electricians?

Uh huh.

You started on the bobbins and you were saying eighteen to twenty women worked on the bobbins, aye?

Ah would think so.

And you were saying that you hadn't been there long when you saw an accident?

It wis mohair we were doin and they were two reels, and ye untangled it and set it off for tae come up and go through the drum and get made intae a bobbin. And she wis doin this and the yarn hanked on the shaft and it pued her in.

Pulled her wrist in?

Her hand wis lyin on the floor.

Cut her hand right off?

Took it right off.

Dear, oh, dear. That would be a very serious accident?

Oh, that wis.

So what happened? Was she rushed to hospital?

Oh, she wis rushed away to the hospital.

Was she alright? She recovered?

Oh, aye, oh, aye. She went aboot. She had nae hand. She went aboot. It wis a Peebles woman, aye. It wis somebody fae the yarn-store that came through wi a canvas bag and lifted it up and put it in!

The hand? Oh, dear. That must have been most upsetting?

Oh, it wis horrible.

Did you get any time off, you know? Did the manager come and say, 'Now girls,' you know, 'you can have the rest of the …'?

No that Ah can think o.

… no. You just had to carry on. Did accidents happen quite often in your experience in the mill?

No. When Ah went on tae the weavin ye often got a flyin shuttle. Ah've had a flyin shuttle on ma head. An Ah've had yin on the arm.

Struck you on the head, aye?

Aye. Ye got that.

Was that, forgive my ignorance, was that because the shuttle worked loose on the machine? It just came off?

It didnae get a proper hit and it hit off the boxes and stotted up in the air.

Was that quite painful then?

Aye, very sore it wis.

Were you ever off work with that?

Ah wis only off work once when Ah worked in the mill, wi an accident. And it wis the webs. We used tae get yer web off an ye got a help tae lift it off intae the passage. And the men hadnae been round tae clear them away and Ah went in in the morning. And it wis wintertime an ma toe o ma boot caught on and a went down and hurt ma knee. And ma knee came up like a balloon. And Ah can remember ma neighbour went away for the boss. Ma boss then wis Willie Logan. He came fae Gala. 'Och,' he says, 'it'll be aaright'. And Ah wis that angry at him, Ah kept on workin. Ah came home at dinnertime and ma son come home. And Ah had made his dinner and Ah wis sittin. He says, 'What's goin' on?' Ah showed him.

He says, 'Are you jist home?'

Ah says, 'Aye'.

He says, 'Well, ye're no goin back'.

Ah says, 'Aye, Ah Ah'm'. (laughs)

But you didn't go?

Aye! Ah walked along there wi him and there were two houses along, before ye got intae the mill. One wis Mackenzie the joiner's house and the other wis Renwick. They both worked in the mill and she wis the First Aid. And Alan and Jean Renwick were awfy friendly and she came to the door. And ma son says, 'Go and have a look at ma mum's knee'. She says, 'Effie, ye're no goin tae yer work. Come on!' And we went up tae the mill, tae the personnel officer. She phoned for the doctor. And as soon he saw it he says, 'Oh, you'll need to go down to the Peel'. So they got somebody frae the mill tae take me down tae get the bruised blood taen off. An Ah wis off ma work for nearly seven weeks!

Did you get paid during that time?

No, Ah wis a widow and Ah had a pension. So because Ah had a pension … When Ah came back to Peebles and went intae the mill, Ah had £3 widow's pension a week. And Ah went intae the mill and if Ah made more than £3, Ah had tae send ma widow's pension book tae Gala, tae get 6d. off o every shilling off ma pension.

Aye, beyond the £3?

Uh huh.

And did that happen often?

Oh, aye.

Can you remember what your wages were? I mean, I appreciate it would go up and down a bit because you'd be on piece-work rate?

Aye, it depended on what kind o work ye had.

But was it considerably more than £3 by the time you got …

Oh, aye! Ye'd send your book away every week. And Ah went round an Ah said tae Miss – her name's on the tip o ma tongue. What did ye caa her?

Personnel?

Personnel officer. Ah says, 'Could Ah cut ma hours?' Ah says, 'Ah'm havin tae send ma pension book tae Gala every week'.

'Oh,' she says, 'you want to get your money from the government. You don't want to work for it'.

That's whit she said to me.

So you didn't get anywhere, and you just had to continue sending your pension book?

Uh huh.

Crazy?

Uh huh.

Would you have preferred to work part-time maybe, if that was possible?

Even if they'd let me start an hour longer in the mornin, ye ken?

Aye, just to make sure you got, aye, just to get the maximum amount you could earn without losing from your pension?

Aye. Well, it wis crazy, wasn't it?

But they weren't prepared to consider that?

No. Now what Ah think she did say wis, the tuners depended on the weavers for their pay. So Ah could understand that in a way, but ye were workin aa thae hoors and ye werena gettin the money.

So am I getting the right picture, that you found that Ballantyne's, as employers, were really not very sympathetic?

No.

They weren't prepared, really, to come and go a bit with you?

No.

Do you know why that would be?

Ah don't know. Ah'll tell ye. There's two brothers got the mill now. And since they took over the workers have been far better off, far better off.

How did you find Ballantyne's as employers then, you know, in your personal experience?

Well, Ah was on the Hattersley when Ah went in.

That's the particular weaving machine?

Yes. And Ah wis on one loom. Everybody had one loom. And then they started up for two looms. And Ah had a bash.

That's to say, they made you?

Work two looms instead o one.

Was that with the agreement of the union?

It must haa been.

Did you get extra money for that?

Oh, well, aye. If you made it you got it.

Aye. So it was piece-work again?

Piece-work.

How difficult did you find looking after two looms, compared with one loom?

Well, actually it depended what kind of work you had in. You would maybe have a good job or a bad job, ken?

What was a good job, then?

Worsted. That wis a guid job. It didnae break a lot. With a bad job, ye were sometimes puttin ashes and soap in (laughs) to make it go.

Aye. So a bad job would be using a particular kind of wool that was liable to break, was it?

That's right.

And what kinds of wool would those be then?

Ye see, this is where ma memory's gone. Ah ken what Ah want tae say and Ah …

Aye, don't worry about the details, you know. It's just that your dealing with …

Rubbish. You couldnae understand it bein made intae a cloth and it bein wearable.

Cheap? Cheap, breakable, easily breakable?

But then Ballantyne's went in for quantity, no quality.

Did they?

Oh, aye.

They claimed to have produced very high quality cloth, didn't they?

Eh, Sportex, things like that.

That was good quality?

That wis good quality.

…

Ah wis made redundant [in 1971].

1971, about twenty-five years ago?

Oh, aye.

Now why were you made redundant? Was the mill taken over?

No, it wis gaun doon. We used tae work three shifts: day shift, back shift and night shift.

Women as well?

Women as well. And then, oh, for a long time we worked shifts. And then they cut oot the night shift and we were doin day shift and back shift. But they wanted the same output as they were gettin on three shifts, on two shifts.

And they didn't succeed in getting that?

Of course they couldnae get it!

So then you were made redundant?

Oh, there wis redundancies before Ah wis made redundant. But Ah could never understand why they paid off a widow and kept on married women, ye ken? Because Ah ended up, when the Dobcross came in, ye were lookin after four looms.

When was that roughly? Two or three years before you were made redundant?

Oh, aye!

Several years?

Oh, aye. They were Hattersley, then the Dobcross and then the Sulzers.

Aye. Was that a German machine?

Ah think so. And there were a lot o us no wantin tae go on them.

Was that because it was too demanding?
> It wisnae shuttles, it wis bullets.

And what was the difference then? More difficult to work?
> They went quicker.

So you were being driven harder and faster all the time?
> Uh huh, uh huh.

As the machines changed, you were expected to produce more and more.
> Uh huh.

But without commensurate increases in wages, I take it?
> Ye see, there's a lot o things that Ah cannae remember, but Ah can always mind that Ah got an awfu lot mair tax off than aa the rest o them, because Ah had a widow's pension and a pay. And if ye were off ill, they aa got rebates. Ah never got a rebate.

No, it was your pension that suffered.
> If you had a pension, you didnae get a rebate.

Anthony French went into the finishing department and described this part of the process to Ian. Anthony went on to work in various jobs, both within and outwith the Ballantyne and Thorburn mills and also shared his thoughts on pay and conditions and unions.

Anthony French, b. 1929, pay and conditions

Aye. So, you left the woods when you were about seventeen, roughly?
> Uh huh. An then went to the mill.

So that would be 1946, just after the War?
> Uh huh, uh huh.

Now which mill did you go in to?
> Ballantyne's. March Street.

How did you get the job?
> Well there wis plenty. Ye jist went up and seen whoever it wis in those days. It would jist be the manager. And ye jist asked for a job an ye probably got a start because, well, as Ah say, the War wis jist aboot finished an there wis plenty work for everybody. Plenty!

So what job did you do when you first went in?
> Ah wis in the finishin department. That's the only place Ah wis ever in, was the finishin department. Where they finished aa the cloth.

And did you find that work interesting?
> Aye, Ah wis quite happy in there. Ah wis quite happy.

And again, can you remember what the wages were in that year or so?
> Ah think, if Ah mind right, Ah might've had aboot, then, maybe aboot £2 a week, if Ah wis lucky. If Ah wis lucky.

So that was a wee bit more than you'd been getting in the woods?

Aye, mair than the wids.

Would that have been a reason for you moving from the woods?

Ah cannae remember if it wis money or no. Because in thae days ye didnae get your pay anyway. It wis jist handed ower tae your mother. It wis handed over an ye got maybe half-a-croon.

Aye. Pocket money?

Aye. Uh huh. The money was always handed over.

Over to your mother, aye. So just remind me, what were you doing when you started in the mill again?

The finishin.

The finishing, aye. And what was the nature of the work that you did there?

Aye, well, the pieces would maybe have to get pressed an everything like that, when they went intae a roller. Or they maybe have tae get cropped. An they got sprayed wi water an everything like that, afore they got pressed. That involved aa that.

So that you were learning the tricks of the trade?

Ah wis learnin aa that, uh huh. Ah came back. In '47, Ah went intae the mill. Where did Ah go fae there? Ah think Ah went to the railway in the early fifties, maybe.

Aye. So you were in the mill maybe three or four years after you did your Army service?

Aye, aye. An Ah think Ah went there maybe aboot the '51 tae the LNER.

…

Aye, Ah went tae Thorburn's in '59. Tweedside.

Tweedside mill. And that was the one that burned down?

That's right, in '65.

'65, so was that when you left the mill?

Well, we hud tae cos it wis burnt. We were still there for aa it wis burnt down. Because Ah wis in the wool store and we could still produce the wool side. But for aa the rest o the mill it wis burnt down but it didnae affect the wool side. Our side wis aaright. So we carried on that way for aboot anything up to a year, then we wis aa transferred over tae Damdale. An then it wis bought over by Henry Ballantyne. An then Ah went to March Street.

So you went to March Street about '66, roughly?

Uh huh.

And then, did you remain in March Street until you went into the building industry?

Yep.

Now, thinking to Damdale, what differences did you find between working in Damdale and working at Tweedside?

It wis the difference again, Ah wis on the finishin again at Thorburn's, at Damdale.

Your work, your own work had changed?

Uh huh. Uh huh. Ah came fae the wool-store side back tae the finishin side.

And you didn't mind that?
No. Ah didnae mind it.
Because it was work that you were already familiar with from your March Street days?
That's right. That's right. And once again, there wis only the three o us in the warehouse, you know whit Ah mean? So there wis nae problems.
No, no. What was the atmosphere like in Damdale? Was it just as friendly as Tweedside had been?
Good. Uh huh. Good. Aye.
Again, you found it was more relaxed, the management was more competent, more efficient, more sympathetic than at March Street?
Ah think the manager at Damdale might have been a wee bit more stricter, Willy Hounam.
And then you were only about a year in Damdale, when that was bought over by Ballantyne's? Was that right?
Uh huh. Uh huh. Henry Ballantyne.
And all the workers were moved up into March Street?
Uh huh. Uh huh.
So you had completed the full circle?
That's right.
Began in March Street, Tweedside, Damdale and back to March Street?
Uh huh. Uh huh.
And that would be roughly about 1966/67? When you went back to March Street?
Aye. An then Ah went tae the buildin trade.
But you remained in March Street for about three years?
Maybe, maybe aboot three years. Three or four years, aye.
Were you not very happy in March Street? Was that why you went to the building trade?
No. Ah got a chance o a drivin job wi the buildin trade an maybe more money. So Ah jist took it.
No. And of course, by that time you'd been working in the mills, first Tweedside, then Damdale and then March Street for about eleven years? So again, maybe you felt you could do with a change? Was that the position?
Well, Ah think the boss o the buildin asked us if Ah wanted a job drivin an Ah thought, well, Ah'll grab it.
…
Ah wis in the mill union for years and years and years.
Aye. Had you become active? You said you were a shop steward?
Ah wis a shop steward in the mill at March Street. Ah wis a shop steward at Damdale.
Damdale. So you must have become a shop steward about 1965–66?
Aye, Ah wis.
Not long after the fire at Tweedside?

Aye, that's right.
Aye. But you weren't a shop steward at Tweedside?
No, no.
It was after you went to Damdale?
Aye.
Now thanks very much indeed for all your time and trouble, Mr French. You were a shop steward, you were saying, for, did you say twenty, twenty-five years?
Twenty-odd years, aye.
Twenty-odd years, aye. Tell me about the strength and weaknesses of the unions that you worked with. First of all the Textile Workers, you know, the Dyers and Textile Workers Union. Was that strong in Peebles in the mills?
Well, there wis no union strong. Ah always felt that the management could always turn ye round about. And ye always felt, it's like the present day, that if somebody says 'Boo!', the union would just say, 'Right then, that's it. We're snookered'. An Ah believe if ye turned roond and says, 'Come on, let's go out the gate!' and ye turned round, Ah think ye'd be on your own.
Aye. That's what I was going to ask. Why was it easy for management to say, 'Boo!' and get away with it?
Because Ah think everybody was feart they'd get their books.
Was that because there was really very little tradition of trade unionism in Peebles?
Ah think if you had demanded a strike or ye advised your workers on a strike, you would've got seventy per cent o them workin. An ye might've got thirty per cent standin by.
So that was a fundamental weakness? Was there, in your recollection, much or any victimisation in the mills, of workers like yourself who were activists in the union?
Ah don't think there was so much victimisation but Ah think there wis always that worry that if ye were too pushy they would get ee.
Did you personally ever suffer in that way?
No, no, no.
And you never felt that you were put under pressure?
No, no.

In the final extract in this section, John Lunn reflects on the changes in men's and women's roles in the mill during his working life.

John Lunn, b.1936, men and women's roles

March Street had a lot o women because they had a lot o weavers, the women.
No women tuners?
No. But it wis women that did the actual weaving. Even when Ah wis at March Street the people who we'd say are the weavers, were aa women. But the tuners that set the looms up, put the beams in and aa that, it wis aa men that did that. If there were a breakdown, the mechanics, if you like … a tuner

is a mechanic on a weaver; a carder is a mechanic on cardin machines. In other words ye look after breakdowns and that and make sure everything's right. All the tuners, aa these people were aa men but the actual weavers themselves, who watched the looms and made sure that everything was runnin right, it wis women. And they served their time for that. It wis an apprenticeship. And the same wi the darnin and the finishin, it wis mainly women that did aa that.

There wouldn't be any men darners?

No. And the same when ye went up tae hosiery, the men gave out the work and aa that. It wis aa the foremen and aa the chargehands were men. But it wis actually women that wis doin the work.

And has that changed in more recent years? Do you get women?

Oh, ye get a lot o women managers and forewomen.

Aye. That's been something that's changed in your working life?

That has changed, aye. Dyers an that. Girls serve their time now. And designers, Ah would say cardin is mainly men. Although, durin the War, when Ah first started, there was one woman worked in the cardin. But again, that wis due to a shortage o men. And she wis quite good at it and she'd never be paid off. And the same in the spinnin, there wis only one woman that worked in the spinnin. But again, she'd been there durin the War and she jist carried on. There was a quite distinct[ion], you know, windin was a woman's job and cardin and spinnin were men's jobs. And weavin wis a woman's job. Darnin wis a woman's job.

Aye, aye. Quite interesting. A fairly rigid division between the sexes in the various tasks within the mill?

Oh, aye.

Industrial Relations

Before moving on to hear more from workers at Ballantyne's Caerlee mill, some extracts which relate more specifically to industrial relations within the mill are set out here.

Ian asked each of his interviewees about any union activities and was met, for the most part, with a fairly tepid response. Some interviewees had no knowledge of union activity within the mill while others said they simply paid their dues with little or no expectation of getting anything back. This may be because the paternalistic attitude of the Ballantynes and Thorburns may have fostered a feeling that the bosses were already acting in the best interests of their workers so no further action was needed. In addition, the mills were the main employer for the area so where else would you get employment if you didn't want to accept the conditions being offered in the mill? A third reason for the apparent lack of engagement with trade unions, put forward by one of Ian's interviewees, was that the mill workers lacked the clout of, for example, the miners. If the miners stopped working, the country quickly felt the impact whereas the mills had a history of periods of inactivity with no evidence of impact beyond the consequence of shorter hours for the workforce.

This first, short extract from Effie Anderson, is illuminating.

Effie Anderson, b.1925, union membership

Just one last question if I may. Trade unionism: you were a bit scathing.
    Oh! The only reason that Ah wis in the union wis in case o accidents. And when Ah had that accident wi ma knee, Ah never even thought aboot claimin. Never thought aboot it. And it wis Arthur Simmond's brother, he wis the union official, and [Arthur] came over to the house tae see how Ah wis and he says, 'Have ye thought aboot claimin?'
    'Ah never even thought aboot it, Arthur.'
    He says, 'Well, Ah think ye should'.
    And Ah wis off, Ah think it wis almost seven weeks (laughs) and Ah got £150.
Compensation from the firm?
    Uh huh.
It was their fault. Now, you joined a union?
    Aye.
Were there many workers in the union?
    Well, (laughs) for a wee while, Ah wis collectin the union. And, oh, there wis wee meetins, ye know, and they wanted a closed shop. And Ah can remember this other girl and I, we went roond everybody, and we ended up gettin a closed shop.
Was that a few years before you were made redundant?
    That's right. Oh, aye, a long time, a long time, aye!
But do I get the impression that the union wasn't really very strong?
    No, no. They agreed wi the bosses aa the time.

In a similar vein, we have this account from Margaret Melrose.

Margaret Melrose, b.1907, union membership

Was there a trade union in the mill when you first began?
    Well, Ah wouldna say it wis great but Ah wis in the union (laughs)
Aye. What union was that, Mrs Melrose?
    Ah couldnae even tell ye. It wis jist the union, they jist caed it.
But you joined as soon as you went in?
    No. They had tae come an ask me. (laughs) Ah didnae believe in payin oot for somethin Ah wasnae gettin. (laughs) You were usually makin your own wage when they asked ye. Yince ye'd been in a wee while.
So was it when you got onto the weaving side that you joined the union?
    Uh huh.
Not when you were working on the pirn?

No, no.
So you must have been working there for maybe three or four years before you joined the union?
> Aye. Ah wisnae long in the union, Ah dinnae think. After Ah wis mairried, Ah never wis in the union.

This next account, from Hume Davidson, covers a number of salient points, particularly his assertion of the belief that the attitude of the bosses was one of 'take it or leave it'.

Hume Davidson, b. 1928, trade unions

What about the strength or the weakness of trade unionism in your forty-five years in the mill? You know, is it your recollection that trade unionism was becoming weaker or stronger or remaining just much the same?
> Ah think it maybe got a wee bit stronger but it wis never dominant here because [if] it wis a trade likes o the miners, they mattered, didn't they, ken what Ah mean? If they stopped diggin coal aa the country suffered. But if we stopped weavin, there wis nobody, nobody [to be affected right away]. So ee paid your union and ee got your annual rise. If ye wasnae pleased wi it, you went on strike, well, you very seldom got a strike because you kent, if you striked, they would've said, 'Take it or leave it!', so …

Did you personally ever go on strike?
> No, Ah dinnae think sae.

You were never on strike in the forty-five years you worked in the mill?
> No.

And you don't recollect any strikes taking place?
> Ah think there were maybe strikes on the hosiery side. They were a wee bit mair dominant.

Were the hosiery workers a bit more militant or trade union?
> Ah, well, aye. They had a wee bit better wages than us, too.

But it was always a fairly weak union in your working life?
> Exactly.

Walter Scott's account reiterates the points made by Hume Davidson, and speaks of the general apathy towards union activity.

Walter Scott, b. 1924, trade unions

Now, can I ask, were you ever politically active as a young fellow?
> No.

Did you have any interest in politics?
> No. No. And Ah still dinnae have tae this day!

No, no. You were never a member of any political party?

No, no, no. In fact, if Ah'd onything tae dae wi it Ah'd bloody scrap the bloody lot o them. Ah'd make a coalition government and put aa the brains thegither tae sort it oot. But that's another subject.

But you were never much interested in political issues as such?

No, no.

You never joined a party?

No, no.

Now what about trade unions and the mill?

Yes, Ah wis a member o the trade union.

As soon as you went? When you were fourteen you joined a union did you?

Aye, well, more or less. The union man came and approached me.

Now what union was that?

That wis the Bleachers and Dyers Union.

Aye, aye. Were they the union that organised all the workers in the mill, who wanted to join?

Yes.

Aye. Was there another union? Maybe the Transport and General or the General Municipal Workers?

No then.

Not then?

Later on in life they did join the Transport and General Union.

Aye. But when you went into the mill first there was only the one union?

Only the one.

And anybody could join that?

Oh, aye, aye.

I mean, you didnae have to be a dyer or a bleacher?

No, no, no. Anybody in the mill could join the union.

Now I know it's a long time ago and you were just a young laddie before the War: is it easy to recall roughly what proportion of the workers would be in the union at that time? Was it as many as a half or a third or two-thirds?

Oh, Ah would say, at least two-thirds. Most o the workers wis in a union.

Before the War?

Aye.

In the March Street mill. And you wouldn't know about the position, except maybe through your father, in the Damdale or Tweedside mills? In Thorburn's mills?

Ah never heard him discussin much aboot that. No that Ah can mind o. Ah thought it wis a guid thing when Ah came hame and telt him Ah had joined the union, ken. Ah don't think it ever did us any bloody guid. Although they were supposed tae negotiate the wage rises and conditions and this, that and the next thing. But if the Ballantynes says 'You're gettin thruppence o a rise', that's what ye got, ken.

Aye. The union was fairly weak then was it, in your experience?

Oh, aye, oh, aye.
Why was it weak do you think? I mean, if most of the workers were in it?
Ah mean, if the union had said right, 'We'll call a strike for mair money or somethin like that, ye would get very few in [March Street] would go on strike.
Why was that then?
Cause Ah think they were too feart for their job. And that wis how in thae days management could pey what they liked.
So management knew that, at the end of the day, most of the workers would refuse to go on strike, even if the union called them out?
Uh huh.
And was it your recollection that most of the workers were really just quite unwilling to go on strike under virtually any circumstances?
That's right, aye.
Do you remember before the War taking part in any strike in the mill?
No.
Was there a strike?
Never.

Betty Muir remembers that she was expected to join the union when she first joined the workforce at the March Street mill.

Betty Muir, b. 1922, union membership

Now what about trade unions? Did you join a union when you entered the mill?
Oh, aye, yeah, yeah. Ye had tae.
As soon as you entered the mill?
Yeah, ye had tae.
Even before the War?
Aye. Ye had tae join a union.
So you joined the union as soon as you went into the mill?
Aye, Ah think so, Ah'm sure Ah did cause Ah remember the cards.
Aye. I had formed the impression that the union was very weak before the War?
Aye, it was but if ye didnae join it ye were aa that wis bad. So me, rather than have rows, Ah joined.
Did someone come and ask you to join?
Aye, yeah.
Were you active in the union?
No.
Were there any meetings that you went to?
Oh, aye, jist within the mill, aye, if they wanted to do anything. But Ah jist let them get on wi it, ye ken. Ah paid ma dues an that wis it, as far as Ah wis concerned.
Do you remember any union meetings being held in the mill during working hours?

> Oh, aye.
>
> *Before the War, I mean?*
>
> No, Ah cannae remember that.
>
> *And did you join as soon as you were fourteen?*
>
> Ah'm sure Ah did, aye. Ah'm sure that wis kept off your wages as well. But it wis only 2d. or something at that time, aye, that was kept off your insurance.

Again this account, from W. Lockie Robson seems fairly typical. You joined the union and paid your dues, but you were never an active member.

W. Lockie Robson, b. 1932, union membership

> *Aye, aye. That's great. Now can I ask about trade unionism? When you went into the mill did you join a union?*
>
> Aye.
>
> *So you joined as a laddie. More or less as soon as you went in?*
>
> Well, more or less, aye. …
>
> *And can I ask, did you become an active member?*
>
> No, no.
>
> *Always been a rank and file member?*
>
> Uh huh.

In these next two extracts we hear from Robert Gray and his wife Margaret who were much more active in the union. Robert had been a serving trade union official and he was keen to share and discuss his thoughts with Ian.

Robert Gray, b. 1926, trade union activity in the mill

> Ah never remember a union before the War at Caerlee. Mind you, havin said that, well, Ah've answered your question. When Ah went in there as a boy, Ah didn't know anything about a union. But havin been involved in the trade union movement so deeply in ma latter life Ah know that there were union members within the mills in those days. But the local representative had to go round their doors at night collectin their money. Ah found that out much later, yes.
>
> *But you never heard your father, who worked in the mills, or your brother or your sister or any of your mates or their parents talking about trade unionism before the War?*
>
> Never, never, never. No, no, no.
>
> *So it simply didn't exist at all, as far as you're aware?*
>
> As far as Ah'm aware, it jist didn't exist, no.
>
> *Did veterans tell you in later years that this is what had happened? That the organiser went round the doors at night, in the dark of night?*
>
> That's right, yeah.
>
> *And this was presumably because of fear of management?*

Well, Ah think so. Ah think it would be. Ah mean, that's the only thing that Ah can make out o it, was that there was such a resentment aboot trade unionism. Ah mean, even after the War, Ah mean they certainly werenae welcomed wi open arms, you know. You had to fight to establish the union. You fought for everything you got, really.

Just before we come to the post-war period, can you recall any stories or hearing anything about men or women, young or old, being victimised for trade union activities in Innerleithen before the War?

No, no, no. Ah'd be very surprised tae hear if there was any union activity in this area prior to the War.

So you hadn't yourself had any previous union experience before you went off to the Forces. But your experiences in the Forces made you maybe union conscious, or at any rate aware of some of the differences of a social class nature: officers and other ranks.

Yeah, Ah would say that possibly.

So you came back after the War and did you plunge in immediately to the union?

No, no, no, no. It was a long, long time after. It would be somewhere in the middle fifties.

Now what was the union concerned?

The union concerned was a Yorkshire-based union, which was called the Dyers, Bleachers and Textile Workers.

Was it just your daily experience at work that got you interested in trade unionism or was it some particular individual interest, you know, maybe a book that you'd read?

No, Ah think it was just that experiences at work that informed me, you know how things go. That you go along to meetings and there are things happen in factories and aa the rest o it. And if you have your say that you sort o said, 'Oh, well, you know, if you feel that, you better see if you can do it', sort o thing, you know. But the trade union movement, of course, as you know yourself, that if you get involved in it, the deeper you get involved, the more interested you become in it. That's just really what happened.

So was it a case of the union forming after the War?

There was organisation in Caerlee when Ah come back [in 1947]. Bud Smith. He was the collector. But, you know, if you'd any problems, well, you just told him and he got in touch wi a lad wi the name o Jock Samson. He lived in Peebles but he worked in Innerleithen over in Waverley mill. And he was the sort o contact man. He eventually became branch secretary but he wasnae branch secretary then. It was a lad wi the name o Gilroy in Peebles that was the branch secretary then. Everybody ran to Jock wi anything that wis wrong, you know and he wis the man that had the contact with the full-time officials who, under the Dyers and Bleachers, were in Glasgow, you know, Bath Street in Glasgow. And Jock wis the man that ye had to see if ye wanted a full-time official.

So you became involved really just as a result of your work, in the usual kind o way?

That's right. Ah wis appointed a shop steward and it jist aa went fae there, you know. Shop steward, went on to the branch committee and …

Presumably you were one of the folk that got up and spoke your thoughts when it was necessary to do so?

Oh, aye, aye.

Can you remember was there any particular incident maybe, where you felt you really had to get up and say something or do something? Maybe some conflict or difficulty?

Oh, there was quite a few occasions that, you know, there was sort o problems up there. Ah can remember one occasion that Arthur Oddy, this managing director, came back from America and that he said that he'd had a very, very difficult selling season. And the 6d. an hour that he had put on to the piece-work rates when things were good, he was takin back. And nobody can ever remember the 6d. goin on! So there was a bit of a rumpus then. But, Ah mean, the trade union strength in those days, ye jist had to accept – you could make a noise about it – but ye jist had to accept it and that was that. It was accepted. There wis numerous things, you know, throughout the years that happened. Ah would say that there was sort o maybe forty per cent, you know, of the people that Ah worked beside were in the union. But the majority weren't in it.

So with 300 workers roughly, you would have thought that somewhere about 120, 130, 140, something like that, were in the union?

Yeah, aye, uh huh.

And there were women as well as men in?

Yes, aye.

And again was it that the women formed the majority of the 300 workers?

Yes. It's always been that up there.

So was that reflected in the membership of the union, when you came back? Or were there more men than women in it?

Ah think there'd be more men than women in it then. Yeah, Ah think so. There would be some women in but Ah don't think there would be a big presence.

Was part of the problem in getting more women into the union that some women, were working part-time in the mill?

There was quite a lot o part-time women in those days.

When you came back from the Forces?

Yes, aye. Quite a lot o part-time workers.

And was it that as part-timers they couldn't see so much point maybe in joining a union?

That was always that, well, call it a reason, call it an excuse, Ah don't know, that that's what they said, you know. Ah've always said that, you know, there are no good reasons why you don't join a union, there are only excuses.

And presumably they got some sort of pro-rata subscription offered them, if they were working, say, a half-week or a half-day? They didn't pay the full union contribution? They'd pay a half?

Ah think they did but, Ah mean, it was coppers in those days.

You would no doubt get some workers who were adamant that they would not under any circumstances join a trade union for one reason or another?

Oh, yes. Oh, aye.

You became a shop steward by 1957–58?

Oh, somewhere aboot that. Aye. As Ah say, Ah went from there and Ah got on to the branch committee, Ah eventually became branch secretary, district chairman, and eventually a full-time official with the Dyers, Bleachers and Textile Workers.

Fine. Now the branch encompassed what [area]?

Peebles, Innerleithen and Walkerburn.

There's no history of long established trade unionism [in the Borders]. The farm workers wouldnae be well organised. The forestry workers would be in a union but …

Aye. The farm workers in the Borders, again Ah talk from experience with being with the Transport and General Workers, the farm workers in the Borders, as ye probably know, are very, very poorly organised, trade union wise.

So you became shop steward and then you became branch secretary. So roughly when would that be that you became branch secretary?

Let us think. Aboot '60, somewhere aboot there. Ah went full-time in January 1968, and how long would Ah be branch secretary prior to that, Margaret? Seven years? Aye.

Quite a few years, aye. And that was an elective position? You were elected branch secretary were you?

Aye it was done at an annual general meetin of the branch, you know.

Aye. And that wasn't a full-time job obviously, by definition?

No, no, no, no, no.

You just worked away at that in your spare time?

That's right. Jock Anderson's still doin it to this day.

That's great. So your work as branch secretary involved contacting workers, shop stewards in all the mills in Innerleithen, Peebles and Walkerburn?

That's right, and because of the nature o the union, because of the full time officials bein in Glasgow, they encouraged the branch secretaries to get involved in local negotiations rather than sort o just call for them every time. So that, that's where Ah got ma experience in sort o dealin wi employers and that type o thing.

Aye, aye. So you'd be involved pretty well daily, weekly in negotiations with employers?

Quite a lot. Quite a lot, yes, aye. Ah wis at the call o March Street mill in Peebles, Waverley, Leithen mill, and Walkerburn. And various sort o committees and things outside, you know, that you've got to go to.

Aye, once you're in a position like that, you get elected on to other committees, sub-committees and so on. Now was the employer on the whole willing to give you time off to attend to trade union work of this sort during working hours?

They never objected.

So if you got a phone call from, say, Waverley mill to say, 'We've got a problem here. Can you come over and sort it?' There was no difficulty?

That's right. Well, Phil McGlasson was ma foreman at that time and aa Ah needed to say was to Phil, 'Look,' you know, 'Ah've jist got that phone call. There's a problem down the road. Ah'll need to go down there'.

'OK, then just away ye go.' No, they never objected to the time off, no.

No, no, no. So that was quite reasonable?

Oh, aye, it was. They were good in that respect, yeah.

Did you ever feel that, you know, there was even any suspicion that you were being victimised or discriminated against in any way by the management because of your trade union activities?

No, no really. Ah never gave it much o a thought, really, that. The only thing Ah can add tae ye is that when Ah did eventually decide to go full-time and go into the trade union movement, that one o the directors o Caerlee mill said to me, he says, 'Well, that's the reason that we never done anything about you because we knew you'd be goin on'.

Your commitment was always to trade unionism and not to your own personal career?

Uh huh. That's right.

Just tell me what was involved mainly in the work of branch secretary? You were at, as you say, the call of your members.

Yeah.

But also ordinary workers who knew you personally and maybe wouldnae understand the niceties of procedures and routines and just said, 'Hoi!'.

(Mrs Gray: That's right, yeah.)

The normal duties o any secretary, you know, you handle aa the branch correspondence. You keep the minutes and aa that. But, plus the fact that you was also acted as the branch treasurer. And that you'd collectors in aa the mills and that, you know, Ah had ways o gettin aa the money bags and the books in. And…ye had tae get this in every week, check aa the books to who has paid and count the money and bank it in the Co-op Bank. This kind o thing, you know.

Now that must have involved you in a great mass of work then, mustn't it?

Oh, aye. Margaret and I— We used to get thir books in, some on a Thursday night, cause Thursday was the pay day then. And then on a Friday we used to get the rest in, and we used to sit on a Friday night and a Saturday. And she would check some books and Ah'd check the money and then once we'd got it aa checked, Ah'd total the money up and get it aa ready for bankin, you know. Oh, aye.

So every night presumably was devoted to writing minutes, correspondence. Did you have a lot of correspondence with the active members? If a member wrote to you and said, 'Oh, this is terrible!' and such and such, you'd have to go and investigate?

That's right. Ah mean, a lot of it was somebody writin in and doin their nut about something and aa the rest o it and Ah felt well, that's a wee bit out o ma experience and aa the rest o it, Ah would just pass it on to Glasgow, you know. But, Ah mean, that had to be done within your day.

You had to make a judgement?

Yes, aye, aye.

And you're doing all this at the end of a hard day's work yourself?

Well, Ah think we quite enjoyed it, didn't we Margaret?

(Mrs Gray: We did. The thing that used to bother me about it was if there was trouble in the mill, some o them could be quite nasty to me about the union. That used to bug me. And it was nothing to do with me, you know.)

No, no. That always happens. You're the wife of the union man, so you get it as well as him!

And this is the disadvantage, forgive me for saying so, of living in a small town, where everybody knows you. In a big city like Glasgow or Edinburgh, you know, you'd be living somewhere, where the workers, very few of them, would know you personally or know where you lived? In a small town it's doubly burdensome, I'm sure, to be a branch secretary or, even worse, the wife of a branch secretary! (laughter)

(Mrs Gray: It was quite difficult at times of trouble, yeah.) (laughs)

We didnae have a phone in this house until Ah became a full-time official.

Ah, Ah. Because I was going to say, you know, did you find the phone a bit troublesome?

Ah found it very troublesome then (laughs) once Ah got it in, aye. Ah had a shop steward once that worked permanent night shift in a factory in Hawick – Wilson & Glenny's in Hawick. He was a terrible man, that, always had something , you know. And he got into this habit … He finished his shift at six o'clock in the mornin and he got into this habit just aboot three-quarters o an hour or half an hour before he was due to finish his shift, of phonin me up. (laughs) Ah took it till couldnae stand it any longer! (laughs)

Oh, that's terrible! Utter lack of consideration!

(Mrs Gray: And on the other side, you could get some quite nice people.) And his argument when I got on to him one day was, 'I want away home to ma bed!' (laughs) Ah missed ma sleep an aa!

Did you ever take part in a strike? Or was there ever a strike in any of the mills in Peebles?

Ah don't think Ah ever took part in a strike. Well, Ah once took part in a stoppage o work where they put a time-study man on at the gents' toilets to see how long people spent in the toilet. So Ah downed tools. But that was the nearest I ever was to a strike. That would be in the fifties sometime, yeah. Just when the work-study was startin to come to the fore, you know. But as far as strikes goes, that, yes, Ah had strikes in the mills here but Ah was a full-time official by that time.

Yes. You personally as a worker in the mill never took part in one?

Other than that, no, no, no.

Because this seems to have been a general feature, as you will know better than I do, that I don't think I've spoken to anybody in Peebles, Walkerburn or Innerleithen so far who himself or herself had taken part in a strike.

Oh, well, but there's plenty o them!

There must be some around, as you say.

Because, Ah mean, the Caerlee, the first one up there, it was an all-out strike. They were out for aboot sort o ten days. The next one was a limited section because by that time we'd got aa this industrial relations sort o ballyhoo forced upon us. And they said that they would, you know, take action rather than a total strike, you know. And they selected days, you know. For example, like on a Tuesday night, we says: 'Right then, we're on strike tomorrow mornin.' Well, you've to terrorise the management, of course, you know. So there's quite a few. Waverley have been on strike.

But these are more recent years, I gather, if it's the present legislation you're talking about?

Well, yes, aye, but, mind you, we've had industrial legislation for quite a number o years now, you know.

But as a trade union official obviously you were drawn in quite a few times?

Yes. Oh, aye, aye, aye.

And mainly the strikes that took place were over consequences or outcomes of legislation? The anti-trade union legislation?

No, no, no really. The first one, when it was the all-out strike, that was due to what happened in Ireland. The Irish factory were on strike and they started layin off people up here because the Irish factory was on strike. So we jist said 'Well,' you know, 'you're not on'. And it lasted Ah think aboot ten days. It was a case o puttin pressure on the management. You see, they had a factory in Ireland which done a certain amount of the process. But a lot o the finishin processes had to come back here. And because this income o work wasnae comin, they started layin people off up there. Well, we said, 'I'm sorry, but unless ye get Ireland sorted out we're no prepared tae accept that people are goin tae suffer here simply because ye cannae sort yourself out in Ireland'. Ah cannae remember what that strike in Ireland was about. You see, the management had a very, very poor industrial relations thing in Ireland in particular. Ah mean, there was a good few stoppages o work over there. Coleraine, up in the north, aye. But, but their industrial relations record in Ireland was very, very poor. Very poor indeed.

Aye. Of course, from what you were saying and what other people have told me, too, Ballantyne's were a firm or a family or grouping of families and firms, they really hadn't encountered trade unionism until after the Second World War? It was very uncommon for a strike, or similar industrial action short of a strike, to take place in the mills in Peeblesshire [before the War].

That's right, yeah. Ah don't think it would ever take place prior to [the] War. And, you see, Ah mean, [in] other sections o industry you might be drawn intae that, but other sections o industry just did not exist in those days. The whole area was solely dependent upon textiles. And that's to the misfortune o the place at the present moment because the Border textile industry has just disappeared. Practically disappeared.

The textile workers have always been very reluctant to look upon trade unionism as a strength. They didnae realise their own capabilities if they could have been 100 per cent organised.

Margaret Gray also gave her own interview to Ian.

Margaret Gray, b. 1933, union membership

Did you join a union when you went into Caerlee or soon after that? Or was it some time after that?

It wis quite a wee bit after that.

But before you were married?

Oh, yes, aye, oh, aye.

Maybe in your early twenties?

Aye, Ah would say, och, Ah would say before that, aye.

Aye, around twenty or late teens?

Yes, aye.

After you'd been in the mill two or three years?

Uh huh, I would think so, yes, uh huh.

And how did you come to join the union? Did somebody come round and ask you to join?

It was a friend of ma mother's and she plagued me and plagued me and Ah said, 'No, Ah'm no joinin the union'. And Ah thought oh, tae hell, Ah'll give in tae her. An then ye suddenly realise that ye should've been a member.

What were the grounds of your resistance to joining?

Oh, jist young an daft, Ah think! (laughs) Young and daft, yes, yes. Ah would think that's what it would be. Ah'd nothing against them cause Ah didnae know.

Had your mother been in the union?

No, no. Nor ma granny, no, no, no.

So there was no family tradition, experience?

No, no, no.

And at that stage it was the National Union of Dyers, Bleachers and Textile Workers?

Dyers & Bleachers and Textile Workers, aye, yes.

And to begin with did you just pay your dues?

Oh, yes.

But didn't play an active part?

Oh, no, Ah never really played an active part in it. Ah jist helped Bert at times.

You did something better and married someone who was active?

(Laughs) That's right, yes, aye, yes.

But you were never yourself a collector, a shop steward or secretary or chairman?

Oh, no, no. Ah wis asked a few times because Ah've always been quite an outspoken person. But Ah thought one in the family's enough. (laughs)

That doesn't sound very complimentary somehow? (laughs)

Well, Ah really mean it in a nice way.

I know what you mean. And of course, as you say, you were involved, because your husband was telling me last week, what was involved in being an activist in the union. Your private time was taken up with folk phoning and comin to the door and all the rest of it.

Yes, that's right, aye, yes, aye, yeah.

Were you ever involved in strike action at Caerlee?

Yes, uh huh, yes.

What about at Murray Allan's? Was there ever any industrial action there that you were involved in?

Well, Ah wis never involved in it but they took action because o pay. They stopped workin overtime and these sort o things. But Ah never worked overtime. It was a long enough day for me anyway withoot workin overtime. Ah never got involved.

By the time you retired what were your hours?

Quarter-to-eight to half-four.

Aye, so in your working life the working day had shortened by an hour, roughly?

Uh huh, uh huh. I ended up on a thirty-nine hour week.

(Mr Gray: You went frae a forty-five hour week doon tae a thirty-nine hour week.)

And you retired at the age of sixty, you started work at sixteen, so that was over forty-four years, the working week had shortened by six hours?

Uh huh. Not a lot!

Not a lot but better than nothing?

Better than nothing, yes, aye, yes, yes, definitely.

It's quite a difference between forty-five and thirty-nine?

Uh huh, uh huh.

There really is. Forty-five is really quite a lot?

(Mr Gray: Ah think when it was cut frae forty-eight doon tae forty-five.)

It would be some time after the War?

(Mr Gray: Yeah, it was. You see, ye were talkin there, askin ma wife about workin Saturday mornins. That's when Saturday mornins were really sort o done away wi as part of the normal workin week and it was reduced fae forty-eight down tae forty-five. And was that no – there were three hours came off the workin week. To make up for the four hours that they worked on a Saturday mornin that's where the quarter-to-eight start in the mornin came in.) Ah wis goin tae say. Aye, Ah've got an awfy feelin Ah worked a forty-eight hour week.

When you first began?

Aye, it runs in ma head that, but Ah could be wrong – your memory fails ye at times.

Textile workers always worked longer hours than most other folk, you know?

Yes, that's right, yes, aye, yeah.

But it did gradually come down. Sometimes, you know, an hour was knocked off, sometimes a bit more than that, and so on?

Yes, aye, uh huh, yes.

Now looking back on your working life, do you have any regrets about having become a textile mill worker rather that a nurse or a hairdresser or whatever?

No really, no really.

You got a lot of satisfaction out of what you were doing?

Yes, aye. Well, Ah did what Ah wanted to do. We've made a good livin out o it. Ye had your ups and downs. Ah don't know, maybe lookin back now I might … No, Ah don't think Ah would have done anything different.

And then it's a question of opportunities, as your husband was saying, too?

Yes, that's right.

You know, if you live in Innerleithen and you don't want to, or you can't afford to travel to Peebles or to Edinburgh or Galashiels, then what is there to do?

Uh huh, uh huh.

You know, there's textiles, shops, domestic work, maybe a wee office job here and there, but nothing very much. That's it?

Uh huh, no, no. No, Ah think it's been aaright really, yeah.

Good. Well, thanks very much indeed Mrs Gray, that was very interesting. Aye, that was very interesting and I'm grateful to you. And, as I say, it's once we try and fit all the bits of the jig-saws together that the picture emerges.

The Ballantyne Caerlee Mill (hosiery)

We now return to mill processes, this time with a focus on Caerlee mill. Robert Gray started at Caerlee aged fourteen, in 1940. His father and brother also worked at Caerlee (his brother was a hand knitter until he went to the RAF during the Second World War). This extract is a good introduction to the processes at Caerlee and also explains something of the impact of the Second World War on the mill. Robert says more about the importance of Caerlee in the wider fashion markets. He also discusses the specialist machines and processes which were introduced to Caerlee over time.

Robert Gray, b. 1926, working at Caerlee

Coming at last to the work: you start work in Caerlee mill…
That's right.
… at fourteen. And what were you doing? What was your first job in the mill?
Ma first job in what they called the bar-fillin, was puttin the ribs on tae bars for the power frames, as it were then. And that wis a job that ye jist, ye got put in there until such times as there wis a sort o knittin machine, you know, available for you, a hand-knittin machine. Or if ye wis goin tae go on to the frames, until there wis a vacancy for somebody to train you, you know.
So that was a normal sort o job for a young lad or a girl starting, to do at that time?
Well, the girls didnae do it in those days actually. It wis a male that done the knittin, you know, when Ah first started there. There was a couple o women come on after that but not at first. That was the normal thing. But the women aa went intae the finishin processes, you know.
Right, right. And how long did you work at the bar-filling then roughly?
It would only be a matter o months, if it was months. It wisnae very long. It was more or less just until ye learned how to do the damn thing.
And learned something about the mill?
That's right. And Ah think to a certain degree, it was more a way o sort o induction you know, jist tae get ye in there and get ye used tae things.
And then you went on to do what?
On tae a hand-knittin machine.
Now just tell me, because you're dealing with an absolute ignoramus here about hosiery, you know, just describe the machine, please, the nature of the machine? What exactly did it do? How big was it?
Oh, it would be about what, about a metre, a metre in length, somewhere aboot that length and stood aboot, oh, three feet [above the floor], you know. And it has two beds wi needles on it, you know. And it depends … ye can only work one bed, you can work two beds … aa sorts o different patterns on it. And there wis a big sort o handle that ye pulled and this brought the head along to sort o make the needles come up and catch the yarn and knit the garment, whatever ye wis knittin, ye know. We used to knit hose for plus-fours, you know. And a certain amount of ladies garments, you know.
Twin-set things?
No, not so much the twin-sets. It wis aa heavier stuff, you know. It was after the War that cashmere became the main product up there, aye, aye.
And at the time you were beginning, of course, the War had been on for a year. So had the War affected the production in any way or the nature of what was being knitted?
The War did affect it because, well, the markets dried up, right. And they

started makin a lot o those great, big sort o sea-boots, we used tae call them. You know, they were the big, white liners for puttin inside wellington boots and what not.

Aye, aye, for the Forces?

Yeah. Ah mean, the place eventually closed down.

Roughly, when would that be? '42, maybe '43?

Aye, uh huh.

So you would have been in the mill maybe about a couple of years?

Aye, somewhere aboot that, aye.

And you went off to the Forces in 1943? And the mill was closed?

Oh, it was closed then, yes, aye. It was closed then.

So what happened to your job? Were you unemployed then?

We got jobs in the forestry. You know, there was a lot o forestry round aboot here. We got jobs in there jist until I went off to the Forces.

Now what I should have asked earlier, too, was how did you get the job at Caerlee?

Ah often say this, when Ah see the youngsters sort o sittin about the town doin nothing and no jobs for them and this. Ah often say that, you know, in ma days it wis totally different. Ye could choose the mill that ye wanted to go into. Because, you know, they were encouragin youngsters tae get in, you know, and …

You had four mills at that time. Was that right?

Yeah, that's right, uh huh.

Just at the beginning of the War?

Uh huh.

So did you deliberately choose to Caerlee?

Ah deliberately did because Ah had a couple o ma pals were in there already, ye see.

How did you find the work on the knitting?

The work? Before the orders dried up because of the War and the markets disappearin, ye know, and aa the rest o it, the work was very varied. So, Ah mean, it wasnae a monotonous job. Ah mean, one day you could be knittin the stockings for plus-fours. Another period it could be ordinary socks or you could be knittin a garment, you know. It was quite varied. Ye even knitted gloves at some point in time, ye know. Ah never done very many scarves.

So there was a variety about the work?

Yes, aye, there was.

You found the work interesting itself?

Well, as interesting as work can be, like, at that age, you know. Ah mean, certainly, as Ah say, it was never borin. Ye know, it's no like, it wisnae like sort o some o the other jobs that Ah seen in other factories and aa the rest o it much later in ma life. But Ah often wonder how some o them done them. They were that repetitive and sort o, ye know.

Aye. There was a wee bit of scope for individual initiative and so on?
   Oh, yes, aye, aye.
Did you feel that you were being hard driven by management as a laddie?
   No, no really, no. Ah don't think Ah wis hard driven. The only thing was that ye went in and ye wis trained on any old yarn, jist knittin anything that ye kind o wanted to do. And once ye got an order to do, once they felt you were good enough to knit an order, you then had to strive to get on to piece-work. Because they then wanted you on piece-work. They wanted you off o this marvellous set-wage o 10s.2d. a week, ye know – 10s.2d., a lot o money!
That's what you began with?
   That's what Ah began with, aye. (laughs)
And you still had that when you went on to the knitting machine?
   Well, yes, aye, aye, that's it. That was the sort o youngster's rate, you know. And, you know, you had to strive to get on to piece-work.
Aye. So there was a pressure on you to develop your skills to the point where you could get on to piece-work?
   Yes, Ah suppose there was a certain amount of pressure put on to you. But tae a large degree, it was very much left to your own devices, you know, to get on tae it. Ah mean, there were people who went in who couldn't get on to it. Well, they jist didnae last. They had to go, you know. They wouldnae pay them this 10s.2d. forever.
Aye, aye, that's right. There was an expectation that sooner rather than later you would move on to higher and better things?
   That's right. Uh huh.
That's great. So you were doing this until the mill closed down?
   That's right.
When you first started there, when you left school, roughly how many workers would be employed at Caerlee?
   Hell, that's difficult to say. See, there was two parts o Caerlee at that time. There was a spinning part and a ... whew! Employees there at that time? Probably 150, 200, something like that, ye know. Ah would think it would be more women, more women than men. Because Ah mean, the men in those days really only done the knittin and the sort o, you know, the millin and boardin and that type o thing. The heavier work. Once they were garments and that kind o thing, or even before they were garments, in the seamin and bindin, you know. Ah mean, look at the size o that seamin and bindin department when (to Mrs Gray) you were in it. There must have been about what, thirty, fifty folk – girls in there?
   (Mrs Gray: Yes. It would be about fifty. Aye, Ah would think so.)
Maybe something like three-fifths women, two-fifths men? Out of the 150–200 or so?
   Yeah, aye, somewhere aboot that.
Not as many as two-thirds women and one-third men maybe?

It could damn near be it because the amount o women that the amount o women that were involved in the finishin department – there was a terrific amount o women in there, aye.

So you came back. And did you go back on to the knitting machines?

Yes, aye, Ah went back on to the knittin, aye.

Virtually the same job you had?

Well, to start with, yes, aye. But then, but then, as Ah say, the industry had changed a bit. It was a much more sophisticated industry Ah came back to as to what Ah left. By this time they were opening up big markets in America. And there was a managing director up there with the name o Arthur Oddy. At that time he must have been a brilliant salesman, the man. Well, maybe sellin in a seller's market, of course, in those days. He used to go away to America and he got some fantastic orders.

From before the War?

Yes. And then they were goin intae aa different type o things that from what they used to call an ordinary flat-bed knittin machine, Ah eventually transferred and was trained on what they caed an Intarsia machine [a Swiss machine].

And what was the difference between that then and the machine that you worked on?

One, it was jist a single-bed machine and every thread was hand-laid in, you know. You developed the pattern by puttin the threads in by hand and jist pullin the hand intae the thing across the top tae knit the coarser yarn in. And then you progressed – well, you'd a pattern in front of you, a graph and you jist – each line across the graph was a row o knittin and each dot on the graph was a needle in the machine. So you jist followed the pattern.

And that could be done fairly quickly?

No, it was a very, very slow … very, very slow and laborious job, aye. A very interesting job because, you got such a lot o different patterns in it, you know.

So you're making more jerseys maybe by this time?

That's right.

Presumably by this time the plus-fours were going out of fashion?

Oh, they were away, aye. There was nothing like that then, no, no, no, no. We did knit what they cried hose, wee socks. For the American golfers. But they matched the garment, you know.

Aye, the set?

Aye.

Aye, they certainly were extremely popular garments weren't they in those days? I mean, I was just a laddie at the time but I can dimly remember, don't ask me how, that whether it was on the radio a lot, that knitwear was doing extremely well in export sales?

Oh, yes, aye. Knitwear went through a boom period, you know. That right up, Ah mean, oh, Ah'd say, oh, certainly right up through the fifties anyway, you know. There was hiccoughs in it. There was hiccoughs in it in the sixties and there was more hiccoughs in it in the seventies, you know.

Yes, yes. Fashions were changing, I suppose?

There was hiccoughs in it in the fifties as well. Because when Margaret and I were married, Ah was workin one week in three and Margaret was workin three days a week, you know.

Short-time working, aye. Expansion was certainly not continuous?

No, no. It wasnae then, no.

Much of what you made was exported, was it?

Oh, yes. Almost totally. Almost totally to America really. They were so dependent on America in those days that jist aboot everything went there. There was a certain amount, you know, went down to the big stores in London. But there again, most o it was indirect export, you know. Because, well, Ah don't think, (laughs) many people in this country at that time could afford to buy them.

John Brown started at Caerlee mill at the age of fifteen and soon earned more, as a hand knitter, than his father. This was a part of the process which was highly skilled and particularly well paid. However, as John was to discover when he went on to work on the frames, not all Caerlee wages were so well paid.

John Brown, b. 1920, working at Caerlee

Now, so did you have any ambitions as a laddie? You know, maybe to become an engine-driver or a seaman or a ploughman?

No, well, as Ah said previously, Ah got a prize for woodwork. And Ah can remember goin up tae Innerleithen and that and round the joiner's shops (in fact, ma mother took me) for tae be an apprentice but, see, there wis nothing. So Ah had ma name down in Walkerburn mill as well, of course, but Ah had ma name down at Ballantyne's.

That's Caerlee mill? Did you go in and say, you know, 'Have you got any jobs?'

That's right.

And they put your name on a waiting list, was that it? Was that how it worked?

Yes, aye, we were on a list. Because Ah can always remember there wis a few o us left the school at fourteen. And, well, we were all lookin for jobs. And there was a chap, Tom Ballantyne, and he got a job up in the bar-fillin, that's the ribs. That was Caerlee. And he got a job and then, aboot a couple of month after, Ah got on tae the bar-fillin.

So you started when you were fifteen? You were unemployed about a year?

Started when Ah wis fifteen, yeah, on ten shillings a week.

And you had your name on the list for a year?

Ma name wis on the list.

Did they send for you and say, 'Now, look, son, there's a vacancy'.

　　　　Yes, aye. The bar-fillin. That's what you usually started wi.
What about girls? Did they start on something else?
　　　　No, the girls could do the bar-fillin as well.
Aye. And what were your hours when you first began?
　　　　The hours were eight o'clock in the morning tae half-five. And you got three-quarters o an hour for lunch. That wis your lunch.
Did you get a wee tea-break in the morning?
　　　　Yes. A canteen break. You used tae get mornin and afternoon but Ah think they stopped the afternoon one.
Was there a canteen in the mill?
　　　　Oh, yes. Ah can remember ye used tae get a lovely lunch there. And, you know when Ah started there first, you used tae take a flask o tea and maybe two or three sandwiches, something like that. A Thermos flask. But some o them jist had sort o cans and they used tae put them on this sort o heater thing and it heated up. But Ah had the Thermos flask. But anyway, oh, they thought this canteen wis great.
Was that just after you'd gone there they started up the canteen?
　　　　Yes. Yes, it wisnae long after.
But that would be about 1936 or so? '35–'36?
　　　　It would be. Oh, there wis two ladies. What nice ladies they were. And grand cooks And you know the price for your lunch? 6d.! They started it off at 6d. Of course, Ah think the firm would sort o subsidise it.
They must have done?
　　　　Oh, they must have done. But it went up tae 9d. After a wee while it went up tae 9d. But, oh, you used to get a lovely lunch.
So did you stop taking sandwiches and get your lunch in the canteen?
　　　　Oh, yes, yes.
And was it a two-course, three-course lunch?
　　　　It wis a two-course anyway.
When you carried the sandwiches, you would get your dinner from your mother, when you went home at night? But then once you went into the canteen and got your lunch there did you not bother with a cooked meal at night?
　　　　Oh, no. Oh, no … just a plain tea, Ah suppose.
And then did your wage go up after a wee while, from the ten shillings with which you started?
　　　　Oh, yes, aye. Ah think Ah wis only on the bar-fillin aboot maybe six month. An then Ah got on the hand knittin, which wis a good job if you were workin. You sometimes had to wait till the post came in in the mornin, for tae see if there wis any orders. But Ah wis actually, well, Ah wis jist a young lad and Ah wis gettin a bigger wage as ma father, who had worked for years and years.
Once you got on to the hand knitting?
　　　　Once Ah got on there. £3 or maybe more a week Ah wis makin.

At the age of fifteen or sixteen?
    Yeah.
Aye. Because you started hand knitting when you were fifteen and a half?
    Aye. Ah think Ah wis only on the bar-fillin aboot six month. But, of course, it wis piece-work, you see.
In the hand knitting?
    You wis makin your own wage.
And was it quite difficult work to learn?
    No. This wis jist plain, plain work, which wis jist a plain machine. But, of course, the quicker you went, well, the more money you were earning. But Ah wis only on that for what, about a year. An Ah got the chance to go on to the frames, you know. Which, Ah took it, but Ah maybe made a mistake because ma wages dropped and Ah wis only gettin aboot £1.50 or something, you see.
That was a big drop?
    Ah maybe should've stayed in the hand knittin. Anyway Ah went on to the frames. And you had to serve an apprenticeship for that.
For the frames, aye.
    However, … of course, well, the War came, you see, … Ah wis on the frames.
You went off at the age of nineteen, in 1939?
    Uh huh.
Can you remember what your wage was roughly when you went to the War? Was it still about 30s. a week? It would fluctuate a wee bit, of course.
    It wouldnae be too much more. Ye see, just before the War, they reckon in Walkerburn mill, some o them in the machine-room, they were gettin under £2 a week. And they were married men.

Here, John describes, in detail, the different jobs and processes he encountered within Caerlee on his return from war service.

And you went back to the Caerlee?
    Aye, Ah got a job back there.
And what were you doing? The frames again was it?
    No, Ah went back, Ah went on tae the knittin. But they started Intarsia. Ah don't know if you saw some o these lovely garments, Intarsia knittin. And there wis four o us started on that. And, oh, it wis, it's individual in-layin threads, you know. It's an individual thing. And, oh, it wis a great success. It wis a great success. They couldn't get enough o it at one time. And they'd get an order in and they jist used tae repeat it. But there wis more and more chaps came in. And they said, 'Oh, we'll buy machines'. But they put a night shift on. And they said, 'Oh, it will only be for six months'. It lasted seven years!

Aye. So these years immediately after the War were really very, very busy years in the mills?

Oh, they were busy.

There was no unemployment then?

There wis, slightly, but not very much.

No. Pretty busy, certainly compared with before the War?

Oh, definitely. But, Ah think the Intarsia started '51 and it wis, as Ah say, oh, aye, they couldn't get enough of it. Couldn't get enough of it. We used to get fifteen shillings for doin a night-shift. That was extra, like. Aye, fifteen shillings, which wis only three shillings an hour. It wis never a job for night shift. Cause it wis concentration. Ah mean, eventually they got counters and that. You used to count, you know, how many rows you wis doin, you had tae count everything in your head and you sometimes had three different counts.

Were you making good money in those days?

Well, we thought it wis good money.

Certainly better than before the War?

Oh, definitely. But the allowance wasnae very good for night shift.

And how did you work the shifts then? Was it night shift once a month or …?

It wis every other week. We used tae start on the Sunday night, nine o'clock, finish at half-seven in the mornin. It was a long night. Aye.

So it was alternately day shift and night shift? Just the two shifts was it?

That's right, yeah.

Now again, roughly how many workers were employed at Caerlee after the War? Was it just the same as or more than before the War?

Oh, there'd be more, Ah think. Maybe aboot 250 to 300.

And again were the balance of the sexes much the same?

Of course, Caerlee, there'd been out-workers, you know. They've run buses from Loanhead and round about.

So there was a shortage of workers after the War?

Oh, yes, aye, they couldn't get workers.

They brought mainly women, was it, they brought in?

Still, they still are yet. Workers come from Galashiels and all round about.

But you didn't get that before the War?

Oh, no, no, no, no.

So you remained in the Caerlee until you retired, Mr Brown?

Yes. Ah took early retirement [in 1982].

When you were sixty-two?

Yes, for to help ma wife. She's terrible with rheumatoid arthritis. Ah always liked the job.

You enjoyed the work, uh huh, aye. Found it satisfying work?

Oh, definitely.

Now just finally looking back on your working life, do you have any regrets about having worked in the mill? You know, would you rather have become a joiner or a football player?

Oh, well, the wages they get now, right enough, football players or that! No. Ah wasnae cut out for that. Oh, Ah've no regrets at all because, on the whole, Ah must admit Ah quite enjoyed ma workin life. Cause it wis up tae yourself. It wis up tae you. You got your order, you got your chart and ye wis left to it. You see, all these years we worked night shift we never had a foreman. There wis never anybody in charge. You wis jist left to it.

There was a sense of freedom?

That's right.

You didn't feel that management were breathing down your neck all the time?

That's right. The foreman used to come in at nine o'clock and say, 'Right!' And he wis off and we wis left to it. No, no, Ah must admit, no, Ah quite enjoyed ma job. Yes.

Well, I'm very grateful to you, Mr Brown. Thanks very much. I hope I havenae disrupted your day for you. That was very kind of you.

In the first part of this next extract, Andrew Brunton tells Ian about his working life. He would have preferred to stay working outdoors rather than go back into the mill although, in the end, his working life as a frame worker lasted almost half a century.

Andrew Brunton, b. 1928, frame-worker, Caerlee

So you got the job in the forestry, the timber supply?

Uh huh, they were aa goin intae that, ye ken. A lot o the folk that didnae want tae go intae the mill, which Ah wisnae very keen tae go intae the mill tae start wi. Ah jist didnae fancy the mill.

You preferred to be outside rather than be in the mill?

Uh huh. But then again, what dictates is wages. So rather as … ken, Ah could've went tae the Forestry Commission efter the War. But Ah didnae, cause they were makin bigger peys in the mill. So Ah worked in the mill for forty-eight year an Ah cannae say Ah ever loved it, ye ken. It wis a job an it wis life, ye ken. Ah had guid days, bad days, like everything else. But Ah think aa ma life Ah'd have preferred tae have worked ootside.

Now you worked away in the timber supply then for about three years? Then when you were seventeen what happened?

Well, the hosiery had opened by this and they were recruitin, ye ken. They were lookin for workers.

This would be the end of the War by this time?

Aye. So Ah jist went there an got a job at the Caerlee mill. Ah got a job on the hand knittin.

That would be quite a change in your working life?

Oh, aye, aye. From the freedom o the open air an everything an then stuck in one position day efter day, aye.

How did you find that?

Oh, it wis a wee bit frustratin, ye ken, aye, uh huh. But, ken, like, Ah mean, ye've got tae … when ye're hand knittin, ye're coontin and ye've got tae concentrate, ye ken. Ye've got tae pey attention tae what ye're daein.

Now what were your hours in the Caerlee mill when you were seventeen years old?

Now, Ah'm tryin tae think, eh. When Ah first sterted workin, we worked forty-eight hoors a week. That wis normal week. An when Ah finished workin, they were workin what, thirty-eight, thirty-nine, somethin like that, ye ken. Well, actually, Ah wis workin thirty-seven and a half because Ah wis on shifts an that, ye ken. An the hoors were kind o adjusted tae suit the shift workin, ye ken.

Picking up the interview again after Andrew returned from National Service, his account of work in Caerlee, where he remained until 1993, includes many details about processes and changes over several decades.

Did you go straight back into the mill [in 1949]?

Intae [Caerlee] mill, aye.

The hosiery?

Uh huh.

You would have a few days at home with your leave and then you went to work?

That's right, that's right, uh huh.

Did you think of changing your job at that time?

No, Ah'll tell ye, when Ah wis in the Airmy it kind o came intae ma heid, ken, whether tae stay on in the Army or what, ye ken. But Ah didn't.

What I wondered was whether you'd thought of maybe going back into the forestry or trying something different again?

Oh, no. No, ye see, then you're stertin tae think money, ye ken. Ah mean, that's where the money wis bein made, up in the hosiery. Ken, even mair in the hosiery as what there wis in the other mills round aboot. That's where the money wis bein made, so, ken, there were really nae option, ye ken. But it's jist like miners, ye ken. Like, in a minin village, what do they dae? Go intae the mines, ye ken. And the same here, ken. Except for other, ken, like, if ye were a tradesman or that or maybe got abilities tae dae things, ye ken, ye'll further yoursel. But maist folk come intae the mill. Ye see, a lot o folk in the mill are clever enough, ye ken. But that's …

Aye. Oh, it demanded skills didn't it, working in the mill? Many of the jobs?

Uh huh. Uh huh.

But it sounds as if you were just a bit reluctant to go back in?

Ah, well, Ah dinnae ken. Ah jist accepted it, ye ken. It didnae, it didnae prey on ma mind or onything. Ah went back intae the old job Ah had. An Ah wis in there a few month an then they approached iz and says, 'Would you like to learn the frames?', which is a bigger job, ye ken. An Ah thought, aye, that'll be aaright. So Ah finished up as a frame-worker aa the rest o ma life.

Well, tell me what the frames were and what frame-workers did.

Right. The hand knittin is you're either cawin the machine or the kind o specialist kind o job, Intarsia knittin, which is quite an intricate thing. And Ballantyne's, Ah think their machines originated in Switzerland. And before the War, there werenae mony o the Intarsia knitters. But gradually, a lot o the guid Intarsia knitters were aa poached away tae other mills – doon tae Hawick an different places. An Intarsia knittin's quite a big thing now, ye ken. An that wis where big money wis made. But Ah wanted the frames an Ah wis a frame-worker. The frames, well, when Ah first went on to the frames, they were, they were auld frames and kind o belt-, they were belt-driven the first yins. Six division, ken, it had six, ye knit six pieces at a time. If ye're daein fronts, ye're daein six fronts. Six backs, an then you've six sleeves, six sleeves. That's a complete jersey afore they're sent on tae be joined up.

Aye. So that's what you were making mainly was jerseys?

Jerseys, aye, aye. See the machines, when Ah first sterted on the machines, on the frames [the rate would be] thirty courses a minute. That's thirty rows o jersey in a minute. When Ah finished, they were daen eighty-two or some-thing, eighty-three, eighty-four.

Nearly three times as many?

And bigger machines. But they were automated. But even being automated, ken, the faster the machine, the faster you've got tae gaun an aa, ye ken what Ah mean. But as ye stert tae get aulder, on these fast machines an that, ye're nippin up an doon aa the time. Oh, it's hard work, aye.

You've got to concentrate? You've got to concentrate all the time?

Aye. Quite hard work. It's no hard work, when you compare it to a manual worker, ye ken what Ah mean. You're havin tae keep your mind on your work, ye ken. Ah retired as a frame worker.

Aye. So that was from 1949 until 1993?

Uh huh. Forty-eight years Ah've worked in the mills.

Forty-eight years, that's a long time!

Aye.

Half a century. Did you ever in those years think of switching to something else, maybe entirely different, outside the mill?

No, no. But Ah mind o … Doreen's got a brother in New Zealand. An things wis kind o slack here an … And Andrew had a friend who was in a hosiery ower there. An Ah did write but Ah didnae send the letter away. Ah wrote the letter. Ah swithered, cause Ah'd … Ah'm tryin tae mind if Ah'd twae bairns, ye see, ken.

You had twins to begin with, aye?
>We had twins and lost a bairn.

Oh, I'm sorry to hear that.
>An then we had a younger son, eleven year between them. An Ah cannae mind if it wis before Andrew wis born. But Ah had this letter written, an things wis kind o sticky up there, ye ken. But Ah eventually jist tore it up, ye ken, aye.

You didn't actually post it. It was a big step to take, to emigrate?
>Well, this is it.

…

And, of course, you were working overtime sometimes when the mills were busy?
>That's right. Uh huh.

Now conversely, were you ever unemployed, after you came back from the Army?
>Never unemployed but Ah wis laid off, ye ken – short-time. Well, whit happened, well, ye ken, like, ye sometimes got it mair often as others, ye ken. Like, ye'd maybe lose markets an that, ye ken. At one time, Ballantyne's selt aa the jerseys they could make, nae bother, nae problem, tae aa the biggest department stores in America: Saks, Lord & Taylor an aa these, ye ken. There were aye, aye plenty work and there were aye plenty overtime. At other times, ye'd jist maybe get this period o time when there wis a dip. So Ah used tae go tae the tattie pickin, ken. Or Ah went [grouse] beatin at the shootin … Or Ah went tae the ferm an gied them a hand wi the harvest. It's only been a few times in oor lifetime Ah've been laid off in forty-eight years.

There was hardly ever an occasion, in those times you were laid off, when you were off for an entire week?
>No, Ah dinnae think so.

It was more short time?
>It wis short time. Uh huh.

…

Aye. Now what about the wages. You know, looking back over your forty-eight years in the mill, did the wages improve distinctly during that half century?
>Aye, aye. Oh, aye. Well, oh, aye. Ken, like, as Ah say the hosiery were aa better peyed as the other mills. In fact some o the other mills, ken, the Waverley an some o these now, they're no peyed very guid wages at aa. But Ah've worked piece-work aa ma life, ken. Oh, except the last twae year. That wis on a time job, the last twae year, ye ken. Jist, ken, wi bein older an that, ye ken.

So it was possible to make a bit extra money if you wanted to do so?
>Well, aa ma life Ah've earned ma maximum, ken. Ah'm no sayin, ma maximum wasnae the top wage. Some o them were, ken, ye get quicker workers an faster workers. A lot depended on what kind o work ye wis on. An ye often depended on folk, ken, like, ye depend on bar fillers for puttin

the ribs on the bars an that, ye ken.

Aye, there's a certain division of labour? You're not doing everything yourself?

That's right. Uh huh. But, as Ah say, ken, ye get faster workers than what others is. But on the frames, there werenae sic a big difference. On the hand knittin, the speed an that could vary quite a lot, ken. But on the frames, the speed o the machine dictated how fast you could go. Oh, there were always rows about the rates, ye ken. Like, see, there again, Ah wis on aboot the American influence. Ah can mind when the time-study first sterted. Before that, they used tae have a person knittin, ye ken, an then, dependin on how long they took tae make the jersey, that kind o gave ye the statement. . But on the machine, on the frames, an that, your statement wis based on the speed o the machine. Ah mean, ye still could get faster workers or folk that were prepared tae no take a meenit, ye ken whit Ah mean. These kind o things, uh huh.

Now did you find at times it was frustrating because you were being driven too hard?

Och, och, sometimes ye were on the verge. (laughs)

Things got a bit fraught did they?

Oh, aye! A bit fraught! There's a lot o the rows goes on up in the hosiery, aye. Cos it's sic a … it is a kind o frustratin job.

Is it a noisy factory, the hosiery?

Well, Ah've got a hearing-aid an that's doon tae the noise on the machines. Uh huh.

Aye. So it was always pretty noisy?

But Ah got compensation for this. A lot o them have never got compensation.

Really?

Uh huh.

Bob Anderson had a less straightforward working experience. His interview includes interesting details about working practices in the New Zealand mills, where he spent time as a young man. Towards the end of this account, he reflects on the upsetting events towards the end of his career when, having worked as a knitting foreman for seventeen years, he was replaced by a far less experienced worker.

Bob Anderson, b. 1931, working at home and abroad

That's great. So you got the job – and, remind me, it was Caerlee?

Caerlee, aye, aye, aye.

Now what were your hours there then when you first began?

Well, oo worked frae eight o'clock tae half past five, aye.

And you had an hour – was it an hour or three-quarters of an hour for your dinner?

Three-quarters o an hoor, aye, aye.

And did you work on Saturday mornings to begin with?

Yes, oo did, aye, aye.
From eight till twelve when you finished?
Till twelve, that's right, aye, aye.
So you were working roughly about forty-eight, forty-nine hours a week when you first started?
Aye, aye.
Now what was your wage, can you remember, when you first began?
Ah think it wis aboot seeven pound ten or somethin like that. That's right, aye, aye, aye. And then of course, efter that ye went on tae piece-work, ee see.
Aye, you could make a bit more?
Well, jist actually they had a ceilin. Ee see, oo wis only allowed tae make aboot 5s.9d. an hour, and if ee made over that they cut the statement. And then once Ah wis off the plain machines – Ah wis on the plain machines, Ah had tae make ma pay on the plain machines.
Plain knitting?
Aye, aye. And then efter that oo wis on tae the Intarsia knittin, which is the fancy knittin.
Yes, that was much more complicated work wasn't it?
That's right, aye.
You couldn't start on that because you had to be trained?
No, no. Ye had tae learn the rudiments o the knittin first.
So how long were you on plain knitting then?
Aye, maybe jist say, say aboot six months, a few month. Then oo went on the Intarsias. And oo only got eight weeks tae make your pay on the Intarsias. And after that they sterted the night shift.
Aye. Was that constant night shift?
No, week aboot, which wis worse. It wis supposed tae be for six weeks and it wis aboot six year. And oo started, oo started on the Sunday night at nine o'clock tae half past seven in the mornin. We started at quarter tae eight tae nine o'clock at night. So the machines wis only stopped quarter o an hoor in twenty-four.
The demand was enormous for the product?
Oh, aye, oh, aye, aye, uh huh, uh huh.
But, I mean, it must have been very unsettling for your personally, because you'd never worked shifts before?
No, no. It wis … Ah never liked night shift, never liked it. But there were one thing: Ah could sleep through the day, which other people couldnae. Some o the mates wis terrible. They couldnae sleep. They were shattered by the end o the week.
So you didn't have that difficulty?
No, no.
But it must have cut you off in many ways from your social life?

Well, it did, aye. And then when oo got married Ah wis on that and aa, and Ah hardly seen the bairn. (laughs) Ken.

When did you get married?

'59 Ah got married, aye. At twenty-seven, aye.

Aye. So you'd been working in the mill for about five years by the time you got married?

Aye, that's right, uh huh, uh huh.

Do you mind if I ask, did you meet your wife in or through the mill?

No. But within that time Ah went away tae New Zealand in 1955 tae the end o '57.

Ah, right. So you'd only been in the mill about a couple of years was it?

Uh huh, well, '52 to '55. Ah jist wis a bit unsettled, ken, so Ah went away tae New Zealand.

So you mentioned that you came back to be best man at your brother's wedding?

Aye.

And that was where you met your fate?

That's right, Ah met the wife.

(Mrs Anderson: Ah had lived in Innerleithen aa ma life. Ah kent him. He wisnae like a stranger.) (laughs)

So you never went back to New Zealand again?

No, no, no.

And then did you go back into Caerlee Mill?

Aye. Uh huh.

And much the same job?

Aye, on the night shift, aye, aye, uh huh.

Did you feel it difficult to settle down after the better working conditions?

No, it wis … Ah never thought anything aboot it really, no.

So you were back on the night shift And were conditions much the same? Because you'd only been away a couple of years?

Aye. It wis jist much the same. It wis the same money for night shift – fifteen shillins.

It hadn't increased in the three years you'd been away?

It hadnae improved on it, no. Because oo complained. Fifteen shillins for workin night shift a week wis terrible really.

That was per week?

Aye, that wis a week, aye, aye, fifteen shillins in auld money. And oo wanted it up tae £1, and the manager says, 'Oh, no. You'll buy a lot o sandwiches wi fifteen shillins'.

Now what about the union?

Oh, aye, the union.

You weren't in a union until you went to the mill?

No, no, no, no. No, as soon as Ah went tae the mill everybody jist then joined the union.

Did somebody approach you and say, 'Now what about joining the union?'

Aye, well, everybody. As soon as ye went intae the mill somebody did, aye.

Was there a shop steward?

Aye, oh, aye. There were a shop steward in every department.

So you joined as soon as you went in after New Zealand?

Aye. And when Ah went tae New Zealand Ah asked for an affiliation card, because they're terrible strict oot there the unions.

Aye, aye, it was maybe a closed shop was it?

Aye, well, actually it cost ee a lot o money tae join a union oot there. But wi me havin an affiliation card Ah got right in, ye see.

Aye, aye, of course. Thanks to being a member of the T&G?

Aye, that's right, aye, aye.

So you carried on in the union when you came back?

That's right, aye, Ah went back intae the union, that's right.

And did you become active in the union, did you become an office bearer?

No, no, jist a member, aye, aye. Then when Ah come on tae the staff – efter Ah come off the knittin Ah went on, Ah wis the foreman in the knittin flat, ee see, for a long time – for seventeen years.

So when you came back, you got married, you went into the mill again.

Aye, Ah wis paid off, aye. Shortage o work, aye. Last in, first oot, ee see.

So then you worked for the council and you worked in a plastics works?

Aye, aye, up the Leithen Road. It's still up there, the Leithen Road, aye. So Ah worked in there for what – a year, a year and a half?

And then you got back into Caerlee?

Aye.

Aye, things had got a bit busier again?

Aye. They sent iz a letter. Ah jist newly changed intae the plastic works and Ah got a letter fae the mill tae go back, and Ah says, 'Oh, well, Ah'm no goin tae bother'. But Ah wis promised a lot o overtime in the plastic works and Ah got one night. And Ah jist said, 'Oh, well, Ah'm goin back intae the mill'. There were a job come up in the mill on the washin place, washin the jerseys, and Ah applied for that. And the boss came in and he says, 'Ah,' he says, 'what are ye efter?'

Ah says, 'Ah'm wantin a job'.

'Oh,' he says, 'Ah'll gie ye a job, but no in here'. He says, 'Ah'll gie ye a job in the knittin'.

Aye, which you would much prefer?

Aye, the washing is a skilled job really, ye have tae use experience, sizin and everythin like that.

Aye, but you prefered the knitting anyway?

Ah liked the knittin, aye, aye, aye. Ah got back in there, and that wis me.

And then you remained there until you retired?

That's right, aye. '61 Ah went back intae the mill and Ah wis there till Ah retired.
That's fifty-five years, aye?
Aye, uh huh.
And you were saying that you became a foreman?
Ah wis a foreman in the knittin flat for seventeen year.
Aye, till you retired?
No, no, no. (laughs) Ah got shifted oot o that.
Sorry, I was going to say, just to get the timing roughly right. You went back to the mill – eleven years, then you became a foreman, seventeen years.
Actually, Ah got off the knittin tae dae the prototype samples in the samples room, afore Ah became a foreman. Ah wis daein that for twae or three year, and then they offered iz this job in the knittin as a foreman. So Ah wis a foreman seventeen years.
Seventeen years. So you must have been a non-foreman for about eleven years before that?
Aye, something like that, aye, aye.
Eleven, seventeen and seven makes thirty-five?
Aye, that's right. Within that time Ah wis daein the prototype samples in the sample room, ee see.
Aye, aye. That's great. So that was the experience you had. Now was the fact that you were replaced by a younger person as foreman connected in any way with changes in the ownership of the mill?
No, no. It's the same owners. But the management wis aye changin! (laughs) Ah dinnae ken what. Ah kent ma job backwards. Tae tell ye the truth, Ah don't know why Ah wis replaced, because it wisnae that Ah didnae ken ma job. But what Ah think it … one thing Ah think it wis wis that Ah kent ma job too much. They wanted somebody they could tell what tae do and when tae do it and aa thae kind o things.
Aye, you were maybe too independent in your attitudes?
Aye, that's right, aye.
That can be fatal, too.
Aye, that's it, aye, aye. But the man that replaced me wis … he didnae ken the job at aa. He wis goin tae start fae scratch.
It must have been an upsetting experience for you?
Oh, it wis terrible, it really wis, aye. Ah wis shattered. So wis the wife. Ah wis shattered. Cause there were nae need for it.
No. There was no explanation given of course?
No, oh, no, oh, no, no. They jist said— There were another job in the mill, which wis in charge o the baton store, which was aa the things that make up jerseys, ye ordered, and thae kind o things. And it wis either take that or out the door. But Ah wisnae the only yin. They din it wi two or three jist the very same, ken. And really that job Ah went on tae, baton store, it was quite guid.

Ah quite enjoyed it really, because Ah wis on ma own. Ah jist ordered the stuff, and thae kind o things, aye. Oh, aye, Ah wis away on ma own. Ah finished there, ken.

But it's the sense of humiliation you suffer.

Oh, it was, it really wis, aye. Everybody in the mill wis shattered, aye, when the notice came up. Ken, the notice went up on the notice board, they were really shattered, ken.

You never applied for a job in any of the other Innerleithen mills?

No, no, no.

In this next extract, W. Lockie Robson reflects candidly on his forty-five years at Caerlee and provides some interesting details on working the binding machine.

W. Lockie Robson, b. 1932, working at Caerlee

So what happened when you left school? Did you start in the mill right away?

Aye.

Did you go up and ask for a job?

Uh huh.

Which mill did you go to?

Caerlee.

Aye. Why did you go to Caerlee? Do you remember?

Oh, Ah don't know. It didnae make ony difference.

Aye. Were there any, maybe some of your pals were going there, were they?

No.

Because there were other mills?

Uh huh.

At that time there was what, the Leithen Mill?

The Leithen, the Waverley and the top mill.

The wee one. That was Beckett and …?

Aye, Beckett & Robertson.

Robertson, as well as Caerlee?

Uh huh.

It wasn't that Caerlee was the nearest to you? Where you were living?

Well, at the time it wis.

Aye, it was. It was actually nearer than Leithen, was it?

Aye. Because by that time, durin the War, we moved up into the Hall, the Memorial Hall. Father took over as caretaker.

Now again forgive my ignorance, is that, that's the big hall, which I've just passed coming up there, aye?

Aye. Aye.

And was there a wee house attached?

Aye, we got a nice house. They made it into a museum when we moved up

here. Father wis still in charge o the Hall, when we moved up here.
That's great. So Caerlee was really just more or less at your back door?
Across the road, aye.
So you started there in 1946 would it be?
August '46. Ah left at the summer holidays like.
Aye. You had your holidays and then went in. Now what was the work you were doing first?
Frame flat bar-fillin. It wis a terrible job.
Was it? Tell me about it then, what did you do in bar-filling?
Well, you know, it's the bit at the bottom of your jersey. It wis run on tae points and then transferred on tae a frame. Ye see, ye had tae get every stitch on tae thae points. And Ah hated the job.
Was it a sort of fiddly, finicky job?
Oh, terrible!
So how long were you doing that particular task?
Aboot three month.
Aye. That was the normal?
No. Actually, ye wis supposed to do aboot three year. Ah threatened tae leave. Ah wisnae gonnae dae ony mair. So Ah got put on to the knittin flat.
What was your wage, when you first began the bar-filling?
Oh, I got twenty-five shillings the first week. It wasnae piece-work wi bar-fillin.
No. So you got twenty-five shillings a week for the three months you were doing that?
Aye.
Now what hours did you have?
Quarter to eight tae five o'clock, half-five and lunch wis quarter past twelve tae one o'clock.
Quite a long day for a laddie of fourteen?
Uh huh. You got a fifteen-minute break in the mornin and a break in the efternin.
Aye, that's great. Did you work Saturday mornings?
Aye, it wis overtime. Ah sometimes did, sometimes did.
Aye. So by that time, they'd passed the five-day-week by the time you started?
Uh huh, uh huh.
So you escaped from the bar-filling after three months and you got on to the hand knitting. And did you prefer that?
Aye.
Aye, aye. And could you make more money at that, too? Would that be piece-work?
Aye. Well, Ah jumped fae twenty-five shillings a week tae aboot £3, which wis quite a lot. It wis a good wage then.
For a laddie of fourteen, that was really quite good?
Uh huh.

Now just tell me, what was the work? What did the work involve? I know nothing about textile mills, I'm afraid.
>Well, Ah sterted off on the bindin machine. Ah wis on it for two or three month. Then Ah went on tae another plain machine.

Aye. And the binding, was that a matter of stitching arms to the bodies?
>The actual bindin wis the bit that goes doon for the cardigan, ken, where ye get the button holes in it?

Aye, aye. And the buttons, the button holes go into that, aye?
>Ye done yairds at a time on it.

Aye. Did you find that a bit boring? A bit repetitive?
>Ach, well, it wis a wee bit. But what job isnae efter a wee while?

Aye, I suppose so. And then how long did you do that work?
>Jist two or three month on the bindin and then Ah went on tae a bigger machine, doin the fronts and backs and sleeves.

Uh huh. So you were gradually progressing through the making of garments?
>Aye.

Was it a formal apprenticeship you were undertaking?
>No.

You just ... the procedure was, as a young lad, you started here and then you were moved to there after a while?
>Aye.

And the amount of time you spent doing a particular job depended partly on yourself?
>Uh huh.

And your first task was not a congenial one, so you moved on as quickly as you could?
>Uh huh.

So did you go back to what you'd been doing before you went off to do your National Service?
>Uh huh. More or less. And then they got awfy busy on the Intarsia machines and Ah got put on tae that to train on it. Ah've been on it ever since.

And you've enjoyed that work?
>Aye.

So you came back at the age of twenty [in 1952]. And, from what you were saying, I gather you're fairly soon to retire in the summer, in May?
>Uh huh.

So again, that's thirty-five years you'll have been working, sorry, forty-five years, I beg your pardon, forty-five years you've been working in the mill by the time you retire?
>Uh huh. Well, it's actually fifty. Your National Service counted as unbroken service. So, actually it was fae 1946.

Of course. So you've been working on the Intarsia pretty well throughout those forty-five years? And you've enjoyed that?
>Aye.

Satisfying kind of work?

Uh huh.
    Aye, aye.
High quality hosiery?
    Aye, aye.
And certainly very popular?
    Uh huh.
Do you know where the main demand has come form? Is it from overseas or from home?
    Mostly overseas. Likes o now our biggest thing is Italy, Japan. We dinnae dae as much for America now as we used to.

W. Lockie Robson also provided this detail about working hours and change over time in the Caerlee mill.

Now what about conditions of work? When you first started, you began, I think you said, at eight in the morning and you worked till half-past-five?
    Uh huh.
Have the working hours changed?
    Aye, they've changed quite a lot.
Tell me about that then, please.
    Well, before they changed the hoors again, most o the time Ah worked quarter to eight. Then it went fae half-five tae five o'clock. And then it came doon tae half-four. It wis always quarter to eight in the mornin. Whereas now, we start at half-seven to half-four. And that gies ye the difference for the efternin, Friday efternin off.
Aye. You get Friday afternoon. And you welcome that personally?
    Oh, aye.
It gives you a longer weekend?
    Uh huh.
Have you ever suffered from unemployment?
    Aboot two weeks since Ah joined the place.
Aye. That's pretty good, then, in half a century?
    Uh huh. Aboot twice.
Aye. And on each occasion it was only for a short time?
    For a week. Ah did mair overtime in that place than ye ever did short time.
Now what about the wages? Do you feel that they have improved?
    Well, Ah wouldnae like to say. Ah think they'll jist be aboot more or less the same maybe. Maybe even less than what they used tae be.
So that piece-work has meant that management has depressed the rates?
    Aye, a wee bit.
Aye. You know, compared with when you first began?
    Uh huh.

Margaret Gray's mother and grandmother were both keen to support her through a secretarial course but Margaret was determined to go into the mill. More specifically into the hosiery because, as she told Ian, she had two grannies who had been weavers and she had seen how they had experienced 'very, very long days and very tiring days'. It is clear from this account that Margaret's job, as a point seamer, was a highly skilled one – as her husband is keen to reiterate. However, after twenty-six years at Caerlee, Margaret went to work at Murray Allan, reflecting that by then, and under different owners, Caerlee had changed and the atmosphere was very different.

Margaret Gray, b. 1933, working life

So when you were a girl did you have any particular ambitions?
> Yes, Ah did, Ah did. Ah was quite interested. I would like to have been a nurse or a hairdresser. But Ah had a spell in hospital an that knocked the nursin right oot ma head.

So you left school without, I gather, bursting into tears and sadness!
> That's right. (laughs) Quite glad to leave, yes, uh huh.

And did you start work immediately in the mill?
> I would do, yes, uh huh, I would do. And I was working when Ah went into the hospital.

Now how did you get the job in the mill?
> Ah think it was jist that when ye left the school, ye jist went to see aboot gettin a job.

Aye, you went down yourself to the office? Do you remember doing that?
> Yes, uh huh, yes, uh huh.

Had some of your pals maybe gone?
> Well, we all went.

You went in a wee group?
> Yes, uh huh, uh huh, yes, yes.

And it was quite easy to get a job at that time?
> Yes, no problem, yes, yes, yes.

And your mind hadn't turned to other possibilities, maybe getting a job in an office or typing or something like that?
> No. Ma mother didnae want me to go into the sportswear. Ma granny was quite willing, and ma mother, to send me to Skerry's College[14] in Edinburgh. Oh, but Ah wouldnae have any o this because all ma pals was goin in and, well, that was it.

You just decided you weren't going to do that?
> Ah just decided I wasnae … well, we'd have to travel to Edinburgh every day,

---

14 Skerry's College was a series of colleges which primarily prepared candidates for Civil Service examinations across the UK and Ireland.

which was quite a big thing when ye was that age, you know.
That's right. It's quite a long way. There would also have been quite a lot of cost for your mother and your grandmother.
   Yes, yes, that's right, aye, yeah, yeah.
And the fees as well, because Skerry's was a private college.
   That's right, aye. They obviously knew they had the money to do it or something. I don't know. They were quite keen because ma mother really tried very hard for me to go but Ah just wouldnae.
Did you ever come, you know, later on to feel, 'Oh, I wish I'd done as my mother and grandmother wanted'.
   Some days when I was fed-up in the mill, yes. Ah think as you get older, yes, I thought 'Now, Margaret, you should ha done that, you should've,' you know. But Ah mean it was just fleetingly thought.
So you got started in the mill?
   Uh huh.
And that would be 1949?
   It would be aboot there I would think.
Now can you remember what your wages were when you began?
   Thirty-five shillings a week, yes.
That was quite a good wage for a girl then, wasn't it?
   Aye. Well you're in an apprenticeship, you know, for when ee was learnin ee run the messages.
Aye, 'gofer', the usual thing.
   That's right.
Did you sign, or did your mother sign a formal apprenticeship indenture? Was it as formal as that?
   No. I dinnae think so. I wouldnae think so.
No. It was just an understanding that you did this and that other job. And then eventually you'd graduate on to something else.
   Uh huh, aye.
Now what about the hours, when you started – what were your hours of work?
   (Mr Gray: Eight to twelve and then one to half-five, I think, but I'm no sure.)
It was quite a long day for a young girl?
   A long day, yes.
And you worked Saturday mornings then, too?
   No.
Well that wasn't quite so bad. So that would be, if my arithmetic is right, that would be eight and a half hours per day, so it's about forty-two and a half, forty-three hours per week you were working.
   (Mr Gray: We were workin aboot a forty-five hour week then, Ah would think.)
   Aye, aboot forty-five hours, yes.
It was quite a long day. So what were you doing, I mean, apart from running messages?

Was there some particular task?
   Yes I was training, the machines in the seaming and binding. Yeah, yeah.
Did you find the work interesting, you know, taking it in the round?
   Yes, yes, Ah did.
You werenae sighing to get back to the school again?
   No, oh, no, no.
And of course you'd be working beside people, some of whom at least, you would know?
   Oh, aye, we knew them all really. Yes.
Now which mill was this, that you started in?
   The Ballantyne's Sportswear, the Caerlee.
The Caerlee. Was it known locally as Ballantyne's Sportswear?
   (Mr Gray: That was the name of it.)
   It was actually referred to as the hosiery.
   (Mr Gray: It was actually The Ballantyne Sportswear, Caerlee Knitting Mills.)
   That's the proper name, yes.
Aye, the full Sunday name. But the others were tweed mills. That was the only hosiery one?
   Yes. That's right. It was always referred to as the hosiery.
   (Mr Gray: That's right.)
So it wasn't deliberate choice that you went to the hosiery rather than any of the tweed mills?
   I was wantin to go into that. Because I think both ma grannies havin both travelled to Peebles as weavers Ah saw how they had very, very long days and very tiring days. Because they stood aa day an things like that. No, I would never have went to the tweed mills unless it had been the only job available, I would ha hud to have did that, you know, yes, yes.
You made a deliberate decision to go to hosiery.
   Oh, yes, aye, yes, aye.
Good. So you did this sort of general dogsbody work for a year, two years?
   About a year maybe. It might not even be that. You see, Ah started in the summer now, maybe if was an intake at Christmas or something. The next intake, somebody younger as you got the job.
You were pushed upwards and onwards? That was the way that things progressed, that people came in on a school leaving date or whatever – mainly the summer. So after a few months you moved on to the next stage of learning in the mill. And what was that? What did you do?
   Well, ye just learnt the job till ee got proficient enough to make your own pay.
Aye, but what job were you learning?
   The seaming. Ye could've went anywhere in the mill. But that was the job that Ah got offered. I enjoyed it. It was a very happy atmosphere in the place cause everybody got on well. We used tae sing at oor work an things like that. It was nice. It was good. It changed through the years of course, you know.

Was that quite common that you sang at work?
  We used to, aye, yes. I don't know aboot the men but the women did.
Aye, because where you were working would be mainly women, was it?
  It was all women, it was all women, aye, yes.
Now what did you do when you were seaming?
  Sew the sides on a machine, you know, for the skirt right up to the cuff, yeah.
And your task was to sew the bits together into one garment?
  Yes, that's right, aye. The binder puts it thegither first. They join it across the top and put the sleeves in. Right?
And then the seamer does the rest. Sews up the sides. And you found that quite enjoyable, interesting work?
  Yes, aye, Ah did, yes.
There'd be a variation presumably in the kinds of garments you were working?
  Oh, yes.
Aye, ye werenae working away at the one thing for weeks at a time?
  Well, it was the same principle all the time, you know.
Aye, but different colours and different sizes, shapes and fashions?
  Oh yes, aye, yes aye. Aye, that's right, different …
  (Mr Gray: You dinnae mind me sayin somethin?)
  No, Ah need some help.
  (Mr Gray: It's a case of, she's makin it sound quite simple really, this seamin business. It is quite simple tae dae wi the modern machinery. But in those days it wis what they cried the old point machine. An it wis a circular machine with, like a needle stickin out. An each sort o, each row of stitchin had to be matched up the side by that points.)
  Oh, yes, it's quite an intricate job.
  (Mr Gray: Point seamin is something that is, I would say, non-existent today. But the reason Ah'm sayin this is because she's sayin that, you know, she had to learn the job. She was aboot a year almost before she got a machine, you know, permanently on a machine. The job had to be sort o taught in a proper manner because everything had to match in those days.)
It would have been a very difficult job. It demanded concentration.
  Oh, yes.
  (Mr Gray: It was quite a highly skilled operation in the industry in those days.)
  I mean, really, at one point in time when the mills were slack, just to give you an instance, o the seaming job, Bert and I decided we would quite like to emigrate. Which, Bert went for an interview, the knittin, things like that. And they were very interested. But as soon as he told them what his wife did, they were more interested in me than the knittin side. An, well, we wouldnae go on that understandin, cause a man had to be the breadwinner.
Where were you thinking of emigrating?
  New Zealand.

So you actually got an interview with a New Zealand immigration official?
>Oh, yes.
>(Mr Gray: Oh, we went that far and aa the rest o it. But they were far more interested in Margaret the more they learned.)
>Uh huh, once they knew what job that I did.
>(Mr Gray: Ah mean, aaright, they would haa took me. But we went with the expectation that Ah wis goin for a job and Margaret wis comin with us.)
>Uh huh, that's right. No the other way round.
>(Mr Gray: No a case o she wis goin for a job an Ah wis goin wi her. An that wisnae sort o on at all.)
>No, we decided against that. It was the best decision really.

But what strikes me, forgive me, as a complete ignoramus, is that you would be put on to that kind of work, which demanded a high level of concentration and skills. OK, I mean, no doubt to begin with you'd make a few errors. You'd maybe practise on something to begin with? But to move from leaving school and within a short time into doing that work …
>Ah wouldnae say it's bred into you, but there was very few people couldnae master these skills, you know … you learnt quickly. Of course, you're young.

And I mean, you were there with other girls who'd started when you did.
>We had a very, very good teacher, a very good teacher. She wis a great boss.

Was this a forewoman?
>Uh uh, yes. She was excellent.

What was her name?
>Beatrice Rae. She was a super person.

Then did you work on seaming for some time after that?
>Oh, a good, good, good number of years, and then they introduced a machine for doing it quicker, which was a Rimoldi. They put me upstairs, and it was men that learnt me to do this machine. And then I came back into the flat, which I learned somebody else and then they done away wi the point seaming. So Ah was transferred to another job beside a lot o other people that wis put throughout the mill, you know. Because, well, by that time I was married.

So by that time you'd been working in the mill for eight years or thereabouts, seven or eight years.
>Yes, aye, yeah, yeah.

So you had a lot of experience?
>Yes, uh huh. Then Ah got transferred on to the passing, which is, ye examine everybody's work, which is quite … it's not a skill but you've got to be very careful, you've got to know what you're looking for.

You couldn't possibly do that without a lot of years of experience? So, you were then doing the passing?
>Yes, uh huh.

How many passers were there employed in the mill, roughly? Half a dozen? Two or three?

Oh, there wis more is that. Nine or ten Ah would think.

(Mr Gray: Ten. Ah wis thinkin there wis two different tables there.)

And these were all women were they?

Yes, uh huh, yes.

No men were ever employed in that particular job?

Never known it anyway, no.

That was the general case, was it, in the mill that certain tasks, only men or only women were employed in?

Yes, that's right, yes. I think the only thing we eventually came to [men and women doing the same job] was the knitting.

(Mr Gray: Oh, that was much later.)

That was much later, yes.

But in the first ten years or so that you worked in the mill, there was this segregation?

Uh huh.

And you were paid by the piece presumably?

I was paid piece-rates on the seaming but the passing, when I first went on to it, no. It was a set wage, a time rate. And then it eventually got to piece, and the quality of it went out the window. You could see, I mean, I suppose I would see it in me, I would see it in other people, that would say, 'Oh, tae hell, if she's goin to throw it off, I'll throw it off'. Ye know? But Ah mean, ye had standards. Ah mean, Ah had standards that Ah thought, 'Right, that is it'. Ye know, I jist wouldnae let it go, ye know.

Aye. But it is very difficult to resist that feeling isn't it? Aye.

Very difficult to resist it, yeah.

Why should you bother if your colleagues are not to the same extent?

That's right. If ye didna do above a certain thing, I mean you could get bad work and your efficiency would fall, an ye got intae trouble for it. Yeah that was a job that should never have been, never ever have been piece-work. Never! Yeah, yeah.

So you did the passing for quite some time? A few years?

Oh yes, aye.

(Mr Gray: Ye did the passing up until ye retired, really, because ye changed mills.)

That was your specialism as it were. Did you find that work tiring?

Ye stood, ye stood.

You stood? All day?

All day, aa day, yes. Oh aye, the whole day.

You weren't allowed to sit or you just couldn't sit because of the nature of the job?

Ye couldnae sit, no, no.

It must have been quite sore on the back and the legs, that?

I suppose so. In the end ye got used to it, yes.

(Mr Gray: Plus the fact that once ye'd examined and measured the garments and aa the rest o it, you folded it an put it into its final whatever.)

Ye folded them an put them on to the next part of the process.

Aye, so there is a certain amount of movement in the job and you're turning round and walking away?

Aye, yes, plus the fact that if you found a mistake, ye took it back to the person that made the mistake. So that broke the monotony a wee bit, ye know, frae standin. Yes.

It certainly must have been quite tiring for a long time, I would have thought, if you're standing these quite long hours.

Uh huh, yes, that's right. An then of course, ye had great big lights, you know, which was warm, yes.

Aye, I was going to ask about the temperature. It was quite warm?

The temperatures were quite high, yes, aye.

Especially in the summer no doubt?

Yes, that's right. An if you opened a window, somebody would complain aboot a draught, ye know. (laughs)

So it couldn't have been a very comfortable sort of job that you were doing?

Och it was alright really. It was something you just got used to. Ye never felt it in the end, you know.

Well, that's great. So you got married, just remind me, when you were twenty?

Twenty-four. Ah was still seaming when I was married at twenty-four, yes. Then Ah went on to the passing.

And that remained your job for the rest of the time?

Yes, uh huh.

Now, when did you leave the Caerlee mill then, roughly? Or what age were you, roughly when you left the Caerlee?

I'll tell ee, I can tell ee, it wis twenty-six years in the hosiery, and the rest o ma workin life was in Murray Allan's.

You were twenty-six years altogether at Caerlee?

Twenty-six years at Caerlee, uh huh, that's right.

And you were saying the reasons you changed, you were fed up? Was there anything specific?

Ah jist, Ah jist, after twenty-six years Ah thought, 'Ah'm needin a change'. Ah was fed up. And Ah saw they were lookin for a passer at Murray Allan's, cause it was a comparatively new firm, you know, two or three years it had been goin. And I applied for the job and got it. So that was it, you know.

Of course, around that age, forgive me for saying the obvious, (laughter) I think we all feel when we get to that sort of age, you know, we've been doing this for so many years, 'Oh my God, am I gonna be having to do this till I retire?' I think a lot of people, don't they, feel a bit restless around that time?

BORDER MILLS: LIVES OF PEEBLESSHIRE TEXTILE WORKERS

That's right. But Ah think it was more the factory, you know, I was jist fed up wi it. There was lots o changes in management. The place wisnae the same. (sighs) Ah just don't know.

When you went at first, you were just a young lass and you wouldn't know a great deal maybe about the mill until you'd been in there a few years anyway.

That's right, yes.

Was it your impression that things had gone on in pretty much in the same kinds of ways for a long time? And then in later years, the pace of change speeded up? You got new managers, new techniques, new machines.

Yes, yes, uh huh.

Was it partly that, you think, that made you restless?

Yes, Ah would think so, yes, Ah would think so. An Ah jist didnae like the changes. They sort o forced you into doin things that went against the grain to do in the job, you know. The managers didnae seem to bother about ye. The atmosphere was different. You wis jist a number in the end, jist a number, and they couldnae hae cared less.

And was that because there were new managers had come in?

Aye, yes, Ah would think so.

Accidents at Work

As we have already heard, the mill could be a dangerous place to work. In this extract Robert Sanderson recalls the dangers of working on the carding machines.

Robert Sanderson, b. 1929

Now, not many more questions to badger you with and I hope I'm no tiring you?

No, no.

Accidents in the mill.

It didn't happen very often but, you know, it did happen.

Take Damdale first. Can you recall any accidents there?

Ah remember one o the painters wis paintin the ceilin or something one day and he got caught in the shaftin. And he got whirled round the shaft and thrown off. And he wis virtually stripped, you know. But that was the worst one. He wisnae killed or anything, you know, but he got pretty badly hurt at the time.

Was he sent to hospital?

Oh, aye, aye, aye. He wis off for a long time. But, you know, he recovered.

Were there any particular occupational hazards?

Aye, there's been one or two who've lost fingers and that on some machines. Ah know a chap, well, that wis in one o the Ballantyne's, he lost his hand on the cardin machines, you know. Got crushed.

Was carding the most dangerous job in the mill?

Sometimes Ah think, you know, when the wool's goin round these cards, you know, a thick, sort o wire brush thing. If ye see something, a foreign object on it, ye tend tae try and pick it off, maybe. And if it catches your hand, it's under the roller before ye can react. You know, you're no supposed to touch anything. But you know, Ah think it maybe catches your eye and you think, 'Ah dinnae want that in there!'

Aye, it's instinctive?

Aye. And that has happened. And one or two others have lost bits o fingers, you know, on the looms, you know, bangin into them.

So carding and the weaving are the most dangerous aspects?

That's right, yeah. But Ah've never seen anybody killed or anything like that, you know. There's one or two have collapsed and died, you know. But, you know, aye, things like that.

Aye, natural causes, as it were?

That's right, yes.

But not industrial injuries?

No, not industrial.

In this next extract, Hume Davidson recalls some health and safety related stories including his own close shave. He also reflects on the First Aid provision at Ballantyne's, which, thankfully improved over time.

Hume Davidson, b. 1928

Ah remember once – Ah often think aboot it yet – there wis a foldin machine. It folded the yarn – the cloth. After they wove it, it wis milled in the mill house. Now there wis a dryin machine that the cloth went through and it dried the piece o cloth, 100 yards or 50 yards. And it went through this machine wi hot pipes and it dried it. Well, it come out, it wis a brittly feel, dry, and they hung it over the dam to regain moisture, ee see. An it wis a, it wis a big shed, wi spaces on the floor and the water wis underneath, ten feet deep below the turbines. And the water come up and the cloth got regained, the moisture regained. Well, they took the cloth off o there and they put it intae a foldin machine tae get it folded, tae take it tae the finishin. And Ah remember Ah wis goin tae the engineers one day and the machine wis foldin, workin away and when Ah come back, one o the assistants says, 'You've never been as lucky in aa your life!' Ah says, 'How's that? What's wrong?' Well, Ah must've put ma hand on a bar when Ah passed. And this bar went back and forrit like this. And this wis a metal bar here and this wis a metal bar that wis … and he reckoned it could've took ma finger or ma hand clean off!

Oh, aye. Dear, oh dear!

And, Ah mean, they wouldnae have that nowadays. It wid've been covered.

Now that must be one of the differences you saw, between your last days in the mill and your early days in the same place? Safety was very much more emphasised?

Well, Ah often think aboot it yet. Imagine what kind o life Ah would've had if Ah'd had a hand off or a finger or aa ma fingers. And it wis daist (snaps his fingers) through the split seconds, Ah must've put ma hand on it and never knew that Ah'd done it. (laughs)

No, no. Terribly dangerous.

Ah often think aboot it. Oh, God!

Was there any kind of medical provision provided by the mill itself?

Aye, well, when I worked in the mill there wis a man had a bottle o brandy for (laughs) you know. And then eventually they made a First Aid room in 1949. And there were a medical room wi a settee in it.

Was there a nurse?

No. There wis somebody nominated that wis maybe good at caring. And then eventually they were sent away tae do a course, which Olive done sometimes.

(Mrs Davidson: We went to the Red Cross, we were sent intae Leith … Ah went doon there and you had to sit exams.)

It sounds as if it must have been a Ministry of Labour training centre or something like that?

(Mrs Davidson: Yin o the times that Ah went, we went tae the Carlton Hotel and sat exams. We went for a week's course then we sat exams there and you got your certificate for the next three year.)

Aye. Would it be St Andrew's Ambulance, do you think, that organised it?

(Mrs Davidson: Well, that yin that oo went tae at the Carlton Hotel wis.) But in the early days, there wis, as Ah say, a bottle o brandy or Ah remember the guy run doon years ago wi the glass o brandy for somebody that had collapsed and he had died. And he says, 'Oh, too late!' And he drunk it hissel!' (laughter)

I can understand that! (laughs)

Aye, that wis true.

But there was never any nurse?

No. Ah remember an old lady. She wis a VAD [Voluntary Aid Detachment] person and she did it, you know. But that wis as far as it went.

(Mrs Davidson: But if you needed a doctor or a nurse you got somebody to phone the offices and they phoned Innerleithen and oo got a nurse or a doctor down, ken whit Ah mean?)

But Ah know in the fifties and sixties, it wis daist 100 yards along the road there, they had a wee clinic. The Innerleithen doctors came down tae Walkerburn. So Ah remember one day a fisher came in tae the weavin shed. 'Take that oot ma finger, man!' And it wis a hook, right over the barb. And Ah got ma pliers oot and then Ah had a look at it and Ah said, 'Ah would tear your finger tae bits'.

'Oh, it'll no maitter. Get it oot!'

Ah says, 'Look,' Ah says, 'there's a doctor along, see thon hut along yonder, that's a doctor'. So Ah sent him along tae the doctor. (laughs)
Quite right, too. It's not just a matter of yanking it out.

In this last extract, Olive Davidson provides us with a vivid image of the mill environment and the dangers of flying shuttles.

Olive Davidson, b. 1934, flying shuttles

I was going to ask you about your injury. I believe the shuttle simply flew out, as shuttles were prone to do and struck you on the elbow?

Uh huh.

Were you off work then for a few days or a week?

No. Ah worked on the gang with this other lady, you see. And her shuttle, Ah must've been at this end and it struck me.

(Mr Davidson: That's what Ah wis always frightened for in the mill, when somebody brought visitors round, especially if they had a baby in their arms. And thae shuttles, well, they were aboot that size (he indicates 18 inches long) … they were heavy and they had sharp points on the end.)

Yin o the women Ah used tae gang aboot wi, she'd a right hole there (in the palm of her hand. She used tae catch the shuttle before it went intae the box and, ye ken, there's a sharp point on it.

(Mr Davidson: There was one person Ah remember gettin injured. He wis an old fellow, a First World War man and he had a peg leg. And he worked in the office but periodically had tae come round the looms. And he tripped one day. Well, the looms had some safety devices on them and, ee see, when a shuttle went into the box it lifted a lever. And, in turn, it lifted a rod. Now if it didnae get lifted it got put intae a block and jammed. They called it the jammin block. And he tripped one day and this rod that went intae the jammin block, it went through his hand!)

Well, I mind there wis a wee man and you caed him Sandy Grierson. He worked in the tunin. He wis a right wee man. And he used tae sometimes sit at the end o the looms. There wis a bench.

(Mr Davidson: The tuners, by the way, you had a section of looms, aboot ten. And if aa your looms wis goin ee could sit down and watch them goin.) (laughs)

Aye. And Sandy wis obviously sat, and Ah always remember this. Ah wis weavin away and the shuttle flew right oot and it knocked his hat. He aye had a bonnet on. And it knocked it clean off and the shuttle went right through the windae and intae the dam, ye ken. And Ah thought, 'Good God!' But Ah aye mind o that. And Sandy's face, because he wis half sleepin thon way, sittin on the bench. And he went, 'Oh!' ken. (laughs)

No wonder. He was lucky because if it had struck him on the face! And it was liable to happen without warning at any time?

    Oh, aye, aye, aye.

How frequent was that, that shuttles flew out?

    Oh, well, shuttles flew out quite often. The looms were four and you had a guard here so as if the shuttles came oot, it wouldnae hit the other folk in the other gangs.

(Looking at a shuttle) *Oh, that would give you a terrible crack, as you say, with a pointed metal end. That's a dangerous thing to be flying about that. It's a projectile.*

    (Mr Davidson: (laughs) Ah wis on aboot quick reflexes and Ah wis on aboot left-handed folk wis supposed tae have quicker reflexes than right. And ma mate up at Innerleithen, he finished up the manager at Peebles but he wis a tuner in that mill doon there. And there were one flew oot one day and he caught it. He put his hand up and he caught it.)

6

Reflections and Looking Forward

Before he pressed stop on his recording machine, Ian always asked his interviewees if they had enjoyed their working life and whether they felt any regrets; or whether they should have made different choices along the way. The replies were likely to have been – in part at least – what he expected to hear. Ian had set out to collect material about an industry in decline and had asked people to reflect on how their communities had been changed by this. The interviews reflect a strong sense of community, both within and out of the mill. Hardly surprising then, that the reflections shared with Ian express a feeling of sadness for the loss of the sense of community once shared among the large workforce. A feeling of belonging that was created largely through a shared work experience that had persisted for many generations. There is also regret that the mills are no longer there to provide stable jobs for the local young people. Many are unhappy that the communities have evolved as commuter towns for Edinburgh, or as sleepy places to which people retire.

Alongside these more sombre reflections is a strong sense of pride expressed by many interviewees, who felt that through their working life they had been able to make a strong contribution to both their families and communities.

At fifty-eight, Wilma French was the youngest of Ian's interviewees and also one of the only ones still to be working in a mill when the recordings were made. Her interview with Ian contains interesting details about the experience of living and working in Peebles from the mid-1950s to the time of the interview. When she left school at fifteen, Wilma followed her two sisters into Damdale mill where she trained to become a darner. Outwith the mill, her social life revolved around dancing which, once she was earning her own wage, was her favourite way to spend her free time.

Wilma's account reflects the changing experience of women in the mill. She went to the mill from school and left work only when her first child was born, which was already an innovation. When her children were very small, she was able to work on webs at home before returning to the workplace when her youngest started school. Wilma also talks about women being appointed to more senior roles within the mill and she herself held a supervisory role when she spoke to Ian. Wilma's working life included time at both a Thorburn mill and a Ballantyne mill.

Wilma French, b. 1938, interviewed 6 December 1996 and 14 February 1997

Now, what was your first job when you left school then?
>The mill.

Aye. How did you get that job?
>Well, Isobel and Margaret [her sisters] both worked in the mill at the time. And, well, Ah jist said, 'Was there any jobs goin?' And that wis it. Ah jist got a job at Damdale, Thorburns.

Now you left school when you were fifteen?
>Fifteen, aye.

That was the minimum school-leaving age, so that would be 1953?
>Right, aye.

And you went straight into the mill? You left the school on the Friday and started on the Monday?
>Uh huh.

Your sisters spoke for you, was that it?
>Aye. Uh huh.

And what was the work that you did when you first went in?
>You went on to the in-giving.

So tell me about that?
>Well, it's the start o the weavin process, where the threads are on beams. And they go down through – it's like a sieve, in a way – and the threads aa go through that. But then you have to put them through. Somebody sits at that side with a hook and you're puttin the threads through and they pu it through. Right?

And the other person hooks them? Aye.
>It's a cam, it's called. That's what it goes through.

This is the sieve-like thing?
>Yes, aye. It's like threads wi wee metal bits in the middle. And this thread has to go through that metal bit. So that's where ye start off, well, we did in these days anyway.

Did all girls start off doin that?
>If you were gonnae be a darner, yes.

Right. Was that your ambition?
>Well, that's what Ah wis gonnae be, wis a darner.

Aye. You wouldn't know maybe much about mills when you started?
>Well, except ma sisters talkin about darnin. Yeah, aye.

Aye. So that attracted you from the sound of it?
>Ah suppose it did, aye.

And this was the normal route towards becoming a darner?
>Aye, ye started in there, in the in-givin and then ye went on tae the shadin and the pickin and learned that.

Now what was the shading and picking then?

Well, once the material's finished, there's always maybe wee white bits or wee black bits. They have tae come out. Or the shadin, the material can be different shades o grey or different shades o black or whatever. An ye can shade it to make it look similar. You make it look even lookin. So Ah wis on that for a while.

And how did you do that then?
It's a thing like a crayon.
I see. So you sort of dye the thing by hand, as it were?
That's right, aye, uh huh.
And that's fairly straightforward work?
Oh, yes, aye. Uh huh.
You don't need a lot of training, or do you?
Well, you do need a bit of trainin. Aye, ye do, definitely, aye. Aye.
And then the picking?
Well, there was people that did that all the time.
Picking out imperfections, was it?
Yes. Uh huh.
So you did each of these things for maybe a few months?
Aye. Yes.
And this was part of your training?
Aye. Uh huh.
And then did you graduate to darning after you'd done that?
Then you'd go into the corner and you learned to do the patterns. That's where you learned your darnin in these days, doin the patterns.
Now what did that involve then? Forgive my dreadful ignorance.
Aye. No, well, it wis the two older women that were in the corner at these days. And they would jist teach ye tae darn. It's as simple as that.
Now darning to me, as an ignoramus, means getting a needle and thread because my wife refuses to sew buttons on. But your kind of darning is different from that?
It's totally different. You're puttin the weave back into the material. If there's a bit missin, you're puttin it back in, that way. With a needle and thread. Uh huh. Yeah.
So it's really repairing any broken bits in the cloth?
That's right. Uh huh.
And that would be quite a skilled job would it?
Yes, it can be.
Aye. Presumably there are some bits of darning that are easy or more difficult to do than others?
Oh, aye. Definitely. Oh, definitely.
As a young lass, you started with the …?
The easy ones, uh huh.
Aye, and worked your way up over a number of years?

That's right.
So that's how you qualify as a darner?
In these days. Uh huh.
Aye, aye. That's grand. Now when you started work in 1953, or I suppose it may have been even early '54 if you were fifteen in October?
Aye. Uh huh.
When you started work, what hours did you work?
We worked fae quarter to eight in the mornin to half-past five.
And that was the standard working week at that time?
Uh huh, uh huh.
Now what about Saturdays?
No so much when ye were startin. Once ye got on tae the darnin an ye learned the job, you would work Saturday mornins and you would work overtime at night. But not when you were trainin.
But as a girl it was a five-day week?
Aye.
The five-day week must have come in because, I think, earlier on people worked on Saturday mornings as purely a matter of routine?
That's right.
Now did you get any kind of approach from a trade union when you started work? Or did that come later on?
Ah think it came once you were out your time and you were actually a darner.
How long did that process take then, to work out your time as a darner?
At least three years. At that time.
Did the union person, the man or woman, come to you or did you go to them?
Ah cannae remember. Ah think it would maybe be, the older women were in the union and they said, well, maybe you should be in the union. And you would go and see and get a form and fill it in.
Aye. Was there ever any discussion about trade unions or trade unionism? Maybe during your tea-breaks or …?
Aye, well, Ah suppose there always was, yes. Aye.
Maybe at a time when wages were being discussed or shortening of hours? That sort of thing, was it?
Uh huh. Yeah, yeah. Aye.
And what was the union that you joined: the Dyers, Bleachers and Textile workers?
Aye, yes, that's what it would be, uh huh.
That was the only union, was it, in the Damdale?
Aye, Ah'm sure it was, aye. Uh huh.
How many darners were there in Damdale?
Might've been, what, fifteen, twenty maybe.
So that was a fair number of the workers out of the eighty, ninety, a hundred in the

mill? Who were the most numerous group in the mill?

    Had tae be darners and weavers.

Aye. The weavers were about the same were they? About fifteen, twenty?

    Aye. Had tae be, aye.

Aye. So between the two groups, you constituted almost the majority of the workers? Maybe more than a third of the workers? And then what were the other groups of workers?

    Well there wis shaders, pickers, birlers, women that jist took the knots out the pieces. And latterly in life, there wis markers, who marked the pieces for us tae darn them. Before, we marked and darned our own pieces. But in later life the cloth wis laid on tae tables and the girls marked the pieces an we jist darned them.

That would make the job less interesting maybe, did it? Maybe not?

    In a way it did. Cause it meant you were sittin all day long once that happened.

More specialised work, too?

    Yeah.

Aye. More division of labour really?

    Aye, it wis, aye.

Whereas at one time you'd done a whole process?

    Aye, latterly … ye jist did the one.

Would that be after you were married? Maybe when you were in your thirties or so, Mrs French?

    Not even as long ago as that, no.

In the last ten, fifteen years, maybe?

    Once Ah had ma family, Ah went back to work, and Ah went intae Ballantyne's, they had birlers. And then a few years ago they did away wi all them and there's only darners now and we do everything. So it went a full circle really.

Yeah. They've really been quite considerable changes in your working life on the whole?

    Uh huh. Yeah.

So as you were saying, you worked in the mill from the age of fifteen until you were married?

    Ah got married jist after ma twenty first birthday.

So you were there about six years roughly?

    Uh huh. Uh huh.

Of course, you were earning money in the mill?

    Uh huh. Aye, but you had to give most o your money tae your mum.

That was my next question. Did you give your pay packet to your mother?

    Uh huh.

Unopened?

    No. But Ah had a certain amount Ah had tae give her.

For bed and board?
> Yes, aye, uh huh.

Aye, aye. And so you gave her what you were due for bed and board?
> Aye.

And kept the rest?
> That's right.

Some people just handed their pay packet over.
> No, Ah didnae have to do that.

No, no. And of course, you had older sisters, who were working so your parents, at that stage, would be presumably better off?
> Than they had been. That's right. Uh huh.

And the money that you retained for yourself was a reasonable sum that enabled you to buy your coffee and put a penny in the jukebox and go to the dancing twice a week?
> Well, aye. And save up for your clothes. You died if you didnae have new clothes, aye.

And did you buy these clothes in Peebles or did you go up to Edinburgh?
> Sometimes here, but a lot o the times we went to Edinburgh. Uh huh. Aye. Not every Saturday. Jist when you'd saved up enough money to buy somethin.

Now once you got married, did I gather from what you were saying, you stopped work in the mill?
> Ah worked for two years after Ah got married.

It was no longer the common thing, you know, before the War, I think, when women got married, they immediately stopped work? Was that the case?
> No, not always. Usually, it seemed tae work that they worked until they had the family. And then they stopped.

But you can't recall married women working in the mill with young children, when you were a young girl?
> No when their kids were wee, no, no. Ah think maybe once the children got to school age, the women came back to work. Well, Ah had Susan first, '62. Lynne came in '64 and Ah went back to work when Lynne went to the school.

And did you work full-time then?
> No, Ah worked part-time.

The mill was willing to take you part-time?
> Oh, yes, then. Then, aye, definitely.

So there was no difficulty in finding part-time employment?
> No, no. Ah darned at home when the kids were awfy wee. Ah had webs in here and sat and darned in here. It wis fae Thorburn's tae start wi, and then it wis March Street. An Ah think that's why Ah got back quite easily because Ah had been darnin at home.

Now were there any forewomen in Damdale? Or were all the foremen men?
> Men tae start wi. Later on it wis women.

All the people with responsibility were men. But when you were roughly what age, did you start to get women foremen?
>It would be at the time Ah wisnae workin, that Nan took over. When ma sister had went back tae work, it wis a woman foreman then.

It would be in the 1960s by the sound of it? Sometime after '62?
>Aye.

And certainly there was a woman foreman, at least one, by the time you went back?
>Aye, uh huh [in 1969].

That would be March Street, of course?
>Yeah, it wis. We had a man to start wi, when Ah went back, an then it wis a woman.

Heads of department have always been men, in your working life?
>Aye. Yeah.

First in Damdale and after your children went to school, in March Street mills?
>Yeah. Uh huh. That's right.

Now, when you went back to work, after your younger lass went to school in 1969, you went, of course, to March Street because both Damdale and Tweedside had gone. And Damdale was closed down about a year, two years after that? Taken over by Ballantyne's?
>Uh huh.

And the workers went up to March Street. When you went to March Street then in 1969, can you recollect, you know, noticing or feeling any differences from what you had previously experienced in Damdale?
>Well, the mill was much more modern for a start, wasn't it? Cause, Ah mean, we still had wooden floors and everything in Thorburn's when Ah wis there.

So it was a much older building was it, Damdale?
>Aye. Oh, Damdale wis an old building.

So were working conditions better at March Street?
>Aye. Uh huh.

In what sense were they better?
>Well, as Ah say, for the floorin for a start, it wisnae wooden floors. It's no cement but it wis a solid floor rather than a wooden floor. But it wisnae cement. And it made a difference, because in these days, when you'd finished a piece and you rolled it up tae take it away, ye jist lifted the end. Two girls, one at each side, and ye pull it along the floor. So if you were in Thorburn's and it wis a wooden floor, that sometimes caused problems.

Because the cloth would catch and there was a danger of ripping it? So maybe you weren't allowed to drag it along the floor?
>Sometimes ye werenae. It depended on what kind o materials you were workin with. Aye. In Ballantyne's it wis different. It didnae matter then.

Now, anything else? Was the light better in March Street than it had been in Damdale?
>Definitely. Definitely.

So what sort of lighting had they had in Damdale?
> In Damdale, when we started darnin, ye had fluorescent. Ah wis gonnae say fluorescent lights above.

Not the sort of winkie-blinkie kind that started to flutter when the thing was running down? It wasn't them?
> No, no. It wisnae them at aa. It wis a single bulb. An it wis on a thing that you could pull up and down. And it literally sat in here. You're darnin here and the lightbulb wis there.

Right against your cheek.
> Aye. That's right.

So in March Street, on the other hand, you had what kind of lighting?
> When we went to March Street it wis the strip-lighting.

Aye, neon or fluorescent lighting? A much brighter light?
> Oh, aye.

Ballantyne's was a much more comfortable place to work was it, from the point of view of light and temperature?
> Yeah, definitely.

Was there any difference in the atmosphere? You know, sort of maybe less friendly or more remote? You wouldn't know everybody when you went to March Street, in the way that you tended to know the people in Damdale?
> Well, actually at that time everybody in Peebles knew everybody else. So you really did know the most o the girls, aye.

That's great. Now what about the union? When you went back to work, you'd been a member of the Dyers, Bleachers and Textile Workers at Damdale.
> Uh huh.

Did you resume your membership when you went to March Street?
> Aye but it wis the Transport and General Workers.

Were you ever an active member?
> No.

You wouldn't be with a family, you wouldn't have time … And you're still working in the mill, Mrs French?
> Uh huh.

In your working life, have you ever been on strike?
> One day.

Oh! Was that at Damdale?
> It wis at March Street.

March Street. After you went back?
> Ah cannae remember the reason for it. It wis the whole country wis asked tae have one day's strike for some reason?

Oh, it was maybe the Industrial Relations Act or something like that?
> Ah cannae remember what it was at all. Ah never went tae ma work. That wis the only time in ma life.

It was nothing to do with the mill specifically?
>No really, no, no.

No. You can't recall ever any difficulties arising in the mill, which almost led to strike action? You know, people got really worked up about it and said, 'Oh, we'll need to come out on strike!', even if they didn't actually come out on strike?
>Yeah. Well, jist when it came to time for wage rises. There's always been arguments about it until the last few years or, och, I don't know how many years. But before that, there wis always arguments about wages because they always said they'd never any money when it came to time for wage rises.

People would start to say, 'Oh, it's time we had a wage increase'. And that's when tensions would rise?
>Yeah. To me, that would be the biggest arguments in the mill.

Aye. But it never came to the point of having a strike?
>No. They used to talk about it but it never happened, no.

Never came to anything, no. Your husband was saying earlier, that there was this unwillingness on the part of most workers, you know, if the chips were down, actually to come out on strike. Was that your recollection?
>Uh huh. Aye. Uh huh. Yeah.

We were saying, in Peebles if you didn't work in the mill, there wasn't really much choice of other employment?
>No. Cause, well, it wis aa hotel work an things like that. An a lot o the women didnae want to do that.

I mean, how was work in the mill regarded by women like yourself? Was it seen as a kind of plum job; a more desirable job than most others?
>Not really. Not really, no. No, not really.

What did young women like yourself think of as a better job within Peebles, than working in the mill?
>Well, Ah suppose they used tae say if ye worked in a shop ye were kind o posh, in these days. But the wages werenae good. A lot o people in Peebles have started off workin in the Hydro.

I see. But was it your impression that girls, young women like yourself, [regarding] hotel work, wouldn't be keen on going there unless they had to?
>Aye, that kind o thing, that's right.

They would rather work in the mill?
>Uh huh.

And that though there were some attractions in working in a shop – they were posh, and so on – the wages in fact were not as good as you could earn in the mill?
>That's right, that's right, uh huh. And, Ah cannae remember what the reason was Ah left the mill for, but Ah went back tae shop work and Ah wis only there about six months or something and Ah went back tae the mill again.

That was Damdale?
>Aye, uh huh.

Aye, aye. So maybe was there an incident and you got fed up and felt you could do with a change?

Ah jist cannae remember, but Ah jist remember o doin that.

Aye, that's interesting that in the course of talking about these things you remembered there was this period – before you were married when you left the mill and went to work in this shop that you'd worked in as a schoolgirl?

Uh huh, that's right, aye.

But you went back to the mill?

Aye, uh huh, yeah.

Well, I'll keep one eye on the clock, because I hadn't realised it was marching on. I'll make a quick dash for the bus. So looking back on your working life have you enjoyed working in the mill?

Sometimes yes, sometimes no. I enjoy my work. I enjoy what I do. Sometimes you get too much aggravation.

And that has been increasingly so?

Yeah.

And this aggravation or pressure comes from?

Well, the mill nowadays wants everything yesterday. They want everything yesterday.

More so than there used to be?

Yes, uh huh. And, well, Ah'm kind o the boss now in ma bit and Ah do the runnin around. The gofor, aye, that's what Ah am, yeah.

You're under a lot of pressure?

Uh huh.

Well, I hope the pressure eases off for you, Mrs French.

Aye, I hope sae, tae. (laughs)

Well, thanks very much – thanks very much to both of you. It's very good of you.

Despite the imminent departure of the Edinburgh bus, the interview resumes briefly to record this detail about the Mount hostel.

Well, the Mount wis connected wi the Thorburn mill, and it wis girls that came frae Fife and through the west, and they came tae stay in Peebles tae work in the mill. And they had this hostel for the girls, and it wis up on The Mount. Above the Dalcusha [Dilkusha]. It wis an old Thorburn's house at one time, wisn't it, Tony?

(Mr French: It wis an estate.)

Aye. It wis jist two women that ran it.

They were employees of the mill?

Yes. And these two women did the cookin and the cleanin and aa thae kind o things. And the girls stayed there through the week and went home at the weekends.

Uh huh. And you stayed there yourself?
>Ma sister and I stayed there jist for about a year.

Because you were living at that time down in the railway cottage?
>Yes, aye. And, well, when the railway finished ma dad lost his job eventually and went to stay at Carstairs. So we stayed at The Mount for a year.

Aye, aye. Now tell me about the house then. Roughly how many rooms? It was a long time ago.
>There'd be two wi two beds, rooms wi four beds, and Ah wis jist gettin reminded, there wis one wi six beds in it.

So did you share a room with your sister only?
>Ma sister, tae start wi. And then later on there wis four of us in the one room, aye. But Ah remember they were great big rooms. It wis an old, old house.

Yes, you had a fair bit of space each?
>Yes, uh huh.

That's good. Now did you pay something, or was it deducted from your wages?
>Aye, it wid come off our wages.

And did you get all your meals there?
>Ah think ye mair or less seen tae your ain supper. Ye wid get the tea made and then anything else ye got yersel.

A cup of cocoa or something of the sort?
>Aye, that's right.

Was it quite comfortable?
>Oh, aye, yes.

Quite warm? Not a damp house?
>No, no. It wis a well kept place, it wis, aye. And there wis a great big lounge, a great big fire on every night for us aa tae sit in if we wanted tae.

A coal fire, aye?
>Or you had your wirelesses up the stair.

And it was specifically the girls and women who didn't have anywhere to live in Peebles? Or lived too far from Peebles to make travel.
>That's right aye. And ye had tae work in Thorburn's mill.

You were there – just remind me – what year roughly?
>'55, Ah think.

And do you know when it closed?
>Well, we would be the last lot that wis in it. Ma sister and I went back home because ma parents moved back here. But the girls that were there then were the last lot. So it could maybe have been 1960-ish.

So it was probably open for about up to fifteen years altogether? From the end of the Second War to about 1960 – somewhere about that, roughly?
>Aye, aye, I wid think that, roughly, yeah there were the two women that looked after it. One did the cookin and the one did the cleanin.

Were you allowed visitors there?

Yes, we were. Ah cannae remember o havin any, but, yes, we were allowed visitors.
You know, some places they might have strict rules, say, against men visiting?
Oh, there wouldnae be men in, no, no. Other girl friends, aye, but no men, no.
The food was quite good?
Yes, it wis very good, aye.
And as far as you know that was the only hostel of its kind in Peebles? None of the other mills had a hostel of that sort?
Not that Ah know of, no, no.
Some of the girls presumably would be there pretty well throughout the time it was open, for ten or twelve years?
Oh, aye, yes. Oh, there's one o the girls that works wi me the now wis in The Mount. She wis there a lot longer than me.
There was no limit put on the time you could live there?
No, as long as you were in the mill you could stay there as long as you liked.
Can you remember how much you paid?
Oh, Ah think it wisnae … It wis about twenty-five shillins, sort o thing.
It was a fairly small sum because you were getting all your meals there? And full board and lodging?
Yes.
It was very reasonable? Did you feel it so at the time?
Oh, at the time we quite enjoyed it, once we got used tae it, we enjoyed it.
Well, that's great. Well, thanks very much, Mrs French.
Oh, you're welcome.
And again my apologies for taking so long.
Oh, it's aaright. (laughs)
Thanks a lot.

Other Voices

While Wilma was reflecting on a time when the mills were the main employers in the area, Duncan Murray shared his thoughts with Ian about the more recent decline in the industry across many border communities.

Duncan Murray, b. 1918, Border mills

Well, Ah don't know, but when Ah retired, there wis a chap down there, quite high up in textiles. And he told me, he said, 'Well,' he says, 'Ah think maybe another fifteen years and the Borders have had it for textiles'.
It certainly looks like that?
Uh huh. Ye see, they were startin away … losin the cashmere to China.
So at the moment there's only the bit of March Street mills left? The other two mills have long since gone?
Yes, they were gone long ago.

REFLECTIONS AND LOOKING FORWARD

And in Innerleithen. Is there anything in Innerleithen?
> There is, there's, what used to be Waverley mills is cloth mills now, but that's synthetic stuff.

Man-made fibre? It's not wool?
> It's aa man-made. No, it's no wool. And Walkerburn, nothing now.

There's nothing at all at Walkerburn?
> It finished. It's closed. It's all knocked down.

Now what about Galashiels? There's still one or two mills there?
> One or two but not … there's nothing like what they used to be.

The same applies to Selkirk, doesn't it? I was down there yesterday.
> Selkirk, aye, Selkirk's the same.

It's terribly sad.
> Hawick is the same. They've suffered, oh, aye.

Kelso used to have some but that's all away?
> It's away, aye, oh, aye.

So it really has been an industry very much in decline in your working life?
> It has, oh, yes, definitely.

It's quite sad.
> So it is.

When you think of all the skills, including your own as a dyer, that have all been lost. And, no jobs for people? People, presumably, living in Peebles have to go to Galashiels or Edinburgh or move?
> They have to move. Yes, that's right. Or go abroad. It's sad, mind, because Peebles wis a town where there wis plenty o work.

Aye, it's a sad commentary.
> It is.

While Duncan reflects on the impact of new producers on the mills, in this next extract Peter Lavin reflects on the role of innovation which led to the first wave of reductions in the size of the workforce needed to keep a mill functioning.

Peter Lavin, b. 1922, a job for life, innovation and decreased workforce

Now of course, employment in textiles in Peebles, … has fallen off very considerably. First of all the two mills were closed: the one burned down and the other one was closed. And then in March Street only about one-third of the workers are employed there now who were there when you first started. Before the War there was 300, 350. Now it's 100?
> Yeah.

So what are the reasons for that decline?
> New machinery comin in. Well, tae gie ye a rough idea, Ah looked after what they caed the web windin and the cone windin. Makin thae big bobbins, you know. An there wis twenty-four girls between the two places. An when Ah left there were only four daein the same job, cause they brought in this new-

fangled machine an it used to rip the stuff oot.

So it's quite a serious loss of jobs for quite a small town like Peebles?

I mean, that wis only one department. Ye lost aboot, say, nineteen tae twenty girls. Now if you think o it, if they keep that up, they'll be naebody workin in a wee while at aa. (laughs)

(Miss Margaret Lavin: Ye see long ago when ye got a job in the mill, ye were there, that wis your job.)

That's right. Well you're examples and maybe your sister, you were there for life, weren't you?

(Miss Lavin: Nowadays they're in and out.)

Now looking back on your working life, do you have any regrets about having worked in the March Street mills or the Peebles textile?

No, no really. Everything wis aaright. I mean I got on aaright with the management and everythin you know.

Were relationships between management and the workers on the whole quite good?

Ah think they were quite good, uh huh.

You were saying you had no regrets about working in the mill?

Oh, no, Ah got a livin out o it an – well, Ah'm existin. (laughs) Ah mean, Ah wisnae very highly paid, it never wis highly paid.

No, no. And it was always the lack of alternative employment in Peebles?

Well, there's nothin really. If ye're goin to be employed, you've got to go into Edinburgh or somewhere.

And that's very expensive isn't it?

An Ah think they're jist aboot as bad in Edinburgh tryin tae get jobs as what they are here.

Aye. Has Peebles itself changed in your lifetime?

Oh, yes.

In what ways then?

Well, Ah mean, there's aa the different housin schemes that's taen up more ground and more people comin in. An there's an awfu lot o folk come in here frae Edinburgh. Ah think, because it bein a quieter place, ye know, they jist rather come through here and stay than travel through. Well, what, half-an-hour takes ye there in a car, doesn't it?

That's right, even less than that. The bus took about forty minutes for me.

Aye, well, better stayin here an enjoyin the quietness. Well, ye have yeer vandals nowadays. We never had that before but we've got some o them makin trouble. But Edinburgh, the hustle an bustle, ye'll ken yersel. But when people are gettin up in years an gettin ready to retire …

Yes, there seem to be a lot of retired people here?

Yeah, there is.

That's a change from your younger days, when you were a young man?

That's right, uh huh.

John Lunn also reflected on changing working practices within the industry which he had witnessed during his working life.

John Lunn, b. 1936, changing technology

That's wonderful. Thanks very much for all your time and trouble. Extremely clear throughout. Now looking back over your life, which continues in the mills – any comments, you know, changes that have taken place, differences between the 1950s when you began and now?

> Oh, there's tremendous differences. Working conditions have changed completely.

For the better?

> Well, in some respects for the better. There were mills, and Ah don't think there is now, where they were sort o homes fae homes. Ah mean, obviously they would never survive in a modern era. Ah would say most mills now are equipped wi modern machinery. Ah mean, as Ah said probably before, Ah worked through a revolution. When Ah first started workin, Ah mean, some o the machines that ye used, some o the cardin machines both in Innerleithen and in Gala had what they caed wooden rollers – wooden cylinders. Ah mean, Ah scrapped a machine in Gala and it wis built in 1879.

And that's in the mid-1960s?

> And that wis in the 1960s. It wis nearly a hundred year old. In fact, when Ah wis at Selkirk in 1963 we'd a machine runnin in the blendin and it had been built in 1860. So, Ah mean …

A damn good machine! (laughs)

> They were good machines but they werenae fast. The biggest thing is the actual speed o the machinery. Machines now are really fast.

Everything's been speeded up?

> Everything is actually goin faster and faster. It's the speed o the machines that has been the biggest difference. As Ah say, we put machines in in the Waverley, when Ah wis there in 1976. And man for man, the men were producin something like about ten times [the work]. Cause, we'd over a hundred workers only producin somethin like 10, 15 ton o yarn a week. And suddenly ye'd six men could produce 25 ton o yarn a week.

Huge and rapid change?

> Huge. Aye, and that wis overnight. Ah mean, up until 1956, or round about that, most mills had never changed for a hundred years. They literally had not changed for a hundred years. They were usin conin machines that were ninety year old. Windin, they were spinnin on tae little spindles. Ye only got maybe about a quarter o pound o yarn on a spindle. Now, in the 1970s and eighties, the type o spindle that they use, they're gettin five kilos on a spindle as against half a pound. Now it means that the time that the men actually have to stop the machine tae take the spindles off, tae take these bobbins off,

is minimal. When Ah started workin, if your spinnin run at fifty per cent you were lucky because they filled up and that was it. Ye had tae stop it. You'd tae tie in and do various other things. Now if the spinnin isnae runnin about ninety-five per cent, they're askin questions.

Aye. There's been this huge revolution?

There's a huge revolution in efficiencies and size o machinery, size o spindles. Obviously, bearins are different. Now, everything runs on roller-based bearins and that. So you can get huge speeds: 10,000 revs, 12,000 revs is nothin. But before, all you had wis a piece, a spindle, and it run on an oil bath. So if it wis runnin any more than about a couple o thousand revs, it wis red hot. Even the cardin machines in spinnin, they're all electronically controlled. They speed up, each bit speeds up and slows down, all in proportion. When Ah first started, it wis a big six-inch broad belt. Ye started the machine wi a broad belt and ye'd tae start every bit individually. And you'd a line-shaft and ye had tae oil the line-shaft. You'd tae go up and oil the line-shaft. Things have changed. Now you go in and press a button. Before, you had tae start all these belts. Maintenance is a lot easier. Nowadays they come along and they say 'Oh, it's no runnin'. And they pull out a plug and they put in another plug, printed circuit board, and the machine starts up again. In the old days, you had tae maintain aa your belts, your pulleys, aa your line-shaft, everything. That wis aa part o your work.

Despite all this innovation, the border mills decline. Myra Little shared her own very personal views on her working life with Ian, including her strong feeling that the Ballantynes could have saved the mills.

Myra Little, b. 1936, working life and reflections

Before I go, can I put one final question to you? Looking back on your life in the mills, you know, what are your feelings now? Did you enjoy the work? Did you feel you wasted your life? What do you think, Mrs Little?

No, Ah've no feelin Ah've wasted ma life. Ah feel it wis an experience. And you cannae feel you've wasted your life because that wis jist life. That was life. And Ah thoroughly enjoyed ma stake warpin. Tae me that wis an experience, it really wis. Ah like aa these sort o complicated things that you've tae think on. Somethin that you're goin tae achieve somethin at the end o it.

Great. And, of course, your interest and your proficiency in maths and sums at the school maybe there's a link there. You know, with the complicated patterns and all that?

Aye. It aa comes intae the same, same as ma cross-stitch and everything like that. It's aa intae that.

Now, given that the mills have been so badly run down in the Borders, Walkerburn not least, there's nothing at all left in Walkerburn, what's your feeling about that?

Ah think it's disgustin. Ah think actually if it hadnae been a sort o wee family

feud wi the Ballantynes, Ah dinnae think the mill here would've finished.
It would still have carried on?
It wis jist a wee sort o family disagreement and thing. They couldnae agree, Henry and Jeremy and them.
The directors of the firm?
Aye. Uh huh.
So that was the reason the mill ended up with Dawson International?
Aye. It aa bottled doon tae that, didn't it, Archie?
(Mr Archie Little: Well, Ah don't know. They had space at Dalkeith for a lot o the stuff doon here. Ah shifted it up tae Dalkeith.)

Like Myra, many of Ian's interviewees had enjoyed their working lives. They had worked hard and worked well and were able to look back with a sense of pride and certainty on their working life. As Walter Scott, who was emphatic in his assessment of his own fifty years of experience, stated, 'Ah've no regrets'.

Walter Scott, b. 1924, changing attitudes to work

Well, that's great. Now just to finish with because I don't want to keep you back. Apart from your war service in the Fleet Air Arm, you worked in the mill from the age of fourteen to the age of sixty-five. That's half a century. Looking back on it now, what do you think of your experience? Do you have any regrets about having worked in the mill? Did you enjoy your work?
No, Ah've no regrets. The mill's been good to me, aye.
You enjoyed the work?
Ah enjoyed the work. Uh huh. Ye get the biggest half o them nowadays, that come in there on a Monday mornin: 'Roll on bloody Friday!' Now that wis never the attitude when Ah wis a laddie.
Dropped, aye. Personal responsibility, personal morality?
There wis never a person came intae the mill on a Monday mornin wi dirty overalls. Everybody came in wi clean overalls on a Monday. Now?!
So it's morale? Morale has fallen for some reason?
Definitely, definitely.
I mean, you found the work satisfying, all the years you worked there? You enjoyed what you were doing?
Oh, aye.
You felt you were doing something worthwhile and got satisfaction out of it? But you don't think that's the case now?
No now. Oh, working conditions in there nowadays is a bloody cakewalk!
Aye, compared to what they were in your young days?
Aye. Ah mean, men in the millhoose there, they were up tae their bloody waists in water, wi pails o sodae and pails o this and that. Now it's a case o jist press a button.

Aye. It's all mechanised and automated. And much easier now the manual labour and the hardships have gone?

Aye. Definitely.

That's a big change in your lifetime, aye?

Definitely. Oh, aye … Ah've no complaints.

I mean, looking back on it you don't say, 'I wish I'd become a fireman or an engine-driver?'

No, no, no. No complaints.

Well thanks very much indeed, Mr Scott. That was excellent.

You're welcome.

Andrew Brunton told Ian that he was happy he had chosen to stay in Innerleithen rather than head to New Zealand, but also expressed his concern about the lack of local employment opportunities for young people.

Andrew Brunton, b. 1928, opportunities then and now

The only question that occurs to me to ask you is, looking back over your half century [at Caerlee], forty-eight years there, you know, what are your thoughts now? Did you enjoy the work? Did you get a lot out of it? Do you wish that you'd done something else entirely different, or what?

Oh, well, everybody thinks they could've done somethin. But Ah telt ye that Ah wrote that letter, Ah wrote the letter oot tae go tae New Zealand. An Ah says tae Doreen, Ah says, 'Doreen, it'll no maitter where oo go, oo'll have tae work'. So better the devil ye ken as the devil ye dinnae ken. So Ah stayed here. Twae young bairns, ye ken. Ah dinnae think Andrew wis born then.

That's grand. I mean, at the end of your working life, you didn't feel, 'Oh I wish I'd stayed in the woods' or 'I wish I'd become an engine driver or a seaman' or something like that?

No. Ah dinnae ken.

You didn't have a strong feeling of that sort? You'd enjoyed the work?

Och, as Ah say, everybody, ken, the gress is greener, ken, sort o thing, ye ken. But, ye could've went and done something else. An Ah hear folk complainin aboot their job an Ah think you've no much to complain aboot, you, ye ken. They're stuck in the mill aa day. But there ye are, they're daein a job that maybe Ah thought wis guid. But they aa have their problems.

That's right. That's right. The grass is greener, as you say.

An Ah mean, Ah handled ma work, ye ken. Ah got on aaright an Ah had freends. Mind, efter aa thir takeovers an efter aa this time-study and things, things got tighter and tighter, ye ken. There werenae the same carefree atmosphere that used tae be in the mills, ye ken.

Yes, yes. But, you know, looking at the mills now, there are only two left in Innerleithen, Waverley and Caerlee, the one where you were. Are you sad at the realisation

REFLECTIONS AND LOOKING FORWARD

that the textile industry has gone down?
>   Oh, it's terrible. Ah mean, Ah telt ye, Ah spoke to that laddie there. He says, 'Ah wis supposed tae be in over Christmas and they've kept us on longer'. That laddie disnae ken how long he's goin tae be in a job. When the mills were aa goin there were a job for everybody. Ken, Ah mean, they could find ye a job, ye ken – maybe a menial job, but ye were bringin in a wage. You were bringin in a wage. An ye were off the street. Ken, ye see them goin aboot now, and they're young men walkin up and doon the street through the day. Ah mean, Ah'm walkin up and doon the street but Ah've earned ma retirement, ye ken what Ah mean. But Ah feel sorry for them. Ma eldest laddie, he wis oot o work for quite a while. An he'd three bairns. An he had tae traivel up and doon tae Gala tae the Job Centre doon there. He had tae report every week. An he wrote letters an never ony success. Eventually he got a job doon in the Borders General Hospital.

But he had been a mill worker?
>   He'd worked in the mill, aye. Uh huh, uh huh. But he'd had twae or three jobs. He worked in the Region for a while. He wis made redundant oot o that, ken. He's been aboot six or seven year doon at the Border General. But he's nae money. He has tae buy a car afore he can traivel up an doon, ken whit Ah mean?

Aye, it's very expensive? As you say, you and your wife got the best years because you were never unemployed?
>   Nae doubt aboot that, nae doubt aboot that, aye, uh huh.

It's a really sad world for young people.
>   Oh, aye. What's the answer?

Many of the interviews Ian made reflect the fact that many were fortunate enough to be able to place a priority on quality of life. Looking back on his own working life and how Walkerburn had changed over the decades, Eric Pearce told Ian that he was sure he could have earned more money and ensured better financial security away from the mills and Walkerburn but, he said, 'money's not everything'.

Eric Pearce b. 1927, working life and Walkerburn

>   The mill buildings themselves have all been demolished and they're now into various units and some of them are doing quite well. But there's very little prospect for youngsters nowadays in Walkerburn.

And there are quite a number of people are there who travel daily to work from Walkerburn?
>   Oh, yes, there's a vast exodus every day.

And is it mainly on the bus, public transport, or motor car?
>   It's mainly motor cars, I gather. The place seems to be getting littered with motor cars nowadays.

So you've really seen quite a big change in Walkerburn in your lifetime? You came here when you were eleven years old, Eric, to live?

Uh huh. Yes, there were no motor cars up and down the street like you have nowadays, parked head to tail. When you go along that avenue, one side of the street's completely lined with motor cars all the way down. It's happening everywhere.

That's great. Now looking back over your working life?

I did my fifty years, aye.

Almost exactly fifty years, Eric? Because you retired as soon as you were sixty-five, did you?

Uh huh.

And you'd entered the mill just short, I think you said, of your fifteenth birthday.

Uh huh.

Now looking back on your working days in the mill, what thoughts do you have now?

Well, as I say, the first half was quite enjoyable. The second half wasn't particularly enjoyable and I did have second thoughts ... that I'd picked the wrong trade.

Sorry, you didn't feel that so strongly in the first half of your working life as in the later years? Is that right?

That's right. It's later on when you look at, let's say, your pension prospects and what's going to affect your retirement and so forth. Originally we had a pension plan in this mill but it was peanuts. I mean, it wasn't up to much. And gradually you moved into the different companies, they had stronger ... likes of pension plans and life insurance guarantees and so forth. So that you gradually built up as you went through it. But I think I could have done better in something else than the textile trade.

Occupational pensions in textiles are not all that good, Eric?

No.

No, no, no. So not only did you suffer, I gather, from a sense of frustration and restlessness in your later years in the mill, but also your financial prospects once you retired were not as good as they would have been had you started off or transferred much earlier to some other occupation or industry?

That's true, yes. We've no financial worries. But, I mean ... I know for a fact I could've been, let's say, in a higher income bracket if I'd been in a different industry.

But then that might have involved leaving Walkerburn and that's another decision isn't it?

Yes, I've no complaints, I like Walkerburn. I like the friends, neighbours, everything that I'm doing. I mean, I've lots of occupations that I like doing. I'm a keen fisher, a keen bowler, and do all these things.

So there are always pros and cons aren't there? You know, what you might have gained financially or in satisfaction with the job you might have lost by having to leave Walkerburn.

Oh, I always say money's not everything.
No. Well, that's great, Eric.

We conclude this chapter with an extract from Ian's conversation with Bob Anderson. Like many of Ian's interviewees, Bob enjoyed a high level of job satisfaction, in his case particularly from his work with the Intarsia knitting at Caerlee. Whilst he was sad about the changes he has seen in Innerleithen, with a high number of commuters who 'dae nothing for the toon', he was resolutely upbeat about his own working life and experience: 'Ah fair enjoyed ma life' he told Ian.

Bob Anderson, b. 1931, Innerleithen and reflections on a working life in the mill

Yes. So Innerleithen was a much smaller place?
Oh, jist a village, aye, jist a village. You know, you knew everybody in Innerleithen. (laughs) You couldnae dae nothing wrong cause they went and telt your mother. (laughs)
Aye. You felt big brother's eye was upon you all the time?
That's right, aye. That's right, aye.
But now it's more spread out?
Ah dinnae ken. But there's an awfy lot o folk now that jist sleeps in the place. They work in Edinburgh. They jist commute every day. And Ah aye feel it's sad because they dinnae dae nothing for the toon. They dinnae even shop in the toon. They dinnae even buy petrol in the toon.
No, no. That's the universal experience of the time?
That's right, that's it.
For villages and small towns, aye.
Aye, aye, aye.
Now that's great. Looking back on your life in the mill, what are your thoughts? Do you have any regrets? Would you rather, looking back now, have spent your time doing something else than working in Caerlee?
Ah've never thocht aboot it. Ah really enjoyed ma work. And Ah liked the folk Ah worked aside. Ah got on awfy weel wi folk, ee ken. Ah wasnae ill tae get on with, Ah suppose, but Ah enjoyed it. Aye. Ah enjoyed it.
You could take a real pride in it.
Oh, aye. Well, the likes o that Intarsia, it wis aa made wi your fingers, ee ken, and …
Very skilful.
Oh, it wis nice tae see a pattern gettin made, ken.
And you would know these were going out all over the world?
That's right, aye. When Ah went on tae piece-work in the plain machine one o ma first orders wis a black twinset for the Queen Mother.
Really?

>Aye. (laughs) But it wis only on paper ... Black, aye, for the Queen Mother, aye, a black twinset.

So the orders came from the highest circles in the land?
>Oh, aye. Oh, aye, oh, aye. We used tae get a lot o film stars roond the mill and everything like that.

Can you remember any film stars who came?
>Well, there were Frankie Lane. Judy Garland. Nat King Cole. Aye. Oh, there were quite a few, aye.

Well, that's great. Well, I cannae think of anything else to ask you. You've given an excellent account of your working life. Was there anything that you wanted to say?
>No, Ah dinnae think sae. Ah aye enjoyed ... jist that Ah enjoyed, Ah fair enjoyed ma life. Ah really have, really.
>
>(Mrs Anderson: You're quite happy to be retired!) (laughs)
>
>Oh, Ah'm quite happy tae be retired, aye.

Despite discussing a declining industry, a number of the interviewees believed that the mills had been capable of developing and changing over the years, most notably during the First and Second World Wars. Given the trajectory of mill fortunes highlighted in the text so far, perhaps the Peeblesshire mill industry may yet be revived.

APPENDIX I

The Mills and Mill Owners

For much of the period under consideration in this publication the Ballantyne and Thorburn families were the main mill owners in Peeblesshire. The Ballantyne family were active in expanding and changing their portfolio; often moving plant and workers around seeking to thrive in an increasingly competitive world market. This appendix gives a brief overview of ownership and production across the three communities of Peebles, Innerleithen and Walkerburn, based on the information shared with Ian during the interview sessions.

Peebles

Name	What was done there	Owners/Notes
Damcroft Mill		Thorburn family
Damdale Mill	Spinning, weaving, ware-room	Thorburn family
Damside Mill		Thorburn family
Lowe Donald & Co., later Holland & Sherry	Tweed warehouse	Founded and run by the Thorburn family
March Street Mills	Drawing and weaving, darning and finishing	D. Ballantyne & Bros Co. Ltd, later Frasers, then Baird, then Dawson International
Tweedside Mill	Carding and spinning	Thorburn family

Innerleithen

Name	What was done there	Owners/Notes
Caerlee Mill	Hosiery – cashmere, Intarsia lambswool, camel hair	D. Ballantyne & Bros Co. Ltd Full name: The Ballantyne Sportswear, Caerlee Knitting Mills
Cleikum Mill		Murray Allan of Innerleithen Ltd (specialised in cashmere, est. 1971)
Leithen Mills	Spinning (woollen) Supplied Walkerburn and Peebles with yarn for weaving	D. Ballantyne & Bros Co. Ltd
St Ronan's Mill, known as the tap (top) mill		Originally owned by Beckett & Robertson, later bought over by D. Ballantyne & Bros Co. Ltd
Waverley Mill	Spinning (woollen) Supplied Walkerburn and Peebles with yarn for weaving	D. Ballantyne & Bros Co. Ltd

Walkerburn

Name	Owners/Notes
Tweedholm Mill, known as the wee mill	Dalziel, then Henry Ballantyne & Sons
Tweedvale Mill, known as the big mill	Henry Ballantyne & Sons

APPENDIX 2

The Interviewees

ORDERED BY INTERVIEW DATE

The material included in this book comprises only part of the Peeblesshire mill workers collection. This appendix provides a brief summary for each of the interviews and can be used to gain an insight into the wider range of themes and experiences shared with Ian as he made his fieldwork recordings.

Mr Duncan Adam, b. 1917, Peebles
Interviewed 8 November 1996, aged 80 (1h 33m 32s and 33m 57s)
In this interview, Duncan Adam reflects on his life in Peebles and Innerleithen. He was born in Peebles, where his mother and father both worked in the mills, his mother as a weaver and his father as a warper. Duncan's father, a soldier in the First World War, was killed at Festubert, north of Arras in 1917 and he talks about the impact this had on the family. Duncan left school at fifteen to work as a clerk in March Street in Peebles. He talks about his long career in the mills, which began in 1931. He retired aged sixty-five and his only break in employment was for his own war service, 1941–46. He progressed from clerk to manager and reflects on his different jobs and how the mills changed over the decades: in culture, ownership and technology. Duncan also reflects on his early home life, schooldays and holidays and how the mill communities have changed over time.

Miss Margaret Lavin, b. 1919, Peebles
Interviewed 12 November 1996, shortly before her 77th birthday (1h 33m 50s and 9m 38s)
In this interview, Margaret Lavin first talks about her father who was 'on the throssle' in March Street and had served in the First World War. She left school in 1934 and immediately started at the same mill, as an in-giver. Margaret talks about her apprenticeship and working life as a drawer (and later chargehand) and about her time in a munitions factory near Chorley during the Second World War.

Mr Peter Lavin, b. 1922, Peebles
Interviewed 12 November 1996, aged 74 (48m 39s)

In this interview, Peter Lavin begins by talking about his early life in Peebles. He left school at fourteen and was taken from the school gate, by his uncle, to March Street to secure a job. Key subjects discussed in this interview are Peter's Second World War experiences and his time in the mills. There is a particular emphasis on the unions and how working conditions changed over time.

Miss Betty Muir, b. 1922, Peebles
Interviewed 12 November 1996, aged 74 (1h 33m 37s and 11m 12s)

Betty Muir left school just short of her fourteenth birthday, with a special exemption so that she could start work rather than return to school for the spring term. She talks a little about her home life and schooldays at Halyrude and Kingsland primary schools, but the majority of this interview focusses on her forty-six-year working life at March Street and her Second World War service with the WAAF.

Miss Minnie (Benjamina) Lavin, b. 1925, Peebles
Interviewed 22 November 1996 aged 71 (1h 5m 6s)

Minnie Lavin left school one Friday afternoon, aged fourteen, and started work in March Street on Monday morning. She worked there until she retired, first as an in-giver, then a pirn-winder and then a weaver. She talks about her working life and how this changed over time in a discussion which encompasses changes in production during the Second World War and gender issues relating to employment practice and the War. Towards the end of the interview, Minnie talks about how she gave her mother her wages and would then receive 6d. back in return. This was enough for two visits to the cinema (at a time when Peebles supported three picture houses) and some sweeties. Other subjects discussed include holidays and away-days.

Mr Duncan Murray, b. 1918, Galashiels
Interviewed 22 November 1996, aged 78 (1h 32m 50s and 43m 06s)

In this interview, Duncan Murray begins by describing his early life and childhood. His father was a forester at Holylee Estate, outside Walkerburn and Duncan recalls that his parents were keen for him to stay on at school but he was determined to leave. He secured a job at March Street, aged fifteen, and worked in the pattern shop until he turned sixteen, when he secured an apprenticeship as a dyer. Duncan remained in the mills for his entire working life and his interview contains detailed information about many aspects of mill life, including: working conditions; different parts of the milling process; changes in mill ownership; gender roles within the mills; employment opportunities and emigration and health & safety in the mills. Duncan also talks about his experiences during the Second World War. Deployed to Dunkirk, his platoon was captured and Duncan spent five years as a POW before being liberated by the Americans.

THE INTERVIEWEES

Mrs Effie Anderson, b.1925, Peebles
Interviewed 28 November 1996, aged 71 (1h 18m 30s)

Effie Anderson's mother had been a 'Jennie' at Tweedside and wasn't keen for Effie to choose the mill. However, after several tries in other jobs, Effie went into the mill, on the bobbin machine, when she was sixteen. She moved to Kelty when she married but returned to Peebles and to the mill after the early death of her husband. She worked for the Ballantynes at March Street until she was made redundant, after twenty-six years. Effie talks about her working life (including pay, health & safety, change over time) as well as family, holidays and her time with the forestry at Cademuir – near the start of the Second World War.

Mr Robert R. Sanderson, b. 1929, Peebles
Interviewed 28 November 1996, aged 67 (1h 33m 15s and 40m 6s)

Robert Sanderson left school at sixteen and started working in the office at Damdale. His entire working life was spent in the mills and he retired from March Street on his sixty-fifth birthday. His father, grandfather and an aunt had also worked in the mills. Like his father, Robert had a love of football and he played professionally for Hibernian Football Club. In this interview, Robert speaks about his early life in Peebles, his time in football and at National Service and describes, in detail, different aspects of mill life including: milling processes; gender roles; industrial relations; mill life and change over time.

Mr Anthony (Tony) French, b.1929, Peebles
Interviewed 6 December 1996, aged 67 (1h 24m 2s)

In this interview, Anthony French talks about his childhood and working life in Peebles. He was brought up in the town and enjoyed a varied working life which included being a trainee baker, a woodsman, a millworker (at both Damdale and March Street), a railman and a local authority employee. As well as his working life, topics covered include: housing, football, national service and industrial relations.

Mrs Wilma French, b.1938, Peebles
Interviewed 6 December 1996 and 14 February 1997, aged 58 (1h 3m 5s)

Wilma French went into the mill when she left school, aged fifteen. Her father was a railwayman and she stayed at Caledonian Cottages, known as the Callies, until she married. Apart from time off to have her family, Wilma has been in the mills (Damdale, March Street) most of her working life. In this interview she recalls the training needed to become a darner and describes how the mills and mill processes have changed over time. Wilma, who was still working at March Street when this interview was recorded, also talks about the Mount hostel in Peebles where she stayed for a while. Other themes covered include: social life and dancing, holidays, shopping and other job opportunities (or lack of) in Peebles.

Mr Walter Scott, b. 1924, Peebles
Interviewed 6 December 1996, aged 72 (1h 33m 38s and 26m 10s)

In this interview Walter Scott begins by talking about his childhood in Peebles, especially his home life and his early working life when, from the age of twelve until he went into the mills, he delivered newspapers before and after school. Walter's father, grandfather, aunts and future wife had all worked in the mills and so, alongside his own working experiences, Walter is able to reflect on change over a number of decades. He joined March Street from school, shortly before he turned fourteen, after going up to Joe Euman's home to ask if there were jobs going. Walter relates many anecdotes and shares information from fifty years of experience in the mills, which includes time spent at other Ballantyne mills in places such as Forfar and Renton. Walter also speaks in detail about his Second World War experiences. He served with the Fleet Air Arm as a mechanic and this took him to many parts of the world including Scapa Flow and Murmansk, when he was involved in escorting convoys.

Mr Hume Davidson, b. 1928, Walkerburn (born in Peebles hospital)
Interviewed 13 December 1996, aged 68 (1h 33m 33s and 1h 35m 59s)

In this interview, Hume Davidson talks about his life and work in Walkerburn. Hume's grandfather came to Walkerburn in the 1870s, around twenty years after the Ballantynes opened their mill there. At the beginning of this interview Hume describes the work his father and grandfather did at the mill and he talks about some of the Ballantyne-owned houses he lived in as a child. Hume spent most of his life working for the Ballantyne family, first as an apprentice gardener and then, after National Service, in the Walkerburn mill. In this interview, Hume, accompanied by his wife, talks about the central role the Ballantyne family had within the Walkerburn community and the impact this had on various aspects of life. Towards the end of the interview, Hume talks about salmon poaching at Walkerburn and about other wild harvests.

Mrs Myra Little, b. 1936, Edinburgh
Interviewed 18 December 1996, aged 60 (1h 34m 2s and 42m 12s)

Myra Little was born in Edinburgh and evacuated to Selkirk in 1939. The family decided to settle in the Borders and Myra's father, a civil servant, transferred to the Selkirk Labour Exchange where he worked as a manager. Myra describes her early life in Selkirk and her first job, at Woolworths. She recalls that many girls were keen to go into the mills as the pay and conditions were better and Myra soon got a job at the pirn machine with Gibson & Lumgair, a tweed textile mill at Waterside. Aged eighteen, Myra married Archie Little and moved to Walkerburn where she got a job at the Tweedholm mill. This interview contains interesting information about life in the Selkirk mill and also her move to Walkerburn and millwork there. Overall, Myra spent thirty years doing mill work and has much to reflect on. Latterly, she worked on the stake warping, which was her favourite job. As a highly skilled female worker, Myra is also able to provide interesting reflections on gender roles and wage parity in the mills.

Mr Archie Little, b. 1927, West Bold, near Walkerburn
Interviewed 10 January 1997, aged 69 (1h 23m 53s)

Archie Little spent most of his working life driving lorries for the Tweedholm mill in Walkerburn as an employee of the Ballantynes (although this changed with successive new owners over later years). In addition to his working life, the main themes here are his own Second World War service and his father's service in the First World War. He also talks about his early working life, on The Glen Estate in the early years of the Second World War, his love of sport, and how Walkerburn has changed over time.

Mrs Olive Davidson, b. 1934, Edinburgh
Interviewed 10 January 1997, aged 63 (31m 17s)

In this short interview, Olive Davidson speaks about her early life in the centre of Edinburgh, where she was raised by her granny. She describes the family home and talks about her early working life at Roland Carbondale, Thistle Street. At the age of seventeen, Olive moved to Walkerburn to care for her great aunt Mary, who had retired to the town and lived in one of the mill cottages. Olive subsequently worked in the mills for a period of forty years until retirement.

Mrs Margaret Melrose, b. 1907, Innerleithen
Interviewed 17 January 1997, aged 89 (1h 27m 20s)

In this interview, Margaret Melrose recalls her childhood and working life. She was born in Innerleithen to a large family. At least two sisters and three brothers, in addition to Margaret, spent time working in the mills. Margaret recalls the living conditions growing up as well as her first married home, which was an attic with only basic facilities. Margaret worked at the Waverley mill but was unable to return there after she married because they had a policy of not employing married women. She also worked at Damdale mill and Caerlee hosiery and reflects on over fifty years' experience of working in the mills.

Mr Andrew Brunton, b. 1928, Innerleithen
Interviewed 17 January 1997, aged 68 (1h 33m 23s and 21m 12s)

Andrew Brunton was born into a mill family with ties to Innerleithen dating back to the 1700s. He left school at fourteen, in 1942, and went to work at the forestry for the remainder of the War, after which he went to work at the Caerlee mill. Apart from his National Service, with the Royal Signals, he was in the mill for the rest of his working life – some forty-eight years. As well as giving a detailed description of his working life at Caerlee and the changes he witnessed, Andrew also recalls his early life, schooldays, forestry work and his National Service – part of which was spent at Celle, in Germany.

Mr Robert Gray, b. 1926, Edinburgh
Interviewed 24 January 1997, age 70 (1h 33m 56s and 1h 19m 59s)

In this interview, Robert Gray talks about his early life in Innerleithen, where he lived with his parents, brother, sister, uncle and granny. His mum, a trained cook, was often away from home during the week. The family lived in Chapel Street and then moved to new council houses on Montgomery Street and he recalls life at home and at school. In 1940, he left school and went to work first in Caerlee mill and then the forestry, before signing up to train with the Parachute Regiment. Robert talks about his military training and his time in Asia and Palestine. He returned to Innerleithen and the Caerlee mill where he continued to work and had an increasing role in the trade union movement, eventually becoming a full-time union official. This interview has a particular focus on his trade union work and political views.

Mr Phil McGlasson, b. 1906, Patna
Interviewed 24 January 1997, aged 90 (1h 33m 37s and 1h 9m 58s)

In this interview, Phil McGlasson recalls his early life and the family's move to Innerleithen when he was a child and his father secured the post of bandmaster with the St Ronan's Silver Band. Phil, along with several siblings, was involved in the band and, at the time of this interview, he was still president of the band. Phil recalls the Army taking over his school early in the First World War. His father served in the First World War, as did his half-brother John William, who died of injuries sustained at the Battle of Ypres in 1917. Phil started work in Caerlee mill, Innerleithen, when he was fourteen years old. Like many, he finished school on the Friday and started work on the Monday. Aside from his own Second World War experience, Phil spent his life in the mills and retired in 1971. He is therefore able to reflect on over fifty years of mill operation and this interview explores both his personal working experiences and more general trends of activity and change in the mill industry. Phil also reflects on other working experiences he had when he was younger, such as the week he spent as an under-butler at Lord Glenconner's house, The Glen.

Mrs Margaret Gray, b. 1933, Peebles
Interviewed 31 January 1997, aged 63 (1h 10m 15s)

The main theme of this interview is Margaret Gray's working life at both Caerlee mill and then later at Murray Anderson where she was a seamer and then a passer. She talks about her apprenticeship and working life, reflecting on changes in mill ownership, working practices and industrial relations over time. Other aspects of life covered in this interview include schooldays, domestic life and recreation.

THE INTERVIEWEES

Mr John Lunn, b. 1936, Innerleithen (born Peebles hospital)
Interviewed 7 February 1997, aged 61 (1h 33m 18s and 1h 11m 26s)

When John Lunn was interviewed, in 1997, he was working as a carder in Gardiner's mill, Selkirk, a job he first did at Waverley mill in Innerleithen, aged fifteen. In between times, in a career spanning over forty-five years and including time in management, John had worked in a number of mills in different towns in the Borders and extending over to Ayrshire. He considers his own working life as well as reflecting on those of his parents and grandparents: his father's family had strong connections to mill work while his mother's family were farm workers. In this detailed interview, John reflects on change over time in the mills across a number of themes, including: working hours, pay and conditions; different mill processes; gender roles within the mills; unions and industrial action; and changing technology, ownership and management. Outwith the mills, this interview contains information about housing, education and health.

Mrs Nellie Nisbett, b. 1908, Moffat
Interviewed 7 February 1997, aged 88 (14m 32s)

Nellie Nisbett's family moved to Innerleithen when Nellie was thirteen. She was the eldest of four girls and, when she left school at fourteen she went to work in the Caerlee mill. In this brief interview (not referenced in the text of this book) Nellie recalls working 'at the darning … up in the attic'. Her husband was a millworker in Walkerburn.

Mrs Margaret Turnbull, b. 1897, Galashiels
Interviewed 7 February 1997, aged 100 (32m 8s)

In this short interview, Margaret Turnbull talks about her early family life and recalls the domestic surroundings. Her father was a Tweed finisher and the family had spent some time in Tillicoultry, where her father was a foreman. Margaret worked there, as a darner, before the family moved again, after two years. Margaret talks about her time at the Tweedvale mill, in Walkerburn and then later, at Leithen mill, Innerleithen. She recalls the outbreak of the First World War, the increase in khaki production at the mill and the impact of the Second World War on her and the wider community.

Mr Eric Pearce, b. 1927, Innerleithen (born Peebles hospital)
Interviewed 9 February 1997, aged 69 (1h 33m 26s and 9m 6s)

In this interview, Eric Pearce, who worked for the Ballantyne mills in Walkerburn and Peebles for fifty years, talks about the various jobs he did during that time as well as changes in production and management, the role of the unions and the importance of the Ballantyne family. He also recalls his national service experiences and shares anecdotes relating to his early cycling experiences and school choices. Eric also wrote a book about Walkerburn. Pearce, F. W. : *Walkerburn: Origins and Progress* 1854–1987, Meigle Printers, Galashiels, 1987.

Mr John Brown, b. 1920, Walkerburn
Interviewed 14 February 1997, aged 76 (1h 33m 53s and 44m 44s)
In this interview, John Brown, who began his working life at Caerlee mill in Innerleithen, talks about his childhood, war experiences and working life. John won a prize for joinery work at school and had intended to serve his apprenticeship in that trade, but none were available. He was unemployed for a while until his name came up for a mill job. John's parents and his two sisters also worked in the mills. John talks about his childhood in Walkerburn and Innerleithen, his early interest in sport and Sunday observances. He also recalls family day trips to Dunbar, cycling excursions and a trip to London for the rugby. He joined the Territorial Army in 1938–39 and was called up at the start of the Second World War. He served out the War in the ambulance service and came back in 1946 to resume his work in the mill. John talks about his working life and the move over to Intarsia knitting (around 1951).

Mr W. Lockie Robson, b. 1932, Innerleithen
Interviewed 14 February 1997, aged 65 (52m 21s)
In this interview, W. Lockie Robson describes his working life at Caerlee mill. He went to the mill in August 1946, at the age of fourteen, and began on the frame flat bar-filling, which he recalled was a terrible job. Lockie remained at the mill for his entire working life, except for a break to complete his National Service. He also talks about his family life, schooldays, holidays and day-trips and his long interest in fishing.

Mr Robert (Bob) Fraser Anderson, b. 1931, Innerleithen
Interviewed 21 February 1997, aged 65, (1h 33m 16s and 16m 39s)
In this interview, Bob Anderson talks about his family and life in Innerleithen. His family connections to mill work extended back over 100 years and Bob spent most of his working life at Caerlee, where, at the time of the interview, his son worked. Bob talks about his early life and about leaving school at thirteen to help support the family while his father was serving in the Second World War. He talks with affection about his first full-time job, at Pearce's Lemonade factory, about his time in National Service and his decision to go to New Zealand to work. Returning home for a family wedding he met his future wife, Joan, and that set his course for life. Most of his working life thereafter was spent in the mill at Caerlee and he talks about his work and how this changed over time. Bob also talks about the Polish officers who came to Innerleithen during the Second World War, and about how the local community coped during the war years.

Mr James Howitt, b. 1911, Peebles
Interviewed 21 February 1997, aged 85 (1h 33m 49s and 36m 49s)
In this interview, James Howitt begins by speaking about his early life in Peebles where he lived on St Andrew's Road with his parents and younger siblings. He was

a keen reader as a child and recalls various private libraries in Peebles. He enjoyed school and had an early ambition to train as a vet before deciding to leave school at fifteen. He worked for a short time with Lowe Donald, a tweed distributor, before becoming an apprentice at the Ballantyne March Street mill. Like his father before him, James worked in the mills for over fifty years and he speaks in detail about his working life, from apprentice to manager, in a timespan which encompassed the Second World War and the centralisation of the Ballantyne mill operations in the Borders. He also reflects on the decline of the mills and the Border communities.

Mrs Peggy Ferguson, b. 1913, Howgate
Interviewed 12 February 2004, aged 90 (1h 33m 40s, 41m 52s and 5m 53s)
This was the last of the Peeblesshire mill workers interviews to be recorded by Ian. Peggy Ferguson was born in Howgate, at the Milkhall railwaymen's cottages and moved to Peebles as a small child. She talks in detail about her home at Venlaw Court in Peebles, where she lived almost continuously for eighty-four years, first with her parents and siblings and later, in the next door house, when she married and had a family of her own. She also spent a couple of years in Hawick with an aunt who ran a sweetie shop from her front room and made the famous Hawick Balls to her own recipe. When Peggy left school at fourteen, she joined two older sisters and went to work in the mills, in her case to Thorburn's Tweedside mill. This interview contains lots of detail about the different jobs she did and how working conditions changed over time. Peggy also talks about her father and his work as a surfaceman on the railways.

Glossary

AEU	Amalgamated Engineering Union.
ATS	Auxiliary Territorial Service.
Bar-filling ('bar-fillin')	joining the hem part of a knitted garment onto the knitting machine that will knit the main part of the garment.
Beam	fitted to the back of a loom and used to hold the warp, or lengthwise threads. Beaming is also known as warping, skilled task to get the warp yarn ready to roll forward onto the loom.
Binding ('bindin') machine	knitting machine designed to produce long narrow strips of knitted fabric, used for the button edges of cardigans.
Bleacher and Dyers Union	National Union of Dyers, Bleachers and Textile Workers.
Blending	Selecting the right amounts of suitable wools, by type and colour, to fulfil an order and then mixing them by blowing air to give a uniform product before carding and spinning.
Bobbin machine	for winding yarn onto bobbins.
British Restaurant	communal kitchens created in 1940 during the Second World War to feed people who had been bombed out of their homes, had run out of ration coupons or otherwise needed help.
Bullet	the Caledonian Railway Station, like many others, had a large First World War shell converted into a charity donation box in the middle of its concourse which served as a convenient meeting point.

GLOSSARY

Burling ('birlin')	process used to remove surface imperfections, such as knots and loose fibers, from a fabric.
Cam	a projection on a rotating part of machinery, an eccentric shape that converts rotary to reciprocal motion.
Carding	a sharp-toothed drum with teethed rollers working against it to disentangle and align the fibres before spinning. Four of these in sequence make a carding sett.
Cauld	a weir or dam.
Chargehand	a worker with supervisory duties.
Cheviots	a breed of white-faced sheep named after the Cheviot Hills; the fleece produces fine, soft fibres.
Cleek	a salmon gaff.
Condenser	a funnel-shaped piece of machinery on the last carding machine in a sett, to condense the web of fibre into a sliver before spinning. Condenser spinning of wool places the condensed sliver as a roll at the back of the mule/jenny (unlike a cotton mule which takes yarn from bobbins filled on roving frames).
Coning ('conin') machines	spun yarn is wound onto a truncated cone ready for knitting or weaving.
Darners	workers employed to repair (darn) any faults in the finished fabric.
Drawer	worker who attaches weaving beam to the drawing-in frame, and draws each warp yarn, separately, with a hook, through the eye (or loop) of the heald (heddle), and through the dent (or slot) of the reed, preparing it for weaving. Also known as reeding (after the reeds that were initially used to do this).
Dux	top pupil in a school.
Finishing	processes that convert the woven cloth or knitted hosiery into a usable material, especially those performed after dyeing the yarn or fabric to improve the look, performance, or feel of the finished textile.
Frames	knitting machines in the hosiery industry, or spinning frames such as the throstle or the ring frame (as opposed to mule jennies).

Grist ('wis ⅟₁₆th')	a measure of the density of a yarn.
Harris (Harris Tweed)	a type of cloth made of 100 per cent sheep's wool, spun, dyed and prepared in the islands of Harris and Lewis and then hand-woven at home on the islands.
Hawick Balls	Mint, buttery flavoured boiled sweeties associated with the town of Hawick and the renowned rugby commentator, Bill McLaren.
Heddle or heald	one of a set of cords or wires, each with an eye in the centre, through which the warp yarns are passed, as part of the process of preparing the loom for weaving a pattern.
Hydro	The Peebles Hydro hotel and health spa.
Improver	a worker learning to perfect their particular specialism.
In-giving	handing individual warp threads to the drawer preparing the weaving beam for the weaver.
Intarsia knitting	a technique used to create patterns using multiple colours, but unlike other multicolour techniques (such as Fair Isle) there is only one 'active' colour on any given stitch, and yarn is not carried across the back of the work.
Leafs	may refer to the finished woven fabric that has left the loom. If the reader knows the precise meaning of the term please get in touch with the publisher.
Licker-in	a roller on a carding machine, especially the roller that opens the stock as it is fed into the card and transfers the fibres to the main cylinder.
Lifts	refers to the various darning techniques used to correct or mask flaws in the different patterned woven fabrics.
Lookers	workers who check others work; the term Overlookers is usually used.
Magazines	in a Northrop loom a rotating series of pirns ready to automatically fit a shuttle as soon as it is empty, that the weaver must refill from a box of pirns over each loom.
Markers	workers checking fabric for defects and marking it before passing it on to the darners.
Marl	mottled yarn or fabric.

Mohair	yarn made from the hair of the Angora goat.
National Service	An eighteen-month period of compulsory service in the armed forces of the UK for men aged 17–21. Came into effect in 1949 and ran until its abolition in 1960.
Nissen hut	A prefabricated, corrugated steel roofed domed structure used for accommodation of billet forces.
Passing	checking the finished garments and letting them go onto the next process, or not.
Pattern store	All the cloth samples were pasted into big books kept there, and became the source of reference for repeat orders that required particular yarns.
Penciller	worker employed to mask colour flaws in a piece of woven cloth.
Picking	removing stray fibres or threads of the wrong colour from a piece of woven cloth.
Piecer/Piecing	worker employed during the spinning process to repair broken threads, piecing them together.
Pirn machine	machinery used to wind yarn onto pirns that slot into shuttles.
Point seamer	sewing up the sides of garments.
Press shop	area of a mill where the woven cloth went to be pressed, as part of the finishing process.
Qualifying Exam	An exam taken at age twelve to deicide progression into either junior secondary or senior secondary, known colloquially as 'the qualy'.
Queen's Award	The Queen's award to Industry established in 1965 to recognise outstanding achievement in business.
RASC	Royal Army Service Corps.
Ribs	element in shaped fitted hosiery.
Rippin' oot/ Ripping out	preparing the seams of different sections of a garment before they are sewn together.
Scouring	cleaning wool in preparation for spinning and dyeing, taking out the natural oil lanolin.
Seaming	sewing sections of a garment together along the seams.

Shading	matching colours in cloth.
Spinle	spindle which spins yarn, whether on a spinning wheel or a machine.
Sportex	a pure twisted woven wool fabric designed for outdoor pursuits by the French firm Dormeuil in the early 1920s.
Stake warping ('warpin')	warping by hand between stakes pinned to a wall or on a vertical warp mill.
SUITS	Scottish & Universal Investments Ltd.
TGWU	Transport and General Workers Union.
Three times thirty-six cut, Cheviot	refers to the type of woollen yarn used, in this case a very strong yarn.
Throstle	a spinning machine with a continuous action for drawing and twisting yarn, in contrast to the mule or jenny which alternates between spinning on its outward pass and winding on its return pass.
Trap	the pedal under a spindle that the spinner uses to stop it and join up a breakage.
Tuner	worker whose job it was to keep the looms working in optimum condition. Also known (in the jute and linen industries, but possibly wool too) as a tenter who 'taks tent' – takes care – of several looms.
WAAFS	Women's Auxiliary Air Force Service.
Warper	a person who carries out warping or beaming, a skilled task to get the warp yarn ready to roll forward onto the loom. Also used to refer to a warping or beaming machine, or warp mill when set on a vertical axis.
Worsted	fine smooth yarn, spun from long-staple (long-fibred) wool that has been combed, not carded, and the fabric made from such yarn.

MACHINERY

Dobcross loom	fast loom named after the address of the makers, Hutchinson Hollingworth & Co Ltd, Dobcross Works, Harropdale, Diggleworth, Oldham, Lancashire. Manufactured 1860–1967.
Dornier ('Dornair') loom	German firm Dornier, originally an aircraft manufacturer but prohibited from doing so after the Second World War, started manufacturing textile machinery from 1950 as Lindauer DORNIER. A Dornier loom has weft yarn carried by one or two rapiers instead of a shuttle, so can maintain a faster pace, amongst other types.
Hattersley loom	widely used looms, developed by the textile machinery company of George Hattersley & Sons of Keighley, West Yorkshire. Hattersley treadle looms (foot powered) were widely used in Harris.
Hergeth	German textile machinery manufacturer, founded in 1920. Made warping/beaming machines.
Rimoldi	Italian textile machinery manufacturer, established in 1877.
Sulzer loom	Swiss industrial engineering firm Sulzer Ltd, founded in 1775. Sulzer introduced in 1952 a loom that has weft yarn carried by a projectile rather than a shuttle, so can maintain a faster pace, amongst other types. They also made engines.
Tangye engine	engines developed by the firm of Tangyes Limited of Cornwall Works, Smethwick, Birmingham.

Bibliography

Selected Bibliography of works by Ian MacDougall in order of publication, provided by Sandra MacDougall

Interim Bibliography of the Scottish Working Class Movement, Society for the Study of Labour History, Edinburgh, 1965.

Minutes of Edinburgh Trades Council 1859–1873, The Scottish History Society, Edinburgh, 1968.

Essays in Scottish Labour History: A Tribute to W. H. Marwick, John Donald, Edinburgh, 1978.

A Catalogue of Some Labour Records in Scotland and some Scots records outside Scotland, Scottish Labour History Society, Edinburgh, 1978.

Militant Miners: Recollections of John McArthur, Buckhaven, and letters, 1924–26, of David Proudfoot, Methil, to G. Allen Hutt, Polygon, Edinburgh, 1981.

Labour in Scotland: A Pictorial History from the Eighteenth Century to the Present, Mainstream Publishing, Edinburgh, 1985.

Voices from the Spanish Civil War: personal Recollections of Scottish Volunteers in Republican Spain, 1936–1939, Polygon, Edinburgh, 1986.

The Prisoners of Penicuik, Midlothian District Council, Dalkeith, 1989.

Music of Midlothian: Notes to the Music featured on the cassette, Music of Midlothian, Midlothian District Council, Edinburgh, 1989.

Voices from the Hunger Marches: Personal Recollections by Scottish Hunger Marchers of the 1920s and 1930s, Polygon, Edinburgh, 1990 and 1991 (two volumes).

'Hard Work, ye ken': Midlothian Women Farmworkers, The European Ethnological Research Centre/Tuckwell Press/Midlothian District Council, 1993.

Hoggie's Angels: Tattie Howkers Remember, Midlothian District Council/National Museums of Scotland/Tuckwell Press, East Linton, 1995.

Mungo Mackay and the Green Table: Newtongrange Miners Remember, The European Ethnological Research Centre/Midlothian District Council/Tuckwell Press, East Linton, 1995.

Voices from War and some Labour Struggles: Personal Recollections of War in our Century by Scottish Men and Women, Mercat Press, Edinburgh, 1995.

Working Lives: Photographs of Workers and their Work in Scotland 1897–1997, Scottish Library Association, Hamilton, 1997.

'Oh, Ye Had to be Careful': Personal Recollections by Roslin Gunpowder Mill and Bomb Factory Workers, The European Ethnological Research Centre/The Scottish Working People's History Trust/Tuckwell Press, East Linton, 2000.

Bondagers: Personal Recollections of Eight Scots Women Farm Workers, The European Ethnological Research Centre/The Scottish Working People's Trust/Tuckwell Press, East Linton, 2000.

Voices from Work and Home: Personal Recollections of Working Life and Labour Struggles in the Twentieth Century by Scots Men and Women, Mercat Press, Edinburgh, 2000.

Voices of Leith Dockers: Personal Recollections of Working Lives, The Scottish Working People's History Trust/Mercat Press, Edinburgh, 2001.

Onion Johnnies: Personal Recollections by Nine French Onion Johnnies of their Working Lives in Scotland, European Ethnological Research Centre/The Scottish Working People's Trust/Tuckwell Press, East Linton, 2002. Second edition Birlinn Ltd, Edinburgh, 2023.

Mid and East Lothian Miners' Association minutes: 1894–1918, Scottish History Society, Lothian Print, Edinburgh, 2003.

All men are brethren: French, Scandinavian, Italian, German, Dutch, Belgian, Spanish, Polish, West Indian, American and other prisoners of war in Scotland during the Napoleonic Wars, 1803–1814, John Donald, Edinburgh, 2008.

Through the Mill: Personal Recollections by Veteran Men and Women Penicuik Paper Mill Workers, The Scottish Working People's History Trust, Falkirk, 2009.

Voices of Scottish Journalists: Recollections by 22 Veteran Scottish Journalists of their Life and Work, The Scottish Working People's Trust/John Donald, Edinburgh, 2013.

Voices from Lilliesleaf: Spoken Personal Recollections of People, Life and Work, Events and Changes, in Peace and War, in a Scottish Borders Village during the 20th Century, John Donald, Edinburgh, 2015.

Voices of Scottish Librarians: the Evolution of a Profession and its Response to Changing Times (with Alan Reid and David Fletcher). The Scottish Working People's Trust/John Donald, Edinburgh, 2017.

Voices of Scotswomen in Peace and War: Recollections by 19 Scotswomen of Home Life, Employment and War Service, John Donald, Edinburgh, 2019.

Dalkeith: Aspects of the History of a Scottish Burgh, a Selection of articles by David R. Smith (with Neil McVicar and Alan Reid) Hunt Close Publishing, 2019.

Other Resources

Books

Anderson, J. A.: *At the Sign of the Cleikum: Reminiscences of Innerleithen 1926–1932*, Bordersprint Ltd, Selkirk, 1996.

Simm, Fraser: *The Story of Caerlee Mill/Ballantyne Sportswear: An Illustrated History of Caerlee Mill*, Bordersprint Ltd, Selkirk, 2021.

Online Resources

http://www.swpht.org.uk/

Dr Ian MacDougall, a recording of Ian talking about his work as an oral historian. https://www.nls.uk/learning-zone/politics-and-society/labour-history/ian-macdougall/

Obituary: Ian MacDougall, Scottish historian with a special interest in the Labour movement, Ian S. Wood, *The Scotsman* , published 9 May 2020: https://www.scotsman.com/news/people/obituary-ian-macdougall-scottish-historian-with-a-special-interest-in-the-labour-movement-2847232

Border Weave: How tweed is produced in the Scottish Borders showing the different stages involved, from the dying of the wool, spinning and weaving, to the finished product. Director: John Lewis Curthoys. Turner Film Productions. 1942. Ref NLS0482. Held as part of the National Library of Scotland archive, https://www.nls.uk/

Pure New Wool – And Scottish: From Sheep Shearing in Australia to wool being spun and woven in Scottish Tweed mills. Scottish Woollen Trade Mark Association, 1924, Ref NLS0571. Held as part of the National Library of Scotland archive, https://www.nls.uk/

Elizabeth Bryan interviewed Ian MacDougall on 22 February 2018 in the National Museum of Scotland, Edinburgh. It is anticipated that this interview will be available on the SCRAN website in due course https://www.scran.ac.uk/. For access before this resources is live please contact the Scottish Working People's History Trust http://www.swpht.org.uk/index.php

Index

During interviews, it was common for people to refer to mills by the surnames of the owners, especially in the case of the Ballantyne and Thorburn-owned mills. However, as both families owned multiple mills, and ownership changed over the years, it was not always easy to determine which mills were actually being discussed. This is further complicated by different branches of the Ballantyne family owning and operating separate mills in various towns. In conversations, Ballantyne's and Thorburn's can refer to the family, one of the companies, one of the mills or even a group of mills.

51st (Highland) Division 71–76

Adam, Daphne 49, 51, 54
Adam, Duncan 1, 49, 50–54, 371
Adams, Nan 51, 52, 53, 54
Air Training Corps 41–42, 76, 77, 235, 237
– football team 41–42
– Observer Corps 235
Aitken, Tom 26
Allen, Murray *see also* Murray Allan of Innerleithen 204, 205
Amalgamated Engineering Union 146
American armed forces 53, 74, 75, 372
ammunition dump, Leadburn 57
Anderson, Bob 92–94, 153–56, 181–83, 326–31, 367–68, 378
Anderson, Effie 5, 10, 91–92, 178–79, 288–95, 300, 373
Anderson, Joan 93, 328, 320, 368, 378
Anderson, Jock 307
Arbroath 77
Asia 376

Auchendinny 14–15
Australia 90, 247
Australian armed forces 89
Auxiliary Territorial Service (ATS) 81, 86
Ayrshire 127, 377

Bairds / William Baird 6, 191, 192, 194, 203, 213, 214, 215, 240–41, 243, 244, 369
– Bairdtex 192
Ballantyne, Alison 158
Ballantyne, David 143, 168, 169, 170, 172, 178, 191
Ballantyne, Douglas 169, 178, 191
Ballantyne family 6, 10, 24, 27, 28, 47, 51, 101, 106, 113, 115,126–27, 129, 133, 134, 149, 151–61, 162, 163, 167–72, 173, 176, 177, 178, 179, 183, 188–89, 190, 191, 192, 198, 200–1, 202, 203, 206, 208, 212–13, 214, 215, 218, 221, 225, 230, 231, 234–35, 236, 237, 240, 241, 242, 253–73, 274, 276, 284, 287, 293, 294, 295, 297, 299, 302, 311, 313–34, 337, 342, 343, 347, 351, 353, 354, 356, 362–63, 369, 373, 374, 375, 377, 379
Ballantyne, Mrs (Stoneyhill) 114, 116
Ballantyne, Henry (1802–65) 152, 170
Ballantyne Henry 46, 168, 169, 170–71, 172, 188, 191, 213, 214, 234–35, 296, 297, 363
Ballantyne, Jeremy 158, 363
Ballantyne, J. K. 158
Ballantyne, Tom 318
Beckett & Robertson 126, 129–30, 149, 167, 188, 235, 236, 331, 370
Belgium 65
Berwick-upon-Tweed 70, 71, 97, 235
– Magdalene Fields army camp 97
Bevin, Neil 205–6
Birnie, Jimmy 285, 286
Black Watch, the
Blackpool 53
Blackrock mill, Huddersfield
Blackwood Brothers 197
Bombay (Mumbai) 54
– Mahalaximi railway station 54

389

Bonnyrigg 147, 178
Bonser, Clem 165
Bonser, Johnnie 144–45
Borders Co-operative Society 175–76
Borders General Hospital 365
Borders Regional Council 365
Bradford 173, 190
Braemar 188
Brazil 220
British armed forces 22, 58, 59, 66, 71, 74, 75, 79, 80, 81, 110, 125, 238, 246, 305, 306, 315, 305, 306, 315
British Army 36, 52, 55–56, 57, 58, 59, 63–76, 94–98, 100, 113, 141–42, 143, 145, 150, 211, 323, 376
British Restaurant 158
British Road Services 100
Brodie, Alexander 148
Brown Allan & Co., Selkirk 190
Brown, Jim 234
Brown, John 63–66, 109–10, 318–22, 378
Brown, Mrs (John) 321
Brunton, Andrew 31, 94–96, 108–109, 148–49, 322–26, 364–65, 375
– Andrew, brother-in-law 324
– Andrew, son 364
– David, uncle 108
– mother 108
Brunton, Doreen 148, 324, 364
Bryan, Elizabeth 2–3, 7, 8
Burma (Myanmar) 53

Cademuir forest 91–92, 373
Canada 117
Canadians armed forces 89
Cardrona 15, 43
Carstairs 81, 357
Carter, Mr (schoolmaster) 63
Chamberlain, Neville 52
China 211, 258
Churchill, William 64
Clark, Mr 138
Clayton-le-Woods 83
Cleethorpes 88
Clyde, Betty 276, 277
Clyde, River 53, 77
Clydebank 235, 237
Coldstream 42
Cole, Nat King 368
Community Clothing 11
Conservative Party, support for 150, 154, 156, 169, 170

Coventry 60, 61, 141,142
Craig, Jim 46
Crozier, Mr (Caerlee foreman) 143
Cubs, the 27, 41
Cumnock 197
Czechoslovakia 74

D-Day 65, 93
D. Ballantyne & Bros & Co. Ltd (see also Ballantyne family) 126, 231, 235, 369, 370
Dalgleish, Adam 220, 224–25
Dalkeith 43, 147, 173, 178, 191, 193, 272
Dalziel 126, 370
Davidson, Hume 4, 25–28, 37, 43, 55–56, 96–97, 110–16, 153, 156–61, 185–86, 200–2, 301, 343–45, 345, 346, 374
– Wat, uncle 113
Davidson, Margaret 23–24, 379
– Hawick Balls 23–24, 379
Davidson, Olive 4, 26, 27, 111, 112, 113, 114, 157, 158, 159, 160, 161, 186, 200, 344, 345–46, 374, 375
– Mary, aunt 27, 375
Dawson International 6, 106, 153, 156, 170, 173, 190–91, 194–95, 197, 203, 213, 214, 215, 241, 272, 363, 369
– Dalkeith mill 191, 193, 194, 363
Derbyshire 67
Dewar, Miss 262, 264
Di Rollo family (from Musselburgh) 57
Dick (Caerlee mill) 132
Dobcross loom 134, 200, 288, 294
Donaldson, Brian 206
Dornier loom 202, 288
Dreghorn Barracks 67
Dryden, John 110
Dunbar 45, 378
Duncan, Mrs 122–23
Dundee 284
Dunfermline 184, 185
Duns 42
Dutch East Indies, the 69
Dyer, James (Jim) 218

Earlston 60, 63, 172
East Grinstead 61
East Kilbride 106
– Ballantyne mill 106
Edderston 33

Edinburgh 16, 44, 45, 47, 52, 61, 67, 70, 79, 81, 85, 90, 98, 101, 146, 158, 184, 203, 309, 313, 335, 247, 352, 359, 360, 367, 374, 375, 376
– Beechmount Hospital 45
– Caledonian Station 85
– Carlton Hotel 344
– Corstorphine 45
– George Street 52, 97
– Leith 344
– Moray House 158
– Polmont 61
– Portobello 44, 45, 62
– Princes Street 85
– Scottish National Portrait Gallery 8
– Skerry's College 335–36
– Waverley Steps 44, 45
Edston 33
Education Board 114
Egypt 79, 101
Elizabeth the Queen Mother, Queen 367–68
Eshiels 15, 19
– Eshiels Cottages 15
Ettrick 105, 106
Euman, Joe 42, 124, 165, 284, 285, 289, 374
Europe 52, 249
Exton 81

Factory Acts 122
Fairgrieve, Alex 269
Fairgrieve, Sir Russell 265, 268, 269, 271
Fala Hill 273
Ferguson, Helen 15
Ferguson, Janet (Nettie) 15
Ferguson, Mary (Mamie) 15
Ferguson, Margaret (Peggy) 7, 9, 13–25, 379
– Elliot, uncle 19
Ferguson, Sarah (Cissie) 15, 16–17
Ferguson, Tom 17, 24
Fife 289, 356
First World War 4, 10, 14, 19, 46, 49, 50–51, 52, 54–55, 60, 63, 101, 116, 129, 152, 169, 269, 345, 368, 371, 375, 376, 377
– Battle of Festubert 50, 54, 371
– Battle of Ypres 376
Fleet Air Arm 76, 77–79, 363, 374
Fleming, Sandy 268
Forestry Commission 322

390

INDEX

Forfar 183, 184, 374
– Ballantyne's 183
Forth Rail Bridge 61
Forth, River 61
Foulkes, Mr 195, 196
France 54, 60, 65, 71–72, 73, 93
– Arras 50, 371
– Cherbourg 71
– Le Havre 71
– Normandy 64, 65
– Rouen 71
– St Valery-en-Caux 71–72
Fraser, Sir Hugh (*see also* House of Fraser) 6, 191, 203, 213, 214, 215
French, Anthony (Tony) 35, 37, 97–98, 161–62, 163–67, 295–98, 356, 373
– Ina, aunt 161
French armed forces 75
French, Wilma 9, 162, 164, 166, 347–58, 373
– Isobel, sister 347, 348
– Lynne, daughter 352
– Margaret, sister 347, 348
– Susan, daughter 352

Galashiels 28, 39, 45, 64, 101, 117, 143, 146, 147, 152, 160, 163, 173, 174, 176, 177, 188, 190, 193, 204, 205, 206, 217, 226, 244, 263, 265, 266, 272, 273, 292, 313, 321, 359, 361, 365, 376
– Co-operative Society 176
– Gladstone's shrinking works 191
– High Street 265
– Job Centre 365
– Scottish Woollen Technical College 225, 263
Gardiner's Mill, Selkirk 198, 377
Garland, Judy 368
General Municipal Workers Union 302
General Strike 1926 136, 145
Geneva Convention 65
George V, King 157, 158
George VI, King 158
George Roberts, Selkirk 172, 199
German armed forces 71, 72, 77, 78, 93–94
Germany 66, 72, 73, 95, 249, 375
– Bad Bramstedt 66
– Bergen-Belsen concentration camp 95
– Celle 95, 375
– Dortmund 73

– Hamburg 66
– Lüneburg Heath 66
– Munich 74–75
– Wiesendorf 95
Gibson & Lumgair, Waterside 249–53, 374
Gilroy, Mr (union branch secretary) 305
Glasgow 16, 23, 189, 254, 305, 307, 309
– Bath Street 305
Glen House and Estate, The 102, 103–104, 138–40, 375, 376
Glenconner, Lord 138, 376
Glencorse Barracks 94
Glenormiston House and Estate 150
Gloucester 85–86
Göring, Hermann 66
Gray, Margaret 37, 68, 202–7, 211, 304, 307, 308, 309, 311–13, 316, 318, 335–42, 376
Gray, Robert 36, 37, 66–70, 145, 167–70, 202, 203, 204, 205, 211–13, 304–11, 312–18, 335, 336, 337, 338, 339, 340, 341, 376
Grierson, Sandy 345
Grimsby 87, 88, 89
Grossart, Cis 176–77
gunpowder factory, Roslin 9, 14

H. Ballantyne & Sons (*see also* Ballantyne family) 126, 370
Haddington 54
Hagan, Hugh 2
Hardie, Walter 46
Harris 219
Hattersley loom 134, 181, 200, 288, 293, 294
Hawick 23–24, 106, 141, 188, 199, 309, 359, 379
– Croft Road 24
– Trinity School 24
Heart of Midlothian FC 267, 269
Heath, Edward 113
Hepworth's tailors 249
Hergeth warping machine 202–203
Hibernian FC 41, 267, 373
Highland Home Industries 172
Hitler, Adolf 52
HMS *Campania* 77, 78
Hoggie's Angels 3
Holland 56, 65, 72–73
– Blerick 56
– Eindhoven 56

– Helmond 56
– Venlo 56
Holylee Estate 372
Hounam, Willy 297
House of Fraser (*see also* Hugh Fraser) 6, 240, 369
Howgate 14, 379
– Milkhall cottages 14, 379
Howie, Jimmy 192–93, 258–59, 262, 268
Howitt, James 11, 218–44, 378–79
Howitt, Mrs (James) 226
Hull 88
Hutcheson family 188, 212, 235

India 53, 96
– New Delhi 96, 97
– Red Fort 97
Industrial Relations Act 354
INNERLEITHEN 9, 13, 15, 29–31, 39, 40, 43, 44, 47, 54–55, 63, 66, 92–94, 108–9, 113, 117, 118, 120, 126, 127, 128, 129, 137–38, 146, 147, 148–49, 151, 155, 160, 169–70, 174, 176, 177, 178, 181, 182, 187, 189, 193, 196, 198, 199, 204, 205, 212, 213, 215, 222, 233, 234, 235, 237, 256, 257, 259, 261, 262, 276, 286, 305, 307, 310, 311, 313, 331, 344, 346, 359, 361, 364, 367, 370, 371, 375, 376, 377, 378
– Adam's washhouse 30
– Bond Street 29, 30–31, 39, 137
– Caddon Court 31
– Caerlee Mill (aka The Ballantyne Sportswear, Caerlee Knitting Mills) 29, 36, 47, 92, 93, 126, 127, 128–35, 136, 140, 141, 142–48, 149, 167, 168, 173, 178, 187, 188, 189, 204, 206, 211, 222, 232–33, 235, 257, 258, 299, 304, 305, 308, 310, 311, 312, 313–42, 364, 367, 370, 375, 376, 377, 378
– Chapel Street 376
– Chapel Street washhouse 30
– Cleikum Mill 370
– Co-operative Society (includes bank and store) 137, 138, 141, 176
– Fire Brigade 200
– Forsyth's baker 63, 130
– golf course 129
– High Street 204
– Hogg & Robertson engineering works 149, 187
– Horsburgh Street 30, 31

391

– Jimmy Stewart's sawmill 149
– Kirklands Farm 100, 101
– Leithen Mills 92, 126, 129, 134, 146, 149, 167, 182, 183, 187, 188, 235, 236, 307, 331, 370, 377
– Leithen Road 43, 149, 329
– Leithenside School 37, 128
– Masonic Hall 204
– Maxwell Street School 37
– Memorial Hall 40, 137, 331, 332
– Miller Street 30, 92, 93
– Montgomery Street 31, 376
– plastic works 329
– police station 108
– Red Roofs 236
– Robert Smaill's Printing Works 149
– Russell's chemist 108
– St Ronan's ('tap') Mill 126, 129–30, 146, 149, 167, 188, 235, 236, 331, 370
– St Ronan's Silver Band 376
– St Ronan's Terrace 168
– Taynuilt 236
– town council 155
– Waverley Mill 93, 126, 129, 131, 134, 146, 149, 167, 168, 183, 187, 188, 189–90, 191, 195–95, 198, 213, 215, 222, 226, 228, 229–30, 232, 233–34, 235, 236, 237–43, 254–57, 258–59, 261, 262–63, 266–67, 268–69, 271, 276, 305, 307, 308, 310, 325, 331, 359, 361, 364, 370, 375, 377
– Waverley Road 108
Innes, Mrs (landlady) 34
Intarsia knitting and machine 317, 320, 321, 324, 327, 333, 367, 370
Isle of Man 206
Italian armed forces 118
Italy 61–62, 334
– Cassino 61
– Messina 61
– Rome 61
– Sicily 61, 62
– Veriano 61
ITC Catterick 95

Japan 162, 172, 205, 334
Japanese armed forces 69
Java 66, 69, 70

Karachi 96
Kelso 117, 118, 359
Kelty 289, 373
Kerr, Roy 64, 65

Kilmarnock 181, 197
– Glencairn school 181
Kilwinning 197
King's Own Scottish Borderers (KOSB) 56, 67, 70, 71–76, 97, 98, 269
Kinghorn 63–64
Korean War 240

Labour League of Youth 5
Labour Party, support for 62, 154, 156–57, 170
Laidlaw & Fairgrieve Ltd (see also Dawson International) 156, 258, 265–66
– Dalkeith 173, 191, 272–73
– Galashiels 263, 173, 190, 266, 267, 268, 269–70, 271, 272
– Selkirk 173, 190–91, 270, 271–72
– Walkerburn 173
Lanarkshire 184, 185
Lancashire 81, 87, 195
– Chorley 81, 83, 371
 – munitions factory 81, 371
– Clough Mill, Shaw 195, 241, 243
– St Helens 87
Land Army 81
Lane, Frankie 368
Langholm 101
Lavin Margaret 6–7, 55, 80–84, 274–80, 360, 371
Lavin, Minnie (Benjamina) 3, 6, 58–59, 276
Lavin, Peter 6, 59–62, 66, 118–20, 209, 210, 275, 277, 359–60, 372
Leadburn 14, 57
– ammunition dump 57
Learmond, Mr 143
Leatherhead 64
Leigh-on-Solent 77
Leithen Water 39, 148, 149
Lennel Hill Farm 117–18
Lesmahagow 106
Liberal Party, support for 154, 156, 157, 169, 170
Lincolnshire 88
Litchfield, Mike 205–6
Little, Archie 5, 10, 100–107, 363, 374, 375
Little, Duncan 102
Little, Myra 46–47, 103, 105, 106, 201, 249–53, 362–63, 374
Loanhead 273, 321
Logan, Willie 292

London 45–46, 75, 378
– Euston railway station 46
London, Midland and Scottish Railway (LMS) 81, 85
London North Eastern Railway (LNER) 85, 120, 150, 296
Lothian, Marquess of 160
Lowestoft 64–65
– Palace cinema 64
Lunn, John 29–31, 38–40, 117–18, 187–98, 258–73, 298–99, 361–62, 377
Lunn, Margaret 192

Macmerry 77
Malaya (Malaysia) 69
Marks & Spencer 192
Marlborough 64
MacDougall, Ian ii, 1–11
MacDougall, Sandra 2, 4, 5, 7–8
McGlasson, Bob 130
McGlasson, Frank 130, 141
McGlasson, Hannah 130
McGlasson, John William 130, 376
McGlasson, Meg 128, 131, 132, 136, 138, 139, 140, 141, 142, 143, 148
McGlasson, Philip 127–48, 308, 376
McGlasson, Tiz 130
Mackenzie, Mr (joiner) 292
Maclean, Sir Donald 169
Mediterranean Sea 79
Meldons, the 42
Melrose, Margaret 8–9, 40–41, 55, 254–58, 300–1, 375
– brother Dawson 55
Middleton Moor 273
Middleton Toll 273
Midlands, the 192
Midlothian Council 3
Midlothian District Council 4
Midlothian 159, 160
Miller, Jock 124
mills in Peeblesshire:
– Caerlee, Cleikum, Leithen, St Ronan's and Waverley see under Innerleithen
– Damcroft, Damdale, Damside, March Street and Tweedside see under Peebles
– Tweedholm and Tweedvale see under Walkerburn
Milne, Bert 290
Ministry of Labour 344
Ministry of Home Grown

392

INDEX

Timber Production 105
Montgomery, Field Marshall 66
Moodie, Wills 46
Mountbatten, Lady 97
Muir, Betty 31–32, 35–36, 84–91, 99, 123–25, 162, 176–78, 207–11, 280–84, 303–4
– Mary, sister 32
– Stewart, grandfather 32
Muir, Marion 177
Muir, Peggy 124
Munich Agreement 52
Munn, Gurney 138
Murray Allan of Innerleithen 204–6, 312, 335, 341, 370, 376
Murray, Davie 16
Murray, Duncan 42, 59, 70–76, 213–16, 358–59, 372
Murray, Ella 16
Murray, Jessie 16
Murray, Miss (teacher) 38
Murray, Peggie 16, 124
Murray, Ruby 16
Murray, Tommy 16
Musselburgh 21, 57, 113
– Fisherrow 21

Nan (forewoman, March Street Mills) 353
National Library of Scotland 2, 217
National Service 49, 54, 59, 94–98, 150, 245, 246, 249, 323, 333, 373, 374, 375, 378
National Union of Dyers, Bleachers and Textile Workers 231, 253, 298, 302, 305, 307, 312, 350, 354
New Lanark 171
New Zealand 90, 247, 260, 324, 326, 328, 329, 338–39, 364, 378
Newbattle Abbey College 1
Newcastle 64
Newtongrange 159
– Lady Victoria Colliery 159
Nicoll family 267
Nisbett, Nellie 377
North Africa 61, 62
North Berwick 45
North Sea 235
Northern Ireland 98, 143, 310
– Bangor 98
– Belfast 98
– Coleraine 98, 143, 310
– Holywood Barracks 98
Norway 64

Oddy, Arthur 147–48, 306, 317
Oder river 74
Odhams, printing firm 240
Orkney Islands 60–61
– Scapa Flow 60, 77, 79, 374
– South Ronaldsay 60

Palestine 66, 69, 376
Parachute Regiment 67–70, 376
Parslow, Johnny 65
Paterson, George 215
Pathhead 113
Patna 127, 376
Patten, General George 75
Pearce, Eric 29, 38, 43–44, 151–53, 170–76, 185, 365–67, 377
Pearce's Lemonade factory 378
PEEBLES 9, 13, 15–23, 24–25, 28, 31–35, 39, 44, 45, 47–48, 57, 62, 75, 77, 81, 120, 124, 126, 127, 147, 150, 160, 161–62, 169, 170, 171, 172, 173, 174, 176, 176, 178, 182, 189, 198, 201, 202, 212, 214, 218, 220, 222, 228, 231, 232, 233–34, 235, 236, 237, 245, 256, 257, 259, 261, 280, 283, 284, 289, 290, 291, 292, 298, 305, 307, 310, 313, 337, 346, 347, 352, 354, 355, 357, 358, 359, 360, 369, 371, 372, 373, 374, 376, 377, 378–79
– Biggiesknowe 17
– Bonnington Road 150
– burgh hall 42
– Caledonian Cottages 373
– Castle Warehouse 119
– cemetery 120
– Checkland Street 120
– Co-operative Society 15–16, 44, 62, 176
– Connor Street 34
– County Hotel 5, 289
– Cross Street 33
– Cuddy Bridge 17
– Dalatho 17, 23
Dalcushie Hotel 184
– Damcroft Mill 126, 198, 369
– Damdale Mill 126, 149, 151, 161, 162, 163, 167, 179–81, 184–85, 198, 199, 245–47, 257, 284, 296–98, 302, 342, 347, 348–51, 352–54, 355–56, 369, 373, 375
– Damside Mill 126, 181, 198–99, 369
– Dilkusha 356
– drill hall 42, 60
– Eastgate 40
– Edinburgh Road 17, 23
– Eliot's Park 40, 120
– Empire cinema 42, 122
– Ex-Servicemen's Club 51
– Gateway store 161
– Gladstone Place 120
– Glasgow Road 120
– Goodburn's 20
– Graham Street 33, 34, 122
– Greystones 150
– Halyrude Primary School 35–36, 372
– High School 36, 37, 38, 39–40, 41, 55, 114, 115, 117, 118, 119, 110, 124, 128, 218, 277
– High Street 5, 15, 28, 91, 120
– Holland & Sherry, textile merchant 126, 161–62, 369
– Innerleithen Road 33
– Kelly's, newsagent 120
– Kingsland Primary School 48, 55, 372
– Kingsmuir Hotel 184
– Labour Exchange 81, 91
– Lowe Donald, textile merchant 126, 161–62, 218–20, 369, 379
– March Street 120
– March Street Mills 6, 24, 48, 50, 51, 80, 81, 84, 85, 90, 122, 124–25, 126, 134, 151, 161, 163, 164–65, 170, 171, 172, 176, 177, 179, 182, 183, 184, 185, 188, 189, 192, 199, 207–11, 213, 214, 215, 218, 220, 221, 222, 223, 229–30, 231–33, 234, 236, 237, 239, 245, 258, 259, 261, 262, 274–80, 281–88, 289, 290–95, 295–96, 297, 289–99, 302, 303, 307, 351, 352–54, 358, 359, 360, 369, 371, 372, 373, 374, 379
– The Mount hostel 184–85, 356–58, 373
– North Street 32
– Northgate 35, 122, 123, 165
– Nursing Home 29
– The Playhouse cinema 42
– Post Office 15, 40
– railway station 120
– Rosetta Road 120, 150
– St Andrew's Road 120, 378
– Somerfield store 161
– swimming baths 17–18, 27, 34, 35
– Tontine Hotel 5
– Tweed Bridge 184
– Tweedside Mill 24, 126, 151, 161, 162, 163–67, 178, 179, 185,

393

199, 247, 284, 288, 289, 296, 297–98, 302, 353, 369, 374, 379
– Venlaw Court 15, 16, 18, 22, 23, 379
– Venlaw Hill 237
– Wemyss Place 120
– Young Street 120
Peebles Hydro 48, 357
Peebles Rovers 41
Peeblesshire County Council 137
Peel Hospital 292
Penicuik 1, 14
Perthshire 71
Plora Wood 109
Poland 52, 73–74
– Auschwitz concentration camp 75
– civilians 75
– Ober (Upper) Silesia 73, 74
– Poznań 73
– Silesia 73
– Toruń 73
Polish armed forces 186, 189, 378
Polish immigration to 92–93, 239–40
Port Sunlight 171
Preston 81, 83
Pringle, Dougal 137, 138
Pringle of Scotland, Hawick 173
Probus Club 113

Qualifying Exam 37, 38, 39, 119
Queen's Award for Industry 145

Rae, Beatrice 339
Rae, Robert 192–93, 195, 196
RAF (Royal Air Force) 41, 51, 52–54, 57, 58, 59, 66–67, 71, 95, 96, 234, 238, 245, 313
RAF East Fortune 89, 235, 237
RAF North Coats 87–88, 89, 90
RAF Pocklington 96
RAF Ringway 67
RAF Turnhouse 89
RAF West Raynham 96
Red Army 74
Red Cross 65, 67, 344
Reid, Alan 2
Reid, Susan 2, 7
Renwick, Alan 292
Renwick, Jean 292
Rhine River 73
Rimoldi 339
Risley munitions factory 81
Robert Noble, Hawick 172, 199
Roberts, Noble and William Brown 172, 199

Robson, W. Lockie 3–4, 304, 331–34, 378
Roland Carbondale 375
Rosewell 159
– Co-operative Society 160
Roslin 9, 14
Royal Air Force see RAF
Royal Army Service Corps (RASC) 57
Royal Artillery 60
Royal Corps of Signals 94, 95, 375
Royal Hospital for Sick Children 38
Royal Infirmary of Edinburgh 44–45
Royal Navy 52, 66, 68, 70, 86, 234, 238
Royal Scots 50, 59–60, 63–66, 95, 96, 97
Royal Scots Fusiliers 96
Russell, Geordie 44, 45
Russell, Sandy 108
Russia 77
– Murmansk 77, 79, 374
Russian armed forces 79, 95

Saighton Camp, Chester 97
St Andrew's First Aid 344
St Cuthbert's Co-operative Society 160
Samson, Jock 305
Sanderson, Robert 41–42, 47–48, 55, 149–51, 179–81, 184–85, 198–99, 245–49, 342–43, 373
Saughton Jail 113
Schofield, Phil 195
Scott, Dick 34
Scott, Jack 34
Scott, Walter 33–34, 44–45, 57–58, 76–79, 120–23, 183–84, 284–88, 301–3, 363–64, 374
– Jenny, aunt 285
– Meg, aunt 285, 286
– Nellie, great aunt 77
– Wull, uncle 33
Scottish & Universal Investments Ltd see SUITS
Scottish Working People's History Trust, The 2, 8
Scottish Worsteds and Woollens 170, 172, 203
Scouts, the 27
Second World War 5, 10, 22, 25, 27, 28, 36, 41, 44, 45, 46, 47, 49, 51–54, 55–94, 99, 100, 108, 110,
116, 117, 118, 125, 136, 141, 142, 145, 146, 147, 148, 150, 152, 154, 157, 168, 169, 175, 176, 177, 182, 184, 186, 189, 198, 202, 211, 212, 214, 215, 218, 223, 234, 235, 236, 237, 238, 239, 240, 243, 280, 283, 285, 286, 295, 302, 303, 304, 305, 311, 313–14, 315, 317, 320, 321, 322, 331, 357, 368, 372, 373, 374, 375, 376, 377, 378, 379
– Battle of Arnhem 67
– Bruneval Raid 67
– Dunkirk evacuation 71, 81, 91, 372
– munitions work 80, 81–84, 100, 371
– North Africa campaign 61
Selkirk 28, 46, 47, 106, 173, 190, 191, 193, 196, 198, 199, 214, 359, 361, 374, 377
– Labour Exchange 374
– Woolworths 253, 374
Simmonds, Arthur 300
– brother 300
Simpson and Fairbairn's, Earlston 172
Singapore 69
Smith, Bud 305
Smith, Sir Alan 190
Southampton 71, 75
Staffordshire 77
Steel, David 156, 170
Sternok, Captain Julius 92
Stevenage 90
Stirling, Jim 46
Stirlingshire 106
SUITS 170, 171, 203
Sukarno (Indonesian president) 69
Sulzer loom 202, 288, 294
Switzerland 324
Symington 81

Territorial Army 54, 59, 60, 63, 378
Thatcher, Margaret 5
Thomson, John 187–88
Thorburn, Alistair 150
Thorburn, David Hunter 150
Thorburn family 10, 24, 126, 127, 149–51, 161, 162, 163, 167, 173, 178–79, 180, 184, 198, 199, 212, 236–37, 245, 256, 257, 258, 284, 285, 287, 295, 296, 299, 302, 347, 348, 352, 353, 356, 357, 369, 379
Thorburn, Hunter 248
Thorburn, Sir Michael 150

INDEX

Thorburn, 'Millie' 150
Thorburn, Sir Ronald 162
Thorburn, Colonel. W. Hunter 149–50, 162
Tibet 211
Tillicoultry 377
Todd & Duncan, Kinross 190, 241
Torquay 89
– Grand Hotel 89
– Toorak Hotel 89
Transport and General Workers Union 105, 231, 302, 307, 329, 354
Traquair 140
– sub-Post Office 140
Turnbull, Margaret 3–4, 9, 54–55, 377
Turner, James 46
Tweed, River 34, 35, 40, 109, 149, 235
Tweedside 42
Twickenham Stadium. 45, 46

Uniroyal 203
United States of America 162, 249, 254, 306, 317, 318, 325, 326, 334
– Boston 254
– Lord & Taylor store 325
– Saks Fifth Avenue store 325
University of Edinburgh 1, 8
– Centre for Research Collections 8
– European Ethnological Research Centre 1
– School of Scottish Studies Archives 1, 8
Upper Lyne 77

VE Day 75, 82, 84, 90
VJ Day 82, 84
Voluntary Aid Detachment (VAD) 344

Walker Burn 43, 112, 159
WALKERBURN 9, 13, 25–28, 40–41, 46–47,, 64, 66, 96, 100–103, 106, 109–16, 126, 127, 137, 149, 156–61, 169, 170–72, 173, 174–76, 178, 182, 212, 214, 215, 307, 310, 344, 362, 365–67, 370, 372, 374, 375, 377, 378
– Barn Walls Hostel 185–86
– Beattie housing 159
– Co-operative Society & store 101, 102, 105, 159–61, 175, 176
– council housing 159
– Dalziel's Brae 185
– Dryden's barbers 110
– Gaberson Farm 152
– Galashiels Road 25, 27, 101
– Henry Ballantyne Memorial Club 107, 157
– High Cottages 152
– Jubilee Road 27, 159, 185
– library 107, 157
– Mackay's chemical works 159
– mill housing 25–28, 29, 153, 159, 171, 185–86, 374
– mills 110, 111, 151–53, 158, 159, 170–71, 172, 174, 177, 178, 182, 200, 213, 214, 250, 258, 307, 318, 359, 374
– Tweedholm (wee) mill 46–47, 101, 106, 107, 126, 185, 200, 370, 374, 375
– Tweedvale (big) mill 29, 126, 200, 370, 377
– Montatza 100, 101
– Peebles Road 159
– pictures (cinema) 40–41
– police station 111
– Post Office 175
– Primary School 37
– railway station 46, 109
– Rathburn Chemicals 174
– Stoneyhill 114–16, 157
– the strawberry field 186

– tennis courts 28
– Tweedholm Avenue 110
– Youth Hostel 186
Wallsend 46
War Graves Commission 56
Watson, Alan 101, 102
Watt, Susan 283
Weir, Jimmy 140
Wells, Mr (March St) 84
West Bold 103, 375
West Calder 44
West Dumbartonshire 183
– Alexandria 183
– Bonhill 183
– Dumbarton 183
– Renton 183, 184, 374
– Ballantyne's 183
– Vale of Leven 183
West Linton 14
Weston's Biscuits 154
William Brown's, Galashiels 172
Wilson & Glenny, Hawick 107, 172, 309
Wilson, Tommy 116
Wolverhampton 87
Women's Auxiliary Air Force (WAAF) 81, 84–90, 372
Women's Royal Naval Service (WRNS) 86
Women's Timber Corps 104, 105
Woolwich Arsenal munitions factory 81
Worthing 65

Yarrow 105, 106
YM football 41
YMCA 42
York 100
Yorkshire 238, 241, 247, 305

395

TITLES IN THE REGIONAL FLASHBACK SERIES:

Stranraer and District Lives
Voices in Trust
Edited by Caroline Milligan

Whithorn
An Economy of People, 1920–1960
Edited by Julia Muir Watt

Lochmaben
Community Memories
Edited by Isabelle C. Gow and Sheila Findlay

TITLES IN THE FLASHBACK SERIES:

An Orkney Boyhood
Duncan Cameron Mackenzie

From Kelso to Kalamazoo
The Life and Times of George Taylor
Edited by Margaret Jeary and Mark A. Mulhern

From Land to Rail
Life and Times of Andrew Ramage 1854–1917
Edited by Caroline Milligan and Mark A. Mulhern

Galoshins Remembered
'A penny was a lot in these days'
Edited by Emily Lyle

Going to the Berries
Voices of Perthshire and Angus Seasonal Workers
Roger Leitch, edited by Caroline Milligan

The Making of *Am Fasgadh*
An Account of the Origins of the Highland Folk Museum by its Founder
Isabel Frances Grant MBE, LLD

Scotland's Land Girls
Breeches, Bombers and Backaches
Edited by Elaine M. Edwards

Showfolk
An Oral History of a Fairground Dynasty
Frank Bruce